W9-CXP-358

All-American

ANARCHIST

★ ★ ★

Debonair and carefully attired, Labadie belied the stereotype of an anarchist. (Author's photo.)

All-American
ANARCHIST

Joseph A. Labadie
and the Labor Movement

Carlotta R. Anderson

 WAYNE STATE UNIVERSITY PRESS   Detroit

Great Lakes Books

*A complete listing of the books in this series
can be found at the back of this volume.*

Philip P. Mason
Editor
Department of History, Wayne State University

Dr. Charles K. Hyde
Associate Editor
Department of History, Wayne State University

Copyright © 1998 by Wayne State University Press,
Detroit, Michigan 48201. All rights are reserved.
No part of this book may be reproduced without formal permission.
Manufactured in the United States of America.

02 01 00 99 98   5 4 3 2 1

Library of Congress Cataloging-in-Publication Data

Anderson, Carlotta R., 1929–
    All-American anarchist : Joseph A. Labadie and the labor movement /
Carlotta R. Anderson.
        p.   cm. — (Great Lakes books)
    Includes bibliographical references and index.
    ISBN 0-8143-2707-9 (alk. paper)
    1. Labadie, Jo, 1850–1933.   2. Anarchists—United States—
Biography.   3. Labor movement—Michigan—History.   I. Title.
II. Series.
HX843.7.L33A53   1998
335'.83'092—dc21
[B]   97-42353

Cover photo: Jo Labadie, 1905. (Author's photo.)

To the memory of my mother,
CHARLOTTE ANTOINETTE LABADIE HAUSER,
who adored her father
and inherited the gentle part of his nature.

Contents

✯ ✯ ✯

ACKNOWLEDGMENTS

The genesis of this book came from Edward C. Weber, curator of the Labadie Collection which I first visited in 1984 when my daughter was a student at the University of Michigan. He suggested I write the biography of my grandfather after reading an article of mine about grand juries. In the years since, he has been an unfailing source of encouragement and assistance as well as a personal friend. I am also indebted to librarians Kathryn Beam, Julie Herrada, and Anne Okey of the University's Special Collections Library for their painstaking professional help in locating and obtaining source materials for me. Dione Miles, former reference librarian in the Walter P. Reuther Library of Wayne State University, extended her friendship along with archival assistance. Many other librarians have been most helpful.

It was particularly gratifying to me to receive the support of Paul Avrich throughout the long process of completing the book. He read portions of the manuscript and was always confident that I would finish it and that it would be published. Other scholars who encouraged me, made useful suggestions, pointed me to relevant sources, or gave me articles or manuscripts include Frank Brooks, Randall Donaldson, Sidney Fine, the late Herbert G. Gutman, the late Stuart B. Kaufman, Leonard Liggio, and Richard Jules Oestreicher. James J. Martin, one of Laurance Labadie's few close friends, also offered assistance in the disposition of the books and literary effects of Jo and Laurance remaining in the latter's possession at his death in 1975.

I would like to thank Mark A. Sullivan, a young man who admired and befriended Laurance in his last lonely years. It was he, assisted by Sharon Presley, who knowledgeably sorted through the daunting mass of materials Laurance had stashed away, shipping most to the Labadie Collection but saving for me Jo Labadie's scrapbooks, his personal account book, and hundred of photographs, all enormously valuable in researching this book. He also gave me useful counsel and insights into anarchist philosophy.

I had the benefit of extensive research, genealogical and otherwise, undertaken by Larry Emery, the grandson of Jo's brother, Oliver, as well as Brother Albert Labadie, editor of *Labadie's Family Newsletter.* I received newspaper clippings, photographs, and recollections from distant relatives Emmett, Austin, and Elizabeth Labadie, and from Siphra Rolland.

I owe immense gratitude to my husband, Jim, daughter, Julia, and dear friend George Sherman—editors and journalists all—who spent many hours reading the entire manuscript, giving me invaluable advice. My sons, Chris and Eric, affectionately prodded and encouraged me as the years passed, and I appreciate it.

PREFACE

Some lives are notable because they changed the course of the world. Others played a more subtle role in the movements they helped inspire and form. Reading about these figures, we experience the events of the past in fuller detail and can often identify more vividly than with the stories of the great heroes and villains. Such a man was Joseph A. Labadie.

A Michigan anarchist and labor leader, Labadie (pronounced *La*-ba-die and known as "Jo" most of his adult life) was neither hero nor villain, but he had his day on the stage during one of the most turbulent and formative periods of American society. When he was born in the village of Paw Paw in 1850, the nation was wrenching itself from a rural, craft-oriented economy to one that was increasingly mechanized and depersonalized. As he came to maturity, revolutionary fervor stirred the world's impoverished workers as they watched the new capitalists flaunt gilded lives. Emile Zola described the time and the new social forces being born: "Men were springing up, a black avenging host was slowly germinating in the furrows, thrusting upwards for the harvests of the future ages. And very soon their germination would crack the earth asunder."[1]

Jo Labadie, a born rebel, was one of the country's most zealous in leading the fight for workers' rights and social justice. By the late nineteenth century, he had become Michigan's most influential labor agitator. Through him, the underdogs began to snarl back with a vengeance. Labor was fragmented and at the mercy of employers. Many labor leaders and workers were determined to seek power through solidarity. Labadie immersed himself in countless efforts to revolutionize society. As one memorialist quipped, "Jo was a man who could see something good in every movement that was opposed to the present system."[2]

He was a crusader for the Socialist Labor party, the Knights of Labor, the Greenback party, the American Federation of Labor, the single-tax movement, land reform, and the eight-hour movement. Above all, for fifty years he promoted his brand of non-violent anarchism in pursuit of liberating the individual. After embracing this libertarian philosophy, so endemic to America, he campaigned against protectionism, customs, patent and copyright laws; labor bureaus and labor legislation; compulsory taxation, arbitration, and schooling; and, indeed, anything he believed limited personal liberty. He was convinced that it would all work out if "Uncle Sam" would get out of the way.[3]

Like many reformers and idealists of the 1880s, Labadie was passionately devoted to the Knights of Labor, seeing in its "great brotherhood" the future emancipation of the wage earner. After it disintegrated in a mess of intrigue, denunciations, and factionalism, he was heartbroken and never dedicated himself with equivalent ardor to another labor body.

Until his death in 1933 at age eighty-three, Labadie prolifically wrote, edited, and published for the radical and daily press; was a popular speaker at demonstrations, meetings, rallies, and forums; and maintained a lively and often contentious correspondence with such figures as Emma Goldman, Eugene V. Debs, Samuel Gompers, Albert and Lucy Parsons, Benjamin Tucker, Joseph Buchanan, Alexander Berkman, Terence Powderly, and Henry George.

Frustrated in many of his efforts for social and economic reform, Labadie in middle age turned to verse, from revolutionary paeans to tender love poems. Lines selected from them introduce each chapter of this book.

It was said that not to know Labadie was not to know Detroit. Flamboyant, outspoken, and picturesque, he was both a dissident and a town character. His pen was often barbed, but in person he was reckoned kind, amiable, and witty. Especially noteworthy was his ability to quiet the alarm that the word anarchism generally evoked. Such was his personal charm, that even in the months after the Haymarket bombing in Chicago sent other cities into a paroxysm of terror of its alleged anarchist perpetrators, Detroiters remained calm and continued to cherish their "Gentle Anarchist." For a lifetime, Labadie patiently laid out the evolutionary tenets of his American species of anarchism to church groups, businessmen's clubs, a stream of reporters, and anyone who would listen, with the result that Detroit probably had a greater percentage of people who understood its essence than anywhere since.

Labadie's biography can be written in vivid detail, as those of most of his worthy comrades cannot, because of the wealth of material he and his wife saved. The conviction that he was engaged in events likely to transform the social and economic system imbued him with an acute sense of history.

He was also an irrepressible pack rat, and something of a sentimentalist as well. The ideas and ideals of so many other fighters in humanity's cause, their struggles, triumphs, and tragedies, can no longer be recaptured. Only the bare facts remain; the personal element is lost. Labadie's endures.

The story of his life, deeds, and thoughts is abundantly revealed through the treasure trove of letters, periodicals, clippings, manuscripts, booklets, photos, and circulars once stored in his attic, and now housed in the Labadie Collection of the University of Michigan. His stockpile of documents of social protest has proved a boon to scholars, enabling them to study the early labor movement in detail and draw on rich source materials representing a multitude of radical causes.

After several years of research, it was clear to me that Jo Labadie was not a saint, but a tireless, and sometimes tiresome, crusader. Once he adopted the doctrine of anarchism, he promulgated it with the fervor of a religious zealot. He did not advocate violence, but could delight in puncturing an opponent with a stiletto of words. Like Mark Twain, he affected to be a simple rube when it suited him, although he was a genuine intellectual, despite a lack of schooling. He had a poetic soul, but (as he himself admitted) wrote a lot of "bum" verse, although in the best of it one critic discerned "the sweep of Whitman, the tang of Sandburg."[4] Sometimes he was vain and full of himself; sometimes a bit obsequious to his benefactors.

There is, however, no denying that he devoted a lifetime to fighting for human rights without regard for power or personal gain. Summing himself up five years before his death, Labadie wrote: "I'm a kicker from Kickville, and so long as I have the physical and intellectual strength, . . . I shall kick, and kick like hell."[5]

Before I visited the Labadie Collection the first time, I had heard a great deal about Jo Labadie from my mother, his daughter. She never tired of speaking of him, almost with reverence. My uncle, Laurance Labadie, also an anarchist, said his father was the only person he ever met who was lovable all his life. Although I had not known my grandfather, I began an examination of his life with something less than scholarly dispassion.

I am not a professional historian; my background is in journalism. During more than a decade working on this book, I was able to draw not only on the vast holdings of the Labadie Collection and the archives of many other special collections, but also many of Labadie's scrapbooks, letters and other papers bequeathed to me by Laurance Labadie. I have turned over to the Labadie Collection copies of all materials cited in the book. If the relative ignorance in which I began my research has any benefit, it might be an ability to lead the non-specialist through the convoluted labyrinth of causes Labadie made his own with less bafflement than I felt on first encountering them.

My intention has been to bring Jo Labadie and his time and place to life in a way that will be of interest to the general reader as well as the scholar. I hope I have carried out the wish of Agnes Inglis, first curator of the Labadie Collection, who imagined that one day someone would write the story of "Old Joe . . . who had the Dream and was the poet and the anarchist—to the last!"[6] and that it would illuminate for the reader the great movements in which he participated.

A Knighthood Flowers

Men of Labor, men of mettle,
Let no person govern you!
For his crimes make Mammon settle!
Block the bandit! Dare and do!
—FROM "DARE AND DO," *SONGS OF THE SPOILED*

On a Sunday in early October 1878, Joseph Labadie, a newly married young printer and socialist, strode down Detroit's wide avenues on his way to a portentous meeting in the old Market Hall. Charles Litchman, the Grand Scribe of the Knights of St. Crispin, a once-prominent national shoemakers union, was going to speak. It was whispered that Litchman was recruiting for a new, secret labor organization of a type never before attempted.

This was to be a grand and noble enterprise, as workshop rumors had it, that would welcome all the nation's workers—skilled as well as unskilled—of every race, creed, and nationality, into one big brotherhood of toil. It was said that the mission of this underground society, known to non-members only by the insignia of five stars (written *****), was to end poverty and wage slavery throughout the world, to right all economic wrongs, and to achieve "the greatest good to the greatest number." A great defensive army of labor would be created, mobilized for mutual protection. Its motto: "An injury to one is the concern of all."[1]

The twenty-eight-year-old Labadie was inflamed by these high-principled goals. Along with millions of the country's workers, he had struggled and suffered through the last five years of depression, an economic downturn unequaled in the young industrial history of America. Near-starvation and misery had haunted working people across the country. "The men asked for work and found it not, and children cried for bread," wrote George E. McNeill.[2] Although Labadie had lived among the Indians in the Michigan woods until the age of fourteen, he spent those depression years in Detroit, where he found thousands on relief and the county poorhouse filled with the destitute.

The distress filled him with moral indignation. He was convinced it was wrong for the underdog to suffer so, while the new capitalists flaunted huge accumulations of wealth. It was wrong that the privileged few should feed off the toil of the working people. As he wrote later, he was stirred by "the abuse and insults heaped upon the workers by brutal employers and bosses"; he sometimes wished for the "total annihilation by any and every means at our command" of the ruling class. He predicted a "terrible conflict that is surely coming."[3]

The workers he passed on their day off he viewed as "industrial slaves." No longer proud and independent artisans in their own shops, they toiled in factories, at the mercy of employers who might dismiss them on a whim, especially for attempting to unionize. They had much to avenge, and, perhaps, a new day was dawning.

Labadie was on his way to what became one of the three great passions dominating his life. For the next decade, he threw himself into the fight for labor power and solidarity represented by the Knights of Labor, soon to develop into the mightiest labor organization the nation had yet seen. Simultaneously, he channeled his prodigious energies into promoting an idealized vision of anarchistic society, which became his religion of sorts. And, in the background, glowed his abiding love for his wife, Sophie. His first passion expired bitterly in a few years, a loss to which he was never reconciled. The remaining two endured a lifetime.

As Labadie walked along the riverfront that Sunday in 1878, he could not help but see that times were getting better, at least temporarily. The depression was ending and the city was coming alive again. Mills and factories sprouted up along the Detroit River. The beautiful avenues, cooled by great shade trees, reached outward and the skyline thrust upward. A majestic procession of ships carrying lumber, grain, coal, and ore steamed past. Immigrants, chatting in German or Polish, or with an Irish brogue, streamed in for factory jobs in the reviving industries. Two daily newspapers kept Detroit abreast of world affairs: Afghan regiments advanced on British troops near the Khyber Pass; Bismarck pushed his anti-socialist bill through the German Reichstag; ex-President Grant watched the Dutch trotting races in Paris; and America's South battled a yellow fever epidemic. In Detroit, the papers reported a continuing problem: alcohol-related violence. There had been two murders "caused by liquor" that weekend. One was in a cigar factory, where a drunken cigarmaker threw a heavy wooden cigar mold at a fellow worker.[4]

All sorts of modern inventions arrived in a city considered one of the loveliest in the country. In the Telegraph Building at Congress and Griswold streets, a tiny telephone exchange had just been installed, enabling more than a hundred Detroiters to call each other. Thomas Edison's new phonograph had been on exhibit in Detroit that summer. At night, the city was still illuminated by gaslights but their end was near. As he approached the Market Hall, Labadie faced the Church of the Most Holy Trinity, where, only a few years before, Detroit's first electric light had feebly illuminated the middle altar.[5]

Dodging the horse-drawn buggies, Labadie approached the Campus Martius and Cadillac Square. He walked across rows of flagstones worn smooth by the traffic of many feet toward the Market Hall, where the day before farmers and city folk had engaged in their weekly haggling over wares. He found a large number of workingmen—mostly shoemakers—eager to hear Grand Scribe Litchman, the proselytizing labor leader. Considered "a big gun," he had spoken the previous evening at St. Andrew's Hall on "Labor and Finance." Today's group was uneasy. A number of "roughs" nearby seemed threatening. Were they company thugs? Police spies? Agents provocateurs? Litchman decided it was best for his audience to disperse, but invited Labadie and a few others he trusted to accompany him to his temporary quarters in the house of Otis C. Hodgdon. Hodgdon, a shoemaker, lived on Third Street, north of Grand River.[6] In his parlor, Litchman tried to size up the men before him. Were they the right ones to organize a branch of the secret labor brotherhood in Detroit?

Litchman was an impressive man of twenty-nine, well liked and famed for his eloquence. Favoring a large drooping mustache and pince-nez, he did not look a wage earner, nor was he. He began work as shoe salesman for his father's business in Marblehead, Massachusetts. Later, he and his brother established their own shoe factory. He had hoped to become a lawyer, a goal shattered when the shoe business failed in the depression. With no income, he was forced to give up his legal studies.

Reduced temporarily to shoemaking again, the enterprising Litchman did not remain long with the shoemaker's welts and lasts. He turned to union organizing. He soon became a ranking official in the Knights of St. Crispin, a secret shoemakers' society that in the early 1870s was the

largest and strongest trade union in the United States. A few months before
he visited Detroit for the secret ***** society, he had been named its grand
secretary, the second highest office. Soon afterward, he also was elected to
the Massachusetts state legislature on the Greenback-Labor ticket.[7]

Labadie found Litchman a compelling and persuasive leader. He
had heard Litchman's speech the previous evening and agreed with its
"Socialistic wisdom." Known as the "silver-tongued orator of the labor
movement," Litchman had spoken of the curse of labor-saving machinery, of
the necessity for laborers to own the machines themselves, and of producers'
cooperatives as the only remedy for the nefarious wage system.[8] Labadie,
the Greenback party's mayoral candidate for the upcoming city election, was
also in sympathy with Litchman's work for the Greenback currency reform
movement. But at that moment Labadie was excited by an aspiration that
none of the other causes he worked for—socialism, Greenbackism, or the
printers' union—offered: one big workingmen's union.

In evaluating Labadie at Hodgdon's quarters, Litchman found a well-
read and well-informed man, attributes frequently found in printers. Of
French and Native American heritage, Labadie was carefully dressed and
groomed. Somewhat short in stature, but bearing himself regally, he had
luxuriant black, wavy hair atop a big head, with penetrating blue eyes.
His handsome face was punctuated by a handlebar mustache and goatee.
Usually in a genial mood, he had "a smile that beamed upon you." But when
angered, "his eyes glinted and you saw the unquenchable spirit of the Indian
in him," remarked a close associate.[9] Labadie was highly respected in the
local printers' union. The year before, he was one of the first two American-
born workers to join the Socialist Labor party in Detroit. Coupled with a
reformer's passion was a gregarious, convivial personality that could help
win converts.

In selecting candidates for the newly born ***** Litchman had three
initial questions: "Do you believe in God, the Creator and Universal Father
of all?" "Do you obey the Universal Ordinance of God, in gaining your bread
by the sweat of your brow?" "Are you willing to take a solemn vow binding
you to secrecy, obedience, and mutual assistance?"[10] We do not know how
Labadie, a budding agnostic, reconciled these theological requirements with
his own beliefs.

Litchman picked Labadie, shoemaker Hodgdon, and a man named
Miller to initiate on the spot.[11] Of the three, Labadie was destined to become
the most important Michigan labor leader of his day; Hodgdon served as a
good soldier and Miller sank into oblivion. Litchman motioned them into

Hodgdon's bedroom and revealed the secrets of the organization they were about to join: the Noble and Holy Order of the Knights of Labor. He outlined its objectives: The Order, as it was commonly called, did not desire to destroy the capitalists, but to prevent "the pauperization and hopeless degradation of the toiling masses" and to secure for them "a proper share of the wealth that they create." Capital had its "combinations" (monopolies or trusts) that "crush the manly hopes of labor and trample poor humanity in the dust." To counteract them and gain collective power, laborers needed to band together into a "universal brotherhood." Solidarity was the key.[12]

The three were sworn to silence until death. Labadie took the oath that he would "never reveal by word, act or implication . . . the name or object of this Order, the name or person of anyone a member thereof, its signs, mysteries, arts, privileges or benefits . . . any words spoken, acts done or objects intended; except in a legal and authorized manner, or by special permission of the Order granted to me."[13]

Then came a part of the initiation Litchman was particularly fond of: an explanation of the secret handgrips, signs, symbols, and passwords. Like many of the Knights, Litchman was a Mason and delighted in the mysterious rituals that imitated Masonic ceremonies, thought to have passed down from medieval stonemasons' guilds. A man enamored of fraternal organizations, he also claimed membership in the Great Council of the United States Improved Order of Red Men, the Grand Encampment of Massachusetts I.O.O.F. (International Order of Odd Fellows), the Royal Arcanum, the American Legion of Honor, and the Order of the Golden Cross.

There was the identifying Grip, given when shaking hands: "The thumb to be placed over the fingers immediately back of the knuckles. Give one heavy pressure with the thumb, and, if returned, answer with two light pressures in quick succession without removing the hand." Or the Sign of Caution, involving an intricately closed hand placed under the chin. Or the Cry of Distress (to be used in the dark): "I am a stranger." Any member of the Order present was to answer: "A stranger should be assisted."[14]

The arcana of the ritual represented more than a pleasure in the trappings of fraternal orders. It served also as a protective device. Some employers were so terrified at the prospect of workers uniting that they fired or blacklisted union members. Rumors were rife that ***** was plotting revolt and terrorism. Detective and strike-breaker Allan Pinkerton once called the Knights "probably an amalgamation of the Molly Maguires [a secret miners' organization accused of violent acts in the mid 1870s] and the Paris Commune."[15]

Labadie was chosen leader of the three initiates and given the responsibility of organizing the first cell of the Knights of Labor in Detroit. On November 18, 1878, he received a commission authorizing him "to go forth, to Cover and Instruct our Fellow Men, wherever found worthy and fitting of FELLOWSHIP" and organize them into assemblies (local unions). It was signed by Grand Master Workman Uriah S. Stephens, who, with a small group of garment cutters, had founded the Noble and Holy Order of the Knights of Labor in Philadelphia nine years earlier.[16]

Labadie began circulating the word surreptitiously. He worked hard to entice a group of like-minded men into what was grandly called the Washington Literary Society. This camouflaged name for Detroit's Local Assembly 901 (L.A. 901, also referred to as Pioneer Assembly 901, or P.A. 901 because it was the first in Michigan) was intended to shield members of the Knights of Labor from a suspicious public. As its number suggests, there were by then nine hundred other local assemblies representing around ten thousand members in the East and Middle West, and the total was nearly doubling annually.[17]

On Sunday evening, December 1, more than a dozen recruits for the "Washington Literary Society" had their first meeting in Detroit. Labadie had already been selected as master workman (chairman). He had persuaded the perpetually obliging cigarmaker and socialist Thomas M. Dolan, one of the old guard of the Detroit labor movement, to act as Recording Secretary.

To this bearded, English-born Civil War volunteer, who proudly wore a Grand Army of the Republic button in his coat, forming unions was old hat. On a tiny lined notebook less than six inches high, Dolan jotted down the minutes in a clear hand. He recorded the group's decision to meet every other Monday at Forester's Hall, 218 Randolph Street. "Brother Walters" was given twenty-five cents to advertise the assembly's next meeting in the *Detroit Evening News* under its Literary Society alias. This was a departure from the romantic practice of convening Knights' meetings by chalking mysterious symbols on sidewalks, fences, and buildings. Dolan collected total contributions of $1.25, representing the approximate cost of lunch for all those present.[18]

Within a month, Litchman had sent the charter to Detroit and new members were taking their places. With a fifty-cent initiation fee and fifteen cents monthly dues, the treasury reached $10. Hodgdon had been elected Almoner (relief officer) of the "Lodge." The Inspector, Outside Esquire, Inside Esquire, and Unknown Knight had also been chosen. As Statistician,

Labadie's lifelong friend Judson Grenell, a fellow socialist and printers' union member, took on the grand project of compiling a report on the status of all the trades in the country. He planned to request questionnaire forms from the Massachusetts Bureau of Labor Statistics, the first such bureau established.

Labadie was already "squawking" about the "excessive rigamarole" involved in the mystical ritual and had written Grand Secretary Litchman (who relished it), asking if it could be cut down. He scorned the secrecy as "more childish than manly." As for the elaborate ceremony, which evoked images of medieval chivalric pageantry, he thought it represented "the habits and the fears and the ignorance of our barbaric ancestors."[19]

By the middle of February, Master Workman Labadie had reluctantly fulfilled his obligation to instruct twenty-one new members in all the rituals as laid out in the *Adelphon Kruptos* (secret brotherhood), a booklet of secret instructions that were to be committed to memory. It was full of talk of the "venerable sage," the "sanctuary" (where the Bible was kept), "inner and outer veils," and the "circle of harmony," and even contained sections in ciphers using words like CPONXEL and IHAWH, sometimes with letters made up or printed upside down. Its scriptural passages and references to "The King of glory" and "The Lord of hosts" reflected the strong religious sentiments of founder Uriah S. Stephens, who had been educated for the Baptist ministry.[20]

When candidates were prepared for initiation, a mysterious figure, the Unknown Knight would appear before them, his face concealed behind a mask and slouch hat, his form concealed in a black cloak. His identity remained a secret until after the ceremony; members were to be known by number, not name. "Mystery was the order of the day," recalled one Detroit Knight. "I never saw a candidate that knew what it was all about."[21]

As for the organization's program, it was humanitarian and high-minded, but murky as to methods. Labadie's job included reading to the initiates the preamble and declaration of principles. These documents set forth an audacious mission: securing for the laborer "the fruits of his toil," making "industrial [productive], moral worth, not wealth, the true standard of individual and national greatness." They called for the establishment of cooperative institutions; public lands for the actual settler ("Not another acre for railroads or corporations"); the end to all laws "that do not bear equally upon capital and labor"; an eight-hour day; prohibition of child labor before the age of fourteen; substitution of arbitration for strikes; equal pay for equal work for both sexes; and other grand demands common to reform organizations of the time. It was hoped that eventually capitalism would be replaced by some sort of cooperative system.[22]

How were these hopes and dreams to be realized? By political lobbying? By boycotts (strikes were frowned on by the Knights' leadership)? By publicizing them and creating a public demand? No one knew. But such vagueness about how to achieve lofty goals for the working class was typical then. In their early days the Knights were, as Norman Ware wrote, "in sympathy with everything and involved in nothing," awaiting the millennium. The local assembly he likened to a congregation living in times of persecution.[23]

Labadie wholeheartedly supported founder Stephens in believing a main objective of the Knights was education—bringing working people together into a labor fraternity for the purpose of discussing "social science" and their rights and duties to each other. "No one would ever think of putting a law case into the hands of anyone who had never studied law," Labadie argued. "No one can ever hope to win the case of social progress . . . unless they know . . . the laws of political economy." With only a few months of formal education behind him, Labadie himself was reading the writings of Adam Smith, John Stuart Mill, Ferdinand Lassalle, Thomas Paine, and François Guizot; in the following year he spent $26.85—nearly two weeks wages—on books.[24]

So it was with great enthusiasm that he obeyed the Knights' injunction to devote at least ten minutes of each meeting to discussing "labor in all its interests." His "brethren" in what he described as a "socio-economic school, where each member is at once both teacher and pupil," were soon being elected to read aloud their own essays. "He who will not work shall not eat" was one of the first, chosen by cigarmaker and avid socialist Charles Erb. Occasionally a member was unprepared—not surprising considering that most were putting in at least a sixty-hour work week.[25]

L.A. 901 was a "mixed assembly," open to workers in all trades, unlike most of the early local assemblies, which were limited to one craft. Founder Stephens's long-term goal was to unite all toilers of whatever craft, creed, color, or political affiliation into a grand labor army. The Knights of Labor was also the first large labor organization to welcome the unskilled into its ranks. Some 95,000 blacks joined the Order, as it was called. Women, however, were not regularly admitted until 1882, apparently because some men claimed they distracted from "serious" matters or could not keep secrets. Labadie found it difficult to get a Catholic into the Knights, "as they were afraid of the consequences." The Roman Catholic Church objected to secret societies with rituals and vows that might interfere with the confessional, and for a long time automatically excommunicated Masons. Farmers were eligible to become members; even employers who sympathized with organized labor could be admitted. Lawyers, bankers, and saloonkeepers were barred because they were held responsible for many of the evils of the social system.[26]

L.A. 901's new Detroit recruits were mainly skilled workers—cigarmakers, shoemakers, and printers—most of whom probably belonged to trade unions as well. But the unions, never very powerful, had been virtually moribund during the preceding five years of depression; men struggling to find work had been in no mood to antagonize employers and little had been accomplished to better their lot. The depression also had put an end to the first efforts in Detroit to establish amalgamations of trade unions. Only in more prosperous times did workers' thoughts again turn to the possibility of massing together for unified action.

Those elected to join L.A. 901's small brotherhood were a stellar crew. During the first few months (the only period for which minutes were preserved), a fair number of initiates were men who became leading players in the unfolding drama of the Detroit labor movement. Several, including Labadie, were to become nationally prominent.

Among them was printer Lyman A. Brant, one of the founders of the Federation of Organized Trades and Labor Unions, a forerunner of the AFL, and also a leader in the International Typographical Union. Judson Grenell, another printer, was later elected to the state legislature, as were Brant and cigarmaker Hugh McClellan. Carpenter Edward W. Simpson and Charles Erb served on the National Executive Committee of the Socialist Labor party (SLP) and as officials in the Detroit Trades Council. E. A. Stevens, an SLP organizer, became a member of the Knights' General Executive Board. Charles Bell was the local printers' union president. Adam Stuermer was an official in the cigarmakers' union. Shoemaker John Strigel, a former official in the Knights of St. Crispin, organized over fifty assemblies for the Knights and remained active in the Detroit Trades Council for nearly twenty years. The enigmatic Philip van Patten, whose only trade appears to have been agitation during his energetic career in social reform, joined soon. He was prominent as both a Knight and the national leader of the SLP. They came predominantly from English, Irish, and German ethnic stock. Curiously, in a city with such a strong French association, Labadie seems to be Detroit's only labor pioneer of French ancestry.[27]

Almost half of the thirty-eight new Knights were socialists, many of them recent converts, who had joined the American wing of the SLP Labadie and Grenell had formed in Detroit the year before. Both organizations reflected the same high-minded humanitarian goals, cooperative spirit, and vision of labor solidarity, and thus attracted the same type of individual.[28]

It may have been Labadie's fellow socialists who were responsible for turning down in the assembly's first months his nomination of Henry A. Robinson, an ardent Greenbacker and later one of the leading lights of Michigan reform movements. The local socialist newspaper, violently anti-Greenback until 1880, had just attacked Robinson as "an audacious, scandalous, impudent, abominable liar" for accusing socialists of wanting to divide the wealth "between people who are lazy and those who work hard." The brethren also may have been suspicious because, while Robinson claimed to be a carpenter, he probably was already studying law. This profession was much reviled by the Knights and sufficient to ostracize one from their ranks. Robinson, however, described himself as a lifelong "champion for the weak, puny and abused . . . a communist—in the best and broadest sense of that term." He later became both a judge and a leading Knight, and was appointed Michigan Commissioner of Labor in 1892.[29]

It is small wonder that in its early days in Detroit, the Order was represented by such a distinguished cast of activists. A sort of underground workingmen's college, it offered no strategy to increase weekly paychecks. With such long-term, utopian goals, the organization appealed only to those most visionary and committed.

Absorbed with initiation rites, labor essays, and general business, L.A. 901 began as little more than an elite, working-class fraternity and night school with religious overtones. When some of the members found the "socioeconomic" discussions too dry, Labadie referred them portentously to "the sphinx of old, which not to solve is to be destroyed." He had no patience with such types. "Go to, with such drivel," he berated them. "We want men, hard-headed thinking men, in this movement and not babies . . . this is serious business we have undertaken."[30] Some, tired of all talk and no action, dropped out, but there appears to have been a steady flow of new blood.

Since the newly knighted were forbidden even to name their organization outside its sacred sanctuary, their crusades for emancipation of the wage slave originally had to be channeled through the socialist or Greenback parties. The trade unions—narrowly concerned with wages, hours, and working conditions for their own members, and not with grand schemes of social reform—were considered too timid or too limited in aspirations to enter the battle.

No real progress was made in furthering the Order's fortunes in Michigan in the first years. Labadie was able to form only one other assembly, in Jackson, where Litchman informed him the miners "wanted organizing." He chafed at the secrecy that made for "slow growth," as he told the new grand master workman, Terence V. Powderly. It was worse than that. Detroit membership dipped to 24 in 1880, 20 dropping out and only 5 joining. But the following year, secrecy was abolished. Soon Labadie and fellow organizers were "honeycombing" Michigan with local assemblies composed of mechanics (as craftsmen were then called), farmers, laborers, and small storekeepers.[31]

In Michigan, as elsewhere, membership climbed steadily and then in leaps, reaching the national high point of 700,000 by mid 1886.

It was a time of great hope. "Labor is awakening from its long slumber," Labadie and Grenell assured readers of their journal, *Labor Review.* "The rising giant is just now stretching and yawning. But his eyes are beginning to open and his sinews tightening; and soon . . . he will sweep away our false systems of finance and unjust system of distribution."[32] Many looked to the dawn of a new era, with a higher, grander, and more humane civilization and the complete unification of labor worldwide.

There were but a few glorious years ahead as the Knights created America's first successful labor organization, the largest the country had yet seen. Except to students of labor history, the Knights of Labor is an all-but-forgotten force today, but in its brief, dramatic existence, it developed labor consciousness as no workers' union had previously done and managed to build the foundations of the modern labor movement. Hundreds of Knights were elected to public office. Massive rallies, demonstrations, and parades were organized. The organization mounted a general strike against Jay Gould's Southwestern rail systems, the greatest strike victory until then in the United States. It inspired Grenell to write: "Its principles are the purest, its object is the noblest, its motive is the most sublime, and its mode of procedure the most peaceful of any great labor organization of which we have any record."[33]

The Order was to have nine more years of vibrant life before dying a lingering death. Labadie struggled for its success, then, disgusted with the plotting, perfidy, corruption, and hypocrisy of its leaders, played a significant role in its downfall. As Michigan's foremost labor leader, he went on to form a new type of labor body, the Michigan Federation of Labor, an AFL affiliate, and to become a well-known figure in the nation's labor movement. In a few years, he also found that the "fever of governmentalism"—counting on the state to solve all social problems—that had animated him as a young socialist firebrand, had been quenched. In its place, Labadie embraced with greater ardor its exact opposite, no government at all, anarchism. But let us go back to the beginning.

★ 2 ★

A Backwoods Boyhood

Oh! for the rhyming, echoing woods,
Where songbirds twitter overhead,
Where dwells the soul of Liberty,
Which proudly strides with a freeman's tread! . . .
Away from the ruthless wheels of trade,
Far from the grubbing, grinding crowd,
I climb and run and plunge like mad,
And revel in freedom, crying aloud!
—"For the Wild Woods," *Sing Songs and Some That Don't*

The southern Michigan woods were dark and heavy with snow on a winter evening around 1860. The boy with black curly hair was bright-eyed with visions of tomorrow's hunt. He huddled near the fire watching the Indian women prepare the meal, wrapping fish in wet leaves and laying the bundles in hot ashes, with mounds of bread dough and some potatoes. A cup of hot sassafras root tea warmed him as he waited his turn to hold a spit of venison chunks over the flames.

The Indian band had set up their night's shelter miles away from any settlement. The boy, Joseph Labadie, had learned how to build one on previous outings. As he later described it, the men first cut a long pole to reach from one tree to another, perhaps thirty feet away, firming it in place with two crotched poles. Joseph and the other children collected pine boughs, which were leaned upside down against the horizontal pole, forming "walls." Under this lean-to they placed a floor of fine branches, then a thick layer of straw. Buffalo robes were thrown atop this gigantic "mattress." There, wrapped in blankets and buffalo robes, the whole band slept comfortably, with the fire built against a front log radiating heat into their forest abode. Joseph's father, an interpreter between the Indians and the Jesuits, slept near him.[1]

For ten-year-old Joseph, living among the Pottawatomi like a member of the tribe was an idyll in the forest primeval. He delighted in the knowledge that some Indian blood ran through his veins. "Them was the happy days!" he would later say, reminiscing on the lost paradise of his childhood. The Indian ways, as he relived them in letters and random jottings, took on a romanticized glow. His memories far transcended the techniques of building a shelter without boards, hammer, or nails, or shooting a deer. They were crucial in forming his view of the ideal society and an individual's place in it. As Labadie later translated the experiences of a wilderness boyhood into revolutionary tenets, he concluded that only when men and women recaptured the individual freedom and self-sufficiency of Native Americans, or of pioneers like his parents, could they be truly happy.

The Indian, far from being the "boob" many people took him for, Labadie wrote, "knew how to wrest a living from nature without robbing his fellows thru interest, profit, rent and taxes."[2] In the early days, ownership of land was unknown to the Indians, except as the white man's concept. They used only what was required for survival and did not claim land beyond that. They did not waste or ravage nature's bounty. They could reach out and reap the necessities of life without permission from some bureaucracy. Chiefs often had little power and no one was compelled to follow them. Individuals lived with the band in a voluntary community, sharing the food and work, but were free to go their solitary way or join another band. No one was subservient to another; no one dominated. The children were seldom disciplined, learning by imitating their parents rather than sitting in a schoolroom.[3]

In truth, this idyllic life had long since passed away for most of Michigan's Indians by the time of Joseph's childhood. Soon after Michigan became the twenty-sixth state in 1837, most of the Native Americans in the Lower Peninsula had been callously rounded up by the United States government under the "Removal Act," torn from their ancestral lands and herded west across the Mississippi River. The young boy did not know that there, in the early 1860s, he was playing Indian with what were but remnants of once-proud tribes.

As Labadie peered back through the gauze of nostalgia, it seemed that in that pristine life he had viewed anarchism in practice. Those unfettered boyhood days represented an ideal he later sought for all people, even in an urban world, where there were no woods full of game or wild berries for the picking. Like the Michigan Indians, Labadie never reconciled himself to government, nor thought others should have to, and in his labor reform efforts, he envisioned the workers, not the government, demanding and ensuring their rights.

Joseph's love of liberty was a legacy from his father, the only legacy he was to have. Anthony Cleophis Labadie was a sturdy, rough, independent man, who thrived only in the wilderness. Like Michigan's early fur traders, he spent most of his life in the forests, used to hardship. He was one-eighth Ojibway, born in 1830 in the Canadian woods near the Detroit River. His family later moved to Paw Paw (then called Lafayette), a town of around one thousand in southwestern Michigan. It was about forty miles from the Indiana border, where relatives had a homestead on Three Mile Lake. There were still about fifty Indians in the locality, many of mixed blood. Around the age of fourteen, Anthony apparently went off to live with them when the mood struck. With his dark complexion and black hair, he blended in well.

Anthony had learned the carpenter's trade, and sometimes earned money painting houses, but always he was lured by the call of the wild. Even Paw Paw was too much civilization for him. He yearned for a log cabin in the wilderness, where fish and game abounded. Whenever he had the opportunity, he traveled with the Jesuit missionaries, serving as interpreter with the Indians of southern Michigan and northern Indiana.[4]

One day a distant cousin, Euphrosyne Angelique Labadie, came to Paw Paw to visit his family. Perhaps the two were already courting, or perhaps romance bloomed at that time. All we know is that soon afterward, they were married by Father Barreaux, who had been a missionary in China. On April 18, 1850, a son was born and baptized Charles Joseph Antoine Labadie. His godmother, an Ojibway, added an Indian name that sounded like "Otwine." Both his parents were twenty years old.[5]

Years later, Labadie proudly claimed that he was the first native-born Michigan anarchist: "I am no dam [*sic*] foreign 'Arnikist,' " he once quipped. "I'm on my native heath."[6] Taking his Indian blood into account, he was, in fact, about as American as one could be. His French ancestors were already in the New World by 1667; they owned land on the Detroit River prior to 1749. Both his mother and father were descendants of Antoine Louis Descomptes dit (also known as) Labadie, one of the most prominent and prolific French settlers in eighteenth-century Detroit. A prosperous farmer and fur trader, variously credited with having fathered either twenty-three or thirty-three children (depending on whose count is accepted) from three wives, he was jocularly acclaimed for bringing the area a tremendous impetus in both industry and population.[7]

Joseph's mother, Euphrosyne, was Antoine Louis's granddaughter by Charlotte Barthe, his third wife, the daughter of a French army surgeon. She was raised in the spacious frame house her father, Louis, built on the vast Labadie estate in East Sandwich, on the Canadian side of the Detroit River, on land conveyed by the Ottawa chief Pontiac in the mid eighteenth century. The family's numerous relatives and friends frequently canoed across from Detroit or drove along the Queen's Highway in carriages for parties. Sometimes Euphrosyne would paddle a stout dugout the half mile or so to Detroit and back alone. The lawn which sloped to the water's edge was made available to local Indians for feasts and pow-wows, celebrations in which the Labadies would often join.[8]

Although he was the great-grandson of Antoine Louis, Euphrosyne's cousin (and later husband) Anthony Cleophis was not raised in similar wealth and comfort. His home was a log house three miles back into the woods at the edge of the 918-acre farm, near the former site of an Ottawa village.[9] Joseph's father came down the family line from Antoine Louis's second wife, Marie, a full-blooded Ojibway, daughter of the chief of a band whose hunting grounds were along the Detroit River. Despite his seventeen years with Marie, Antoine Louis did not value her offspring as highly as those of his other wives. When he died in 1807, Marie's children did not receive a share of the main estate, its farm animals or slaves, who might have been Indians or blacks. Their only legacy was one horse and one cow each, plus some wilderness land. As a result, that branch of the family languished, while the others prospered. Indeed, Joseph Labadie's paternal grandfather in Paw Paw was an illiterate laborer, while his mother's father, Louis Descomptes dit Labadie, was a well-to-do landowner and pillar of society. Perhaps Antoine Louis made a distinction in the legacies to his children because he and Marie were married only in native ceremonies. There are no church records and their offspring are referred to in his will as "natural children."[10]

Sometime in Joseph's early childhood, his parents moved from Paw Paw back to East Sandwich, the site of his mother's upbringing. Euphrosyne's aunt, Cecile, ran a hotel on the riverfront near the Labadie estate with her husband, Augustin Lagrave. Joseph and his family moved to this large log building, and went into the *pensionnat* or boarding house business, their clientele being shipbuilders from Jenkins's shipyard, up the river.[11]

Sandwich was then a settlement of some five hundred inhabitants one and half miles upstream from Windsor, Ontario; the town itself had a population of only one thousand. The Detroit River formed part of the boundary between Michigan and the province of Ontario. The area was fertile, and generation after generation had farmed long and narrow "ribbon farms," typical of French-Canadian settlement, that extended from the river southeast about three miles into a wilderness covered thickly with timber. Most of the families occupying these strips of land had French Catholic origins. A good many were related to the Labadies.

As a small boy, Joseph liked to sit on the grassy riverbank and watch the wind propel the sweeping arms and flapping sails of an old windmill, possibly one that had been grinding flour since 1770. The busy river traffic between Lake Saint Clair and Lake Erie afforded abundant amusement, as scores of barks, brigs, tall-masted sailing ships, and steamers passed by. When his mother wanted to serve the boarders *poisson blanc,* he and his father would haul in a barrelful of the Detroit River's renowned whitefish— the "prince of freshwater fish"—in a few minutes of seining. All the ponies a young boy could want were running almost wild in the back woods, where his wealthy grandfather kept them. The only problem was trying to catch one.

In old age, Labadie kept coming back to the pleasures of these early days. His most frequently recounted memories were of the Indians from Walpole Island, some fifty miles across Lake St. Clair. (It is still an Indian reserve.) These remnants of once-mighty bands—Chippewa, Ottawa, and Pottawatomi—used to camp on the riverbank below his home when they came to Windsor to trade. Nearly one hundred years of friendship and hospitality by generations of Labadies had made them feel at home. These good relations had come in handy some thirty years earlier, the Labadies recounted, when the Walpole Indians went on a rampage, burning farmhouses and murdering settlers, but sparing those who had befriended them.[12] Joseph remembered that sometimes the Indians were even allowed to sleep on the dining room floor, which then became so crowded that he had to go outside and around the house to get into the kitchen.

But this delightful period came to an abrupt end. Industry was courting Detroit, just across the river. A grocer and liquor merchant named Hiram Walker was seeking a site for a distillery and steam milling plant. The Labadie homestead was deemed ideal: cheaper real estate and labor costs than in Detroit, excellent water transportation possibilities, and well-tilled local farms to supply all the grain needed for his enterprises.

Walker began buying up portions of the original Labadie estate from various heirs. In 1857, Joseph's uncle Charles, deputy inspector and collector of inland revenue in Windsor, sold Walker 104 acres, including the house

Joseph's grandfather had built. Walker's new business prospered immediately and the company town that grew around it soon became known as Walkerville. There, Walker eventually set up a little fiefdom, where all who worked for him were obliged to rent his cottages, where he selected the church and the pastor, appointed the police force, and benevolently provided all the amenities he thought his tenants ought to enjoy at no cost. The sale was made against the wishes of Joseph's mother and Charles's other siblings. Thereafter uncle Charley was referred to bitterly as "the man who sold Walkerville to Hiram Walker." For some thirty years, various Labadie relatives tried to bring suit against Walker, the last time in 1909, when the property was estimated to be worth $22 million. Labadie was sure the deal had been carried out "by chicanery." What disturbed him most was that the land was lost to his family, its original settlers after the Indians. "And then to name it 'Walkerville' was a crushing blow; it should have been Labadieville," he fumed, expressing a curiously retrograde sentiment for an anarchist who abjured ownership of land.[13]

Walker wasted no time building his flour mill and the whiskey distillery that was to make him famous. Young Joseph watched in fascination as hosts of workers drove the foundation pilings into the ground. By 1858, lines of wagons loaded with wheat could be seen along the roadway on the way "au moulin de Walker" (to Walker's windmill). Walker remodeled Louis's old frame house and moved in. When Joseph's family was ousted from their comfortable home, the boardinghouse business, and middle-class life, his father was probably relieved for it gave Anthony the opportunity to return to his beloved forests.

The family relocated in the Michigan frontier settlement of Silver Creek Township, Cass County, south of the Labadie homestead in Paw Paw and near the Indiana border. Most of their neighbors were Pottawatomi, whose chief was the college-educated Simon Pokagon.[14] Joseph's father again served as an interpreter in both French and English for the Jesuit missionaries, who had founded their first mission in Michigan in 1668, hoping to Christianize the Indians. He often took his young son along as he roamed the woods in the company of Indian tribes.

The Labadies lived a pioneer existence deep in the forest. On occasion, Joseph walked seven miles to town to get the mail. As a frontier region, land for the homesite was there for the taking. Although there were now at least seven children (four died in birth or infancy), they all crowded into a one-room log house, quite a contrast to their Sandwich home. There was nothing extraordinary about this—families of twenty or more were living in such homes at the time. A cavernous stone fireplace, so large that a bonfire could be built with a log of almost any size, warmed them in even the most frigid temperatures. A bed stood in each corner, with a trundle bed underneath. The woods were teeming with game. Anthony prided himself on being able to shoot whatever his wife wanted to cook—deer, rabbit, squirrel, turkey, pigeons. The children picked wild fruit, to be eaten fresh or dried in the sun.

Though primitive, conditions were not harsh, as Labadie later remembered them, and offered a high degree of freedom and equality.

> With an ax, gun, good health, the knowing how and the willingness to work there was no excuse to go hungry or suffer the inclemencies of the weather. . . . The necessities of life were at hand . . . without being subject to the will of another for the opportunity. . . . A comfortable log house could be built in a few days, the materials for it being easily at hand in the forest, and a bee [community-organized task] could be organized in a short time for its erection . . . we made bees to haul the winter's wood to the different houses in the neighborhood . . . on bob-sleds and ox teams. . . . The exchange of work for work was the rule . . . equality in economic conditions made the neighborhood kin.[15]

It was Labadie's destiny to work in cities all his life, but he always longed for the wilderness. He spent his life promoting an anarchist utopia where survival was simply a matter of hard work, self-reliance, and voluntary cooperation.

The little house in the big woods was the stuff of nostalgia, not least because there were no schools to constrain a boy's wild spirit. Due to the unsettled conditions of his early life, Labadie had no schooling except a few months in a parochial school near South Bend, Indiana, when his father briefly worked as a carpenter for the University of Notre Dame.[16] It is unclear how Labadie learned to read and write, but by the age of sixteen he was able to compose a letter quite adequately. Since his father was barely literate, he could hardly have been the teacher. Probably Euphrosyne, from the richer and more privileged branch of the family, was able to instruct her son. There must have been a Bible in the house, but it was the *New York Ledger,* a popular weekly "which came into my house somehow or other," that Joseph used as reading matter.[17] Both French and English were spoken in the home and Joseph also knew the Pottawatomi language.

Almost the only demand for childhood decorum came during Sunday mass at a homespun local church built by a French priest. There Joseph served as an acolyte, learned a little Latin, and instilled the cleric with dreams of turning him into a fellow Jesuit. Alas for the cleric, Labadie chose the agnosticism of his father over the devoutness of his "saintly" mother, as he described her.

This fairy tale life may not have seemed so charmed to Euphrosyne as it did to her eldest son. Her husband was by nature a hunter and free spirit, not a *pater familias*. Sometimes he was at home and a good provider, but when he felt like it he would go off and let the brood fend for themselves. During one of his father's absences, young Joseph was hired out to a farmer to help his mother provide for the family of five boys. Of a sober turn of mind, she appears in photographs as a stern and sharp-faced woman, quite unlike her genial, irresponsible mate. Her face is gaunt and careworn, her hair tightly pulled back in a bun; she wears granny glasses and a spinsterish high-necked dress. Labadie idolized her. In a poem, "What Is Love?" he wrote of her "grace and meekness, charity and sweetness, affection and generosity." He acknowledged, in the same poem, that his father was "not what I would have ordained." Nevertheless, Labadie remembered him with love and some admiration:

> His hankering for the silent forest, the talkative stream, the exciting chase,
> The log cabin, the rude hearth, the blazing faggot,
> The coonskin tacked to the rustic door,
> The yielding pelts strewn upon the floor,
> The wooden latch and rawhide string outside,
> His unerring gun on the crotches nailed to the rugged beam,
> His thrilling tales turned true from oft telling.[18]

The family probably was little aware of events beyond, from the election of Abraham Lincoln to the secession of the Southern states. But their seclusion did not protect them from the government's long arm. On August 16, 1861, Joseph's father was enrolled as a private in the First Regiment of the Michigan Cavalry. He fought in the Shenandoah Valley and the second battle of Bull Run, though not with distinction. He managed to shoot off his forefinger while loading a pistol, then injured his spine when he fell off a horse during General Banks's retreat from Martinsburg, Virginia, to Williamsport. In 1863 he was discharged as totally disabled. Anthony's disabilities did not cramp his style much. The house was again filled with his cronies, lively with laughter, drinking, and tall story-telling. Hospitality was Anthony's pride, but often his generosity meant his children went hungry. His father's improvidence was probably evident to Labadie then and seems to have stirred in him a concern for the welfare of others, which eventually extended to the workers of the world.[19]

★ 3 ★

Passionate Stirrings

> I am a sprout of the primeval forest
> Transplanted to the sweltering town,
> With its grime and smoke and squalor,
> Where ignorant poverty jostles ignorant wealth,
> And both go to the grave with wasted lives,
> Knowing not the joy of freedom and justice.
> I am a pioneer, unafraid to blaze new paths
> Into virgin forests or realms of social weal,
> Or follow old ones neglected and untrod.
> —"I," MANUSCRIPT

Labadie was soon transported from a backwoods idyll to the "sweltering town," as the above lines from one of his poems attest. At the age of fourteen, Joseph began learning watchmaking in his uncle's jewelry store in White Pigeon, Michigan. A year or two of frustrated fussing with gears and mainsprings impelled Joseph to move on. He rejoined his family, then in South Bend, Indiana, and qualified for a job as printer's devil for the *National Union,* a local weekly. Despite his lack of formal education, his penmanship, spelling, and punctuation were easily on a par with today's sixteen-year-olds, as evidenced by an 1866 letter.[1]

As it has for so many incipient radicals, the printing trade offered Labadie both exposure to a wide range of ideas and the means to disseminate his own. In a few years, he was publishing tracts, labor journals, and revolutionary poetry in the service of a variety of reformist causes. The first recorded example of Labadie's fierce defense of workers' rights—in this case, his own—occurred at the *National Union.* The episode is unique because it almost involved physical violence. As Labadie recounted the story, proprietor Edward Molloy unjustly blamed his young apprentice for some errors. When Labadie objected, Molloy swore at him. In righteous indignation, Labadie grabbed a poker and "I would have brained him . . . if the foreman had not intervened." His job precipitously terminated, Labadie moved on to Schuyler Colfax's *Register*.[2] (Colfax was vice-president in Grant's first administration.)

At seventeen, Labadie began his travels as a "tramp" (itinerant) printer. This hobo-like existence, involving a series of stints in many cities, was almost obligatory in the days of handset type in order to be considered a journeyman printer. It was also a wonderful opportunity for an inquisitive young man from the backwoods to learn about the world. Wandering for the next few years, Labadie witnessed the disparity between the new class of millionaire capitalists and the struggling workers of emerging industrial cities. He observed tenements, misery, and grueling hours of toil. He perceived social upheavals in the making and the role that unionization could play in bringing power to the working class. He developed a passion for social justice that was to dominate his life.

For a young man raised in a backwater of the Midwest, the life of a tramp printer was thrilling. So long as he could satisfy his sparse needs, Labadie was free to follow his wanderlust from place to place as the mood took him, while reassuring himself that in doing so he was mastering the craft. He crisscrossed the northeastern part of the country, working a week here, a month there, for the five years of his required apprenticeship. As a rookie printer, Labadie would pick up jobs at busy publications, only to be laid off as soon as the need disappeared. A day's work often could be had by standing in front of a newspaper office, prepared to fill in if one of the regular printers failed to show up.

His wanderings took him to Boston and New York City and throughout New York, Pennsylvania, Ohio, and Michigan. Business was booming when the Civil War ended, and jobs were not hard to come by. Labadie worked at the *Cincinnati Gazette, Scranton Republican, Erie Dispatch,* and *Jackson Citizen,* with a year-long stint at the *New York World*.[3]

Tramp printing was wearisome, unremunerative, and exasperating, but educational, as Labadie's pal, Judson Grenell, described it. A variety of employers were encountered, "some fair, some tricky." There were many days of "storm and stress." Sometimes the new arrival would find a surfeit of printers and be forced to hit the road again. These hobos were generally "a happy-go-lucky lot, content if they had a dollar or two to provide them a meal and a bed and the still more necessary alcoholic stimulant." Drink was the tramp printer's "staff of life," Grenell wrote, necessitated by a demanding working day of twelve hours or more.[4]

On a morning daily, the work began soon after noon. First came "throwing in the case," that is, distributing the type set the day before into its wooden type cases. Around four o'clock, the printers began composition, selecting each individual letter from the cases. After dusk, this exacting work was continued by gaslight or kerosene lantern. Hand-setting of type went on at least until midnight, interrupted only by a supper break. Some printers remained until early morning, setting the news coming over the wire by telegraph.

Fighting mental exhaustion was a daily battle and alcohol was constantly at hand. Grenell recalled how he would start the morning with an "eye opener," need another "finger or two" in the afternoon, and another before beginning the long hours of the night. After work, an all-night saloon provided the "nightcap."[5]

The hours were by no means exceptional. Most wage earners put in a workday of ten to fourteen hours. Although not necessarily longer than those once worked by independent craftsmen and women, the pace was no longer the worker's to control. Employers, disguising their own self-interests, defended the practice on the grounds that "idleness breeds sloth." It was during Labadie's tramp printing days that the demand for an eight-hour day became the main rallying cry of American labor. Businessmen found this movement alarming, especially since proponents of the shorter working day stressed its purpose was not only more leisure for the enjoyment of life and family. It would also provide time to study the political and economic system so as to check the "corruptions of capital" and reform the social order.[6]

The crusade's leading light was Boston machinist Ira Steward, who inspired the formation of hundreds of eight-hour leagues in the mid 1860s. He anticipated that a cut in working hours with no cut in wages would benefit everyone: workers would have more time to desire and buy products previously considered luxuries, manufacturers would then increase production, prices would fall, more workers would be hired, creating more consumers, and so on. "Whether you work by the piece or work by the day, decreasing the hours increases the pay" went the rhyme that popularized the idea.

During his working life, Labadie participated in countless rallies, demonstrations, marches, and agitation meetings stimulated by the dream of more free time. But the optimistic prophesies of its originators proved illusory. Although President Andrew Johnson signed into law an eight-hour day for federal workers in 1868, it was not until 1919 that even half the country's workers had achieved as little as a six-day, forty-eight-hour work week.[7]

Labadie's first stop after he left South Bend in 1867 was Kalamazoo, where he worked on the *Telegraph,* using a cylinder press with hand power. Here the eighteen-year-old first tasted labor activism by helping form the Kalamazoo Typographical Union.[8] The move probably did not endear him to his boss. Many unionists were discharged and then blacklisted by employers anxious to suppress unionization. But printers had a record of trade organization dating back to the late eighteenth century and it was not easy to stifle their demands. Tramp printers, in particular, were energetic organizers. "Should they arrive in a town where there is no Union they immediately set about organizing one," the *Typographical Journal* noted in 1889, adding that "there are more typographical Unions who owe their inception to the proselyting efforts of the tramp, than to . . . all other causes combined."[9]

As young Labadie tramped the country from Kalamazoo to Boston, he joined the typographical union in each city, paying the dues—"the best investment I ever made"—with relish. His union traveling card entitled him to assistance in finding a bed, a meal, and a job as soon as he arrived. He lovingly treasured the working cards from these early days. A glance at them reveals his itinerary: Erie T.U. (Typographical Union) 77, Scranton T.U. 112, New York City T.U. 6.[10]

In this roaming life Labadie developed not only union consciousness, but social consciousness as well. The printing trade has a history of breeding and nurturing eloquent and articulate champions of social reform. The tramp printer was "certain to be pretty well up in his information touching the leading questions of the day . . . ever ready to engage in a controversy, it making no material difference whether the subject is one of theology or politics, or on matters dramatic, musical or pugilistic," according to the *Typographical Journal* article. In sum, Labadie's tramping days provided some of the education of which he had been deprived. They enabled him to enroll at the age of eighteen as "a modest student of social science," as he put it, by means of discussions, observations of the life around him, and reading the provocative thinkers who influenced him deeply, like Mill, Emerson, and Thoreau.[11]

The time was ripe for such studies. Labadie was born on the eve of a cataclysmic social and economic revolution as the United States transformed itself from an agrarian to an industrial nation. Vast fortunes were amassed by the new capitalist class, powerful monopolies and trusts were formed, and the competitive spirit raged. This phenomenal economic expansion gave rise to explosive social questions. With the introduction of mass production machinery, the artisan in his shop was replaced by the depersonalized factory hand. Once-respected craftsmen found themselves regarded as a commodity, to be bought like any other raw material and tossed out at will. As Labadie saw them, they were the new slaves—wage slaves, displaced, demoralized, and degraded.

The rapid growth of capitalism found the laboring people powerless against the onslaught of big business. There had been sporadic strikes or riots in the past, but most ended disastrously for the workers. Work previously had been individualized, carried out by artisans. It was difficult for the new American working class to come to terms with the Industrial Revolution and learn to band together for self-protection. On his journeys, Labadie saw the growing chasm between the haves and have-nots—those who lived a gilded life and the downtrodden subsisting in squalor. He could hear the rumblings of a volcano of discontent preparing to erupt. He later recalled that he began to be "troubled . . . with that thing we call thought. Before that, I was content with satisfying my animal wants."[12] Radical activism had not been part of his heritage or his frontier upbringing, but he was soon caught up in the momentum of social change.

In 1872, Labadie traveled from New York City to South Bend to visit his family, and then to Detroit to see friends and relatives. His intention was to return to New York, but by then Detroit was a booming town, though not, of course, as lively a metropolis as New York. Life was far more stimulating than during his early childhood in the sleepy hamlet of Sandwich across the river in Canada. Perhaps by this time the twenty-two-year-old was tired of the roaming life and wanted to settle down. Whatever the reason, he got a job at the *Detroit Post and Tribune,* presented his printer's traveling card to Detroit's Typographical Union #18, and, after his five wandering years, began to put down roots.[13]

Detroit was in the midst of astounding industrial growth. Manufacturing establishments were crowding out the small shops of what had once been a city of merchants. In the previous forty years, the population, fed by a steady flow of immigrants, had exploded from 2,000 to 79,000. It had become the seventeenth largest American city. The number of manufacturing jobs had quadrupled in the previous twenty years. Stove making and production of the famous Pullman sleeping cars, Detroit's largest industries before the automotive pioneers came along, depended on iron ore and coal shipped down the lakes from Michigan's Upper Peninsula and from nearby states. Sawmills were fed by deck loads of logs from the state's forests. Thousands of commercial ships, navigating the northwestern lakes either began their journeys in Detroit or passed through it on their way to Buffalo, Chicago, Milwaukee, and elsewhere. By 1880, ten railroads connected Detroit with the rest of the country.[14] Workers were producing drugs, varnish, cigars, shoes, and furniture. Detroit, like most of the country, had embarked on what Mark Twain dubbed the "Gilded Age." Industry, and with it the worship of wealth and status, was king.

The majority of Detroit's working class had been born outside the United States. Canadians and British were the first to arrive in large numbers, followed by the Irish, fleeing the potato famine and British land monopoly. They clustered on the city's west side in "Corktown," and by 1850 formed one-seventh of the population. Most were poor and unskilled when they arrived, but many found jobs in the metal trade and eventually prospered.

By 1860, Germans surpassed the Irish in numbers and within thirty years represented more than four in every ten Detroiters. Waves of German immigrants were also sweeping into other Great Lakes cities like Cleveland, Chicago, and Milwaukee. The latter was known as the "Deutsche Athens," and 70 percent of its population was German by 1890. Nearly half the workers in Detroit's eastside German community were skilled artisans— cigarmakers, shoemakers, brewers, woodworkers, and coopers—but it was harder for them to achieve high-skill positions than the English-speaking immigrants.

Poles were the most recent arrivals, but by 1890 may have outnumbered native-born workers (since Poland was divided between Prussia and Russia, Poles sometimes identified themselves to census takers as Russians, Austrians, or Germans). Most had been peasants back home. They found it difficult to enter skilled trades and, as in Milwaukee and other cities, found work only as manual laborers, earning half the wages of a skilled craftsman.

The poor, however, were not crammed into tenements. Detroit was a city of single family houses, although many laborers lived in outlying shantytowns near brick- and lumberyards.[15]

In 1873, just one year after Labadie's move to Detroit, the boom sparked by the Civil War came to a dramatic end. A devastating financial panic swept the country, followed by six years of widespread unemployment, poverty, and misery, an economic depression felt not only in the United States, but in much of the industrialized world. Blame for the Panic of 1873 was laid on currency inflation, reckless speculation, overly rapid building of railroads, and a host of other unhealthy economic practices. "Vicious and ignorant financial experiments," the *Detroit Evening News* called them.[16]

In Detroit, more than six thousand people went on relief. The number of inmates in the county poor house increased more than threefold.[17] Bread lines formed in many cities. It was said that nine hundred people starved to death in New York City. Radical rumblings grew among the unemployed, but it was a black period for labor unions. Wage earners were reluctant to antagonize employers and union membership declined drastically.

Labor was "used and abused," as Labadie described the times. "When pay day came around the men found [their wages] had been reduced . . . without any notice whatever. Those who would not stand the reduction . . . were discharged."[18] Hordes of hungry tramps roamed the country. These were not adventurous young men out to seek their fortunes or fulfill their apprentice years, but experienced craftsmen desperately seeking work.

During this depression, the worst yet experienced in the country, Labadie's parents and four brothers returned to Windsor from South Bend. His father could not find work and the family was reduced to begging for money from their prosperous relatives. It was not long before Anthony Cleophis was yearning for "woody glens, the gleaming trout streams, the sighing of the mournful pines and the exciting chase." Labadie attributed this discontent to "the blood of his ancestors," meaning the Indians.[19]

The rest of the family, however, found city life alluring. They were tired of the hardships of the backwoods. So, accompanied by his dogs and guns, Anthony bade his family farewell, and journeyed northward into the forests of Kalkaska County. He spent the rest of his life living alone in a cabin on the Little Manistee River, visited occasionally by his sons. He was no hermit, however; his convivial nature, passed down to his children, attracted a constant stream of visitors to his cabin, including "sportes from all partes of the world" to whom he rented fishing boats. Despite the "total disability" that occasioned his army discharge, he managed to go into lumbering and eventually bought over five thousand acres of timberland.[20] He even founded a township and became one of its elected officials. But newfound prosperity and respectability did not turn Anthony into a responsible family man. He provided for his abandoned wife and children only to the extent of occasionally sending a barrel of potatoes or a deer he had shot.[21] At some point, they joined Jo, the eldest son, in Detroit.

During this period, Labadie experienced a tragedy that provoked the first of what was to become, throughout the years, a flood of passionate protest letters to editors. His brother Edward, also a printer, contracted a virulent form of "black" smallpox. Labadie sought vainly for a nurse, since their mother and his other three brothers had become so ill after vaccinations that they were hospitalized. At the board of health, it was suggested that he contact the "poormaster," although Labadie insisted it was a nurse, not charity, that he needed. Edward, by then in a raging fever and delirious, twice escaped from their Orchard Street house by breaking through a window and wandered shoeless through the streets. In the middle of the night, two policemen found him on Michigan Avenue and took him, "half naked and raving like a maniac," to the smallpox hospital.[22]

"I was not aware of the existence of a pest-house until my brother was taken there . . . or I would have had him taken there as soon as possible," Labadie protested in an anguished letter to the *Evening News*. "I wish to draw the attention of the public . . . to the existing negligence in the care of poor unfortunates who are afflicted with this terrible disease . . . and [hope] the authorities will awaken to the sense of duty they owe the community." Edward, whom Labadie "loved . . . as much as man ever loved a brother," died on May 4, 1876, at the age of twenty-two, after suffering for three weeks "all the torture and horrors of the most terrible disease God ever afflicted mankind with."[23]

At the time Labadie was grieving over his brother he was also deeply absorbed in a tempestuous love affair with his cousin, Sophie Elizabeth Archambeau (or Archambault). They had had a discordant relationship as teenagers in South Bend, when Sophie's mother, Laura Josephine Archambeau, lived down the street with her four daughters. Cousin Sophie, two years his junior, prided herself on her fine education, contrasting it to that of the rustic, uneducated Joseph, and ridiculing his use of language. In turn, he accused her of swallowing a grammar book.[24]

Sophie was an exceptionally well educated and pious young woman of twenty-four, a high school graduate at a time when only one in fifty Americans could make that claim. Once a star pupil at St. Joseph's Academy, a parochial school in South Bend, she now was teaching in a parochial school in Belle River, Canada, several miles outside Windsor. Somehow, in the unknown way that opposites attract, their quarrels had ceased and romance blossomed. Every weekend in the mid 1870s, Sophie made the journey to Detroit to see Labadie. In between, they wrote long and fervent letters, hers frequently in French. Labadie's dwelt on his love for her; Sophie's stressed her duty to the church.[25]

In florid, rapturous phrases, "Antonie" or "Antonius," as the twenty-six-year-old Labadie affectedly signed himself, wrote of his "wild, passionate love" which was "eating my very soul for lack of your affections to appease its hunger." He identified himself with "the lovers of old—those we read of in the days of chivalry." If Sophie refused to become his wife, he threatened, he would be happy at the bottom of the Detroit River.[26]

Sophie was adamant that they not marry until he, a lapsed Catholic, was restored to the faith. "I feel *I must save you,*" she declared, "I know we will be so proud of our labors, and how I will hold you up before the world as one who left the world with all its wickedness and joined that faith without which it is impossible to please God . . . I believe that God has brought us . . . together for some great end, and that end is your conversion." He exclaimed that his "passions have been running wild." She proclaimed: "O blessed creed! O Holy creed, O may God increase my faith that I may do right . . . that you might know the Truths He has revealed to us." Labadie was deeply hurt by her demands. "I am not good enough . . . as I am. I must be born again and remodeled before she can take me. She loves me, but she loves a vague ethereal thing she calls my soul better," he reproached her in his strong, confident hand.[27]

Added to this travail was strong opposition from Sophie's family, now living in Detroit. Her mother, who had known Labadie all his life, so strongly disapproved of her daughter's suitor that she refused to acknowledge him on the street. His incipient radicalism could not have been the cause. He was still conventional enough to be a mainstream Democrat, supporting Samuel J. Tilden for president.[28] Mrs. Archambeau, a strong-willed seamstress separated from her husband, might, of course, have taken exception to Labadie's rustic upbringing and lack of education. She probably thought him a bit reckless and flamboyant, not at all like the steady Sophie. There was also the problem of his father, the kind of man who would desert his family and follow a will o' the wisp into the wilderness. Although he did not yet proclaim himself an agnostic, Labadie was also clearly religiously deficient in her eyes.

The most likely reason for her opposition, however, was probably the same one given by the Church. The pair was consanguineous to an even closer degree than first cousins. Not only were their mothers sisters, direct descendants of Antoine Louis's third marriage, but Labadie's father came down the line from Antoine Louis's second marriage to the Sauteuse, Marie. The two lines, which had merged in the marriage of Labadie's parents, would be drawn even closer. Such a marriage was not illegal according to state statutes, but required a special dispensation if the Church were to approve.[29] It was commonly thought that such unions produced diseased, mentally retarded, or handicapped offspring.

Perhaps Sophie was more motivated by love than she revealed in her letters. She eventually agreed to the marriage with or without a church dispensation. When, afraid of her mother and public opinion, she retracted that promise, Labadie vowed to enlist a Detroit priest he knew in their "good and holy cause." If that failed, he wanted Sophie to become a resident of Windsor, where the bishop seemed more amenable.[30]

He begged Sophie to be true to their love, not church dogma:

> Listen, darling, you hold in your hands the purest, truest crystal of love man ever gave woman; it remains in your future actions to preserve and cherish it or throw it to the pavements of tyranny and cowardice to be broken into fragments! . . . Hold strong and tight, and do not let me slip away from you . . . I have made up my mind to marry you, and marry you I will, if you will only be true and not forsake me in the fight. Buckle on my armor, love, and I will go to the battle with a stout heart and the sword of right sharpened for the conflict.

What he would not do in order to receive permission to marry was "bend my knee or humiliate myself, as only a spaniel would . . . [before] loveless, heartless men . . . who, in all probability, never loved a woman in their lives."[31]

Labadie was the consummate romantic revolutionary; Sophie, the devout conformist, absorbed since childhood with school, daily Mass, and sewing. He was handsome, a bit vain, dynamic, and theatrical. She was somewhat plain, domestic, and rather colorless. "Nothing marked her," as their friend Agnes Inglis put it. His thoughts soared in contemplation of grand social schemes. Hers focused on mundane tasks and the approved feminine interests of the time. They did not appear to be soulmates.

His passion apparently prevailed. The two eventually wed in a formal ceremony on August 14, 1877, in St. Alphonse's Church in Windsor. He was twenty-seven, she was twenty-five. Father Dean Wagner officiated, indicating that they must have received a church dispensation in Canada. Their wedding photograph, posed before a painted backdrop of bookcase and fireplace, depicts a full-faced young man in morning coat, with dark hair curling around his collar, a modified handlebar mustache and goatee. Sophie, swathed in tulle and lace, gazes at the photographer with large, wide-set eyes and a sweet and trusting expression. Not shown is her pride and glory—a mane of wavy hair which, when unpinned, cascaded down her five-foot frame and trailed six inches on the ground.

The outcome of the union put to shame any who questioned its durability. It proved incredibly felicitous. The pair lived together in loving harmony for the next fifty-five years. We can only conjecture on what transformed this strong-minded young woman into the docile and supportive helpmate she became.

Sophie lived and died a pious Catholic. Rather than returning to the fold, Labadie developed into a lifelong agnostic. Yet they lived "as near the anarchist philosophy as could be," marveled Agnes Inglis, who knew them well. As Labadie later expressed it in anarchist jargon, "We do not aggress each other's rights. . . . We do not choose to make one the slave of the other." He granted his "companion-wife" perfect freedom in her own affairs (which were pretty tame), even to the extent of planning a career in the priesthood for their son (who, to Labadie's relief, rejected it). She, in turn, as Labadie himself described it, allowed him to "come and go at will; entertain men and women friends as I choose; accompany them on excursions, picnics, to theaters, meetings, churches and wherever I choose to go without opposition."[32]

Labadie was very like his father in one respect. Freedom was the fuel that ignited his soul. Sophie offered him a lifetime of freedom, coupled with tenderness and loyalty. Through his many endeavors and turmoils, she was a pillar of support, even when his actions conflicted with church dogma. When he was the target of ridicule and scorn, she offered comfort. Uncomplainingly, she made the best of their always limited means. While he glowed in the limelight, she was largely content to linger in the shadows. In return, he made the following vow to Sophie:

> To grant thee the right of the rose to follow the bent of thine own nature,
> To assume no authority over thee,
> To be kind to thee and courtly,
> To respect thy whims, wishes, desires, thots, inclinations,
> And to be loyal to thee.
> This is love.[33]

In years to come, Labadie had many dynamic women friends in the labor and anarchist movements, including such firebrands as Emma Goldman and Lucy Parsons. Yet he never swayed from his devotion to his beloved "Mamma." In old age, he declared: "She has been to me very well worth the living."[34]

★ 4 ★

Waving the Red Flag

O workers of the world, unite,
And use your dormant brains!
You have the right, you have the might
To break your slavish chains!
— "WORKERS, UNITE," *SONGS OF THE SPOILED*

In 1848, two years before Labadie's birth, Karl Marx and Friedrich Engels exhorted the workers of the world to throw off their chains. "The proletarians . . . have a world to win," they cried out in the *Communist Manifesto*. It described history as a class struggle that would result in inevitable doom for the oppressive bourgeoisie: "Let the ruling classes tremble." As the apocalyptic pamphlet whipped up fervor, the ruling classes did not waste their time trembling but rather galvanized their powers to crush all incipient uprisings.

But a revolutionary labor movement had been born that was carried to the United States by boatloads of Germans fleeing their country in the crackdown that followed the revolutions of 1848. These exiles, some of whom had worked with Marx, formed Communist clubs and workers' groups in America before the Civil War. In 1872, the International Working Men's Association—the labor organization Marx helped found in London in 1864—moved its headquarters to New York City. This legendary "First International," as it was later called, numbered about five thousand members in the United States.[1]

Marx was, in Engels's words, "the best hated and most calumniated man of his time." Any organization he was associated with was bound to strike terror in American hearts. The First International, however, was not a communist cell, but rather the first international organization of labor, and was by no means committed to revolution. Its members represented a range of ideologies, not necessarily Marxist. What they strove for was economic emancipation of the working classes, to be achieved through international solidarity. There was no unanimity regarding how to bring this about.

Among Detroiters in the 1870s, as in other cities, unease about immigrant radicalism was growing. The crushing of the 1848 revolts had brought the first wave of German political refugees to Michigan. More than twenty years later, still more Germans streamed into the city, attracted by its rapid industrial growth and favorable employment opportunities. Once a Gallic city, Detroit was becoming, in many ways, a Teutonic one. There was widespread apprehension that foreign-born socialists were spreading their alien creed among Michigan's working people.

As the largest ethnic community in Detroit, Germans by 1870 represented 36 percent of the city's foreign-born; they soon made up nearly a quarter of the entire population. The corridor along Gratiot Avenue on the near east side was a Little Germany, with its own businesses, churches, saloons, and newspapers. Socialist sympathies in this ethnic community were strong even before two top-notch German cigarmakers were hired from New York in 1874 by local cigar manufacturer, George Moebs, who was doubtless unaware of their revolutionary inclinations. Recent immigrants Henry Kummerfeldt and Gustav Herzig, as it turned out, were veteran socialist agitators and union organizers.[2]

Tobacco and cigars were two of Detroit's major industries, with dozens of factories and many more small shops. Most of the city's cigarmakers were German men, renowned for the fine craftsmanship they had acquired in the Old Country, and thus highly prized. (A few women found work in non-union cigar factories, but unionists demanded all-male workshops.) Like printers, cigarmakers often acquired an education on the job. Sitting together for long hours stuffing tobacco leaves into smooth rolls, they had a custom of "hiring" one of the workmen to read to them, rewarding him with as many cigars as he would have rolled at his bench. Sometimes the reader chose pages from Marx, or his rival social theorist, Ferdinand Lassalle. In Detroit, Kummerfeldt and Herzig found receptive ears. Within a year, they had established a thriving socialist "section," with meetings attended by 400 to 500 sympathizers, all native Germans, many of them cigarmakers.[3]

It soon became clear to these Germans that if the economic doctrines of Marx and Lassalle were to influence the majority of Detroit's wage workers, the movement would have to be Americanized. Party organizers began scheduling meetings outside the German ethnic communities and addressing audiences in English. One Sunday afternoon in 1877, in front of a small hall on Michigan Avenue opposite the Book-Cadillac Hotel, they posted a sign: SOCIAL DEMOCRATS MEET HERE. WALK IN. ADMISSION FREE. It was at this meeting, or one like it, that Labadie was introduced to socialism firsthand.[4]

Since the young printer had considered the study of sociology—a term that then included all aspects of economic, political, and cultural life—his "hobby" since the age of eighteen, some idea of Marxist tenets already must have come his way.[5] With socialism popularly denounced as a vicious, un-American doctrine that aimed to steal from the industrious and reward the lazy, he probably mounted the stairs with both anticipation and trepidation. He was, in effect, taking his first steps toward radicalism. A man at the hall door was handing out tracts; another shook his hand and welcomed him. Small groups of men stood around, speaking German.

The chairman spoke in English. He was explaining the cause of poverty in the midst of plenty. In the capitalist system, wage workers were continually creating surplus wealth that became the property of the employing class. When gluts in the market occurred, workers were idled until this surplus, of which they had been robbed, was absorbed. To rectify this injustice, workingmen must demand a cooperative commonwealth, with society collectively the only employer. Profit would be eliminated, prices would be no more than the cost of production, and each worker would be compensated in proportion to his individual production. The socialist motto, "To each according to his deeds" ("needs" in a later version), would be put into practice.[6]

Here was a program to inspire a young reformer. Here was a diagnosis of society's most debilitating diseases and a just and beautiful, all-encompassing cure. Labadie had been horrified by the country's misery and suffering in the last four years of economic depression. Socialism offered a remedy dedicated to providing the greatest good to the greatest number and saving the multitudes he saw perishing because they lacked the necessities of life. He threw himself into the cause of state socialism with the same intensity and fervor he exhibited in repudiating it six years later in favor of anarchism and rejection of the state.

What particularly impressed Labadie was the difference between the socialist vision and the narrow program of the printers' unions he had been involved with, which focused on bettering the wages and working conditions of their members alone. Although an active member of Detroit's Typographical Union 18, he knew it sought no permanent solution to labor's problems. Labadie craved an agenda far more sweeping than trade union aims, one that foresaw a complete recasting of society. As he learned more about state socialism, he thought he had found the mold. When he was issued the Socialist Labor party's red card in 1877, he became one of the first two native-born converts to socialism in Detroit. The other was Judson Grenell, later Labadie's co-worker in many radical endeavors. From this point on, their lives were to be closely linked, and Grenell's writings offer many insights into Labadie's role in these turbulent times.

Grenell was a New York–born printer, three years to the day older than Labadie, the fourteenth child of a Baptist minister. He became a "printer's devil," or assistant, at the age of thirteen. After a bit of "tramping," he settled down as a typesetter in New Haven, and served as financial secretary of the local printers' union. At the time there were three women printers in New Haven. Only one, Mary Thorpe, joined the union, a smart move on her part, as it turned out. The union saw to it that thereafter she received the same wages as the men; the other two women received only two-thirds as much. Judson Grenell married Mary Thorpe.[7]

In 1876, Grenell moved to Detroit to take charge of the composing room of the *Michigan Christian Herald,* a Baptist weekly publication. When he first observed Labadie at a crowded union meeting, Grenell was attracted by his aggressive dynamism, so in contrast to Grenell's own reserve and self-confessed lack of "personal magnetism." A drunken printer, big and brawny, was disrupting the proceedings. The sergeant-at-arms, charged with restoring order, hesitated to throw him out. Labadie rushed headlong into battle. Without pausing for official sanction, he announced: "If the union's regularly delegated officer won't do this duty, I'll elect myself his assistant and do the job myself." He strode purposefully down the aisle, all five feet four inches of him girded to confront the drunkard. Much to Grenell's disappointment, the troublemaker fell into a stupor before Labadie reached him, thereby depriving Grenell of the chance to see "Joe 'in action,' a militant exemplification of 'authority.' "[8]

The two novice socialists, Labadie and Grenell, soon found themselves working in the same Larned Street print shop, Gulley, Bornman, and Company. During lunch breaks, they discovered similar humanitarian ideals and economic predelictions. They agreed that the labor problem was international in scope and that trade unions were not doing much to "help the forward march of the human race toward the light," as Grenell liked to quote Victor Hugo. Full of youthful enthusiasm, they resolved to reorganize the industrial world. In the fall of 1877, Labadie and Grenell began the first of many collaborations, when local socialists started publishing an English-language newspaper dedicated to "the economic emancipation of the working classes." *The Socialist* was Detroit's most radical labor paper up to then, and the first to achieve national prominence. Grenell was its editor; Labadie its chief contributor.[9]

Several other English-speaking members joined Grenell and Labadie in Detroit's hitherto totally "foreign" socialist movement. The city had three sections—German, Bohemian, and American—of the Working-Men's party of the United States, formed in 1876 and soon to be renamed the Socialist Labor party. Meeting in Lafayette Hall at 189 Gratiot Avenue, in the working-class east side, the American section included English-born Edward W. Simpson, president of the Detroit Carpenters' Union; veteran unionist Thomas Dolan, who had organized the Detroit Cigarmakers Union in 1863; Charles Erb, of German parentage, who also worked with the German section; printer Charles Bell; and E. A. Stevens, who became an SLP organizer. (All were to join L.A. 901 of the Knights of Labor one year later when Labadie organized it under cover as the Washington Literary Society.) The activities of the SLP were primarily educational, and, to Labadie's relief, entailed no grips, signs, or passwords.[10]

"The interests of the whole people are more sacred than the interests of the individual" *The Socialist* proclaimed on its masthead. One of a handful of English-language socialist papers in the nation, the eight-page weekly sold for five cents a copy and had paid advertising. Grenell and Labadie produced it at night and Sundays, often after a grueling work week. By the light of a kerosene lamp, they stood at a printer's case on the third floor of the Volksblatt building on Farmer Street, writing and typesetting articles simultaneously to save time.[11]

That fall the socialists nominated Simpson for mayor, Dolan for city clerk, and Erb for director of the poor—all native-born Americans—in their first electoral campaign. Coupled with a lack of money and precinct-level organization, the party was handicapped by a heavily immigrant constituency, many of whom did not speak English and were not registered to vote.

Simpson received 778 votes, 6 percent of the total, most from eastside German precincts. As with other elections of the period in Detroit, the count was disputed, since some of Simpson's votes were thrown out in a recount and Grenell once watched an election inspector throw away handfuls of ballots and neglect to tally others.[12]

Every cent received by *The Socialist* was "sacredly devoted to agitation purposes" and "not a single farthing" went into the pockets of its staff, the paper announced. Labadie even paid for his own subscription, his account book shows, delivered to him at his regular job in the *Post and Tribune* composing rooms at the corner of Shelby and Larned Streets. He saved each issue, also stashing in his and Sophie's quarters a great mass of periodicals, tracts, leaflets, letters, newspaper clippings, and odds and ends. Grenell observed that Labadie "seldom if ever [threw] away any printed matter having to do with labor conditions and radical propaganda, no matter how trivial it might seem to be."[13]

The SLP had been established in New York City earlier that year as an alliance of Marxist (trade union) and Lassallean (political) socialists. Soon after its first convention in Newark, New Jersey, in December 1877, *The Socialist* made the exaggerated boast that there were seventy thousand members in seventy-two sections in the United States. (Whatever the correct number, few were native-born Americans.) *The Socialist*'s subscription sales were going so well that it anticipated over eight thousand readers the following year. The paper marveled that the "capitalistic papers" were fiercely "fumigating [*sic*] against communism, socialism, and other isms they know nothing of," when only a year previously, the term socialism had been almost unknown to the average newspaper reader. It stressed that the SLP supported "ballots before bullets," and denied that socialists were arming themselves for a revolution. Yet it warned that if those controlling the means of production tried to further enslave labor, "a bloody revolution will begin that will end only in Labor's complete emancipation."[14]

What exactly socialism meant was then, as now, the subject of fervent debate. It has been said waggishly that there are as many definitions of socialism as there are socialists. There were at the time several competing versions of socialism, and the party was torn by factional disputes. The followers of Lassalle sought the salvation of the workers through a labor party and considered trade union actions futile. They were pitted against the Marxists, who emphasized militant unionism because they felt it was premature to form a workers' party of any power. Most SLP members were moderates; even Marx relied on the inevitability of the collapse of capitalism, and believed socialism in America might come about by democratic means. Among the warring factions were militants—chiefly Germans—who wanted to destroy capitalism by force and sneered at the Americans for being too tame. In turn, Americans like Labadie and Grenell mocked the doctrinaire Old World ideologues "who walked so straight they leaned backwards." Indeed, the long-term failure of the socialist movement in the United States has been attributed by one scholar to its ideological rigidity and refusal to make practical compromises.[15]

The Socialist proclaimed that working people should organize themselves into one great labor body, with each trade union as a section of the party. It held that the "present slavish, capitalistic, competitive system of industry" should be abolished; the means of production, transportation, and communication, as well as land, machinery, and railroads should become the common property of all the people; cooperative production should replace the wage system and the producer should have the right to all that he created; and all class distinctions should be eliminated. Competition, as Labadie saw it then (he later completely reversed his position), was "inhumanizing," based on a "soul and mind destroying selfishness." It was all very well to fight for such limited goals as the eight-hour day, but communism (as he described the SLP doctrine), which he defined simply as "[to] help one another," was "the only permanent remedy I can see for enforced idleness and consequent misery."[16]

The SLP platform also included other "ameliorative" demands, similar to those of the Knights of Labor. They included sanitary inspections of factories, setting up of bureaus of labor statistics, no private use of prison labor, no employment of children under fourteen, equal pay for women, repeal of conspiracy laws, weekly paydays, and a graduated income tax. The party also called for a ban on the importation of coolies, commonly accused of "taking the bread away from the wage-laboring people" by working too hard for too little. Labadie rejected this cry for the prohibition of Chinese immigration, a cry that was echoed by American labor for decades to come. "I looked behind the laborer who worked cheaply and saw the forces that cheapened him," Labadie wrote. Nothing could be gained by "maltreating this man." Instead, he maintained, laborers of all countries should band together to save themselves "from the terrible vortex of capitalism that threatens . . . to plunge us into everlasting ruin."[17]

Though it is unlikely that many Detroiters studied the party platform, the newspapers pronounced it alarming. Socialism and communism were words used more or less interchangeably, and communism, in the 1870s, evoked the Paris Commune—when insurrectionists controlled Paris for seventy-two days. Its popular imagery signified rampages, atrocities, and anarchy. The Detroit *News* branded the SLP "a band of organized fanatics, of whose members, means or purposes but little is known." The newspaper suspected that they were arming and drilling in Detroit in preparation for overthrowing the entire social system.[18]

In fact, the Detroit socialists were quite a merry bunch, leavening their agitation meetings and study groups with a busy schedule of excursions and entertainment organized to raise funds for the cause. From Christmas to late spring, there were monthly balls and masquerades, some in support of such causes as a cigarmakers' strike in New York City or the Workingmen's Aid and Relief Society. In May, the steamer *Steinhoff* took SLP members on a grand excursion to Slocum's Island.[19]

In keeping with his new responsibilities as a married man, Labadie kept a detailed account book which sketches the link between domestic life and social commitment. The couple bought twenty-five-cent tickets for several balls held by the socialists and attended theatrical performances. They spent $4.75 for hay for their horse, $1.50 for a case of homeopathic medicine, allowed such indulgences as billiards, a sleigh ride, dried figs, and cigars. The Labadies gave five cents to a "poor old man" and ten cents to "orphans." Labadie's notations make clear that his job at the *Post and Tribune* was irregular. Some months he worked as few as fourteen or fifteen days, his earnings varying from $31.80 to $78.44 a month. Printers in union shops could earn fifteen dollars or more per week, considerably more than the average worker's nine or ten dollars for a sixty-hour work week. Labadie also recorded several ten-cent fines, commonly given for tardiness or talking on the job.[20] Jo and Sophie found it hard to make ends meet. They were paying his mother room and board (around eight dollars a week) and occasionally buying clothes for his brothers. Even with Sophie's salary as a teacher during these early days of marriage, the couple often spent more than they took in.

Despite the fact that many rank-and-file members frowned on his left-wing activities, Labadie was well liked and well respected in the local printers' union. In June 1878, the Detroit T.U. 18 chose him as one of two delegates to the annual convention of the International Typographical Union (ITU), held in Detroit. At the time, the Detroit local had around 160 members out of a total of some 400 printers in the city.[21] Although it was the nation's oldest craft organization, the ITU was not thriving. Hard times after the Panic of 1873 had nearly crushed the nation's entire trade union movement; its numbers had declined from some 300,000 to perhaps 50,000. The printers' organization had lost more than half its members in four years.[22]

For a young man who thrived on visionary programs, the talk in the convention's Common Council chamber that year seemed dry and tepid. Labadie conceded later that he had "reaped many benefits" from the union, but he was impatient with its "slow, conservative course," never striking at the root of labor's troubles. The ITU did not concern itself much with larger social reforms, although it was always successful in looking after its own. Labadie sat with forty-six representatives from printers' and pressmen's unions in the United States and Canada as they contemplated such specifics as lowering the per capita union tax, setting up an insurance scheme, and how much to fine "rats" (non-union printers or scabs) who rejoined the union. He proposed that the union support efforts to get a new apprentice law setting fourteen years as the minimum age, but his resolution did not come to a vote. Why, he wondered, did printers, who should stand at the head of organized labor, have "one of the poorest organizations in the country?" After his firsthand look at their annual get-together, Labadie suspected that conventions were held "simply to let the boys have a good time . . . the work done is not equivalent to the cost."[23]

The only fireworks exploded after ITU President Darwin L. Streeter launched an attack in his introductory remarks against communists as "worthless vagabonds . . . who seek to incite genuine workingmen to unlawful acts through the medium of paid agitators . . . bummers and barnacles . . . [who] hope for a chance to live at somebody else's expense," according to the report of the proceedings. Labadie surely winced as other delegates joined the onslaught. R. Higgins of Denver proposed that the ITU publicly express contempt for communism. Henry White of Memphis asked the union to oppose all "isms" that were stigmatizing the ITU and interfering with "friendly relations between employers and journeymen."

All printers were not as unenlightened as Labadie feared, however, and dissenting voices spoke up. One delegate objected to appeasing the public's fears, saying the delegates "were not here to put ourselves right before anybody." Another who knew communists and socialists personally found they were "all right." A third asked what right the convention had "to denounce fellow workingmen for holding views which to them seemed just and honest." The committee appointed to study the anti-communist resolutions recommended their approval, but the majority of the delegates opposed such action, calling it "undignified" and "entirely outside the legitimate business of the Union." The *Detroit Evening News* expressed exasperation with that decision and asked how the union—"supposed to be the most intelligent body of workmen in this or any other country on the globe" could have such a "suspicious" and "short-sighted policy."[24]

Labadie was paid $15 for his services as T.U. 18's delegate for the week. A delegate's certificate and other expenses, including an excursion up the Detroit River to Lake St. Clair, cost him $8.34. It could not have been encouraging for the new husband to record an income that month of $40.77 and expenditures of $53.55.[25]

The week of the convention also marked the demise of the Detroit *Socialist* after thirty-three issues. The death blow came when the SLP decided to launch the *National Socialist* in Cincinnati as its official organ. It was a devastating setback for those trying to keep the nearly bankrupt Detroit paper alive. Workers could not afford to buy two papers. But the *National Socialist* ran heavily into debt, and was soon replaced by the Chicago *Socialist*—which hung on less than a year before it used up its entire capital of $2,600.[26]

Grenell had been offered editorship of the Chicago *Socialist,* but declined to move there, a decision he considered providential in light of future events. After the 1886 Haymarket bombing, socialists and dissenters of all stripes were rounded up by Chicago police. "Had I accepted," wrote Grenell, "it is probable that I would have been accused of complicity." The fate of the Chicago's *Socialist*'s staff was indeed dismaying. Assistant editor Albert Parsons was charged with murder and hanged after the Haymarket trial, although it was acknowledged he was not present at the time of the explosion. Editor Frank Hirth, a Detroiter, was arrested in Milwaukee, where state troops killed five workmen and a boy during a demonstration that took place on the same day as that in Haymarket Square. Hirth later committed suicide in Detroit by taking poison.[27]

Undeterred by the failure of their first collaborative publishing effort, Labadie and Grenell went forward with the optimism and belief in unlimited possibilities so characteristic of both radicals and capitalists in the Gilded Age. In the next decade they produced a stream of pamphlets and short-lived periodicals to prod and enlighten the wage earner. These labor journals were read by workers throughout the country and played a significant role in the growth of the labor movement. They were a most effective tool with which to exhort and inform workers, recruit them into labor organizations, explain economic and political theories, communicate the state of trades in various cities, profile labor leaders and radical thinkers, and reiterate the message that labor's hope for the future lay in organization.[28]

★ 5 ★

Strange Bedfellows

I shall speak out!
Like the roar of the sea, I have a message.
There is danger ahead and I would give warning.
The greater the danger the louder the roar,
And my foghorn voice is pitched deep and strong.
I am the spirit of Discontent.
— FROM "FREEDOM OF SPEECH," *DOGGEREL FOR
THE UNDERDOG*

Agitate, educate, organize!" was the endlessly repeated rallying cry of those fighting for the "emancipation of labor." Labadie vigorously
followed this command, throwing himself into a confusing array of reformist
battles. He intended to "speak out," to "give warning." He rarely saw a
cause he did not like—socialism, Greenbackism, the "single tax" scheme,
the Knights of Labor, and, finally, anarchism. Ideologically, he was always
an ardent lover, but not a monogamous one.

As a printer, Labadie found the press his most effective weapon. The
Detroit *Socialist* was dead; it was time for a new publishing venture to
awaken the masses and recruit a working-class army. He and Grenell planned
to stir up the city's working people and make them think, for "when we
can set the people to think, the battle is won," Grenell told the Chicago
Socialist.[1]

Inspired by the success of religious tract societies, they hit on the
idea of printing simple, cheap pamphlets explaining socialism. These, they
argued, the SLP sections could afford to buy in quantity and distribute
throughout the country "like leaves in autumn." The two pamphleteers
reasoned that if each SLP member passed the tracts out free whenever the

subject of socialism came up, "these little messengers . . . cannot fail of converting many."[2]

Calling themselves the Socialistic Tract Association, Labadie and Grenell congregated most evenings with a few socialist comrades to set type by the light of kerosene lamp and tallow dip. Their headquarters, described rather romantically by Grenell as a "dusty garret," was a little printing office owned by the SLP, located above a saloon and a cigar factory at the corner of Gratiot Avenue and Randolph Street. Motivated by the "great truths [that] can be compressed into four pages," the dedicated crew nevertheless found it required "considerable grit and determination" to spend their only free time writing, typesetting and printing by flickering light after a long day laboring at the same task.[3]

The unsigned tracts were written by Chicago *Socialist* editor Frank Hirth and seventy-year-old Pontiac, Michigan, farmer John Francis Bray, as well as by Labadie, Grenell, and others. Bray was a legendary old-time socialist. As a youth, he had been involved in the Chartist movement of the late 1830s, the first attempt of the British working classes to gain political power. He was writing about socialism when Karl Marx was still a law student at the University of Berlin. Marx later called Bray's 1839 book, *Labour's Wrongs and Labour's Remedy,* "a remarkable work" and quoted him at length in *Poverty of Philosophy.* For fifty years, Bray had been espousing his fanciful remedy for labor's ills: the "marriage" of labor and capital. He acknowledged that the metaphoric marriage would be a forced one, "but when the wife—capital—sees how kind a husband—labor—she has, the hate will quickly change to love, and the result of the union will be a perfected progeny of which both alike will feel proud."[4]

Far from being menacing proclamations, the tracts were the soul of moderation. "What Is Socialism?" the first tract, foresaw the gradual evolution of a cooperative commonwealth that would be the only manufacturer, landowner, or "railroad king." Everyone would be his own employer, there would be no depressions, no overproduction, and the earth would be transformed from "a vale of tears" into a "paradise."[5]

Socialism was not an invented system, the tract emphasized, but a discovery of the laws governing the development of mankind. It was based on "scientific truth." (Marx and Engels held that socialism had graduated from its earlier "utopian" phase and had become "scientific," the result of an inexorable historical process.) Socialists did not need to foment revolutions, but only remove obstacles in the way of mankind's natural and inevitable advancement. The new order was nearly at hand, the tract assured its readers;

indeed, if ignorance could be eliminated next week, "we could commence to inaugurate the Socialistic State the day after." To the pamphleteers, it was simply a matter of informing the public of socialism's wonderful possibilities to ensure its ready adoption.[6]

The tracts were sold at cost, at just over a dollar per thousand. "Think of it! *Four thousand pages* of Socialistic reading matter for $1.12!" their advertisement proclaimed. By July 1880, the association could brag that it had printed and sold 210,000 tracts. As Labadie and Grenell stood on street corners handing out free copies, they were perhaps regarded with distaste and horror by those Detroiters who believed the well-publicized warnings of an international socialist conspiracy to assassinate all the world's leaders. Even an advertisement for a medication in the *Detroit News* sounded the alarm while promoting its nostrum: "Beware of Socialists. . . . Beware of any man who seeks to convince you . . . that the world can reach a higher social and moral plane through anarchy and by saturating the flags of the nations in their rulers' blood. Beware, too, of the man who attempts to convince you that there are better remedies for chronic diseases of the stomach and liver than Dr. Pierce's Pleasant Purgative Pellets."[7]

These self-styled "propagandists [for the] left" side of the labor movement (the word propaganda was not pejorative then) donated their time out of love for the cause, although the SLP offered equivalent wages when they were called from their regular jobs to work for the "movement." They often returned the cash to the SLP coffers, Labadie remembered. As he looked back on it in old age, he contrasted the dedication of those early comrades with the labor leaders of the 1920s, whom he saw looking out for their own financial interests, "profiteering on the hopes for the future."[8]

Despite the heroic efforts of the little socialist band and their trust in the approaching millennium, socialism was not flourishing in English-speaking Detroit in the 1870s and 1880s. The SLP, whose membership had surged in the wake of the great strikes and labor agitation of 1877, known as The Great Upheaval, was actually at the apogee of its strength. Its numbers soon began dwindling rapidly. Factionalism was a good part of the problem. Infighting was rife among the political party backers (Lassalleans), the trade union backers (Marxists), and even the bomb backers, who sought worker salvation by means of the *attentat,* or "propaganda of the deed" (as opposed to "propaganda of the word").

Many of these bomb backers were newly arrived Germans, fleeing Bismarck's Anti-Socialist law of October 1878. After the enactment of that repressive decree, newspapers were banned, books seized, homes searched, and party leaders (including socialist members of the Reichstag) arrested and imprisoned in order to eradicate socialism in Germany. In an effort to aid the hundreds of exiles arriving in New York City in early 1879, the Detroit SLP section organized a relief committee and held a Grand Entertainment and Ball as a fund-raiser.[9]

Labadie, though avidly agitating, educating, and organizing for social-ism, was not content to put all his eggs in that basket. Braving the scorn of his socialist comrades, he began stirring the reformist pot of a competing po-litical movement, Greenbackism. This inflationary "cheap money" panacea was one of the many third-party endeavors that, for a brief period, blazed in American politics and then fizzled out. Greenbackers advocated printing large quantities of paper bills, unbacked by gold, in the somewhat naive belief that more money in circulation would cure the nation's economic ills. The movement took its name from the currency with green-printed backs that was first issued by the government in 1862 as a way of borrowing large sums of money to pay the costs of the Civil War. As *fiat* (let it be) money, with no metal backing, it had value only because the government said it did and because people were willing to accept it as legal tender.

Adding more than $450 million in easily printed money to the economy during the Civil War had naturally produced inflation, with higher prices, higher wages, and lower rates of interest. During the depression of the 1870s, many impoverished farmers, small businessmen, and debtors, remembering the days of wartime prosperity, figured that putting even more paper money in circulation would bring back the good times by raising prices and making it easier to pay off debts. It was widely suspected that the Resumption Act, which fixed January 1, 1879, for the government to redeem the war-related greenbacks in coin, was orchestrated by moneylenders who had attained wealth and power from enormous rates of interest and who wanted to raise that rate even further by keeping money scarce. These "money-sharks" and "bloodsuckers" wanted to recall the greenbacks and resume a metal-based currency so as to "enrich themselves by pauperizing and en-slaving the people," claimed Detroit congressman and leading Greenbacker Moses W. Field.[10]

Greenbackism began as an agrarian movement. In time, union leaders and labor activists saw an advantage in joining forces with the farmers to create an independent political party that would destroy accumulated money power as well as enact laws favorable to labor. The early Greenbackers believed that financial reform alone would solve all labor's problems, but saw the advantage of adding labor votes to the campaign. Thus, in 1878, a Greenback-Labor fusion party was born.

Michigan was one of the strongest Greenback states in the country. Detroit's grand old man of labor, Richard Trevellick, one of the nation's first labor lobbyists, helped launch the Greenback party at a Cleveland convention in 1875 and was a leading light in the movement. Henry Robinson (who had been rejected for membership in Detroit's first Knights of Labor assembly) was another dedicated Greenbacker, and had nominated Peter Cooper as the party's first presidential candidate in 1876.

Most Detroit socialists, however, refused to be "bamboozled" into supporting "the Great I AM [Greenbackism] which all are worshipping," the Chicago *Socialist* boasted. They reviled the cheap money program as middle class, perpetuating "the same cut-throat game between the man at work and the man out of work," according to the paper. The labor planks—shorter hours, state labor bureaus, a ban on imported laborers—were just a bait: "None but fools will bite." Grenell denounced the idea of cranking out additional paper bills to solve the nation's economic ills as "unsound, incorrect and sophistical," a mere palliative.

Nevertheless, Labadie was lured to the Greenback cause, ignoring the hostility of his comrades. He found it difficult to resist any project organized to cure society's ills. Many nationally prominent Knights of Labor, including founder Uriah S. Stephens and Charles Litchman, who initiated Labadie into the Knights, embraced the Greenback movement, and Labadie acknowledged it "drew me into its whirl of activities."[11]

The November 1878 elections were something of a triumph for the new fusion party. Its nominee for governor of Michigan received 73,313 votes, nearly as many as the Democratic candidate and more than half the 126,280 cast for the successful Republican. In Scranton, Pennsylvania, Terence V. Powderly, who had replaced Stephens as grand master workman of the Knights, was elected mayor on the Greenback-Labor ticket and, in turn, found himself accused by the local newspaper of attracting workingmen into "the meshes of communism." The party's congressional candidates polled more than one million votes and fifteen were elected.[12]

The election was the Greenbackers' lone moment of glory. The effect of the Resumption Act the following January eventually killed the movement, although Congress permitted the greenbacks then in circulation to remain part of the nation's currency. As the five-year depression ended and prosperity increased, the cheap money star rapidly waned. In 1879, a committee seeking "prominent persons of the party" to run in the Detroit city elections went "into the highways and byways, and nearly everybody . . . declined the honor of being set up as a target for the old parties to shoot at," the *Evening News* reported. Already, the paper was relegating the "Party of Discontent" to "the limbo where repose the old federal party, the know-nothings, the whigs, the barn-burners, the free soilers and others."[13]

The 1879 Greenback-Labor nominating convention, held on a Saturday evening that October at Kittelberger's Hall on Randolph Street was a noisy and turbulent affair, with a mob of about 150 "Democratic ward bummers . . . Socialists and Communists" heckling the thirty-six delegates, according to a newspaper clipping. Labadie was chairman, possibly chosen because he seemed the most Greenback-inclined of the local socialists. Greenback loyalist Henry Robinson recommended support for the Republican ticket, since no financial issue was at stake in the city election, two weeks hence, and the Republicans had shown a willingness to put some Greenbackers on their ticket. Other delegates, protesting that they were tired of being fed "taffy and wind pudding," demanded an out-and-out Greenback ticket. Fellow Knight John Strigel nominated Labadie for mayor, and there was a "lively howl" when a show of hands favored the Republican candidate, William G. Thompson, by two votes. Five of the delegates, "followed by the riffraff which had been so active in interrupting the convention," then stomped downstairs to organize a "seceders' convention," the newspaper reported.[14]

Labadie continued to preside while the remaining delegates, among them pioneer Greenbackers Richard Trevellick and Moses W. Field, decided there were no party questions at issue and thought it opportune to support the Republican ticket. Straddling the split, Labadie then joined the "straight-haired greenbackers" below, who were loudly denouncing the "shyst-greenbackers" above. The dissenters adopted a six-point platform, including public works jobs for the unemployed, and nominated Labadie for mayor. Their campaign leaflet called on voters to support the ticket "of honest working and business men . . . and not the party of political tricksters and bummers." Labadie accepted.[15]

The platform was moderate, but the candidate was not. Labadie's minority view that the Greenback party was "but a wing of the great communistic movement which is going grandly forward the world over" gave some credence to newspaper warnings about communists lurking in the Greenback fold. Labadie believed it was just a matter of time before not only the means of production, but also the products, would be owned in common. Then, according to communism's "beautiful" principles, people would draw from the common fund not in proportion to their work, but to their need.[16]

Labadie expected to lose resoundingly, but he viewed his candidacy as an opportunity to "throw the light into dark places." The *Evening News* generously described the twenty-nine-year-old as a "sober, intelligent and industrious" journeyman printer. Only 110 votes were recorded for Labadie out of nearly 15,000, and Thompson was elected mayor. Labadie, however, was convinced the Greenback nominees had been cheated, as election fraud was commonplace in Detroit. Over-dramatizing the outcome, he raged to Powderly, the new leader of the Knights, that the ballot was futile. He suggested for the first but not the last time that "by force alone" would society's wrongs be righted, although "agitation, organization and intelligence" would pave the way. Labadie never again ran for public office and soon saw government as labor's oppressor rather than its possible savior.[17]

Jo, as he now called himself (dropping the "e" for unknown reasons), and Sophie were living with his mother and grandmother at 121 Porter Street near the city center, walking distance from his job at Gulley's printshop. Sophie taught at a Catholic school across the river in Windsor. Their account book records that she attended church regularly, paying $1.75 every three months in pew rent. She bought a copy of "Mark Twain's Adhesive Scrap Book: Patented by Saml. L. Clemens, June 24, 1873" in which to paste a growing collection of articles by or about Jo. They saw Shakespeare's *Othello* at the opera house, at which Labadie probably wore his new made-to-order suit ($21). He put great store in workingmen being well dressed: "The world hates him who is dirty and ill-dressed . . . we must not beg for respect . . . we must place ourselves in such a position as to command respect."[18]

He also spent liberally on books. By early 1880, his library included *Uncle Tom's Cabin,* the works of William H. Seward (secretary of state under Presidents Lincoln and Johnson), Duncombe's *Free Banking,* Webster's *Dictionary,* Macaulay's *History of England,* Taine's *History of English Literature,* Adam Smith's *Wealth of Nations,* the Koran, several works by Thomas Paine, and *Lessons in Elocution.* He paid twenty-five dollars for an encyclopedia and bought the first of several copies of the newly published *Progress and Poverty* by Henry George, whom he considered the greatest economist of the century.[19]

One of the all-time best-sellers, *Progress and Poverty* had hit the world like a bombshell, exciting millions of readers and edging out the

most popular fiction. This impassioned and eloquent analysis of the ills of
the rising urban world went through more than one hundred editions and
was translated into at least a dozen languages, including Chinese. It was
read (aloud) in the shop where Samuel Gompers rolled cigars; Leo Tolstoy
incorporated its ideas into his novel *Resurrection;* even plutocrats around
the world found it provocative. Its impact on the American labor movement
was enormous.

The book began by posing the seemingly paradoxical question: Why
were the forces of the Industrial Revolution creating monstrous wealth for the
few living in the "House of Have," but increasing poverty for the many in the
"House of Want"? George found his answer in the private ownership of land.
Why, he challenged, should one be allowed to benefit from simple ownership
of land without contributing any goods or services to the community?

The remedy he proposed was simple: not revolution, not nationaliza-
tion, or even redistribution of the land, but a tax on its actual value. This
"single tax," in George's scheme, would make it possible to eliminate all
other forms of taxation. Industry and enterprise would be encouraged by
being freed of taxes, and landowners would find it unprofitable to pay taxes
on idle property while waiting for it to increase in value.

George was no socialist, but a hearty believer in free enterprise. Yet
Labadie was enamored of the book from the first, primarily because of its
"bold, original and revolutionary" approach to land reform, which he came
to believe was the basis of all reforms. Although he considered the private
ownership of land robbery (as did George), and felt it should be available
only to those who were actually occupying and using it, Labadie conceded
that in the single tax George had come up with a most practical solution to
the problem of unjust land distribution.[20]

A fan letter from Labadie in 1881 initiated an occasionally discordant
friendship which lasted until George died in 1897 at the age of fifty-
eight. "The great struggle is now at hand," George responded warmly, "and
therefore it is important that men who think as you and I do should know
each other."[21] In some ways, the two men were soul-brothers. Both left home
as teenagers to make their way in the world, George as a foremast boy sailing
around Cape Horn to Australia. Both began as itinerant printers, working
up to the job of reporter. Indeed, in 1879 George had issued the first five
hundred copies of *Progress and Poverty* himself after it was rejected by
two New York publishers. Both were self-taught, voracious readers, who
scorned academics for writing murkily and turning education into a chore
instead of a joy.

Temperamentally, both were hell raisers, with strong opinions on every subject and a sharp pen, but were not prone to personal animosity. Their passionate humanitarianism was little touched by self-interest. More important, both developed a strong distrust of government interference, making peace with the state only because on the whole it seemed more practicable than overthrowing it. Labadie believed all true single taxers were "anarchistically inclined."[22] George's stress on individualism and the glorification of liberty in his prophetic crusade for social justice doubtless played a significant role in disentangling Labadie from the embrace of socialism.

But that development lay ahead. In January 1880, still a true believer, Labadie teamed with Grenell to turn out yet another socialist paper, a sixteen-page monthly with no name. The rift over Greenbackism had not disturbed their personal friendship nor did any ideological disagreements to come. The heading of the new publication was simply three stars (evocative of the secret "five stars" society, as the Knights of Labor was still known), and the bold motto: "Labor Conquers Everything." It was issued from Labadie's Porter Street home by the "Cooperating Printers of Detroit," which included Henry Poole, a pressman who had worked with Labadie and Grenell at Gulley's printshop and helped issue the socialist tracts. It gained the immediate approval of SLP national leader Philip Van Patten. He moved the SLP headquarters from Cincinnati to Detroit and merged his publication, the *Bulletin of the Social Labor Movement,* with * * *, which became the *Labor Review* and the new official organ of the SLP.

The small format, two-column publication cost seven cents, a significant sum for workers earning ten to twenty-five cents per hour. It featured essays by Van Patten, John Francis Bray, and the editors, as well as instructive fables and news of labor developments locally and worldwide. Serialization of Victor Hugo's lengthy *Les Miserables* under the title, *The Convict,* betrayed a touching overconfidence in the paper's lifespan. It reported on the opening of a workingmen's clubroom ("no Beer House") at the corner of Randolph and Lafayette Streets, where workers could read labor papers, play games, and enjoy ten-cent dinners and three-cent cups of coffee, with all the labor papers "thrown in free." The clubroom was a significant achievement, freeing workingmen from the necessity of congregating in locales like Tim Gorman's Saloon, the "Printers' Headquarters," where they were prone to drink up their wages before reaching home.[23]

The paper covered Detroit's "Beecher Bread and Water Banquet," one of many held throughout the country to ridicule New York preacher

Henry Ward Beecher, who had had the effrontery to question why workers were complaining: "Is not a dollar a day enough to buy bread? Water costs nothing; and a man who cannot live on bread and water is not fit to live." Two hundred attended in their work clothes, sitting at long board tables on which were placed dishes of bread. A small tin pie-plate and tin cup were set at each place. Water was ladled from a bucket into the cups, which were lifted repeatedly for toasts—by Labadie ("To Discontent, the Mother of Progress"), Grenell, Van Patten, Henry Robinson, and others. Robinson was dressed for the occasion as a "capitalist" in high silk hat and swallow-tail coat. "Laughter and fun" is how Sophie Labadie remembered the festivities; and she recalled the thrilling voice of a young lady singing "The Song of the Shirt." Further entertainment was provided by the Socialistic *Maennerchor* (German men's singing group). While enjoying himself, Jo was looking out for potential recruits for the still underground Knights of Labor.[24]

In June 1880, Labadie boarded a train with a group of Detroit radicals bound for the Greenback-Labor national convention in Chicago. Their mission as socialist delegates was to join with the Greenbackers to nominate third-party candidates for the forthcoming presidential election who would "make the corrupt politicians stand back in dismay," according to the *Labor Review*. Like Labadie, the passengers—Grenell, E. W. Simpson, N. L. Barlow, and Van Patten—probably paid the $8.00 train fare from their own savings.[25]

By agreeing to support an alliance with the Greenbackers and other "politically disaffected elements," the little SLP contingent broke with the more ideologically rigid German element. Only a year earlier, the now-defunct *Socialist* had condemned Greenbackers as "scalawags" with an "execrable policy." But just when the Greenback-Labor movement was already splintered and faltering, the American branch of the SLP, prodded by national secretary Van Patten, voted to participate in the coalition this one time in a pragmatic effort to form a viable third party (the German branch wanted no part in the endeavor). Whatever hopes the socialists had for a political solution based on the Greenback-Labor party's incongruous merging of rural farmers, small businessmen, the urban laboring class, and social radicals were seriously misplaced. As Grenell later recognized, it was "a crazy and abortive notion, considering [the SLP's] own disorganized condition." The convention was a turbulent one, in which the socialists had little part. "Their notions were entirely too radical for the farmer element, which predominated," Grenell recalled. The results turned out to be disastrous for both the socialists and the Greenbackers.[26]

On arriving in Chicago, the forty-four socialist delegates—including a number who figured mightily in labor history—met in caucus to compare notes and plan their convention strategy.[27] Peter J. McGuire, the fiery Irishman who organized the United Brotherhood of Carpenters and Joiners and was second only to Samuel Gompers as architect of the AFL, was there. Also present was the redoubtable Chicago labor stalwart and single taxer George Schilling, whose lifetime dedication to a slew of reformist causes is reminiscent of Labadie's own career, and who became his faithful friend. Labadie also first met Albert Parsons (who was executed seven years later for the Haymarket bombing) and his wife, Lucy, one of the few well-known blacks in the labor movement.

As groups of the delegates (including prominent Michigan Greenbackers Richard Trevellick and Moses Field) chatted at the Palmer House convention headquarters, the subject of socialism naturally arose. Labadie, Van Patten, Simpson, and others stood with Terence Powderly, a slender, blue-eyed ex-machinist with a great drooping blond mustache, the new grand master workman of the Knights of Labor and Greenback-Labor mayor of Scranton. They were delighted to hear him support socialist aims and agree to join the SLP. Seemingly insignificant at the time, the conversation proved historic, one that Powderly lived to regret. Labadie remembered it bitterly a few years later, after the Haymarket disaster, when Powderly was frantic for the Knights of Labor to escape any socialist taint. He read that Powderly was "teetotally and fanatically opposed to socialism and is very desirous of bouncing everybody who is socialistically inclined out of the Knights of Labor." To this claim, Labadie publicly professed amazement, recalling that Powderly had been a good, dues-paying member of the SLP and "his card was as red as the reddest card issued."[28]

Labadie had come to this 1880 convention in a combative mood, spoiling for a fight. "There may be an attempt to bar socialists," he wrote E. A. Stephens in a published letter, "but if they do, it will be capital for us. . . . We have outgrown our swaddling clothes and laid aside our toys and we must not jump from that to dotage. We are men in the prime and vigor of life, and we must act like it."[29]

Alas, no such triumphant showdown lay ahead. The Greenback-Labor convention agreed to admit the socialists as a separate body, with the right to vote as a unit on all issues, a right later rescinded. At the same time, the socialists were relegated to second-class status, their proposals virtually ignored. Thomas J. Morgan of Chicago was allowed to present a mildly socialist resolution declaring land, light, air, and water the free gifts of nature to all, and seeking to abolish "any law or custom . . . that allows any person to monopolize more of these gifts than he has a right to." It was referred to a committee and left sitting. The socialists also were prevented from voting as a body in support of women's suffrage, while Susan B. Anthony of the Woman Suffrage Association sat on the platform, "her presence a silent protest against the disinclination to endorse woman suffrage fully and freely," Grenell recalled.[30]

The proceedings were characterized by confusion and loud disputes; " 'points of order' and 'questions of privilege' were thicker than whortleberries in fly-time," the *Labor Review* reported. Frustrated in the attempts to get Morgan's land resolution added to the platform, the socialists walked out at midnight before the last day. In their absence, delegates nominated James B. Weaver, an Iowa congressman, for president, with B. J. Chambers of Texas as his running mate. The socialists, after spending the night in caucus outside, at 6:00 A.M. presented a list of their grievances and threatened to withdraw from the coalition unless their land plank was voted on. Not wanting to lose socialist support at the polls in November, the Greenback-Labor delegates adopted the plank and the convention adjourned.[31]

Despite this shabby treatment, Van Patten, hard-pressed to keep the warring factions of the SLP together, counseled conciliation. He and other SLP leaders like him saw the forthcoming presidential campaign as "a splendid opportunity for making known our principles." The platform, after all, opposed land, railroad, and money monopolies, and contained labor planks calling for enforcement of an eight-hour law, workplace inspection, child-labor restrictions, and the payment of wages in cash (rather than chits redeemable at a company store). They pledged SLP support for the Greenback candidates.[32]

All this compromising was too much for the socialist militants to stomach. Seething with dissension, the SLP splintered into two hostile factions. A radical Chicago group, mostly Germans, bolted and nominated their own candidates for the fall elections. Among them was Albert Parsons, who proceeded down the fateful road to his execution. Some of the dissidents who threatened to depose Van Patten and the SLP leadership were expelled from the party. They formed social revolutionary clubs, began calling for "direct action," including violence if necessary, and drilled with rifles and bayonets in the paramilitary Lehr-und-Wehr Vereine (Teach-and-Resist Clubs), and similar groups. As the breakaway factions launched a new revolutionary anarchist movement, the word "socialist" took on a more fearsome tone to the public.

Meanwhile, the remainder of the SLP membership under Van Patten's leadership voted to swallow their pride and endorse the Greenback-Labor ticket. Labadie, Grenell, and the rest of the *Labor Review* staff decided to go all out for the campaign, and in August turned the paper into a weekly, reducing the price to two cents. They acquired some very conservative readers who even suggested they change the name of the paper because "many workingmen are too aristocratic to read anything bearing on the subject of labor."[33]

The *Labor Review*'s hearty support for the Greenback cause infuriated the SLP breakaway faction. The paper reported that "cliques who are determined to rule or ruin the Socialistic Labor Party" had revived the *Bulletin of the Social Labor Movement* as a competing publication. These "menageries" in Chicago and New York, afraid of the "more Americanized ideas" shaping SLP policy, then managed to convince the National Executive Committee to switch support to the new rival paper in the interests of harmony, according to the attacked *Labor Review*. Cut off from SLP funding, the Detroiters were forced get financial help from the pockets of their Greenback friends. Labadie later captured such internecine turmoil in doggerel:

> They jawd and glared, and jawd agin,
> An' pounded fist with fist,
> Denyin' t'others's right ter call
> Hisself a socialist.[34]

At a Greenback Michigan state convention, some four hundred delegates nominated a full slate of candidates. The *Labor Review*'s business manager, Henry Poole, ran for justice of the peace in Wayne County. The paper cheerily predicted that "victory will crown our efforts. . . . The Republican Party is dying and in its last agonies."[35] Instead, Republican James A. Garfield took the state with over 185,000 votes, although Greenbacker Weaver managed to garner nearly 35,000 votes, the second largest state support in the nation. Of over nine million votes cast throughout the United States, the party polled only a little over 300,000, less than one-third of the million who had supported it four years earlier.

The Greenback-Labor party was to make one last stab at the presidency in 1884, but after a dismal showing at the polls, gave up the ghost. The SLP under moderate leadership was similarly gasping for breath. Section after section joined the more militant social revolutionary movement, centered in Chicago. By the end of 1883, it could count no more than 1,500 members nationwide. The *Labor Review,* once again installed as an SLP organ with the slogan "To Each According to His Deeds," railed against the Chicago "malcontents" and "Eastern revolutionists."[36]

For a time, Labadie continued to write prolifically in support of socialist principles. He served on the party's National Board of Supervision in Detroit until fall 1884. But little by little his faith in socialism's economic salvation of the world was being undermined. He publicly confessed that he might be "undergoing a kind of mental evolution . . . and where I will be next I don't know." He also admitted that he was increasingly attracted by the idea of "voluntary association taking the place of the present coercive State." It would not be long before he would horrify his socialist comrades by defecting to the anti-statist camp, an enthusiastic convert to anarchism. The progression was one duplicated by others who took their places in the emerging anarchist movement in both its evolutionary and revolutionary versions.[37]

As he raised his eyes to the dawn of a new anarchistic society, Labadie imagined that all would work out for the best because it was in the nature of completely free human beings, interacting with each other, to make it so. But he was a practical man as well as a utopian. For the next few years he concentrated on both creating a potent labor movement and keeping it from relying on the government to help.

$\star\, 6 \,\star$

Toward One Big Union

What Labor makes Labor should own,
And nothing his who has not sown—
The fish to him who wields the hook,
And naught to either drone or crook.
—FROM "PRESUMPTION'S WRECK,"
SONGS OF THE SPOILED

Before the age of thirty, Labadie was well primed to launch salvos in the war against social and economic injustice. The necessary ammunition was at his command: outrage, fervor, grit, and perseverance. All he lacked was an effective battlefield. The Order of the Knights of Labor was still camouflaged, the SLP was in disarray, and the typographical union was lackluster and battle-shy.

A romantic, a utopian, a millenarian, even (as social historians call those who envision a future like the religious millennium, when righteousness will prevail)—Labadie was all of these. But his were not just head-in-the-clouds dreams. Unlike many idealists, he had a strong pragmatic streak and the ability to achieve practical goals. He recognized that most workers were more attuned to the cries of "more, now" than "better, eventually." He knew it was easier for the rank and file to grasp the theory of "bread-and-butter" unionism—and obtain higher wages, shorter hours, and better working conditions within the existing economic system—than to contemplate a radical restructuring of the social order in some vague future. His strategy was to organize all the workers ostensibly for immediate gains, then to consolidate the various organizations into one grand whole for reforming the social order. Along the way, the workers could be enlightened about the evils of monopolistic capitalism. Thus a peaceful, instead of a bloody, revolution would ensue.[1]

For the next few years, Labadie focused his efforts on unifying the various labor bodies into the Knights of Labor. He aimed to prevent labor's energies from being diverted and watered down through a proliferation of unions. The ineffectual Greenback-Labor effort had shown that creating a new, labor-oriented political party would be no easy task. Nor did socialist candidates generate much enthusiasm at the ballot box. Labadie tried to stir up the wage earners to mobilize by means of a profusion of pamphlets, labor papers, discussions, and speeches, but the response was often lukewarm, especially now that times were less harsh. Despite the failure of so many of their enterprises, Labadie and his fellow Detroit labor pioneers did not get discouraged. If one project failed, they tried another; if one publication was entombed in the newspaper graveyard, they eagerly gave birth to a new one.

Not long after becoming a socialist, Labadie took the lead in a practical venture, an attempt to unite all Detroit trade unions into a city-wide assembly, or federation, called the Labor League, that would achieve strength by massing forces. Cigarmaker and self-described "Karl Marx socialist" Charles Erb, and printer Charles Bell, another socialist, joined Labadie in this endeavor.[2]

The concept did not originate with Labadie, nor in Detroit. Municipal trades assemblies had their genesis during the Civil War. By that time, it was clear that most local unions, acting alone, had neither the funds nor the influence to challenge the power of employers' associations then being formed to destroy the budding trade union movement. Blacklists, lockouts, and "yellow dog" contracts (agreements employees were forced to sign, stating they would not join a union) were favored weapons of these employers. Against them, unionists in individual trades had little recourse. To counterattack successfully with strikes, boycotts, and intense organizing, the trade unionists realized, they had to band together and reinforce each other's actions with financial and moral support. These early federations of craft unions emerged simultaneously in every major industrial city. They represented a leap forward in the evolution of the American labor movement, then in its infancy. They were, on a municipal level, the forerunners of the American Federation of Labor.

A trades assembly organized in Detroit in 1864 by Thomas Dolan and Richard Trevellick had been a potent force for a few years. At one time, it had nearly five thousand members from fourteen unions, an astounding 10 percent of the city's entire population. But like most other union activity, it languished during the depression of the mid 1870s, when daily economic survival seemed more important to the average wage earner than fighting for labor's cause.[3]

Some fourteen years later, when Labadie attempted to revive the trades assembly around 1878, labor was again hungering to stand up to the boss. Only a handful of national trade unions had withstood the hard times; they were in no position to offer much support to their members. To strengthen their position, federation of the crafts on a city-wide basis was the logical first step. But Labadie and his socialist comrades had more in mind than just achieving tangible gains for the city's craft workers when they organized this Labor League. They envisioned it as a funnel through which socialism could "permeate all the trades." If all unions were united into one gigantic body, they could be "used as is an army by a skillful general" against the enemy ranks, as *The Socialist* put it. Then "shoulder to shoulder . . . let us storm the citadels of oppression and march to victory."[4]

With talk of "The recent alarming development and aggression of aggregate wealth," and the necessity to "secure to the laborer the fruits of his toil," the Labor League's platform appeared to copy the principles and demands of the Knights of Labor, which Labadie joined around this time, even using identical phrases. Actually, both platforms were copied from a version set forth by a precursor, the Industrial Brotherhood, a secret labor federation of the mid 1870s.[5]

Like so many of Labadie's ventures, the Labor League's lifespan was short. Initially, representatives from the unions agreed to the controversial proposal of an emergency fund for strikes, layoff relief, and the like of member unions. But some unionists balked at the obligatory contributions and refused to pay up. Matters deteriorated further, and less than a year after its birth, the League expired, only a few dollars remaining in its treasury.[6]

Undaunted, Labadie and carpenter E. W. Simpson, another ardent socialist, began agitating for the same cause a few months later. This time, the effort caught on with the creation of a city-wide trades council in March 1880. Finally, Labadie's new paper, the *Labor Review,* exulted, the city's unions, which for over five years had led a "half-dead existence," were "awakening . . . to the fact that the ill or good fortune of one trade affects all other trades; and . . . where employers are tacitly united to keep down wages, employes must combine to keep them up."[7]

With the new Detroit Trades Council, Labadie was not aiming for an enduring organization. By then, he had joined the Knights of Labor, a tempting rival to socialism in the hierarchy of his affections. As an organizer for the Knights, his charge was to enlist all the workers of the world into

a grand labor army to end "wage slavery" through cooperative production
and land reform, although not to overthrow capitalism. His enthusiasm for
a trades assembly was related less to its narrow goal of federating craft
unions than to luring new recruits into the more all-encompassing Knights,
an organization that would not limit its ranks to skilled craftsmen, but would
welcome all workers. Since he could scarcely build up that still-secret body
except by whispers to the trusted, he would attempt to entice workers by
boring from within another group. The Trades Council became his recruiting
ground; from there he aimed to tunnel the elect into the inner sanctum
of the Knights. It is ironic that the Trades Council, to Labadie merely a
stepping-stone toward the one big union of his dreams, still prospers as the
Metropolitan Detroit AFL-CIO, while his beloved Knights of Labor has long
since been relegated to the dustbin of lost causes.

Labadie was one of fifteen delegates from six unions—the carpenters, cigarmakers, shoemakers, painters, ship carpenters and caulkers, and
printers—who met in March 1880, at Kittleberger's Hall, to form the new
Trades Council. Representing fewer than 350 unionists, they declared,
"Single-handed we can accomplish nothing, but united there is no power
of wrong we may not openly defy." Former Labor League treasurer John
Strigel, an idealistic German-born shoemaker who died penniless after a
lifetime of fighting for labor's cause, contributed the $5.60 he had been
guarding since the Labor League breathed its last. Printer Francis B. Egan
was elected president, to be replaced by Labadie a few months later.[8]

Egan, a Republican who was to be elected to the state legislature in
1884, was considered a conservative, but most of the leading lights in the first
years—such men as Philip Van Patten, E. W. Simpson, Adam Stuermer, E. A.
Stevens, Lyman Brant, Hugh McClellan, Strigel, Erb, Bell, and Grenell—
were not just trade unionists, but socialists or Knights, often both. Possibly to
allay the fears of workers leery of radicals, the body's preamble proclaimed:
"We are no theorists; this is no visionary plan, but one eminently practicable."
A year later, the Detroit Council of Trades and Labor Unions, as the new
federation was formally called, could boast 31 member unions, representing
over 4,000 workers out of a population of 116,000. It was soon to become
and to remain the "life blood of the labor movement of Detroit," chronicler
David Boyd wrote in 1938.[9]

Seven months after its founding in October 1880, the Trades Council
was sufficiently confident to hold a giant, torchlight parade to display its
strength publicly. Fifteen hundred workers marched through the city center
for nearly two hours to the beat of five bands in what the *Labor Review*

incorrectly headlined, "The Biggest Thing of the Kind Ever Seen in Detroit." (At least four thousand had taken part in a parade on July 4, 1865, organized by the first trades assembly.) Marchers held aloft banners with such mottos as "Stop the robbery; labor must have all its products," and "Each for himself is the bosses' plea; union of all will make you free." The printers, illuminated from behind by a strong calcium light were at the head of the procession. Their slogans advised, "The Trades Council is the Workingmen's Legislature," "Mutual Aid," and "Amalgamate." The painters swung Chinese lanterns under the demand, "Down with monopolies." "Children belong in schools, not in factories," asserted the banner of the Knights of St. Crispin. Embellished with a coiled serpent, it cautioned, "Don't tread on me," an amusing warning from this shoemakers' union.[10]

A grand ball at the Music Hall followed. Flags and banners were lavishly draped across the stage and around hissing gas lamps and balcony pillars. Jo and Sophie, she likely wearing the new earrings that had cost Jo nearly two days' wages from the print shop, danced to the music of the Great Western Band. The *Labor Review* recorded that stones were thrown at the cigarmakers and that "politicians attacked the demonstration and ball like a pack of wolves," but thousands of spectators lined the streets for the event.[11]

Reckoned a huge success, the parade also created dissension in the ranks. The Trades Council, in its caution, had excluded the SLP from the procession to avoid any taint of radicalism. Although party members were allowed to march with their unions, they were incensed at the "narrow and illiberal spirit" shown by a body that owed its very existence to ranking SLP members like Labadie but refused to let the party banner be held aloft.[12] From its inception, the Trades Council endeavored to please all its broad-based constituency, from revolutionaries to defenders of the status quo, to avoid rash moves, to stay away from political endorsements, and to achieve a balance between practical action and theoretical discussion.

Shortly after the parade, the *Labor Review* folded. With the defeat of the Greenback-Labor party in the November election, it no longer enjoyed financial support from that quarter. Labadie and Grenell, however, were still keen to establish a self-supporting labor journal that would compare favorably with the city's commercial press and mirror the rising success of the Trades Council. In April 1881, they put out the first issue of the *Detroit Times,* with the help of Charles Bell, a fellow Knight, socialist, and printer.[13] A sophisticated effort, the four-page, six-column weekly had pages as large as those of a modern daily. It was the most ambitious labor paper yet attempted in Detroit, already exhibiting the high standard of journalistic skill Labadie and Grenell were to demonstrate and refine in years to come.

Labadie and Grenell launched their new paper with two big interlocking stories: a mass meeting of the Trades Council at the new Central Market Hall on Campus Martius (where tightrope walkers and patent medicine vendors also drew crowds) and plans for a major boycott against the *Detroit Free Press* for maintaining a non-union shop. Surprisingly, the Detroit Common Council had given permission for several thousand unionists to dedicate the new public gathering place and hear German socialist agitator F. W. Fritsche, who was on a speaking tour of the United States. His mission was to denounce Bismarck's attempts to crush the Social Democratic party, and to raise funds for the approaching election of the German Diet. Also on the program was the eloquent *eminence grise* of Michigan labor, Richard Trevellick, who spoke for over an hour (as was his wont), interrupted only by the entrance of a contingent of 250 striking iron molders, to great applause. Their union's leader had just been arrested in Pennsylvania for conspiracy on the grounds that men who combined to resist a wage cut were conspiring against their employers. The *Times* lauded the "manly bearing" of these boisterous arrivals, which it claimed refuted the contentions of the *Free Press* that they were "a bloodthirsty and ugly gang" of communists.[14]

Labadie was another featured speaker. He urged the audience to join the typographical union's boycott (a term that had just come into use) against the *Free Press* for its twelve-year refusal to employ union printers and pay union wages. "Just as long as it 'boycotts' us, we will boycott them," he roared out. Fifteen hundred copies of a "Black List" circular were distributed, listing *Free Press* advertisers who should also be boycotted.[15]

The *Times* was greeted enthusiastically, and immediately became the official organ of the Trades Council. Early Sunday morning, newsboys gathered at John Eby's printing office at 48 Larned Street, where Labadie sometimes worked, to get copies of the first issue of the five-cent paper. By 7:00 A.M., all fifteen hundred copies had been sold, indicating that about 10 percent of the city's industrial work force had bought one. The jubilant editors announced they would increase the run, double the number of pages, and form a stock company to increase their capital. This, all within the first month of publication. They were able to attract advertisers like J. L. Hudson, offering heavy Kentucky jean pants for eleven dollars; W. H. Elliot, with summer silks at fifty cents a yard; and W. C. Coup's New United Monster Show, admission fifty cents, featuring the "Great Paris Hippodrome" with some two hundred chariots and horses.[16]

Labadie was ebullient about the paper's future. He recorded that Sophie spent an astounding $15.75 on silk for a dress (Victorian gowns were voluminous). He bought a suit for $35, although he was earning no more than $64 per month. Looking good meant a great deal to him. He considered the "saving theory" fallacious, the idea that "to prosper in this world we must save our wages; live within our means; wear poorer clothes; eat cheaper food and enjoy less of the luxuries which labor produces." He believed that the rate of wages kept pace with the standard of living workers required; those who were content with little, like the Chinese, were the poorest paid. "Consume all you produce," was his motto, spend a lot, and you will be forced to demand a lot.[17]

Once more, Labadie's confidence in his enterprise was unwarranted, this time monumentally so. The *Times* publishers soon realized their beautiful typography was too expensive. Again they learned by "trial and error, especially error," as Grenell remembered ruefully, the perils of putting out a workers' publication. Their wives expressed resentment over the money and time they spent to improve life for the workers instead of their own families.[18] Added to Labadie's financial burdens were expenses for his and Sophie's mutual grandmother, Marie Victoire Berthiaume Labadie, widow of Louis Descomptes dit Labadie, who had been living in their Porter Street home for several years. Marie Victoire left a staggering one hundred fifty living direct descendants, including ten children, when she finally died at age eighty-six, but somehow only Jo and Sophie were assigned to her care during her last years.

A mere six weeks after the *Times'* inauguration, lack of capital forced Grenell, Labadie, and company to sell out to promoter J. F. Burnham, who published the *Sunday Herald,* a society paper. Soon afterward, the Trades Council withdrew its support from the new ownership, "owing to political intrigues of its editor, who thought to sell the labor vote."[19]

But the war on monopoly capitalism still had to be waged, and Labadie's urge to publish was inexorable. Almost immediately after the *Times'* death, Henry Poole again came forward to help Labadie revive its antecedent, the *Labor Review,* as a monthly organ of the SLP. The two mustered sufficient funds to breathe life into a socialist-oriented *Labor Review* for four issues in 1881, and then for two more in 1882 before they were forced to give it up for good.[20]

One issue honored "the great philosopher" Karl Marx, who, in the admiring words of the editors, "has cast into the boundless ocean of human thought pebbles of logic that stirred it to the very depths and promise soon to raise a storm." It was followed by one profiling John Swinton, a foremost social crusader of the era. Swinton, a great admirer of Marx, had walked with him along the beach at Ramsgate, England, and heard the old man sum up the nature of existence: "Struggle!"[21]

Fifty-two-year-old managing editor of the *New York Sun,* Swinton was one of those who "love humanity better than themselves," as Philadelphia printer William H. Foster commented to Labadie. A bushy-browed man of "stalwart frame, massive head and striking features," the crusading editor was a former abolitionist who had risked his life to teach Negro slaves to read and write in an underground chamber. He had presided at the mass demonstration of the unemployed in New York's Tompkins Square in 1874, where unarmed men, women, and children were clubbed down by platoons of police. He had organized a subscription for John Brown's widow, defended Walt Whitman against charges of immorality, and led protests against a wide array of injustices.

After telling a gathering of fellow New York journalists that they were "intellectual prostitutes . . . the tools and vassals of rich men behind the scenes," Swinton quit his $8,000-a-year job at the *Sun* in 1883, and poured his life savings of $40,000 into a four-page weekly he called *John Swinton's Paper.* The paper was full of vigorous denunciations of social wrongs, "pithy, cutting, . . . keen, striking things" that Labadie applauded. During the four years it lasted, it was the most influential labor journal of its time. Labadie was a frequent contributor.[22]

Putting out a labor paper was a heartbreaking proposition, as Labadie was learning only too well. The time, energy, and money contributed by a few dedicated individuals might have seemed amply rewarded, had they found a wide readership of enthusiastic supporters. But the average worker had limited interest in discussions of economic and social wrongs or long-range projections for some nebulous, rosy future, and was reluctant to use hard-earned wages to subscribe. Swinton had to abandon his noble effort after it "destroyed all my means and my health," he told Labadie. Workers and trade unionists throughout the country lamented the loss, but their support had been expressed more in words than in cash.[23]

By the early 1880s, Labadie was developing into a lively, lucid, and persuasive writer, tempering his outrage at injustice with witty and sarcastic commentary. Hampered by a paucity of formal education, he had originally lacked the facility to express his wealth of ideas. Some elements of style he absorbed from a printer's daily exposure to the written word, but much of his writing ability he credited to Sophie. As a professional teacher, she took pains to correct his work without discouraging him, then had him write the corrected text over and over until it seemed natural.[24]

Women activists were not unknown in the labor movement of the day. But Sophie saw her role as a helpmate, not a participant. Jo was grateful that she "entered largely into the spirit of my studies," and their friend, Agnes Inglis, counted her an ideological ally, who "felt deeply the wrongs of society." Sophie remained behind the scenes, yet even in the cramped households of their early married life she always found a place for the mounting pile of Jo's labor materials, campaign ribbons, and the Beecher "bread-and-water banquet" menu.

Sometimes Jo would blue pencil an item, "Save this," and she did, even when she disapproved of the contents. Why had she saved the writings of atheists, Labadie Collection curator Inglis once asked her. Sophie replied simply, "They thought it was true." As a Catholic, she must have been troubled by her husband's freethinking. Yet she compared Jo to Abou Ben Adhem in Leigh Hunt's celebrated poem, who, finding that his name was not written with those who love the Lord, asked the angel to "write me as one that loves his fellow-men." The next night the angel came again: "And showed the names whom love of God had blessed, / —And, lo! Ben Adhem's name led all the rest!"[25]

The early 1880s were busy times for Labadie. His evenings were a round of meetings, rallies, debates, lectures, and related social events as well as writing, editing, and printing his successive publications. He served as Trades Council president, Master Worker of L.A. 901, and member of the Board of Supervision of the SLP National Executive Committee, then located in Detroit where leader Van Patten was living. In addition to his regular job and work for the Detroit labor press, he contributed articles to other Michigan newspapers, and was widely published in many of the thirty-odd labor papers in the country.[26]

On Sunday afternoons he and other Trades Council members held educational debates at 222 Randolph Street in the city center near the river at what they called "The Free Public Lyceum." They argued over protectionism versus free trade, the land question in Ireland, the relation of socialism to the trades unions and to the church, whether strikes did more harm than good, and the March 1881, assassination of Russian Czar Alexander II, which fed the fires of public alarm about radicals—both transplanted and homegrown. Apprehension mounted when only four months later, the newly elected President James Garfield was shot by Charles Guiteau. Members of the Detroit Common Council seized on the shooting as a chance to denounce socialists, nihilists, and communists. All this, despite the fact that the assassin was no revolutionary, but a stalwart Republican, embittered because he had not been appointed American consul in Paris. Labadie protested to the *Evening News* that socialists especially deplored the attack on the president because it gave "blatant demagogues . . . an opportunity of riding upon the wave of ignorant prejudice."[27]

Labadie's many and varied activities had not helped him do much to further the fortunes of the Knights of Labor in Michigan. After the first burst of enthusiasm for Detroit's Pioneer Assembly 901, interest languished. A hard core of the committed reformers and labor activists that Labadie had rounded up in its Washington Literary Society incarnation stayed on, but it was nearly impossible to entice new members, even by luring them from the newly formed Trades Council. Obligatory secrecy was still the great handicap. There was no way Labadie could publicize the clandestine organization and its aims. As a commissioned organizer, he was supposed to inveigle prospective recruits to the meeting place of a group unknown to them, for which they had been chosen without their knowledge. There were no practical accomplishments he could point to; once the esoteric, mumbo-jumbo involving invisible "Inner" and "Outer" Veils," "Globes," Lances," rapping, and hand and body signs were attended to, the assembly would turn to "the discussion of labor in all its interests." Understandably, only a small band of workers welcomed evenings spent in such vague ideological debate. Even some of the original members were losing interest. In 1880, two years after the Knights came to Michigan, only twenty-four remained. Counting fifty coal miners Labadie had organized in Jackson, this made a grand total of seventy-four Knights in the entire state.[28]

Nationwide as well, secrecy was taking a severe toll on the Knights. For more than ten years, subterfuge had been used as a survival tactic to protect members from the blacklist and other victimization by employers. Intended as a safeguard, the policy had backfired, rousing public suspicions of another sinister organization like the Molly Maguires, ten of whose members were hung in the late 1870s, accused of terrorism, sabotage, and murder, and suspected of plotting to overthrow the government. The Knights' secrecy also fueled the antagonism of the Catholic Church. The church took special exception to the scriptural passages in the Knights' ritual and the candidates' oath—sworn on a Bible—to reveal nothing of the persons or objects of the order, nor its "signs, mysteries, arts, privileges or benefits," a vow which appeared to interfere with confession.[29] There was a large Catholic population in Detroit, and Catholics were often faced with abandoning the Knights or the church.

It seemed that the Knights' were withering away when they held their fifth annual convention in Detroit in September 1881. Numbering fewer than 20,000 nationwide, the Order had lost one-third of its members in the preceding year. Survival, it was clear, required getting rid of the religious overtones and some of the secrecy so dear to the heart of founder Uriah S. Stephens. Terence V. Powderly, the new grand master workman, was eager to do exactly that. Delegates agreed to discard the "five stars" ruse, and to make the name of the Order public, minus its "Noble and Holy" prefix. A simple promise would hereafter replace the oath in the initiation pledge, and use of the Bible would disappear. The signs, grips, and passwords would remain veiled, but Labadie scoffed at these cherished secrets as "of no consequence."[30]

Once the Order's grand mission could be revealed—of enlisting all workers, including the unskilled, into one big labor organization with the motto: "An injury to one is the concern of all"—membership jumped rapidly. Reveling in its newfound popularity, Powderly chuckled in a letter to Labadie, "I don't think God is in any way offended at us" for leaving His name out. In an effort to improve the Knights' reputation, Labadie invited "broad, liberalminded clergymen" to meetings "to see for themselves whether we are the bad men we are generally supposed to be." He hoped the ministers could "lend us the influence which surrounds men of education and refinement."[31]

In a comparatively short time, Labadie recalled, he and the other organizers "spread out over the State, and honeycombed it with assemblies" of Knights. Detroit's L.A. 901 added 131 recruits in 1882. Fifty-seven, however, just as quickly dropped out, some doubtless exasperated with the emphasis on classroom-like discussions in what historian Norman Ware called "the first *bona fide* experiment in adult education in America." Labadie acknowledged it was also a lot to expect those who were already paying dues to a craft union to duplicate the time and money for the Knights.[32]

It was a period of hope and experiment. In Detroit, Knights' assemblies of shoemakers, trunkmakers, painters, and bootmakers were organized in rapid succession, followed by tailors, brass workers, ship carpenters and caulkers, telegraphers, plasterers, coopers, and an assembly of mixed trades. Any ten workers who wanted to form a local assembly were invited to contact Labadie at 44 Canfield Street, where he and Sophie were now residing. They could be of any color, creed, or nationality. Women were not only admitted, but encouraged to join at a half-price (fifty-cent) initiation fee. Manufacturers and employers were welcomed, as well as farmers. Only those associated with idleness (bankers and speculators) or corruption (lawyers, gamblers, and liquor dealers) were shunned.[33]

Soon the Knights had sufficient following in Detroit to form a central body—District Assembly (D.A.) 50—to which each local assembly in the city sent delegates. Matters prospered to the extent that its master work-man, Francis B. Egan, could be paid a salary and devote full time to the office. By 1887, D.A. 50 represented around 10,000 Detroit wage earners of both sexes, more than one-third of the work force. Other cities were experiencing similar membership explosions. During the first years, there were only occasional squabbles between the Knights and the Detroit Trades Council, no charges of "dual unionism" (two unions competing for the same workers) or the type of jurisdictional disputes that caused trouble later. The two organizations even shared many of the same people as officers. They differed to the extent that the Trades Council sought more immediate gains, while D.A. 50 was emphasizing class solidarity and long-range social and economic reforms.[34]

In early 1883, having loosely concluded that "the objects of both bodies are identical," D.A. 50 joined in the publication of the Trades Council's new official organ, *The Unionist,* which had replaced the *Labor Review* the year before. The publication was edited by Grenell, with Labadie as a contributor. The eight-page paper was rife with virulent attacks on what was commonly referred to as the "Yellow Peril." Like almost all labor leaders of the day, Grenell's compassion for the underdog did not extend to Chinese immigrant workers, who were branded unfair competition because they were willing to work more cheaply and tolerate poorer living conditions than white workers. In a sorry chapter of American labor history, Knights' leader Powderly ruled that its acceptance of workers regardless of race, color, creed, or sex did not extend to Asians. He not only rejected them as members but indicated they were unfit even to live in the United States. He was not alone. The SLP also supported a ban on coolie labor. Samuel Gompers, president of the American Federation of Labor, declared that the Chinese were filthy, immoral, vice-ridden and racially inferior. *John Swinton's Paper* called them "human locust[s]," "alien pagans," "men who live like vermin." Prominent Western labor agitator Joseph Buchanan, who claimed to believe in "the international brotherhood of man," wrote that Chinese workers could not be assimilated, and admitted that he should probably amend his fraternal spirit to "The Brotherhood of Man, Limited."[35]

Readers of *The Unionist* were warned they might contact leprosy if they smoked non-union cigars made by "Chinamen and scabs." Despite counting only seventeen Chinese in Detroit, the paper harped on the threat of cheap coolie labor and compared "Ye Chinaman" to fleas, hogs, lice, convicts, thieves, and slaves. When Michigan Congressman H. W. Lord voted against the Chinese Exclusion Act of 1882, the paper successfully dedicated itself to his defeat in the next election. "Hip hulah!" it caricatured an Asian as disdaining the American voter—"Mellican man damme foole! He vote for Lorde! . . . Chinaman comee and takee jobbe away flom damme Mellican man. Damme Mellican man starve. Me no caree. Lorde no caree. Hip-hulah."[36]

As millions of immigrants from southern and eastern Europe began streaming into American industry in the late 1880s, craft unionists piled racist scorn on them as well. Samuel Gompers, one of the "old" immigrants from northern and western Europe, proposed a literacy test to keep out "new" immigrants from such places as Italy, Bohemia, Hungary, Poland, and Russia, whom AFL leaders considered "servile and degraded hordes" with "a slavish willingness to work for almost nothing and live on less."[37]

Such ranting against these helpless unskilled immigrants appalled Labadie. He felt that race prejudice played into the hands of the monopolists by dividing the working class. Almost alone in the labor movement, he maintained that it was the right of every human being to live wherever he chose in the world, that America had room for a hundred times its population, and that "No one who is willing to work . . . can be the cause of another's poverty."[38]

For the Knights' leadership, educating the working people was its "holiest mission." Higher wages and shorter hours, the focus of the trade unions, were "petty questions" compared to the eradication of monopoly capitalism and wage slavery. Even President Grover Cleveland was to declare that trusts, combinations, and monopolies were trampling the citizen "to death beneath an iron heel." When it appeared that some of Detroit's new assemblies were floundering in their discussion periods, Labadie and Grenell volunteered as lecturers to liven the meetings. Almost nightly they could be found at halls and meeting places, trying to inflame workers with visions of a future that transcended a few cents more per hour, better ventilation of the workplace, or a longer dinner break. Labadie was reckoned a "good fellow" and well liked, according to a labor paper, so the fledgling Knights probably listened respectfully even if they found his sermonizing a trifle boring.[39]

The message was doubtless the same one hammered home in his columns. Workers must study political economy. "Its laws are as rigorous as the laws of health. . . . If we violate an economic law, the inevitable consequence is industrial disease." The economic system was at fault. Often unions "resisted a reduction of wages, when a reduction of wages was inevitable. They have blamed their employers, when their employers were not to blame. . . . There is a time to raise wages, and a time to reduce wages, and these proper times ought to be known."[40]

In addressing the means of production, so much a part of socialist doctrine, Labadie stressed land as the crucial issue. So long as land was subject to private ownership, "just so long will Labor eat the crumbs that fall from the landlord's table." Echoing Henry George's doctrine, he exhorted the workers: "Let us abolish all taxes except the tax on land values—in other words, let us make the government the landlord." He viewed the real object of the labor movement "to wipe out interest, profit and rent [on land] by the application of the co-operative principle under control of the State."[41]

Surprisingly, Labadie argued that there was an identity of interest between capital and labor. The idea that the prosperity of the worker was linked to the prosperity of his boss sounds especially strange coming from a socialist, appearing to reject the Marxian thesis of class struggle, of antagonism between the proletarians and the bourgeoisie. Yet this talk of natural law and the right of employers to reap a fair return on their investment, spoken in the same breath with demands for the abolition of wage slavery, was typical of Gilded Age radicals. Labadie reasoned that management gained when it paid good wages, because well-paid employees made good consumers. Their mutual enemy was the landlord—"the curse of nations . . . thief of the world," who was robbing both labor and capital of their just reward. He gave this thought a socialist shading by maintaining that it was only when the world's workers had finally become their own employers that the interests of the two could be identical.[42]

Even before he began flirting with anarchism, Labadie put little faith in political action. Economic justice would come from economic pressure— strikes and boycotts—that could be mobilized by a well-organized labor force. Action in the workplace, not legislation, would bring change and preserve it. He saw the pro-labor laws or labor bureaus demanded by many of his labor comrades as merely "soap," or froth.[43]

By his early thirties, Labadie was recognized nationwide as a dynamic and influential labor leader. He was a compelling and effective public speaker, much in demand for his oratorical style and attractive presence.

Short and inclined to pudginess, Labadie was nevertheless a dapper figure on the podium. He combed his thick black hair in a kind of pompadour, curled his mustache into a handlebar and sported the narrowest of goatees on his handsome, slightly fleshy face. "An elegant talker, somewhat original and radical, . . . but always forcible, pleasant, entertaining, smooth, easy and graceful," the editor of the Bay City, Michigan, *Globe* wrote after his appearances in that city.[44]

After an 1882 pre-election rally in Cleveland, the *Labor Star* found him "one of the soundest and foremost thinkers on the Labor question in the country." Despite his doubts about the power of the ballot to right wrongs, he had exhorted five thousand workers gathered in the public square to stick by their friends and vote for candidates who were Knights of Labor. He again sounded the theme that it was not new laws the country needed; there was too much legislation, much of it bad. He was now shifting from paeans to state control to an attack on government surprisingly at odds with the socialist line. He told the throng, which reportedly was shouting "Hear, hear!" and "Bully!" that "Tom Paine said that government, even in its best state, was an evil . . . organized to restrain our evil propensities." He was looking to the day when American workers would have very little government interference. It appears his "mental evolution" from socialism to anarchism had begun.

He went on to say that law-making bodies were relics of a paternalistic system, set up for "those not big enough to take care of [themselves]." Political parties were unnecessary. In the place of presidents, governors, or senates, "the will of the people ought to be the law of the land." Every important bill should be submitted directly to the people for their confirmation or rejection.[45]

A few weeks later Labadie made another startling proposal in Cleveland to a one-year-old organization that seemed to be faltering and of little future promise. He came to its convention not as a supporter of the fledgling organization, but to urge it to disband and merge with the Knights of Labor. Bearing the cumbersome title, Federation of Organized Trades and Labor Unions of the United States and Canada (FOTLU), it aimed to unite all labor bodies into one association. But unlike the Knights of Labor, it sought a federation of craft unions only rather than the entire working class; it was bent on achieving immediate gains, not reforming the economic system. "We must walk before we can fly," the organization's thinking ran, for it made no sense to ignore present problems "in pursuit of some will-o'-the wisp millennium."[46] Its title was the most impressive thing about the FOTLU.

It had not lured many of the important national unions into its fold, nor generated much in the way of funds. It was dwarfed by the Knights. It laid great stress on getting laws to benefit workers, but even with a powerhouse like Samuel Gompers at the head of its legislative committee, it could point to few achievements.

Labadie found a mere nineteen delegates at this 1882 convention, compared to the first year's hundred and seven in Pittsburgh. No one could have imagined that this meager and disspirited bunch represented the seed of the future mighty American Federation of Labor. He was received warmly despite an open letter to the convention, published in the Cleveland *Labor Star,* criticizing the long list of labor laws the group sought. "Remember," he counseled, "that over-legislation has brought the people to the deplorable condition in which they now are." What the delegates should do instead was simplify their platform to two demands: free land and free trade. That these ideas might be characterized as revolutionary should not "deter those who really mean to better the condition of the proletarian class."[47]

Foreshadowing his coming conversion to anarchism, Labadie told the convention he believed that when humans were free from governmental restraint, they would naturally find a solution to their problems. He assured the delegates that it was enough simply to declare these two demands; there was no need to discuss how they could be brought about. When the abolitionists declared that slavery should be abolished, he pointed out, they were not expected to outline how it could be accomplished. Once the nation had free land and free trade, he maintained, effective labor unions could achieve any needed social and economic reforms.

After adopting these two planks on land and trade, Labadie advised, the FOTLU should dissolve itself and merge with the Knights of Labor. There were already too many labor groups, each struggling ineffectually. At one time he had belonged to five, and "the difference between them was about as much as is the difference between tweedledee and tweedledum." If all the groups consolidated, their effectiveness could be augmented "a hundred fold."[48]

The *Labor Star* found Labadie's suggestions "well chosen and well timed." Though the FOTLU did not decide to disband, Labadie's recom-mendations were well received. The delegates voted to strike out the section of their platform favoring high tariffs, which were supposed to protect the worker from cheap foreign labor. "Protection does not protect the laborer," they agreed.[49] Grenell, who was there representing the Detroit Trades Coun-cil, spoke in favor of free land. The FOTLU was not prepared to advocate such a radical concept, but recommended that labor organizations study "this great subject" further.[50]

Following his performance, Labadie—though not a delegate—was welcomed into the fold at the post-convention banquet. Toasts were plentiful, beginning with Gompers's "To the Federation of Trades," and including Labadie's tribute to self-sufficiency, "To Our Self-Made Men." Gompers and Labadie, both hearty, outgoing, and convivial, apparently took a liking to each other from the start. Gompers, the future leader of the AFL, was an eminently practical man who devoted his life to getting "more and more, here and now," for the craft unions. Labadie, free spirit and founding member of the doomed Knights of Labor, was a visionary, who hoped to eradicate injustice for all mankind. Their ideals of unionism differed, but their outlooks converged in a number of ways and they became lifelong friends.[51]

Labadie next carried his pitch for labor consolidation to a much more powerful group, the International Typographical Union. "Let us turn our whole international body into a district assembly of the Knights of Labor," he proposed in an ITU journal in December, 1882. So what if it would destroy the ITU? he challenged. "When a mechanic takes a rough plank and makes out of it a beautiful piece of furniture, he certainly destroys the plank, but he has something more useful in its stead."[52]

As one of labor's avant garde, Labadie was convinced that amalgamation of labor was an idea whose time was ripe; he knew that in unity lay strength, in numbers, power. Workers must stand together to withstand the increasingly concentrated power of "government, corporations, monopolists and a moneyed aristocracy." The time was over, he insisted, when printers could feel insulted to attend a trades assembly where "a smutty blacksmith" might be present. He castigated unionists who were trapped in "a little narrow groove of selfishness." They should be mingling with other working people to break down trade, national, religious, and political prejudices. The "one grand whole" they should be forming, in his view, was the Knights of Labor, a step forward from strictly trade union organization to a grand union of all labor.[53]

It was one thing to ask an apparently moribund FOTLU to disband, but it was quite another to make the same suggestion to the oldest trade union in the country. The subject was not even raised at the ITU's June 1883 convention in Cincinnati. To Labadie's exasperation, President George Clark suggested instead a merging of the two organizations that Labadie was hoping to lure into the Knights—the ITU and the FOTLU. Still, Labadie was in no mood to drop his scheme to convert the ITU into a district assembly of the Knights of Labor, a scheme that became known as his "hobby," but was more like a grand passion. For months after the convention, he argued his case in ITU publications, provoking hot debate and abusive letters. Labadie was accused of sowing dissension in the labor movement, of being opposed to trades unions, and of wanting to strip the ITU of its powers. He proudly pleaded guilty to the first charge. "Human progress is the result of dissension," he responded. It was better to break the bonds of harmony, he wrote, "than be tied with them to a dead and decaying corpse." At the same time, he attempted to placate his antagonists: "I am not going to fight anybody about it, and therefore no one need get their mad up. Keep cool, and tell us what we would lose by the change proposed."[54]

The topic of labor consolidation was becoming hot. The FOTLU had appointed a committee to discuss with the Knights of Labor a "thorough unification and consolidation of the working people throughout the country." By the time the ITU held its 1884 convention, the rival Knights boasted over 70,000 members, including many printers. Pressure was mounting to join with the Knights. But President Mark L. Crawford, himself a Knight, was eager to stamp out any enthusiasm for merging the ITU, "an organization that has battled for almost half a century in prosperity and adversity" with one "that has not yet passed through the fire." Such a move, he warned, would be "suicidal in the extreme," and would turn the ITU's 15,000 members into an "army of demoralized men, whose commanders would be unable to hold them." In the end, Labadie came away pleased that the convention did not "sit on" his scheme, as some of the " 'craft pride' dudes" had anticipated, but rather had instructed the incoming president to discuss the subject with Powderly. He asked Powderly to support the venture, giving him seven reasons why.[55]

His proposal continued to gain momentum. Two years later, when Labadie brought up the subject again at its 1886 convention, the majority of ITU delegates favored merging into the Knights of Labor, provided Powderly would make some concessions. But conflict between the two organizations was growing. The Knights were now being accused of interfering in the affairs of trades unions, of organizing their own assemblies of printers and of accepting "rats" (scabs or non-union members) into the Order. Many felt that the Knights wanted to "gobble up the unions." Labadie still was singing the song of consolidation, but Powderly's autocratic methods and duplicitous blunders had sowed the seeds of the Knights' demise, and the time for the realization of Labadie's cherished big union had nearly run out.[56]

★ 7 ★

Epiphany

But don't bully me, even for my own good,
As I'd rather be wrong and free,
Responsible for my own deeds,
Than subject to your will,
Like a bull led about with a ring in his nose.
FROM "TO YOU, MY COMRADES," *SONGS OF THE SPOILED*

In mid 1883 a legendary and fearsome figure arrived in Detroit on an agitation tour. The mission of fiery German revolutionary Johann Most was "to terrorize capital . . . upheave the social fabric, and bring into contempt the forms of law and organized government," according to the *Detroit Evening News*. Most's inflammatory utterances could well lead to that conclusion.[1]

Recently released from a British prison for extolling the assassination of Russian Czar Alexander II and urging more of the same, Most was the leading apostle of terrorist acts—"propaganda by the deed." He became one of the most feared and vilified men of his time. His single-minded crusade for extermination of the "reptile brood" included capitalists, the state, and all repressive institutions. "War to the throne, war to the altar, war to the money bags," was his cry.[2]

Like many revolutionaries through the ages, Most considered himself a humanitarian but believed that the end justified the means, even if some innocent blood were shed. Temperamentally attuned to violence, he advised socialists to equip themselves with an arsenal of dynamite ("the good stuff"), fulminating mercury, petroleum, and Indian arrow poison, which could be carried in a walking stick. "A little grease, a little acid, as cheap as blackberries . . . [produce] nitroglycerine," he instructed. "This mixed with sawdust and put in a hollow vessel and thrown under a barracks explodes and the devil receives the workmen's foes." It was enough to make Detroiters quake.[3]

Labadie, then one of the city's most prominent socialists, was chosen to introduce the revolutionary orator when he spoke at Arbeiter Hall. The thirty-three-year-old labor spokesman was intrigued to meet this prophet of violence, caricatured in countless cartoons as a bushy-bearded, wild-eyed fanatic, with a bomb in one hand and pistol in the other. What he found was a small, slender, thirty-seven-year-old with a high forehead and intelligent face. Most was dressed, as usual, in a formal dark suit. His manners have been described as "refined" and "courtly." Only the bushy whiskers covering his face conformed to the stereotype. Their purpose, however, was to conceal a deformity that caused the agitator much torment—a disfigured jawbone left from a childhood operation.[4]

A bookbinder by trade and former member of the German Reichstag, Most had been forced to flee to England after the passage of Bismarck's anti-socialist laws in 1878. Now he was hailed as a hero by the revolutionary dissidents who had broken with the SLP. Thousands of radicals packed the halls in New York City, Chicago, and other cities of the East and Midwest to hear his electrifying advocacy of the joy of destruction. No philosopher, but seething with passion, he preached an imminent revolution, which an army of the proletariat would forge with "blood and iron." His journal, *Freiheit,* espoused the doctrine of Mikhail Bakunin, who had been expelled from the First International by the Marxists because he advocated the violent overthrow of existing states to achieve a free anarchist society.[5]

But Detroit was a relatively conservative city. Most of its socialists were leery of violence and looked to a peaceful social reordering. The several hundred people who turned out to hear this Bakuninist were primarily "intelligent and thrifty Germans," who came out of curiosity, according to the *Evening News.* Labadie, who believed in non-violent methods, was not himself a fan of Most. But he asked the audience to abandon preconceived notions and its fear of agitation, for "where there is agitation there is always hope for a better future." The truly dangerous members of the community, he warned, were those seeking to prohibit Most's speech.

The afternoon went off calmly. Most's eloquence could rouse the rabble elsewhere, but apparently left Detroiters lukewarm. The paper found a large majority "agin" him. Unlike newspapers in other cities, which were heaping abuse on the firebrand, it smugly pronounced him "not nearly as alarming as the shadow he has cast before him . . . religion, society, law and order, capital and enterprise are none the worse off for his raid upon Detroit."[6]

Although the German revolutionary left Detroit unscathed, his arrival in the United States triggered a new and more ominous stage of labor militancy. For the next three years, historian Paul Avrich notes, "virtually the whole social revolutionary movement was the expression of the ideas and vision of this one man." He became the leader of the extremists—most of them Germans—who had seceded or been expelled from the SLP and formed the rival Revolutionary Socialistic party. Most not only galvanized them into action with his "cult of dynamite," but produced a practical manual of guerilla warfare. His motto: "Kill or be killed."[7]

Those who knew Most personally, like Samuel Gompers, claimed that he "talked violence but practiced prudence."[8] Understandably, however, his passionate excesses of language produced public alarm that the terrorist tactics of the dread Russian Nihilists and Bakuninist anarchists were about to invade American shores. Most's glorification of European-inspired terrorist anarchism brought a new dimension of horror to the word anarchist, confirming Americans' worst suspicions.

Most and his followers did not originally call themselves anarchists. They considered themselves revolutionary socialists, whose first priority was destroying the established order. It was the remaining members of the SLP, eager to distance themselves from the dissident group, who originally derided its members as "anarchists." When the revolutionaries adopted the name for their own, it was almost in defiance of its stigma. Yet their doctrine went far beyond the classic opposition to capitalism and private property by which socialism is usually characterized. They considered the state an instrument of oppression, thought the ballot futile, and believed that humanity's salvation would come about through some sort of decentralized collectivist system with no institutionalized government after its overthrow. As one member of the group explained it, "politically we are anarchists, and economically we are communists or socialists." Long-range ideology was vague; specifics could be worked out after the revolution. The common note was a belief in a brave new world, colored by a romantic infatuation with violence.[9]

By the time Labadie met Most, he was intensely interested in anarchism as a philosophy. In the process of a profound intellectual metamorphosis, he was gradually sloughing off the skin of a state socialist, in which he had enfolded himself for the past five years, emerging as a proponent of extreme individual freedom in a stateless society. It was clearly a daunting moment for a peace-loving man to begin identifying himself with such a vilified doctrine as anarchism.

Although the economic and social revolution advocated by the socialists was still dear to Labadie's heart, he was abandoning hope that government—whatever its nature—could create the ideal society. The strong sense of individualism forged during his childhood in the backwoods frontier was coming to the fore. His change of heart was not occasioned because Chester A. Arthur, who assumed the presidency in 1881 after Garfield's assassination, was a reprehensible leader. That year Arthur supported a civil service reform act, vetoed a Chinese exclusion bill, and attempted to reduce tariff rates—all actions in line with Labadie's thinking.

Yet Labadie believed that "politics today is synonymous with corruption, rascality and thievery." The "grand old parties" were "rotten to their very cores . . . alive with vermin." Greenback and SLP election campaign failures had convinced him that hopes for an effective labor party were doomed. In common with many socialists of the time, he concluded that political action in the existing system was a waste of time.[10]

Could workers achieve their desires through the ballot box? he asked Most at their Detroit meeting, probably rhetorically. Should they begin to succeed, they would be crushed by the capitalists, was Most's reply. Repressive measures would be enacted by the government and brutally enforced by the militia and the army, as was done against strikers. "Social reforms do not come about by voting," Most assured him.[11]

But the doctrine that attracted Labadie had little in common with Most's brand of collectivist, or communist, anarchism, nor was it of foreign origin. The philosophical, or individualist, anarchism of America came to life, not in some dingy underground cell in Europe, but in the clear, rarified air of Massachusetts. Its seed was the rebellion against authority and cry for liberty of the American revolutionists. It received nourishment from the Bill of Rights, a document that enunciates the actions government may not take, and protects the individual from the will of the majority.

Individualist anarchism was rooted in the same Enlightenment spirit that motivated the founding fathers—a belief that individuals have natural rights and that by the use of reason they can discover and live in harmony with natural laws. ("The best laws, the safest laws . . . the only laws necessary for the guidance of human action are natural laws," Labadie wrote.) It envisioned a utopia where each individual was sovereign, free to live in any manner that did not infringe on the rights of others, so long as others were granted that right equally. The bedrock of this anarchism, as Labadie later expressed it in a maxim, was: "Mind your own business and leave your neighbor's business alone."[12]

Anarchist ideas have been promulgated through the ages. They were uttered by the Chinese sage, Lao-tse, by Zeno, and other Greek philosphers, by William Godwin, and by Leo Tolstoy. But it is logical that the concept of individualist anarchism reached its fullest expression in the United States, where individual rights and liberty were valued as never before. Developing from these values came a pervasive suspicion, even hostility toward centralized authority, an anti-statism of an intensity found nowhere else in the world.[13]

As "no dam foreign Arnikist," Labadie pointed proudly to the anti-government sentiments of individualist anarchism's illustrious forebears: Ralph Waldo Emerson, Henry David Thoreau, and Bronson Alcott, who questioned: "Why should I employ . . . a state to govern me? . . . Why not govern myself?" He detected strong anarchistic leanings in Thomas Jefferson, Thomas Paine, the Free Soil party, and the abolitionists.[14]

Individualist anarchists saw all government as oppressive and majority rule as a tyranny. They provided no blueprint for the stateless utopia; to do so would be, logically, authoritarian, the antithesis of their belief that individuals should be free to work out any system they liked and change it at will. In the ideal libertarian society, people could organize any voluntary associations they saw fit, so long as they did not force others to join them.

A few weeks before Labadie's encounter with Most, he had written to Benjamin Tucker, the leading American propagandist of the doctrine of individualist anarchism, to say he was "much pleased" with it. He admitted that he had been losing the enthusiasm for state control, "which I had when my mind was more a stranger to the study of social philosophy." (He later was said to have claimed, stretching for humor, that his "Marxmanship was never very keen.") But, he told Tucker, he was confused and full of questions. How could anarchism work in practice? How could railroads be constructed? Thousands of problems troubled his mind. They seemed soluable only if the majority could force the minority to conform to its will, which was anathema to the creed.[15]

Tucker printed the letter in his Boston journal *Liberty* in June 1883, along with a confident response. The important question was whether it was true that individual rights transcended those of the majority. "If he finds that it is," Tucker wrote of Labadie, "then let him advocate it through thick and thin and apply it where he can, trusting to human ingenuity to provide for its universal application eventually." What was true was workable, in other words. Tucker admitted that he could foresee difficulties, especially regarding construction of railroads and highways. But he had faith that "when Anarchism prevails, individuals will be much readier than now to make sacrifices for the public good," since "nothing stifles public spirit like compulsion and nothing inspires it like freedom."[16]

As foremost advocate for the cause, the twenty-nine-year-old Boston publisher was eager to encourage a potential convert, four years older than himself, especially one who was an influential activist in the labor movement. He flattered Labadie by saying that he "never dreamed of making any impression upon men like yourself," and referring to him as one of "the most intelligent of the State Socialists." He was happy to fill Labadie's order for two anarchist classics, Josiah Warren's *True Civilization* and Colonel William B. Greene's *Mutual Banking.* Encounters with Warren and Greene had brought about Tucker's own conversion a decade before. As an eighteen-year-old engineering student at Massachusetts Institute of Technology, Tucker had heard both Warren and Greene speak at the New England Labor Reform League, a birthplace of individualist anarchism. Now keen to shape Labadie's thinking, Tucker temptingly offered at half price a "slightly mouse-gnawed copy" of *What Is Property?* by Pierre-Joseph Proudhon, the first to proclaim himself an anarchist. Tucker himself had translated it from the French. Warren's book was advertised in *Liberty* as "explaining the basic principles of Labor Reform," and this may have been its attraction for Labadie. But Tucker told him these were also the principles of "Anarchy," a word Warren himself never used.[17]

Although a belief that the less government the better was not a new one, Warren was the first to put together a coherent libertarian philosophy. He was formulating his doctrine of "the sovereignty of the individual" in the 1830s, decades before Bakunin and Most were agitating for their conflicting version of a stateless society based on a communist structure. A quarter century before Karl Marx was poring over books in the domed reading room of the British Museum, analyzing the evils of capitalism for *Das Kapital,* Warren was trying to correct those evils in experiments with anarchistic communities. He was testing his theories even before Marx's adversary, Proudhon, laid out a similar individualist philosophy which he named "Anarchy" in 1840 in *What Is Property?*

After studying their works, Labadie pointed out that Warren, Marx, and Proudhon were nearly in agreement in their critique of the existing capitalist society. Each sought to abolish "usury," defined as interest on money, rent for land, and profit on labor—money not earned by working for it. But, according to Labadie, where Warren and Proudhon agreed the ideal society could be attained only if each individual enjoyed the maximum possible freedom, Marx envisioned an authoritarian system in which individual desires would be subservient to the collective good. Under this form of state socialism, private property would be abolished. In contrast, both Warren and Proudhon believed in the right to own what one produced. Unlike Marx, they put their complete trust in evolutionary methods.[18]

At the time all three were working out their tenets, the air was heavy with the zeal for social reform. The study of economic processes as they related to industrial capitalism was in its infancy; theorists were groping for solutions to society's problems. In the spirit of an age still reeling from the startling evolutionary theories of Charles Darwin and Herbert Spencer, social philosophers were confident that society likewise could be analyzed and re-formulated using scientific methods.

As the originator of American anarchism, Warren and his extraordinary social experiments merit examination. Born in Boston in 1798, a descendant of Puritans, Warren was no ivory-tower philosopher. A true American-style pragmatist, he was always asking, "Can it work?" In 1826, a musician and band conductor, he moved his wife and baby daughter to Robert Owen's experimental community in New Harmony, Indiana, to observe socialism in practice. When Owen's scheme collapsed after two years, Warren blamed it on a stifling of individual initiative and a demand for conformity that conflicted with "nature's own inherent law of diversity" and the instinct of self-preservation.[19]

He then undertook what historian James J. Martin has called "the first scientific experiment in cooperative economics in modern history."[20] At Warren's "Time Store" in Cincinnati, he carried out a fascinating practical application of the classic labor theory of value, expounded by Adam Smith and others, which held that the value of a commodity depended on the amount of labor expended in its production. Warren felt that the price of an item should not fluctuate in response to speculation or supply and demand, but only reflect the "cost" of making it.

He bought $300 worth of groceries and dry goods, then posted the bills of purchase for all to see. Customers were to pay the cost price, plus a percentage for shipping and overhead. Warren added no profit. The customer owed an equivalent amount of time, payable by his own labor. Payment was made using promissory "labor notes" instead of money, an idea Warren had picked up from Owen. Warren's price as proprietor was calculated on the basis of the time it took to sell the item. A clock in plain sight measured the minutes. Since time was money, customers did not waste it haggling over their purchases; Warren soon reported selling as much in an hour as normally in a day.

A born inventor, Warren also developed an advanced stereotyping process, a high-speed printing press, a new method of musical notation, and a lamp that burned lard instead of oil. In his Time Store he was testing an economic invention. He next tested a new social hypothesis, a model village. In 1835, on four hundred acres along the Tuscarora River in Ohio, he set up the first anarchist community in America, with the aim of achieving the greatest practicable amount of liberty for each resident. In the Village of Equity there were no laws, no rules, and no one had more authority than anyone else. Its six families were successfully running a sawmill when malaria spread through the settlement and it had to be abandoned.

Warren returned to New Harmony to refine his idea of "equitable commerce" in the work-a-day laboratory of another Time Store. This time labor was not valued simply on a hour-for-hour basis but according to how "disagreeable" or "intense" the task was or how efficient the worker. Each person was free to set the value of his own labor notes, but no one was obliged to accept them if they seemed overrated. In 1847, Warren published a summary of his philosophy and social experiments in *Equitable Commerce,* later re-published as *True Civilization.*

Seeking new challenges, Warren established two long-lasting communities, "Utopia," in 1847, along the Ohio River south of Cincinnati, and, in 1851, "Modern Times" in Brentwood, Long Island. These were proving grounds for his theory that "enlightened self-interest" and free competition would eventually produce an equitable society where humans would practice the laws of social harmony because it was in their interest to do so. He believed that human nature became evil only when corrupted by authority or forced conformity.

"Mind your own business" and "Do not harm your neighbor" were the colonies' only laws. Modern Times was a pleasant, well-kept farming town of attractive cottages constructed on the labor-exchange principle. Life there was reportedly harmonious, with no crime or violence. Undesirables left when colonists refused to buy from them, sell to them, or speak to them.

A poor public speaker, the stocky, shy Warren lacked personal magnetism, and initially his efforts received little notice. When they did, however, he was faced with notoriety. Free to live as they liked, the two hundred ardent individualists at Modern Times felt no need to conform to the norms of the society outside. Curiosity seekers reported that the community was a hotbed of "free love" and promiscuity, with women wearing bloomers and masculine attire. This shocking state of affairs got heavy newspaper play and attracted both disapproving gawkers and those eager to join the group. Warren, personally leery of marital experimentation, cringed at the attention. He pointed out that in his community those preferring a conventional marriage were equally free to have one. Weathering the scandal, Modern Times survived until the 1870s and a few of the community people still lived there after the turn of the century.

Though today Warren's ideas may seem simplistic and his experiments primitive, they were not so preposterous at a time when much of the country was frontier or near-frontier. In that semi-anarchist condition there were few taxes or licenses, and only local law enforcement. With government far less pervasive than it is today, any sort of society seemed possible to utopian romantics.

Warren's theories were carried forward by three associates, all Massachusetts-born, of old New England stock, with a ministerial background. Stephen Pearl Andrews (1812–1886), the son of a Baptist clergyman, was a lawyer, a pioneer in shorthand methods, and a brilliant scholar and linguist. He became a disciple of Warren's after fleeing from a Texas mob because of his abolitionist agitation. He elaborated on Warren's principles in *The Science of Society* (1852).[21] William B. Greene (1819–1878) was educated at West Point, and served in the Army campaign against Florida Seminoles before attending Harvard Divinity School. In *Mutual Banking,* published in 1850, he outlined a system of cooperative banking similar to Proudhon's "Bank of the People" (where no-interest loans were provided at cost), using its own currency as a medium of exchange among members. Co-organizer with Greene of the anarchist-oriented New England Labor Reform League, Ezra Heywood (1829–1893) was another abolitionist who studied for the ministry. Like Greene, he was an ardent fighter for women's rights. An advocate of birth control and free love (he called married women "prostitutes for life"), he was arrested and jailed several times for mailing "obscene" literature. A fourth significant figure was Lysander Spooner (1808–1887), a Constitutional lawyer. He rejected the validity of the Constitution in a series of pamphlets titled *No Treason* published after the Civil War when Northerners were charging that the South had acted treasonously. He claimed the Constitution was a contract drawn up among persons now dead and was not binding on later generations.

Benjamin Tucker, the last of the great voices of the American individualist anarchist tradition, became its chief exponent in the nineteenth century. Born in Dartmouth, Massachusetts, in 1854, the son of "radical Unitarians," he possessed a brilliant, logical mind. He read Charles Darwin, Thomas Huxley, Herbert Spencer, and John Stuart Mill in his teens, but it was Warren whom he described as "my first source of light." By the time he was twenty-one, he had translated Proudhon's *What Is Property?* He had also become an editor of Heywood's anarchist monthly, *The Word,* had been jailed for refusing to pay the poll tax (à la Thoreau), and had been seduced by the notorious suffragist and free love proponent Victoria Woodhull, who was twice his age.[22]

Despite his radical reputation, Tucker remained an editorial writer for the *Boston Daily Globe* for years after he founded the anarchist periodical *Liberty* in August 1881, just as interest in anarchism was beginning to grow. He was a skilled journalist, admired for an incisive, lucid, and elegant style, which he seasoned with generous sprinklings of vitriol. Warren's followers were among his contributors. It was heady for Labadie, a self-taught workingman, to be welcomed into this erudite, intellectual company. He remained almost reverential toward the aloof, aristocratic Tucker, who reciprocated by exempting Labadie from his frequent caustic outbursts against almost everyone else.

As "pope" of the movement, Tucker possessed the charisma and leadership qualities Warren lacked. They were sufficient to create hundreds, if not thousands, of adherents or sympathizers in the United States and abroad. *Liberty* lasted until 1908, becoming the longest-lived of any American radical periodical. The motto decorating its masthead was Proudhon's provocative declaration: "Liberty: not the daughter but the mother of order." Less metaphorically stated: liberty should come first; order would naturally result. Its supporters liked to refer to themselves as "unterrified Jeffersonian democrats," prepared to carry the philosopher/president's supposed assertion that "that government governs best that governs least," to its logical ultimate by substituting "governs not at all." Where the founding fathers had regarded the federal government as a necessary evil, the individualists proposed that it was not necessary at all.

Labadie was a reader of *Liberty* from its first issue. Firmly entrenched in what he called the "communist" (SLP) camp at the time, he nevertheless admired the journal's "consistency and bold and aggressive attitude," he wrote in *Labor Review* in 1882. He was also studying Spencer, who upheld "the man against the state"; Mill, champion of individual liberty; the laissez-faire theories of Adam Smith; and Marx, reading a little at a time in order to avoid "mental dyspepsia." As he began delving into anarchist philosophy, he became increasingly leery of "the infallibility of the majority." Individuals should be allowed to "do their own business at their own cost." Within three years of his first exposure to anarchism, he converted from advocacy of an all-powerful state to the conviction that, once unfettered, humans would choose to harmonize with the great natural laws, as the Indians of his childhood had done. His revelation came like a religious epiphany; once the anarchist creed was revealed to him, he believed he had found humanity's salvation. In defense of his flip-flop, he liked to say that "only dead men and fools never change their minds.[23]

Labadie's shifting philosophical affections appear to have had no bearing on his effectiveness as a labor leader or organizer for the Knights of Labor. Radicals of all colorations were plentiful in the labor movement of the early 1880s and their sentiments were listened to respectfully. Labadie's sudden abandonment of socialism coincided with the exit of most of the SLP's membership. Many were now harking to Johann Most's exhortations. The party's fortunes were not improved by the sudden disappearance of its disheartened leader, the brilliant but erratic Philip Van Patten, who left behind a note intimating suicide, only to re-surface some years later as a prosperous architect in Hot Springs, Arkansas. One of his last acts before vanishing was to complain to Friedrich Engels about the damage Most was doing to the SLP and asking if Marx had supported anarchism. Engels responded that Marx had opposed the philosophy "from the first day it was put forward in its present form by Bakunin."[24]

SLP loyalists did not look kindly on Labadie's musings in *Liberty* about a possible change of heart. Anarchism was "a cheap bait for dupes to swallow," a party publication lashed out. It snidely questioned Labadie's "reasoning faculties," in not recognizing that anarchism was contrary to the laws of nature. In time, the majority would discover those laws and "compel the unreasoning, illogical minority to obey" them, the diatribe concluded (precisely what Labadie feared).[25]

Labadie's resignation from the party and from his position as secretary of the Detroit-based National Board of Supervision was expected imminently. Yet he did not sever his connection at once. Always sympathetic to the downtrodden, he may have been reluctant to desert a sinking ship, especially one he had helped launch with such high hopes. Possibly hoping for his change of heart, the SLP issued Labadie credentials as delegate to its convention in Baltimore in December 1883, as representative of the cash-strapped San Francisco section. He was told that the rapidly disintegrating party wanted "all classes of radicals to unite to fight the common foe." Only sixteen dispirited delegates attended. Labadie was not one of them.[26]

Meanwhile, he was approached by Burnette G. Haskell, an enterprising young comrade in San Francisco, who had concocted a grand scheme for merging all the nation's bitterly divided socialist and anarchist factions into one harmonious whole. He wanted Labadie to promote the plan at a congress in Pittsburgh in October 1883 that Most was organizing to create a unified, international revolutionary party.[27]

Haskell was founder of the International Workmen's Association, a Marxian socialist workers' movement based in the Far West and Rocky Mountain regions. As representative of this "Red International" (to distinguish it from the Bakunin-inspired "Black International"), Haskell had been invited to the Pittsburgh Congress. Unable to attend, he delegated German-born August Spies of Chicago, who was working closely with Most, to present the plan in his stead. He named Labadie his alternate delegate, and requested him also "to urge its adoption."[28]

Labadie knew Haskell as the twenty-six-year-old editor of *Truth,* "A Journal for the Poor," which trumpeted the cause of "scientific socialism" while raging against the "mongolian curse" of cheap Chinese labor, a popular bugaboo of West Coast workers. Violence held singular appeal for Haskell, as it did for Johann Most. *Truth* announced matter-of-factly that the paper cost five cents a copy "and dynamite forty cents a pound." Readers could learn about "Dynamite: the Plain Directions for Making It." Haskell once planned to solve the problem of land monopolies by digging a tunnel to San Francisco's Hall of Records and blowing up the place so there would be "an inextricable confusion in land titles."[29]

Haskell was "of brilliant parts but erratic temperament and habits," as Joseph R. Buchanan, a close associate, described him. He possessed a strong romantic infatuation with conspiratorial schemes. Ideological distinctions did not concern him unduly; he published excerpts from Marx, Proudhon, Bakunin, Henry George and Patrick Henry with equal enthusiasm. When he assured Labadie that "our minds so run in the same channel that you know exactly how I feel," the Detroiter was probably dismayed.[30]

Labadie sent his copy of Haskell's plan to his anarchist mentor Tucker for a reaction. In an attempt to reconcile the tastes of revolutionary socialists, communist (collectivist) anarchists, individualist anarchists, and ordinary American workers, Haskell had stirred together a confusing stew. "Tremble! Oppressors of the World!" the document concluded grandiloquently. "Not far beyond your purblind sight there dawns the rose scarlet and sable lights of the JUDGMENT DAY."[31]

"A hodge-podge of sense and nonsense," Tucker sneered in *Liberty,* "perhaps the most foolishly inconsistent piece of work that ever came to our notice." In what can be read as a cautionary message to Labadie, he wrote: "Every friend of Liberty who may go to Pittsburgh is hereby urged to examine this document carefully before giving it his adhesion."[32] Why Haskell chose Labadie as his representative is mysterious. Possibly he was seeking the blessing of the individualist anarchists, since by then Labadie was assumed to be in their camp. Or perhaps he saw Labadie as a persuasive and well-liked figure who would be listened to respectfully by all factions. Whatever the case, Labadie seems to have stayed home.

When Spies presented Haskell's plan at a secret session of the Pittsburgh Congress, it reportedly precipitated a fistfight. Aiming to please everyone, Haskell had pleased almost no one. The twenty-six delegates then drafted a declaration of principles known as the Pittsburgh Manifesto. It decisively rejected the ballot as futile and called for "energetic, relentless, revolutionary and international action" to overthrow the "unjust, insane and murderous" capitalistic system.[33]

The delegates from New York and the East Coast, led by Most, objected to any role for labor unions. But they were outvoted by the Midwesterners who had broken with the SLP and envisioned unions not only as agents of the coming revolution but as the nucleus of the new social order. Led by Spies and Albert Parsons, this group endorsed a combination of anarchism and revolutionary unionism, which became known as the "Chicago idea" and anticipated by two decades the anarcho-syndicalism of the Industrial Workers of the World (IWW), the so-called Wobblies.

For the sake of unity, the two groups of anarchists buried their disagreements. They dedicated themselves to a new organization of proletarian revolt, the International Working People's Association (IWPA). Known as the "Black International," it was considered a direct descendant of the Bakuninist breakaway factions of the First International. It called for a future system of collective ownership of property in a decentralized society. Direct action—force and violence—would be the tactic used to achieve this. In Labadie's and Tucker's lexicon, its members were not anarchists at all, but revolutionary communists, false figures "sailing under the flag of anarchism."[34] For the individualist anarchist, outside both groups, their dogma would result in coercion as surely as under state socialism.

Though hundreds of thousands of copies of the Pittsburgh Manifesto were distributed in the United States alone, Most failed in his attempt to end the war among the radicals. On the contrary, the Pittsburgh Congress produced a sharp division between the "Reds" (Marxian socialists) and the "Blacks" (Bakuninists). Haskell's group remained aloof from the new organization.[35]

The Pittsburgh conference also drove a wedge between the various revolutionaries (mostly German-born) who attended, and the evolutionary-minded American individualists (like Labadie) who did not take part. As for the remnants of the SLP, they wanted no part of the new movement and sent no delegates. Not only were they staunchly opposed to the use of arms, but, unlike all the others, put their faith in the ballot.[36]

Led by such dynamic agitators as Spies and Parsons, the IWPA soon attracted thousands of unionists in Chicago alone and gained considerable influence in the labor movement of the Midwest. Like the SLP before it, its main following was among German immigrants; Parsons was one of the few American-born adherents. The former assistant editor of the SLP's *Socialist* in Chicago, he now edited the IWPA English-language paper, *The Alarm*. Spies put out the German-language *Arbeiter Zeitung* until they both were arrested for the Haymarket bombing two-and-a-half years later.

Over time, Labadie became increasingly confident that he had been cured of his "fever of governmentalism." A sharp deviation in his march for labor's cause lay ahead, as he recognized Powderly's monumental inadequacies as head of the Knights of Labor, but he strode firmly on the anarchist path the remainder of his life. Through an outpouring of writing, speeches, and debates he became an enormously effective propagandist for what he saw as the "grandest of human aspirations." There were times when he doubted that mankind would ever see the complete realization of his vision. He did not expect it to come in his lifetime. But, "come it will," he predicted, "in obedience to the law of necessity."[37]

★ 8 ★

Tempestuous Times

And Nature says the under dog in the fight may bark,
bite, bruise, damage, hurt, tear, growl, injure, lacerate,
aye, even kill if necessary!
The end indeed justifies the means, and the cause of the
workers is defensible indeed.

FROM *I WELCOME DISORDER*, 1911

One wintry day early in 1884, Labadie boarded a train bound for Lansing, the state capital. We can imagine him carefully clad, as usual, pompadour slicked back, goatee neatly trimmed. In a move scorned by some as unprincipled for an anarchist, he had accepted a government appointment as clerk in the newly created Michigan Bureau of Labor and Industrial Statistics. Offering financial security and stimulating work, the assignment marked an unusually happy period in Labadie's life, as well as affording him an opportunity to study his archenemy—the state—up close.

The unsolicited job offer was a surprise for one who had loudly scoffed at labor bureaus as "soap," whose pleasing suds camouflaged the underlying economic evils. He had even opposed the choice of John McGrath, his new boss, as first commissioner of labor.[1] As Detroit's foremost labor leader, he was a logical choice, but not, however, one government officials would likely embrace. Although Labadie was now openly advocating the withering away of the state, he had no compunctions about working for one so long as it existed.

It was the first, but not the last, time he was in the government's employ. Anarchism was a philosophy he hoped would eventually come to pass, whose evolution he might hasten by propaganda. Meanwhile, he lived in the real world and was ready to grab what opportunities it presented.

Thoreau, another pragmatic anarchist, stated it unapologetically: "I quietly declare war with the State, though I will still make what use and get what advantage of her as I can, as is usual in such cases."[2]

Detroit labor circles by no means shared Labadie's disdain for the new agency. A state labor bureau had ranked high in their long-standing demands for pro-labor legislation. They especially liked its "industrial statistics" role, which could document abuses in the workplace and inspire reform laws. The Knights of Labor, the Trades Council, and the SLP had agitated long and hard for the bureau, had formed a third party, the Independent Labor party, to further labor's cause and nominated painter John Devlin and printer Lyman Brant, both prominent Detroit Knights, to the state legislature. Elected with the help of Democratic Party endorsement, the two helped push through the bill creating a labor bureau in mid 1883, making Michigan the eleventh state to have one.[3] (A federal labor bureau was still two years away.)

The clerkship was a financial godsend for Labadie. At $70 a month, it more than doubled his sparse earnings of the previous year. The boom of 1878–82 was over. The nation again was suffering one of the business recessions that characterized the late nineteenth century. Detroit printers could not find steady work. Labadie had been employed for a few months as columnist for Henry George enthusiast Robert W. Oakman, who started up the *The Spectator* as successor to *The Unionist* in June 1883. Grenell was labor page editor. Oakman, eager to make the new weekly a paying proposition, incongruously interspersed such articles as "How to Get Hitched in 20 Languages" with John Francis Bray's "Hints to Agitators," and long arcane arguments by Labadie against classifying labor as a commodity.[4]

Oakman went on to become Detroit Mayor Hazen Pingree's chief lieutenant in the 1890s and a prosperous real-estate developer. (He laid out the twelve-mile-long Detroit boulevard named after him.) His career as a publisher, however, flopped after only six months and Labadie was out of a job. At the time of his Lansing appointment Labadie had no income and monthly expenses of almost $40.[5]

Sophie temporarily stayed in Detroit, where she took over Jo's duties as treasurer of the Trevellick Home Fund, a fund-raiser to buy a home for fifty-four-year-old Richard Trevellick, Michigan's veteran labor activist. Labadie was soliciting donations from Knights' assemblies, trade unions, and individuals across the country to build their beloved "Dick" a house and save him from the fate of all the "labor heroes who have fought against insurmountable odds and fell headlong, worn and weary and despised into a pauper's grave." More than $2,000 was eventually raised and Trevellick was able to enjoy his last ten years in his own home.[6]

Working relationships at the new four-member bureau turned out to be exceedingly harmonious. Governor Josiah Begole had named state legislator John Devlin, one of Labadie's Detroit labor colleagues, deputy commissioner. John McGrath was far from the disaster labor groups had predicted. As a lawyer (a profession much reviled by labor) and chairman of the Wayne County Democratic Committee, he was initially looked on with suspicion. But after the bureau's first two annual reports, the whiskered forty-four-year-old commissioner was lauded by the *Labor Leaf* as one "who feels strongly the wrongs under which the working people suffer" as well as being "one of the best statisticians in the country."[7]

The first report, for example, was poignant in its documentation of the poverty and squalid life of the brickyard laborers at Springwells on the outskirts of Detroit. Polish and German workers, as young as ten, toiled there from sunrise to sundown. Families of six lived in wretched hovels ten feet square, situated on mud banks alongside stagnant pools. The bureau's staff found their rooms "sieves for the chilling blasts of winter," their food mainly "unsavory messes" of boiled pork blood, entrails, heads, lungs, and liver. "The inmates of our houses of correction and our prisons are better fed, more comfortably clad and housed than these people are," the report concluded. "What wonder is it, then, that these men sometimes become desperate and resort to rash measures?"[8]

Labadie's assignment was a fourteen-page overview of the labor movement. He constructed a diagram of the "economic" and "socialistic" groups. In the former category, he placed trade unions, cooperative unions, and mutual benefit unions. The socialist group consisted of social reformers, identified as social democrats, communists, and anarchists. These reformers all "agree as to the wrongs which should be righted," he wrote, "but they differ widely as to the remedy to be applied." In outlining their aims and methods, he noted generously that all "seem to be the expression of the more intelligent class of wage workers." *Liberty* publisher Benjamin Tucker objected to Labadie's separation of anarchists and communists, noting, "Some Anarchists, I regret to say, are communists."[9]

Proud of the first report, "the best volume of statistics ever published," Labadie nonetheless remained ideologically unshaken in his opposition to government-run labor bureaus. He felt unions could do a better job by themselves, and pointed to the data compiled by New York City's Progressive Cigarmakers' Union No. 1. Hoping to lure the Knights of Labor into this field, he prepared a sample statistical account book. "If we cannot do our own statistical work, let us shut up shop and not keep up the cry for statistics," he wrote Powderly. He deplored "calling upon 'the state' to do for us what we can do much better for ourselves."[10]

Another lucky appointment came Labadie's way. While working for the labor bureau, he functioned as labor-page editor for the *Lansing Sentinel,* a paper known for trumpeting social causes. When a Detroit paper contended that a "Communist" had joined the *Sentinel*'s staff, Labadie refuted the claim by praising competition as "that laudable ambition inherent in the human breast to outstrip your neighbor in a fair field." Not competition, but government-supported monopoly and privilege, were the real evils, he wrote. Where, as a socialist in 1882, he had deplored the "crushing effects" of competition, as an anarchist he now fingered central planning and imposed equality for the crushing of ambition and individuality.[11]

The *Sentinel*'s editor, Mr. Fogg, gave him free rein and Labadie took full advantage of it. He introduced his first column, on November 20, 1884, with a bombshell: "The goal of human civilization is philosophical anarchy." This and future columns were sprinkled liberally with quotes from such champions of liberty as Adam Smith, John Ruskin, John Stuart Mill, Pierre Proudhon, and Josiah Warren. Labadie's conversion to non-violent, individualist anarchism was much like adopting a religious creed. There was little he could do except publicize and proselytize, actions he undertook with gusto. Since anarchism was a negative philosophy, which sought to eliminate the state without substituting another structure in its place, he did his utmost to prevent his readers from relying on the government to solve society's problems.

Scarcely an issue of the paper went by in which Labadie did not denounce the legislators busying themselves at the nearby state capitol. He told them the only good they could do would be "clipping the claws of the State," repealing "useless and vicious" laws that granted privileges to banks, railroad syndicates, and coal monopolists, and made possible the enormous concentrations of capital popularly called "trusts."[12]

He did not expect the lawmakers to do this. Even if they started out honest, he expected their heads to be turned by "the temptations that surround them"; any principles they held would "go to the devil." The next batch of legislators appeared to justify his mistrust. Francis Egan and Hugh McClellan, both elected on the labor party slate and warned to stay true to their labor roots, supported a Republican for house speaker instead of the labor caucus candidate. "Political suicide," the labor press called this "betrayal." The prediction was dead wrong; the two prospered. Egan replaced Devlin in the $1,500-a-year deputy labor commissioner's job, after which he worked in the secretary of state's office. Despite much grumbling, the Independent Labor party did not throw him out. McClellan was later appointed city assessor, yet garnered an official position in the Knights' district assembly.[13]

Contemptuous of most of the 130-member state legislature, Labadie complained that "there is much trash written that is called political economy, yet these people never even read the trash." He was convinced that human nature as well as economic and social processes conformed to a universal natural order that could be revealed through rational analysis. When the laws of social harmony were violated—as, in his view, they often were by man-made laws—social ills like poverty, prostitution and crime resulted.[14]

This scorn of the political process seems a curious message for a Michigan labor leader employed in the state labor bureau to be hammering home at a moment when workers were clamoring to have their say in government. Hopes were high for safety legislation, maximum-hours laws, child labor restrictions, and the repeal of conspiracy statutes against unions. Wage earners talked eagerly of a truly independent labor party that would free them from forced coalitions with the major parties. But with the labor movement in the process of organizing itself, there was enormous tolerance for divergent points of view. Labadie had proved himself an effective and trustworthy soldier and his views were respected. His philosophical spoutings may have baffled his readers, but as a pioneer Knight of Labor, the state's first commissioned organizer, first master workman, and a founder of the first district assembly, he possessed impressive credentials and was listened to.[15]

In Lansing, Labadie continued agitating for the one big union that would unite all workers to protect them from exploitation by big business. After snail-like progress in its first years, the Knights of Labor was gradually picking up steam. In Michigan, there were around 3,300 members in 72 assemblies in early 1883. The membership doubled within the year. Labadie had been pushing for a statewide body, and in January 1884 he presided at the first state convention of Knights. Fifty-three delegates, assembled in Detroit, expressed "unanimity of sentiment and purpose" although they represented, by his account, an exceedingly diverse group: gray-haired veterans who had fought with the abolitionists, "moss-back" farmers, hot young agitators, millworkers, miners, doctors, merchants, manufacturers, one black man, and "even those [like Labadie himself] in whose veins coursed the blood of the red race." One delegate reported the distribution of 250 copies of George's *Progress and Poverty* in his town, indicating keen interest in land reform. Others told of building their own labor halls, with amusement and reading rooms.[16]

After organizing a state assembly, delegates passed a high-blown and ineffectual resolution, much approved by Labadie, seeking to abolish "any law or custom" that curtailed the equal right of all to cultivate the soil and work the mines. Labadie also futilely pushed his favorite goal of consolidation, already tried out unsuccessfully on the ITU and the FOTLU, forerunner of the AFL. He suggested to the delegates the creation of a central labor union representing all industrial organizations within Michigan, including the farmers' Grange. The delegates turned it down, preferring to remain exclusively Knights of Labor. Their most practical step was to support a boycott against the *Detroit Free Press* and *Detroit Post and Tribune* until they employed union men and Knights of Labor. Proposals to allow political action through a labor party, lobbying and campaigning for labor candidates, got nowhere, much to Labadie's satisfaction. As an anarchist, he was adamant that the Order stay out of politics and confine itself to the role of "working people's college." Labadie's labor department colleague, John Devlin, was elected state master workman.

In Lansing, Labadie spent his free hours as master workman of a three hundred-strong assembly. He also busied himself seeking out new recruits and confidently predicted that the labor movement would double in two years, which turned out to be a gross underestimate. One Saturday in June 1886, he and Devlin rounded up seventy Knights and chartered a train to Eaton Rapids, a town of four thousand, prepared to organize an assembly there. Their reception was enthusiastic. Thirty-seven signed up on the spot. But names on a sheet did not satisfy Labadie. He kept the recruits on probationary status until they had "intelligent notions of what the movement is all about." On the return trip, the Knights amused themselves with a straw vote on presidential candidates. Greenback-Labor candidate Benjamin F. Butler, a Union general in the Civil War, was the great favorite, garnering sixty-eight votes to Republican James Blaine's two. No one voted for the victor, Grover Cleveland.[17]

Sentiments were also running high against a challenger to Governor Begole in the November 1884, election. Begole had won labor's heart by such acts as vetoing a bill that would permit only landowners to hold public office. His opponent, Republican Russell A. Alger, was heartily disliked. Alger, who had risen from private to major general in the Civil War, was a principal stockholder and director of the *Detroit Post* (formerly *Post and Tribune*), which denied employment to any union member. After failing to get Alger to change these "rat" (scab) conditions, the Detroit printers' union extended its boycott of the paper to the candidate, a man guilty of what Labadie called "aristocratic apings."[18]

To promote the fight, the printers authorized a campaign paper, the *Labor Leaf,* with the aim of burying Alger in his political grave. It failed in its mission, and the victorious Alger ousted Democrat McGrath as labor commissioner just as the bureau was completing its second report. McGrath's replacement, C. V. R. Pond, gave notice to Labadie; Devlin also was replaced as deputy commissioner by Egan, a Republican, amid charges that it was a political payoff for supporting a Republican for house speaker.[19] As the new pro-business labor commissioner was turning out a report highly antagonistic to labor agitation, his predecessor, radicalized by his exposure to labor's woes, was publicly castigating "a system of white slavery which was worse than the black slavery of thirty years ago." Appearing with Labadie, his ex-clerk, at a Knights of Labor meeting, ex-commissioner McGrath acknowledged that the present-day wage slaves were free, "but their freedom only allows them to starve."[20]

Despite the disheartening political developments, the Knights in Lansing were elated to welcome eighteen members of the Order to the 1885 legislature, including Thomas Barry of Saginaw, one of the Knights' ranking national officers. All five Detroit labor party nominees who had run on a fusion ticket with either of the major parties had been elected with more votes than any legislative candidate running only as a Republican or Democrat. But cigarmaker Charles Erb and Labadie's good friend Judson Grenell, who ran solely on the labor party slate, were roundly defeated. Their connection with socialism may also have tainted them in voters' eyes.[21]

After his ouster from the labor bureau, Labadie and Sophie returned to Detroit in May 1885, to find a dismal labor situation. More than one-third of the workers were unemployed. The printing business was sluggish, and, as a union man, Labadie was banned from both the *News* and the *Free Press.* For the next few months, they struggled along with barely enough money for food.[22]

The city was full of destitution and despair. Able-bodied men filled the office of the "poor commissioner," waiting for charity. Labadie wrote in the *Denver Labor Enquirer* of a little girl whose father had starved and been left unburied for five days. Her mother lay helpless in bed with a newborn baby; there was no food or fire. He knew of a cigarmaker's family living two weeks on corn meal and water, and a painter who became demented from lack of food. It made Labadie "bitter, very bitter, against the upholders of the present monstrously unjust system of distributing wealth."[23]

At the Pingree and Smith boot and shoe factory two hundred workers went on strike in mid 1885 because the owners rejected a union shop and had discharged prominent union members. At the same time, the employer proposed a reduction in wages. When negotiations broke down, scabs were hired. Previously such a strike would have been doomed to failure, but the widespread network of Knights assemblies now made it possible to organize an effective nationwide boycott of the firm's boots and shoes. "Boycott Scab Goods!" the *Labor Leaf* implored unionists' wives, worried that the boycott might fail because women were less likely to observe it than their husbands. Their role as shoppers and consumers made them essential to the success of boycotts, then the Order's most effective weapon. Children were admonished: "Don't forget to tell your parents to BOYCOTT SCAB GOODS."[24]

The strike, like numerous others taking place that year, got little encouragement from the Order's national leaders. Powderly adamantly opposed strikes, although he did not forbid them. His goals were loftier, focusing on land reform. Instead of setting up strike funds, he told Labadie, Knights should be buying "good healthy literature that will teach you your rights without making fools of yourselves by striking for them." When the Detroit strikers began planning a producers' cooperative, however, they were in harmony with one of the Order's grand ideals. Within a month, they had organized and incorporated the Boot and Shoe Cooperative Association of Detroit, the only cooperative shoe factory in what was then called "the West." Labadie, along with several hundred others, bought a five-dollar stock certificate in the fledgling company. Sophie bought a pair of its footwear for $3.25, Labadie's account book shows.[25]

The early labor movement was "cooperative crazy," Detroit labor leader David Boyd later recalled. Co-ops were seen as a possible cure-all for the evils of capitalism. Detroit, however, had been in no hurry to hop on the bandwagon. Indeed, with successful cooperatives well established in many other cities, Detroit was accused of being backward. Labadie's influence may have been partly responsible for the foot-dragging. Cooperatives did not conflict with anarchist tenets, but Labadie counseled caution. He cited the inability of workers to save enough capital to compete with established profit-making businesses, as well as expected pressure tactics by competing merchants. Of the thousands of cooperative experiments begun nationwide years before the formation of the Knights of Labor (and during its lifespan as well), he warned, "not one in a hundred have succeeded."[26]

He complained to economist Richard T. Ely that the cooperative endeavor "smacks too much of joint-stockism to be a healthy movement in the direction of equitable distribution." Although it might benefit the cooperators financially in the short run, as a way out of wage slavery, it was "futile." He believed it would throw the middleman out of work and into competition with labor in other occupations; it would not raise wages; it was a labor-saving institution and "have labor-saving institutions benefitted the wage class?"[27]

But the new Detroit co-op was ready to fly. Indeed, for a time, co-ops flourished throughout Michigan, supported by local Knights' assemblies, although not by the trade unions. By the end of the decade, however, Labadie's negative prediction was proving correct. Most of the labor cooperatives had succumbed due to lack of funds, inefficiency, or mismanagement, including Detroit's example. They also suffered from bitter opposition by competing businesses, per Labadie's forecast. The co-op era of the 1880s was the last time the American labor movement seriously involved itself in this panacea for industrial ills.

Strike fever began inflaming the nation's wage earners. The Knights' national leaders under Powderly, despite their hostility to strikes, had to pay heed. The growing militancy was fed by recent victories in local strikes endorsed by Knights' assemblies, which previously would have been savagely smashed. The first show of strength by railway shopmen had shut down the Union Pacific railroad in 1884. The following year, nearly 5,000 striking railway workers, led by Joseph R. Buchanan representing Knights of Labor assemblies on the western railroads, had threatened to paralyze Jay Gould's entire Southwest railroad system, involving 10,000 miles of tracks. Only after the railroad tycoon was forced to cancel wage cuts and layoffs and to end all discrimination against the Knights of Labor was the strike called off.

Organized labor was jubilant over Gould's capitulation. The railroad magnate was one of the most powerful of the turn-of-the century "robber barons." He had bragged contemptuously, "I can hire one-half of the working class to kill the other half." In the wake of this sensational success, workers swarmed into the ranks of the Knights. Tens of thousands were unskilled or foreign-born. Membership spurted to around 100,000 by mid 1885, five times the enrollment four years before. A year later, with over 700,000 members, it was so huge the general officers began to refuse charters to new locals.

Spurred on by this growing sense of power, the unorganized lumber-mill workers of the Saginaw Valley in July 1885 mounted the greatest strike in Michigan in the nineteenth century. For the first time, a massive labor rebellion raised public fears of the kind of bloody clashes in other states. Pinkerton agents arrived carrying Winchester rifles with bayonets. Armed companies of state militia were dispatched to the scene by Governor Alger, himself a wealthy lumberman. Demonstrators were forbidden to assemble. Police shot some; others were clubbed.

But despite the shutdown of ninety sawmills and fifty salt mines with six thousand men idled, violence was contained. Credit for averting major bloodshed went to Thomas B. Barry, a thirty-three-year-old state legislator from the Saginaw Valley and member of the Knights' general executive board, who took over the strike leadership. The men were rushing to buy guns by that time, but Barry successfully counseled them to remain peaceful and obey the law despite the presence of "armed hirelings of capitalism."[28]

The "Great Strike in the Valley" was based on demands for a ten-hour day with no cut in pay. Millworkers complained that there was no work as exhausting as keeping up with the whirling machinery of a sawmill six days a week, "driven eleven and a half hours per day, handling heavy logs, boards and planks, without a moment's rest, like a prisoner in a treadmill." For this toil, most received less than a dollar and a half a day, had no work in winter when the mills were closed, and often were crippled and broken in health after ten years. Barry understood their plight well. He himself had begun work at the age of eight in a knitting mill, putting in eighty-one hours a week. He never attended school. As an axemaker bent on unionizing his fellow workers, he had repeatedly been fired and blacklisted.

Barry, who rivaled Labadie as the most charismatic Michigan labor figure of the era, had sponsored a bill setting ten hours as a legal day's work. It had passed the state legislature, but would not become law until September 1885. The millworkers naively expected it to take effect immediately and were in no mood to wait. "Ten Hours or No Sawdust," they demanded. When Barry—a compelling figure with a mass of dark, wavy hair, a reddish handle-bar mustache, gaunt cheeks, and an intense gaze—attempted to address the strikers he was arrested, bailed out, and repeatedly arrested again, five times in all. He was charged with violating the Baker Conspiracy Law, which in effect prohibited organized strikes by making it illegal to conspire "willfully and maliciously" to interfere with the operation of a business.

Although the Knights' national organization did not sponsor the strike, Powderly decided to visit the scene, where he effectively undercut Barry's efforts by privately urging workers to accept a cut in wages to gain the shorter day. He engaged in a similar betrayal in 1886, when Barry was negotiating the Chicago packing-house strike. As a result, the two became sworn enemies. It was characteristic of the autocratic grand master workman, who abhorred strikes, to try to settle one on almost any terms, even if it meant undermining his own lieutenants.

The millowners, as it happened, were much better positioned to withstand the two-month strike than the strikers. A local Knights assembly began pleading nationally for relief aid, reporting that it had fed four thousand persons and nearly exhausted its resources. By the time the strike petered out in September 1885, the workers had lost some $385,000 in wages. Equally dismaying, many were still working eleven hours or more, since the ten-hour-law now in effect had a loophole allowing employers to contract with their workers for a longer day and thereby waive the limitation.

Despite the unsatisfactory outcome, Labadie and other labor activists saw the strike as a triumph of labor solidarity. They were heartened that thousands of unorganized men of different nationalities—Germans, Poles, Irish, French Canadians—the minority American-born, had been able to improvise such a vigorous, nationally recognized campaign without mayhem or destruction of property. Barry was acclaimed a hero. Images of this "Joan of Arc in timber" with "the face of a dreamer," as one admirer described him, were carried in the fall labor parade alongside those of icons Powderly, Henry George, and Trevellick.[29]

Barry was put on trial for conspiracy. Labadie began organizing a fund-raising drive for the legal defense of "one of our most self-sacrificing leaders," who had prevented the Saginaw Valley from being "deluged with blood." Barry was acquitted, but for Labadie the verdict resolved nothing. He was shaken by the violent suppression of the strike by government troops and warned that capitalists were blithely preparing for their own destruction. By their "hoggishness and their tyrannies and their brutalities," they were driving the laboring people to desperation. He predicted ominously that in some future strike, when troops and Pinkertons were called in, "the soldiers and thugs will be annihilated, the strikers will confiscate the capital of the corporations as contraband of war . . . and when this has taken place in . . . several industries the Revolution will have been accomplished."[30] He was beginning to believe, as he expressed in the lines of verse that introduce this chapter, that "the end indeed justifies the means."

Loose talk of violence was rife as conditions during the industrial depression of 1884–86 bred desperate thoughts. The period was characterized by wage cuts, lockouts, and miserable working conditions. The worker was regarded as nothing but "a pin to a machine."[31] Radical ideas were spreading through the country and not only fanatics were mouthing threats of revolution and dynamite.

Labadie noted with approval the formation of the Detroit Rifles, a workers' paramilitary group. Recruits began drilling with .44-caliber, sixteen-shot Winchester repeating rifles on the outskirts of the city, under cover of darkness. A strong believer in the right of the citizenry to bear arms, Labadie thought it wise for labor organizations to have well-armed police, detective, and military forces. Like the American revolutionists, they might need to defend themselves against an oppressive regime and "the brutalities of the capitalistic Hessians."[32]

Labadie now was working as both columnist and printer for *Labor Leaf* (later *Advance and Labor Leaf*) publisher John R. Burton, who ran a little printshop on the third floor of 50 Larned Street West, next to the old Tribune Building. The one-time campaign paper had survived its failure to defeat Alger and proved remarkably durable, as labor papers went. In five years of weekly publication, from 1884 to 1889, it gained a reputation as one of the country's great nineteenth-century labor publications and came to serve as Labadie's principal forum. He was especially fond of its motto, borrowed from Tom Paine: "The world is my country; to do good my religion." He used the phrase frequently, and his children later recalled it as epitomizing his philosophy. It tallied with his view that patriotism was "a humbug" that kept the world's working people divided and that the church was "in the hands of Mammon."[33] He also liked to quote Paine's sentiment that government, "even in its best state, is but a necessary evil."

Although Burton leaned toward socialism, he was at one with Labadie in objecting to the class consciousness intrinsic to Marxist philosophy. He announced that the *Labor Leaf* was not the organ of a class, "for I hold class distinctions and those of nationality as the worst enemies the country has to contend with." It was also not the mouthpiece of any dogma. Burton welcomed "all shades of liberal thought," resulting in a spirited publication. He and Labadie were often at odds, but his columnist was allowed to say what he liked in his column, "Cranky Notions." Labadie thought its apologetic name appropriate for his "stray thoughts . . . crude and 'jerky' because they come from an unlearned mechanic [craftsman] who has not had the time from the 'demnition grind' to polish them up." There were those like John Swinton, who reproved Labadie for permitting himself to be called a crank.[34] But his good-natured, self-imposed identification with the lunatic fringe helped protect Labadie from being lumped with zealots and extremists. Unfortunately, it also encouraged some to conclude he was not serious, that he was playing the revolutionary for theatrical effect.

The new columnist was predictably rambunctious. He ridiculed readers who believed governments protected them as "wooden headed scrubs." He was torn "between pity and hate" for labor reformers who disparaged radicals, although Burton had just called on unionists to "join hands to crush out anarchists" lest they discredit the labor movement. Burton let Labadie rant. When questioned if it was proper to allow "a rabid Anarchist to fulminate his traitorous schemes," Burton responded calmly that he should have "the same right of free speech as a rabid Republican."[35]

One of Labadie's readers was Richard T. Ely, a pioneer chronicler of the burgeoning labor movement, who became one of America's most influential economists. Then a thirty-one-year-old professor at Johns Hopkins University in Baltimore, Ely had written two books on socialism and in 1885 was preparing one of the earliest studies of American labor. He responded enthusiastically when Labadie sent him a note, although it accused Ely of misrepresenting Proudhon's ideas in the professor's *French and German Socialism*. Ely even conceded that he "may have fallen into slight error in regard to Proudhon." Although admitting he was opposed to anarchism's "policy of destruction," Ely professed "great faith" in labor organizations, and asked Labadie to help him obtain research materials for his new book. What he wanted were labor pamphlets, convention reports, constitutions, manifestos, and other documents.[36]

Labadie generally viewed professional scholars with a contradictory mixture of awe and disdain, but was flattered to be solicited by a college professor and began requesting materials through the labor press as well as sending along documents in his own collection. At the same time, he was dubious about Ely's credentials. How could this academic, working in his ivory tower, accurately portray the plight of those who were starving? To really understand, he chided, Ely would have to "experience the feelings of being out of work through no fault of your own, with a family to support and no money nor credit" and "know the abuse and insults heaped upon the workers by brutal employers and bosses."[37] Clearly stung, Ely responded defensively that he had once wandered the streets of New York, jobless and penniless, "in a most wretched desperate state." It was then that he had vowed "to write in behalf of the laboring classes."[38]

Ely especially wanted information on the Knights of Labor. Powderly did not reply to his letters, and the staff refused to supply official publications on grounds of secrecy. Labadie agreed that the so-called secrets were "of no consequence," and agreed to solicit Powderly on Ely's behalf. "I never met a more pleasant man than Powderly," he effused, and "I am seldom deceived in the character of men." Labadie's self-congratulation was vastly misplaced. However laudable his humanitarian motives, Powderly was also arrogant, vain, vengeful, and plotting. His actions in undermining Barry in the Saginaw strike seem to have escaped Labadie's notice. Perhaps Labadie's emotional investment in the success of the Knights and his cordial six-year correspondence with its leader blinded him to Powderly's many flaws. By 1887, his assessment had so altered that he was publicly denouncing Powderly as corrupt, "autocratic, opinionated and unfair."[39]

Labadie cooperated with Ely despite the unalloyed suspicion and contempt of Benjamin Tucker, Labadie's anarchist mentor. "Quack," "arrant humbug," and "charlatan" were among the epithets Tucker used. Ely was "trying to make literary capital by a pretended and half-hearted friendliness to labor," Tucker charged. When Ely's ground-breaking *The Labor Movement in America* was published in 1886, it incorrectly represented Tucker as an advocate of forcible revolution without, acccording to Tucker, "giving so much as a hint of my constant insistence on peaceful methods."[40]

Ely acknowledged Labadie's help in the preface to his book, describing him as "a poor mechanic in Detroit" who had amassed a library of three hundred volumes by depriving himself of "bodily comforts." Try as he could, Labadie was unable to disabuse Ely of the conviction that "Plague, pestilence, and famine combined are mild evils compared with widespread anarchy."[41] Ely was a Christian socialist who was looking to the church, not an economic revolution, to bring about social redemption.

In the aftermath of the Saginaw strike, Labadie's writings became increasingly unrestrained. He was obsessed by visions of a coming Armgeddon and saw every avenue of escape from wage-slavedom cut off by the industrial oligarchy. If the workers tried cooperatives, they were crushed by unfair competition. If they tried strikes, "assassins and murderers" were paid to suppress them. If they tried political action, their efforts were nullified by "the unscrupulousness of political harpies." Yet governments, customs, and laws were "but ropes of sand when an angry and outraged people throw themselves against them." A little dynamite was a convincing argument to use against "a monster when he has his fangs in your vitals."

He saw the "avalanche of the revolution" poised to crash. Then "the scenes of the French Revolution will be re-enacted, with the heads of the industrial tyrants held aloft on pike poles in the market places so the populace may see what tyranny produces." Labor agitation was too timid; it was unlikely to bring about a peaceful revolution before this terrible catastrophe occurred. Peaceable means should be tried, of course, but it was likely the force of arms that would grant the people their rights.[42]

Labadie's alarming outbursts were uncharacteristic in their violence. Like many at the time, these sentiments were to a large extent empty rhetoric. But Labadie was by no means the only one in Detroit engaging in such wild talk. At one mass meeting in February 1885, a resolution that dynamite was a justifiable means of political warfare was barely turned down, 100–95. August Spies, the militant Chicago revolutionary, came to preach the doctrine of destruction to local gatherings of the International Working People's Association. "Don't keep dynamite in your pocket," the *Labor Leaf* warned, not that there is evidence any Detroiter did. By fall 1885, even Judson Grenell, normally a voice of moderation, was crying out: "When will the masses become aroused? . . . When there is a robber class and a robbed class, what else should be expected but revolution?"[43]

As labor's army swelled, so did the inevitable cries to use its might. Labor agitation surged, with the dramatically expanding Knights of Labor leading the movement. President Cleveland was sufficiently troubled by labor problems to propose a permanent government arbitration board, but nothing came of it. As a wave of boycotts and strikes hit the nation, a notable harmony seemed to bond working people of varying outlooks. The years of 1885 and 1886 were "stupendous," as Agnes Inglis described them in the retrospect of many decades. She marveled that nearly the whole labor movement was clasped to the bosom of the Knights of Labor, including "anarchist, socialist, trades and labor unions,—political and non-political—autocracy versus rank-and-file ideas, saviours and the to-be-saved."[44] Events were building to a crescendo. In just a few months, the drum roll culminated in a catastrophic explosion.

★ 9 ★

A Bomb Is Thrown

> The people wake.
> When their mighty force is spent in wreck and ruin
> They ope their eyes in sodden wonderment they'd done
> so much
> (As a drunken giant sobered, red-eyed, spent,
> Realizes his mad destruction of home and kin)
> And wearily, in sullen sorrow,
> Go back to sleep again.
> "PROGRESS?" FROM *THE RED FLAG AND OTHER VERSES*

The year 1886—perhaps the most pivotal in American labor history—dawned bright and full of hope. A torrent of workers was flooding the Knights of Labor, its membership reaching 700,000 by summer. An unprecedented wave of successful strikes and boycotts in the mid 1880s gave promise that labor was soon to realize its explosive power. An effective third party seemed possible, as labor candidates campaigned in more than two hundred cities and towns. In Chicago, and New York—where Henry George was the candidate—the labor party received nearly one-third of the votes in the November mayoral election. Passions were fired by hopes that the long-awaited eight-hour workday was just around the corner; since before the Civil War, no single issue had infused the nation's workers with more fervor nor more frustration in failing to see their goal achieved.[1]

Michigan had marched in the forefront of the movement, spurred by Richard Trevellick. As president of Detroit's first Trades Assembly in 1864, he began agitating for shorter hours. He was the catalyst for the organization of some twenty-five eight-hour leagues which, by 1866, joined forces in the statewide Grand Eight-Hour League of Michigan. The British-born

Trevellick had quit his job as ship's carpenter at a Detroit dry dock company to serve as chief Washington lobbyist for the National Labor Union, which claimed to represent more than a half million working people and whose primary goal was passage of laws establishing eight hours as a legal day's work nationwide.[2] Victory had seemed at hand in 1868 when President Andrew Johnson signed into law an eight-hour day for federal employees shortly after he was acquitted in impeachment proceedings.

But celebrations were short-lived. "As is usually the case when we pin our faith on government," Labadie reflected retrospectively, "disappointment followed . . . every president since, excepting Gen. Grant, has failed to enforce [the law], notwithstanding each was sworn to uphold and execute the laws of the United States."[3]

Labadie had been intrigued by a rather far-fetched call to arms in 1884 from the insignificant and impotent Federation of Organized Trades and Labor Unions (FOTLU), the embryonic AFL. Having ignored Labadie's pleas to disband and merge with the Knights of Labor, the FOTLU, in what seemed a last, defiant gasp, issued a half-hearted resolution that simply asserted that eight hours should constitute a legal day's work. An arbitrary deadline was set for May 1, 1886; no provisions for enforcing this schedule were proposed.

The growing labor movement was now flexing its muscles, yearning to achieve its long-nurtured dream. The idea of a mammoth eight-hour-day campaign triggered unexpected enthusiasm among radicals and rank-and-file trade unionists alike. No more relying on statutes; unified labor would take action itself. As it became clear that there must be a means for enforcing the demand, support grew for a nationwide mass strike on May 1, a day that at the time had no wider significance.[4]

The Detroit Trades Council immediately pledged its strength to the crusade, and the eight-hour campaign went to the top of its agenda. Labadie stressed the urgency of vigorous agitation. "No time should be lost . . . to prepare everyone for the occasion," he counseled. Employers should be notified, public sympathy aroused, the country flooded with tracts, bills posted on walls, meetings called, articles written. If there were a chance of failure, he warned prophetically, the strike should be called off because a failure would retard the short work day movement for years.[5]

By early 1886, agitation meetings were held almost nightly throughout the city. Prominent Knights and SLP leaders addressed large and enthusiastic audiences in both English and German. August Spies came from Chicago to exhort the local social revolutionary group—which until then had disparaged the shorter day as a compromise with the capitalistic system—to join the struggle. The indefatigable Trevellick went on a three-month campaigning trip, speaking an average of ten times a week.[6]

In mid February, Labadie pushed for the cause three evenings in a row—for the SLP (with which he was apparently still on good terms), the Knights, and the Trades Council. The next month, he encouraged an audience in Buck's Opera House in Lansing to "get a bag of corn meal and some pork ahead, and get into shape to stand off [the] landlords for a few weeks." If the bosses refused to grant the shorter day, they should just quit work "and it would then be seen whether capital employs labor or labor employs capital."[7]

Employers responded to the agitation with understandable alarm. Some voluntarily capitulated. The Pingree and Smith shoe works and the *Free Press*—a "rat" office for twenty years—decided to settle with the unions. Across the nation, tens of thousands of workers swarmed into the Knights of Labor, believing it sponsored the movement. One Detroit assembly initiated 135 new members in a single night in April.[8]

Labadie and others, intoxicated with labor's burgeoning power, warmed to ominous rhetoric. The cry from the capitalists, Labadie exulted in the *Labor Leaf,* was "Go slow! But the cry comes too late. . . . The blind Sampson [sic] of Labor . . . is at this moment tugging at the pillars of the Temple of Capitalism, and its destruction is as sure as that tomorrow will come. . . . It is useless now to try to escape the revolution."[9]

As the fateful day approached, wage earners were poised for the historic leap forward. In the midst of a severe depression, they saw themselves on the verge of a new era when labor would assert its rights and capitalists would bow to its amassed force. Newspapers published hysterical predictions of horrors to come.

The nation steeled itself for a cataclysmic upheaval. But Saturday, May 1, 1886, was an anticlimax. A spirit of bravado abounded, accompanied by a great deal of enthusiastic marching, but there was no revolution or bloodshed. More than 300,000 workers across the country took the day off. Pinkertons and police were poised with rifles at the ready, but the demonstrating workers only paraded peacefully and listened to eloquent speeches.[10]

In Detroit, the weekend passed quietly. But by midday Monday, an estimated 1,500 strikers and supporters were massed before the Michigan Car Works, which had fired a Knights of Labor organizer. The crowd began advancing from factory to factory, gathering up workers and shutting down one plant after another.

The militancy was infectious. The following evening, three thousand workers assembled for a solidarity meeting that spilled into the streets because the hall was too small. The police were ready with an emergency strategy, and some employers were threatening to shoot. But the Detroit police force was considered relatively "humane," and strike leaders were advocating peaceful means.[11]

Not so Labadie. He chose that moment to issue an inflammatory column chastising those who had "not yet learned to hate the law." Humanity had "never gained any great good except by taking the law and trampling it underfoot," he wrote. Jesus Christ, the American revolutionists, John Brown, and the abolitionists were all well-known law-breakers. "Curse the law," he thundered. "What the deuce are we organized for if it is not to overturn the law?"[12] Labadie's sentiments were extreme at any moment; their outrageousness was magnified by their timing one day after the infamous bombing in Chicago's Haymarket Square let loose a wave of terror of anarchism and all things radical. A bomb had been thrown into the midst of police attempting to break up a labor gathering. Police opened fire, causing a riot. Scores of police and workers had been injured or killed.

Headlines in the commercial press on May 5 reported "Riot and Death" in Chicago, "Dynamite Bombs Fired at the Police Officers." The *Detroit News* blamed the "labor revolution" for the "terrible scenes of riot and bloodshed—The anarchists have turned the weapons of dynamite and powder upon the constituted authorities with awful results." Like the rest of America, Labadie must have read the papers with horror. Although he himself had recklessly called for violence, he was shocked at its realization. Two of the accused men he knew and respected, despite vast ideological differences. Police had arrested August Spies at his offices at the *Arbeiter Zeitung,* a German-language publication of the International Working People's Association (IWPA). Only a few weeks earlier Spies had dropped by the *Labor Leaf* offices to chat. He was a handsome thirty-year-old immigrant, cultured and erudite, with wavy brown hair sweeping back from a high forehead and an air of intense conviction and sincerity. As he toured the country's industrial cities preaching a program of destruction, he echoed the threats of his New York associate, Johann Most. Capitalism was doomed; the IWPA planned to hasten its demise.[13]

An intensive search was underway for Albert Parsons, who, with his wife Lucy, had been Labadie's fellow socialist delegates at the contentious 1880 Greenback-Labor presidential convention. They were among the dissidents who had broken with the SLP to launch the Bakuninist-inspired IWPA.

Parsons, now thirty-eight, had unlikely beginnings for an IWPA leader. A former Confederate soldier from a prominent Texas family, he repudiated his upbringing, then fought for Negro rights and married a woman of African American ancestry. The misery of the unemployed after the Panic of 1873 had radicalized him, as it had Labadie.

Of those indicted for the Haymarket bombing, only Parsons was a Knight. Editor of the IWPA's English-language weekly, *The Alarm,* he was reckoned one of Chicago's most dangerous radicals, a charismatic orator and agitator for revolutionary anarchism. Labadie thought Parsons's mind "all befogged" and claimed he had "mixed up in an unrecognizable mass the theories of Anarchism, State Socialism, and Communism." Nevertheless, he considered Parsons and Spies "brave men" who were willing to "suffer and die for justice."[14]

Repercussions from the Haymarket explosion convulsed the nation into a frenzy of fury and vengeance against anarchists. Left-wingers of every hue were denounced as subversives. Wild tales of conspiracies and dynamite plots abounded. A hysterical populace was caught up in the nation's first "Red Scare." Images of the anarchist as a bearded, crazed fanatic armed with a bomb were etched in the public consciousness. Threats of dynamite could no longer be dismissed as radical bluster, editors warned. It had been used, and blood had flowed in the streets. Many pointed to the bombing as the culmination of ten years of labor violence, proof that the labor movement itself was a menace to society, law, order, and government.[15]

The Haymarket affair is perhaps the most oft-told tale in labor history. It is a tragic story of how the unpredictable act of one hothead and the violence that ensued set back the eight-hour crusade and the dearly held hopes that a social millenium was just around the corner. That one deed demolished years of labor advances, throwing the whole movement into confusion and chaos. In its aftermath, eight men were found guilty of conspiracy to commit murder and four hanged in what is now acknowledged as a gross miscarriage of justice.

In the feverish months before the Haymarket bombing, Chicago had become the vortex of the eight-hour struggle, largely due to the energetic agitation of Parsons, Spies, and the other militants in the IWPA. The Knights' leader, Powderly, had done all he could to undermine the campaign for the May 1 general strike. Believing all strikes to be futile and detrimental to labor's interests, he had issued a secret circular warning against the planned demonstrations, disavowing any official support, and suggesting that, instead of demonstrating, Knights could write essays on the eight-hour day. Stepping into the void, IWPA agitators infused the plan with their revolutionary ardor. They roused thousands at lakefront rallies where the red flag of revolution and the black flag of anarchism were both displayed. Some forty thousand workers took part in the eight-hour strike on May 1 in Chicago, the nation's largest turnout.[16]

As in Detroit, trouble did not begin in Chicago until two days after the May 1 strike date. At the McCormick Reaper Works, workers had been locked out for months in an effort to break the union. As scabs were leaving for the day, strikers began heckling and hurling stones. The Chicago police, notorious for brutality, attacked, leaving several workers dead and many injured. August Spies, in fury at the carnage, rushed to his *Arbeiter Zeitung* offices and scribbled out a fiery call for retaliation, the so-called Revenge Circular: "Workingmen, to Arms!!! . . . Destroy the hideous monster that seeks to destroy you." The typesetter added the inflammatory word "Revenge!"[17]

The following night, May 4, a mass protest meeting was held in Haymarket Square. The weather was raw, and only around three thousand people showed up. They were addressed in turn by Spies, Parsons, and British-born Samuel Fielden, a one-time Methodist lay preacher. The speeches were reasonably moderate; Parsons even brought Lucy and his two children along. Mayor Carter H. Harrison rode up on his white horse, then left, convinced the gathering was harmless. He stopped at a nearby police station where a riot squad was on alert and recommended that the precinct captain, John Bonfield, dismiss them.

Instead, Bonfield marched the contingent of 180 officers to Haymarket Square. It was raining. Parsons and most of the crowd had left; Fielden was winding up the last speech. The police commanded Fielden to halt the meeting. "But we are peaceable," he protested, then grudgingly agreed. Fielden and Spies began climbing down from the speakers' wagon. At that moment, someone threw a bomb. There was a terrific explosion. Police shot back wildly. After five minutes of violence, seven policemen were dead or dying and sixty were injured, most, as it turned out, shot by their fellow officers. An unknown number of dead or injured citizens were carried away and cared for secretly.

Who was the bomb-thrower? What did he hope to accomplish? If he was an anarchist, why did he hurl dynamite with such total disregard for the safety of his comrades? Was he possibly an agent provocateur? To this day, his identity remains a mystery. He was almost certainly none of the eight Chicago anarchists who were convicted of murder in the trial that followed.

Labadie disbelieved newspaper accounts from the start. He observed that reporters had "worked themselves up into a terrible state of frenzy, and lies and ignorance come from their pens as slime from a mad dog's mouth." He pleaded with readers of *Labor Leaf* to suspend judgment until the nation's daily press cooled off. Editor Burton backed him wholeheartedly. The May 12 issue accused news reports of being "thoroughly one-sided" and using "the most intemperate language," and insisted that "it is nowhere shown that the anarchists committed any overt act to justify interference with them."[18]

This was an audacious stance. The *Labor Leaf* was one of only a handful of labor papers that repudiated the hysterical press reports. Sickened at the eagerness of most of the labor press to dissociate itself from the reviled anarchists, Labadie lashed out: "I do wish the labor papers would stop distributing the nasty puke the capitalist papers have seen fit to cover their dirty sheets with." Fears of a backlash did not moderate his outpourings; they may even have fanned the flames. "If it is necessary to use dynamite to protect the right of free meetings, free press, and free speech, then the sooner we learn its manufacture and use the better it will be for the toilers of the world," he proclaimed recklessly in mid June. Yet despite these seething words, he foresaw a future when the "stupid public learns the warmth of the Anarchist's heart for Man, then will it honor and applaud those who were fearless enough to brave public scorn and the vilification of a vicious and ignorant press for an idea."[19]

Labadie was monumentally out of touch with public sentiment. Haymarket intensified a horror of anarchism that scarcely dissipated in his lifetime. What stung him most was the reaction of Terence Powderly. The Knights' leader did not pause a moment to determine the facts. The day after the bombing, frantic to protect the Knights of Labor (and possibly himself), Powderly insisted that every American labor organization condemn the "outrage" in Chicago. "Honest labor," he asserted, "is not to be found in the ranks of those who march under the red flag of anarchy, which is the emblem of blood and destruction."[20]

Labadie must have been aghast to read those words. What had happened to the vaunted motto of the Knights—"An injury to one is the concern of all"? Whence had come this sudden condemnation of anarchism? Powderly knew Labadie was an anarchist, yet had worked closely with him for years. Their relationship had been warm and confiding, with photos exchanged and expressions of mutual trust and admiration.[21]

Powderly, as Labadie knew him, had always seemed sympathetic to radical ideas. He had encouraged the Order's monthly journal to publish an article by his Detroit ally likening communism to "civilized" institutions. He had asked Labadie to speak out with him at the 1883 General Assembly on his favorite ideal, land reform, as well as to help defeat efforts to return "God's name" to the Order's ritual. The grand master workman needed "level heads" at the convention, he had told Labadie.[22]

In the slight, balding man with a pince-nez and enormous blond handlebar mustache, Labadie thought he recognized a fellow idealist, motivated by unselfish and high-minded humanitarianism. He was aware, of course, that Powderly, a one-time machinist, was no earthy labor agitator. Of scholarly demeanor, exuding an air of good breeding, Powderly was a most unlikely looking leader "of a million of the horny-fisted sons of toil," in John Swinton's words.[23] Manual labor had scarcely callused his hands before he was elected mayor of Scranton, began the study of law, then gave it up to lead the Knights of Labor.

What particularly pleased Labadie was that they agreed they did not "go much on politics" and opposed the creation of a labor party. Both also were passionately committed to educating the working people. It would be better to have "5,000 men who will read and think in the Order," Labadie wrote Powderly, than "a million brutal, unthinking clods" (the somewhat inflated estimated membership of the Knights at its peak). He proposed that discussion of "the Labor question" at meetings be made compulsory, and that those who refused to "study some way out of wage slavery" be ousted from membership. Powderly seemed enthusiastic, calling the ideas "sound ones." He promised to incorporate them in his 1884 convention address in Philadelphia.[24]

But he did not do so; Powderly "always talked big, but his actions . . . never matched his words." When Powderly, a teetotaler, stood before the delegates in 1884 in his double-breasted black broadcloth coat, he mentioned education only in passing. "Two remedies alone can save us, they are education and sobriety," he said, before launching into a diatribe against the evils of demon rum. Temperance was his greatest passion.[25]

Vain, petty, vindictive, vacillating—these were some of the character flaws of the man who led the Knights of Labor to might and then into insignificance. Labadie initially did not perceive them, despite boasting that he was a good judge of character. Yet a certain mean-spiritedness is obvious in Powderly's petulant complaints to Labadie of machinations against him, of those who "walk on me, spit on me and abuse me like a dog," of the men who "harass me with their grievances by holding their little sores up for me to look at and refuse to let me put plaster on for fear that they wouldn't have something to growl about."[26]

By 1886, the Knights of Labor had an army of working people at the ready. Instead of relishing this force, Powderly was overwhelmed by it. He was not the man to wield it. Alternatively timid, tentative, negative, and secretive, he was consistently guilty of tactical blunders, and the Haymarket bombing brought out the worst in him.

In the aftermath of the Haymarket incident, Detroit remained calm, despite some hysterical moments. At the West Larned Street labor head-quarters, the Dialectical Union, a weekly discussion group, confirmed its dedication to free speech and no taboos of "unpopular subjects" by opening a debate in June 1886, with the dramatic resolution: "The throwing of the dynamite bomb in Chicago was justifiable." Labadie, for the affirmative, asserted that the question was not whether the ideas expressed at Haymarket Square were harmful, but whether the police had the right to suppress them. He declared hyperbolically that the right to free speech must be defended even if it meant killing every policeman in the country. Henry Robinson, an elected justice of the peace, countered that cool-headed men would refrain from making inflammatory speeches when people were excited by strikes. No evil existed that could not be cured by the ballot.[27]

Audience response was sharply divided. The vote on the resolution tied 23–23. Of four reporters sent to cover the sensational discussion, three reportedly sided with Labadie. Their editors, on the other hand, were "thrown into a state bordering on frenzy," over Detroit's "anarchistic" debating forum, the *Labor Leaf* reported. Labadie's fervor in defending the use of dynamite in defense of free speech doubtless caused trepidation within the rather staid group of Detroit printers who had earlier selected him to represent them at the thirty-fourth annual convention of the ITU. Whatever their misgivings, they sent him off in June along with a $25 delegate's fee.[28]

Labadie had been elected by T.U. 18 on a platform calling for the publication of a weekly paper, to be furnished to every union printer in the country and paid for by a per capita tax. Despite their superior literacy, Labadie considered printers a backward lot when it came to economic matters. "Not one in ten" bothered to consider questions "of graver import than merely trade regulations," he complained to his Detroit colleagues.[29]

At the convention in Pittsburgh, to Labadie's surprise, the 120 ITU delegates approved his proposal without a dissenting vote. They agreed that henceforth each unionist would receive *The Craftsman* and be billed ten cents quarterly for the subscription. But Labadie by now had something more portentous in mind—to promote labor consolidation, his leitmotif. Once again, he lobbied energetically for the ITU to give up its separate identity and join the Knights of Labor. It became the main question before the delegates, with many persuaded by his eloquence, according to one account. The new president, William Amison, was elected after supporting amalgamation.

At this event, the ITU came as close as it ever did to merging with the Order. But the committee on relations with the Knights was leery of Powderly. There had been jurisdictional disputes; "rat" printers had been admitted to Knighthood. The committee claimed that either Powderly was being untrue to his promises to keep out of the affairs of trades unions or he was unable to control his own organization. By the following year, the dissension-racked Knights of Labor was competing with the newly formed American Federation of Labor (formerly the FOTLU) for the allegiance of the ITU, a rivalry in which the Order was the loser.[30]

Although the Haymarket bloodshed broke the momentum of the drive for an eight-hour day, Jo and Sophie Labadie did their small part to keep the cause alive. On a lot at the corner of Buchanan and Fifteenth Streets, bought by Sophie with her earnings as a schoolteacher, they built a frame cottage, paying the workers a full day's current wages for eight hours of work. Originally Jo had protested that he did not believe in owning land. "And I don't believe in paying rent," Sophie countered firmly. About two-fifths of Detroit working-class families were buying their own homes at the time.[31]

Sophie was pregnant, and in September 1886, nine years after their marriage, Laura Euphrosyne was born, evidently their second child. So-phie was thirty-five, Jo thirty-six. Cemetery records indicate that an infant, seventeen-month-old Leo Donatus, was buried in February 1880. His exis-tence is puzzling, because Labadie seems never to have referred to him. The account book gives few clues except the notation of $17.84 for "Funeral expenses, Leo" and payments of $27.50 to "Dr. Younghusband" over the next four months, a very large medical bill for the times.[32]

Except for helping with Knights of Labor social events, Sophie, after Laura's birth, devoted herself to motherhood and the family. This seems to have been her choice, not Jo's. He frequently expressed admiration for dynamic women and heartily supported female Knights, who, by 1887, rep-resented an estimated 10 percent of the membership. Women were attracted by the Knights' radical vision of equal rights in the workplace. In 1886, a former knit goods worker, Leonora M. Barry, was appointed to the Order's general executive board, an extraordinarily high labor union office even by today's standards. She was charged with looking into "the abuses to which our sex is subjected by unscrupulous employers." In Windsor, across the Detroit River, the Knights D.A. 174 was headed by a woman, Rose Lemay. Most women were in all-female assemblies, like Detroit's Florence Nightingale L.A. 3102, which pleased those Knights who resisted women in their midst. Labadie opposed this division, holding that in the world of work men and women had identical interests. Besides, he noted, the presence of the opposite sex made men behave better.[33]

In contrast to Jo's dynamically defined outlines, Sophie remains a shadowy figure. Other than during their courtship, no letters or writings until her late middle age have survived, although she carefully preserved every scrap of paper concerning Jo. Like Darwin's wife, she was devoted to church doctrine but lived in harmony with her agnostic husband, "standing by his side and not seen," as Agnes Inglis put it. (Sophie once complained about a photograph of Jo, saying she had been standing right next to him but "I ain't in the picture.") When free-thinkers came to visit and suggested the Catholic Church was "the greatest menace we have," she told Inglis, she just smiled and passed the bread.[34]

Jo's pleasure in center stage was echoed by his brothers. Francis and Hubert, whom he helped support in their childhood, were both in their twenties, professional actors. As the Labadie Theatre Combination, they performed "Nobody's Child," "Monte Cristo," and "Esmeralda" in music halls and opera houses in Michigan and Canada. Seventeen-year-old Oliver soon joined the troupe.[35]

As children, the three younger boys had frequently visited their itinerant woodsman father, Anthony, in the Michigan wilds of Kalkaska County, while their mother remained in Detroit. Untroubled by his failure as a family breadwinner, they loved vacationing at his shanty on the banks of the north branch of the Manistee River, accompanying him on hunting and fishing expeditions. The former ne'er-do-well and failed *pater familias* had finally found his niche. As a pioneer settler in the pine and hemlock forests of the north country, he not only achieved financial success but emerged as an unlikely pillar of the community. He founded the township of Oliver, named after his youngest son. With more than five thousand acres of land, he bragged that he was one of the most prosperous loggers in the area.[36]

Lumbering was hard work, one would think, for a Civil War veteran who had requested a pension increase on the grounds that war-related spinal injuries rendered him unable to perform manual labor. But he was in his element and loving it: "Home is in the forst and the creem off michigan," he wrote his brother in an untutored scrawl. Shortly before his death in 1886 he commented that he did not hear from "home" (meaning wife Euphrosyne) and he did not "give a —."[37]

Jo Labadie no longer had funds to share with his family. With a new baby at home and a house under construction, he was barely eking out a subsistence. "Burton and I are trying hard to keep the *Labor Leaf* alive but it is hard grubbing" he had told Powderly in early 1886. "We sometimes get as low as five dollars a week apiece to support ourselves, and we have never had more than $12." Some months later, with the country still reeling from the Haymarket incident, he was interviewed by a reporter from the *Evening News* while standing at the printer's case setting type. The reporter found him not at all like the "bloodthirsty demon" many imagined him to be. The paper's surprisingly admiring profile noted that Labadie did not have protruding teeth, dirty fingers, or bad breath, but was handsome and well dressed, with "a large, strong-looking head, covered with a good growth of black hair, dressed *a la pompadour* . . . a neatly-curled black mustache . . . and a just as neat goatee." It reassuringly described Labadie's anarchism as grounded in the theory "that all human nature is good, and that men, if left to themselves without the intervention of statutes, would obey the great natural laws." No mention was made of Labadie's sometimes fiery rhetoric.[38]

The *Labor Leaf* office was a convivial spot, luring a parade of visitors. Adjoining two rooms leased by "friends of the labor movement" (including, surprisingly, the new, supposedly unsympathetic, Commissioner of Labor C. V. R. Pond), it functioned as an impromptu meeting place and social hall. Visiting radicals gravitated there to discuss and argue. Unorganized workers came seeking information. At the height of the eight-hour agitation, more than one hundred meetings had been held there in a one month period. Labadie remembered them including "every shade of labor reformer, from the meek and lowly simple trades unionist, the forerunners of the I.W.W., the relentless bomb-thrower, the authoritarian socialist to the evolutionary anarchist."[39]

Henry George, on a lecture tour in April 1886, gave the *Labor Leaf* a copy of his new book, *Protection or Free Trade,* and enlisted Labadie as agent to sell it. Since Burton was a "single tax" enthusiast and columnists Judson Grenell and John M. McGregor both avid disciples, George must have received the warmest of welcomes. Labadie's friend Peter J. McGuire, founder of the Brotherhood of Carpenters and Joiners and a comrade-in-arms of Samuel Gompers, dropped in early that year, "as fat as an alderman and quite gray," although he was only thirty-four. He had apparently veered from a belief in state socialism toward anarchism at about the same time as Labadie and the two lamented the introduction of politics and socialism into union activities.[40]

One evening, around midnight, a crowd of husky horsecar drivers squeezed into the front office so Labadie could organize them into the Knights of Labor. He was outraged that the drivers were treated worse than mules or oxen by a "heartless corporation." Their long and arduous days were unrelieved by a lunch or dinner break; they were forced to eat while guiding the horses. He encountered an unruly bunch, compared to which "a herd of cattle was a highly disciplined body." He found them baffled by the Order's ritual, mysticism, high-blown rhetoric, and complex organizational procedures. He set up a street railway assembly but it met an untimely death. "What could be expected," Labadie later mused, "of men . . . who had no opportunity to meet with their fellows . . . read books or papers . . . or learn the benefits of organization."[41] More likely, these earthy toilers, new at unionism and exhausted at the end of a brutal day, were seeking relief through labor action, not the edification that was the cornerstone of Knights of Labor strategy.

By early 1886, Labadie was troubled that the Order was growing too rapidly. He and other leaders were spread too thin. They had no time to keep in touch with all the assemblies they were founding, and the newly organized were ill-equipped to function independently. Despite smoldering public apprehension fed by the Haymarket episode, the Knights of Labor was now surging to the height of its power and glory. By the summer of that year, in a total population of some fifty-eight million, nearly three-quarters of a million workers nationwide were members, ten times the figure of two years before. An estimated 13,000 Detroiters of a population of 133,000 belonged to either the Knights, a trade union, or both. Combined, they represented over 20 percent of the city's workforce.[42]

Working men and women were sufficiently captivated by the economic corrections they saw ahead to turn out for a five-act play, *Monopoly,* sponsored by the Knights at the Detroit Opera House. The melodrama depicted a strike for a shorter workday, the attempted bombing of a mill by a conniving superintendent who blamed it on radical elements, and a happy denouement, in which the falsely accused labor agitator turns out be be the kidnapped baby son of the now enlightened industrialist.[43]

Ten thousand ebullient marchers paraded four abreast from Grand Circus Park to Miller's Gardens on Monday, September 6, in a grand show of labor's strength and solidarity. Brimming with confidence and daring, Knights and unionists for the first time scheduled a Labor Day parade during the day, unilaterally declaring it a holiday seven years before Labor Day became legal in Michigan. It marked the largest demonstration of organized workers ever held in the state, almost seven times the size of the great 1880 parade. Chief Marshal Judson Grenell led the three-mile-long procession of floats, bands, banners, and carriages carrying the revered Trevellick, female Knights, and representatives of various trades. "Divided we can beg; united we can demand" read one streamer. On the printers' float, a working press turned out miniature copies of the *Labor Leaf* as souvenirs. Labadie was not enamored of all the hoopla, but he recognized that "these flags and ribbons and drums are simply the means of reaching the sluggish minds and stirring them to thought."[44]

Labor's ascendancy seemed inevitable. The Knights of Labor appeared to be riding the crest of a mighty wave. Mixed with the euphoria, however, were the repercussions of the Haymarket affair. A fear of labor militancy pervaded the nation's consciousness. Employers attempted to break the growing power of labor organizations with armed thugs, lockouts, blacklists, and anti-union oaths. After 1886, membership in the Knights would dwindle rapidly, undermined by Powderly's opposition to strikes and the eight-hour movement, his repudiation of the convicted anarchists, and, not least, his monumentally misguided leadership.

Open Warfare

Ah, there is a hurrying of feet!
The life-boats are putting off!
The pirate crew have monopolized the boats and floats
and are sailing away!
Men and women and children are struggling in the waters
of despair!
Our anchors are failing us!
Sauve qui peut!
       "WATCH THE COURTS," *SONGS OF THE SPOILED*

In 1886, a year of both elation and disillusion for the nation's working people, all sorts of things started going wrong. On the same day the Haymarket bombing triggered an anti-radical frenzy, the Knights of Labor suffered a humiliating defeat, losing a major strike on Jay Gould's Southwest railroad system. Only the year before, the Knights thought they had brought the hated "robber baron" to his knees by threatening to halt his entire system with a massive strike. With that staggering victory hundreds of thousands of new members had swarmed into their ranks.

But now, backed up by hired strikebreakers and Pinkerton guards, and supported by state militias, the railroad magnate was determined to stand tough. Knights' leader Powderly vacillated. He hated strikes. Besides, he was indecisive by nature. Keen to break the power of the Knights, Gould was in no mood for negotiations or concessions. Finally, the Knights' executive council stepped into the void and ordered the men back to work. Labadie, a strong proponent of the strike, knew its collapse was a turning point, bound to crush "the spirit of independence and revolt" in "our more timid comrades." Had the ruling Knights been made of "sterner stuff," he charged, they would not have lost "their grip on the railroad monopoly monster."[1] Whether or not victory had truly been within their grasp, the fact remains that after this debacle the Knights never won another major strike.

Another blow to the Knights' prestige occurred at the Chicago stockyards that November. Workers who had won an eight-hour day during the May 1 general strike again went on strike when management reneged on the agreement and reverted to ten hours. Thomas Barry, the hero of the Saginaw Valley strike and now a ranking official of the Knights, was sent from Philadelphia to intervene. He worked out a deal with some of the packing houses, while others continued to be struck. After Barry left Chicago, Powderly, erratic as ever, undercut him by ordering all the men back to work at ten hours. This second betrayal was too much for Barry; he became Powderly's open enemy.[2]

The murmurings of suspicions between the Knights and the trade unions were escalating into a roar. Samuel Gompers, an official of the Cigar Makers' International Union (CMIU) and rising national labor leader, minced no words when he talked to Detroiters one Sunday afternoon in mid 1886 in a speech titled, "Scabs, Knights of Labor and Unions." He was irate that the Knights were supporting a rival cigarmakers' union and attempting to undermine the CMIU. But in Detroit the local Knights and trade unionists were living in harmony and the cigarmaker factions had worked out a "peace pact."[3] The audience in Germania Hall did not receive Gompers warmly and denounced his assertion that every cigarmaker not in his union was a scab.

The cigarmakers' jurisdictional battle was the result of a long-standing feud in New York City. A dissident group had broken away from the CMIU to set up the socialist-leaning Progressive Cigar Makers' Union. For years the two unions engaged in name-calling, intrigue, personal animosity, cutthroat competition, and the breaking of each other's strikes. Early in 1886, the Progressives took the places of six thousand striking CMIU workers (and were branded "scabs") and merged with the local district assembly of the Knights.

Enraged, Adolph Strasser, CMIU president, demanded that the national officers of the Knights denounce this "unscrupulous attack upon recognized trade union principles." Powderly, who cared little for trade unions and was struggling with the faltering Southwest railroad strike, refused to intervene. Such cavalier treatment hardened the inclination of Gompers and Strasser to set up a new labor group dedicated to trade union principles. In December 1886, they disbanded the FOTLU and organized in its stead the American Federation of Labor (AFL), thereby helping push the Knights of

Labor into the abyss created by the turbulent times and Powderly's wayward leadership, and launching Gompers on his triumphant role as labor kingpin (with Labadie as his eventual ally).[4]

Detroit's 1886 state election campaign also turned out to be an ugly, divisive affair, although labor managed to get five of its candidates elected to the state legislature. The Independent Labor party (ILP), which had successfully sent candidates to Lansing since 1882, held a nominating convention that degenerated into charges of trickery, bribery, and general dishonesty. Radical socialists stood against moderate reformers. The SLP wing protested the presence of Greenback-Labor party delegates, who counter-protested. Bitter charges of a political sellout were hurled. There was much opposition to the seating of state legislator Francis B. Egan, who was accused of betraying labor's interest to curry favor with the Republicans and get the job of deputy labor commissioner the year before.[5]

Mindful that all five party nominees who ran on a fusion ticket with either Republicans or Democrats had been elected in 1884, delegates were eager to obtain candidates with major party connections. This infuriated third-party movement purists, who bolted from the hall to set up a breakaway "Strictly Independent Labor Party." They refused to adopt a ticket with candidates endorsed by the "old, corrupt political parties," and vowed to work for their defeat at the polls.[6]

By compromising principle in favor of vote-getting ability, the ILP convention produced a motley ticket. Judson Grenell, who at the time held office in three Detroit Knights' organizations, was one of the few candidates who had distinguished himself in labor circles. *Labor Leaf* editor Burton was so disturbed by what he viewed as rank opportunism that he attacked in print two of the candidates, accusing one of involvement in municipal bribery and graft schemes.[7] This provoked an uproar. The party's campaign committee denounced the *Labor Leaf* and threatened a boycott. An acrimonious debate in the editorial rooms spilled out into the columns. Candidate Grenell accused his editor of poor judgment and of injuring the paper's reputation. Burton countered that it was his own paper and it was "useless to try to bulldoze me into endorsing men I know to be unworthy." Labadie stood with him. He defended the *Labor Leaf*'s "free platform," which was "not run to suit any party or clique," and insisted there was no room in the labor movement for "dishonest men and tricksters."[8]

Though the boycott idea died, the whole affair left a bad taste in Labadie's mouth. Watching the splintering of the old labor comradeship into warring factions convinced him more than ever that labor should stay out

of politics. "The more I see of politics, the more disgusted do I become
with it," he wrote in his October 13 "Cranky Notions" column, while
acknowledging "the excitement that almost irresistibly draws one into its
powerful current, and the opportunities it presents to study human nature."
The Knights could brag that thirty-nine of their number were elected that
November and sat in the 1887 Michigan legislature, but to Labadie, dragging
the "Labor University" into the "dirty pool of politics is only to besmirch it
with filth."[9]

Labadie's friend Grenell, conversely, was "always for politics," as
Agnes Inglis observed much later in summing up his career. Learning from
his defeat as an independent candidate in 1884, he accepted Republican
endorsement this time, and was elected. More and more, he was letting
expediency be his guide. At the age of thirty-nine, his radicalism was fading
fast. Like many of the labor activists of a decade before, he had managed to
discover some good in the establishment. Temporarily giving up his reporting
job on the *Detroit News,* he accepted a Republican patronage position ("a
political plum," he called it in his unpublished autobiography) acquired
through his friend Egan. As deputy oil inspector checking the flammability
of kerosene, he garnered a handsome $1,200 annual salary with plenty of
free time for writing, but found himself accused by his erstwhile comrades of
"selling out." One historian characterized him as "capable of being all things
to all men at one time . . . apt to take the more comfortable way out."[10]

Slender and fair-haired, a few inches taller than Labadie, Grenell was
mild-mannered but nervous; he suffered from a slight stammer. By his own
admission, he had "no personal magnetism or oratorical gifts." Ironically,
only the year before his election, in his August 5, 1885 "Common Sense"
column, Grenell had scathingly denounced laws as "cunningly devised
schemes to enable the few to rob the many." In another article two months
later, he echoed Labadie in looking forward to "the gradual abolition of all
law, until finally there is consummated the dream of the philosopher . . .
anarchism." To his credit, on election, he vowed to introduce few bills,
and except for ballot reform, did in fact propose mainly the repeal of
existing laws.[11]

Despite profound disagreements, Labadie and Grenell never faltered in
their close friendship for more than a half century. Grenell's political career
did not estrange them, even though Labadie once castigated politicians as
"the crown of thorns upon the brow of crucified labor." The two were an
unlikely pair. Cocky, assertive Labadie, with flowing tie and theatrical flair,
trigger-happy for a debate, seemed a mismatch to the moderate, low-keyed,

Jo and Sophie Labadie
after their wedding in St.
Alphonse Catholic Church
in Windsor, Ontario, on
August 14, 1877. (Author's
photo.)

Labadie (seated, far right) with other Michigan labor leaders of the mid 1880s.
(Author's photo.)

Hair was important to both Jo and Sophie Labadie. In 1883, when she was thirty-two, Sophie's hair could touch the ground. (Author's photo.)

German revolutionary and agitator Johann Most. (Courtesy of the Labadie Collection.)

Benjamin R. Tucker, publisher of
Liberty, c. 1887. (Courtesy of the
Labadie Collection.)

Terence V. Powderly,
grand master workman
of the Knights of Labor.
(Courtesy of the Labadie
Collection.)

Thomas B. Barry, leader of the great lumbermen's strike in the Saginaw Valley in 1885. (Courtesy of the Labadie Collection.)

Euphrosyne Angelique Labadie, Jo Labadie's mother. Curiously, although the Labadies took hundreds of photos, there seem to be none of Jo's errant father. (Author's photo.)

Sophie Labadie saved the documents that formed the Labadie Collection at the University of Michigan in the attic of the Labadies' 1890s home at 2306 Buchanan Street in Detroit. (Author's photo.)

Composite photograph of the Haymarket martyrs. Louis Lingg committed suicide in prison; the four others were hanged November 11, 1887. (Courtesy of the Labadie Collection.)

Lucy Parsons, widow of Albert Parsons, who was executed for the 1886 Haymarket bombing. (Courtesy of the Labadie Collection.)

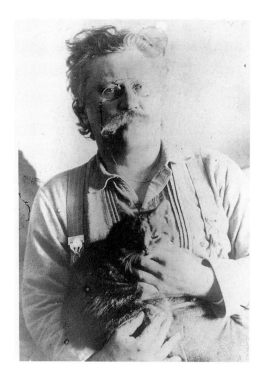

Detroit anarchist Robert Reitzel, publisher of *Der arme Teufel.* (Courtesy of the Labadie Collection.)

Mr. and Mrs. Samuel Gompers on their Golden Wedding Anniversary, January 28, 1917, inscribed: "To my dear Pal Joe Labadie." (Courtesy of the Labadie Collection.)

Alexander Berkman, would-be assassin of Henry Clay Frick. (Courtesy of the Labadie Collection.)

Emma Goldman, "Anarchist Queen." (Courtesy of the Labadie Collection.)

Peter Kropotkin, Russian anarchist and geographer. (Courtesy of the Labadie Collection.)

The Labadie family around 1900. Seated, l. to r.: Mrs. Hubert Labadie; Mrs. Oliver Labadie; Sophie Labadie; Laurance Labadie; Jo Labadie; Mrs. Francis Labadie. Standing, l. to r., Jo's brothers, Hubert and Oliver; his daughters, Charlotte and Laura; brother Francis. (Author's photo.)

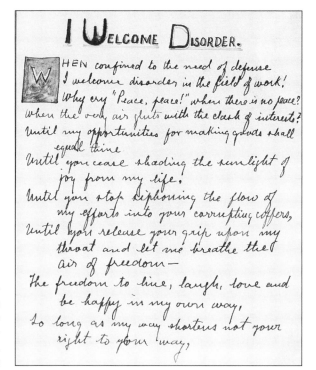

"I Welcome Disorder" from one of Jo's handmade manuscript booklets of poetry. (Author's photo.)

I WELCOME DISORDER.

WHEN confined to the need of defense
I welcome disorder in the field of work!
Why cry "Peace, peace!" when there is no peace?
When the very air gluts with the clash of interests?
Until my opportunities for making goods shall
equal thine
Until you cease shading the sunlight of
joy from my life,
Until you stop siphoning the flow of
my efforts into your corrupting coffers,
Until you release your grip upon my
throat and let me breathe the
air of freedom—
The freedom to live, laugh, love and
be happy in my own way,
So long as my way shortens not your
right to your way,

Advertisement for the Labadie booklets, c. 1911. (Author's photo.)

Detroit newspapers ridiculed Water Board Commissioner James Pound in 1908 for trying to fire Labadie because of his anarchist views. (Author's photo.)

Laurance Labadie, his honey blond curls untrimmed at age six, in *Detroit News Tribune* photo, 1904, illustrates one of Jo's health fads. (Author's photo.)

THE BOY WHO HAS NEVER EATEN BREAKFAST.

Laurance Cleophis, son of Mr. and Mrs. Joseph A. Labadie, of 74 Buchanan street, Detroit, has never been attacked by any of the diseases common to children, and his parents are inclined to attribute the immunity to the "no breakfast" plan, which they have rigidly adhered to for several years.

Carl E. Schmidt, millionaire Detroit tanner and Labadie's benefactor, in 1906. (Author's photo.)

Charlotte, Jo and Sophie's middle child and the author's mother, in front of the Den, Bubbling Waters, c. 1924. (Author's photo.)

Judson Grenell and Jo Labadie in their later years. (Author's photo.)

Socialist leader Eugene Debs around the time of the Pullman strike of 1894. (Author's photo.)

Agnes Inglis with Jo and Sophie Labadie at Bubbling Waters in the late 1920s, after she began working in the Labadie Collection. (Author's photo.)

Jo Labadie, photographed around 1920, adopted the Buffalo Bill look. (Author's photo.)

Sophie and Jo in their Buchanan Street home. (Author's photo.)

The author
with her uncle,
Laurance Labadie,
Berkeley, Cali-
fornia, 1949.
(Author's photo.)

Jo Labadie, 1905. (Author's photo.)

carelessly dressed Grenell. Agnes Inglis saw Grenell as "true, but not intense emotionally." He lacked Labadie's "Dream," she noted, but was "not so self-centered."[12]

Perhaps their puzzling bond endured and strengthened because it was forged at a time of development when undying loyalties are bred. From their early days together, the two had fought side by side in the front-line trenches of labor's battles. They shared a commitment to the pen as their most effective weapon. Both abandoned advocacy of state socialism about the same time. But where Labadie saw salvation in the no-state doctrine, Grenell's ardor was lavished on the concept of a single tax on land to compensate for inequalities in land ownership, together with an unwavering reverence for its proponent, Henry George, whom he esteemed as the most erudite and clear-thinking man he ever met.[13] Whatever his views of the justice of the Haymarket arrests and trial, Grenell seems to have kept them to himself. The plight of the defendants clearly aroused in him no indignation corresponding to Labadie's anguished outbursts.

Nor did Benjamin Tucker, another close associate of Labadie, place himself in the pantheon of those who championed the cause of the Haymarket accused. Indeed, individualist anarchism's high priest appeared nearly as anxious to dissociate his group from the reviled men as did Powderly. He branded them communists at every opportunity. These "falsely called Anarchists" could hardly claim that the bomb would not have been thrown if the meeting had not been attacked, Tucker argued. They had been preaching "wholesale destruction" for years. "Why, then, should they not expect some ardent follower to act upon their advice?" (He confided to Labadie that he knew—he refused to say how—that the package of dynamite police found in Spies's office at the *Arbeiter Zeitung* was not manufactured evidence but "was sent there long ago.") He thundered against those who used "Anarchy's name . . . to secure one of the most revolting of Archies,—the Archy of compulsory Communism." By "adopting the name of the real friends of Liberty" they were confusing the public and endangering "true Anarchists."[14]

Even one of Tucker's closest colleagues on *Liberty,* Victor Yarros, accused him of trying to make anarchism "respectable" in the aftermath of Haymarket, of turning the doctrine into "a sort of spiritual amusement for kid-gloved reformers."[15] But Labadie, uncharacteristically, did not breathe a word of reproach. He seemed over-awed by Tucker's haughty erudition and aristocratic demeanor, an attitude Labadie displayed toward no one else.

The trial of the Haymarket anarchists ended in August 1886. Eight of the defendants were found guilty as conspirators to murder on the grounds that they advocated the overthrow of law by force, and thus inspired some unidentified person to throw the bomb. Five were German-born, one raised in Germany. Samuel Fielden was a native Englishman. Albert Parsons was born in Alabama. No evidence was produced directly connecting them or their advice with the unknown bombthrower. They were sentenced to hang.[16] The *Labor Leaf* proclaimed the verdict "A 'Legal' Outrage." There was not "a particle of evidence" that any of the accused were armed, it protested, nor proof they had done a single act to justify their conviction. The paper called for funds for a new trial "even at the risk of losing sympathy for ourselves."[17] Burton, Labadie, and their allies were clearly in the minority. In the first fires of nationwide rejoicing over this triumph of law and order, theirs was an exceedingly unpopular message.

Labadie's indignation was uncontrolled. By its "oppressive measures," he raged in *Labor Leaf,* the "ruling class" was "urging on a premature and violent revolution" in hope of crushing the labor movement. "Let the authorities not lose their reason in this matter, because if they do they might lose their heads." An Ontario newspaper called on Detroit to muzzle "this fanatical villain . . . who eulogizes the Chicago murderers." From the Cook County jail August Spies expressed his gratitude to Labadie that "in the general stampede of cowardly retreat there are at least some voices who boldly and fearlessly proclaim The Truth."[18]

At the conclusion of the trial, defendant Albert Parsons delivered a rambling, but passionate, eight-hour address, insisting he had broken no laws, had never advocated force except in self-defense, and that the convictions violated the rights of free speech, free press, and public assemblage. Judge Joseph E. Gary then sentenced seven of the men to hang on December 3, and the eighth, Oscar Neebe, to fifteen years' imprisonment.[19]

Lucy Parsons walked to the prisoners' dock after the verdict, took Albert's hand and proclaimed: "My husband, I give you to the cause of liberty. I now go forth to take your place. I will herald abroad to the American people the foul murder ordered here today at the behest of monopoly." Two hours later, she began her campaign to raise funds for an appeal. Since her husband's arrest, she had attempted to support herself and their two young children by dressmaking. The children were sent to stay with friends, and Lucy Parsons embarked on an exhausting sixteen-state tour, resolved to take the case to a "jury" of the American people. She believed many were sickened by the trial, and from the response she received, she was right.[20]

After her first appearance in Cincinnati, she wrote Labadie in unschooled ecstasy that the group of "concervitave Trads Unionest . . .

apploded my utterences to the echo, and excepted me defination of the red flag with *rapture*. . . . Ah! I tell you the people ar becoming hungery for the other side of the late judical farce." By then sentiment was growing that the trial had been a travesty of justice, with a packed jury, perjured testimony, and a hanging judge, and that men were to die for their beliefs, not their deeds.[21]

The tour turned out to be enormously successful; Lucy was a persuasive orator. She addressed more than 200,000 people in sixteen states. More inclined to violence than her husband, she did not hesitate to advocate acts of terrorism and once suggested setting off dynamite in Westminster Abbey. A striking, thirty-three-year-old of black or partly black ancestry, she possessed commanding presence, her black hair and eyes dramatized by a long black dress. She roused audiences by proclaiming that if Parsons should die a martyr, it would only advance the glorious cause, and expressed readiness for the gallows herself: "If a petition were placed before me for mercy, and I knew I could get mercy by the signing of my name, I would say, 'Spring your trap.' "[22]

Eight days before the scheduled December 3 hangings, the Chief Justice of the Illinois Supreme Court granted a stay of execution. Lucy Parsons reached Detroit about a month later, in January 1887. Germania Hall was crowded, with many women and Germans present, as the slender, copperskinned speaker—"impressive and eloquent . . . and deeply and fearfully in earnest"—began to speak. In a soft, melodious voice with a slight Texas twang, she argued that her husband and other leaders would not have brought their wives and children to Haymarket Square if they had known a bomb would be thrown. She described the atrocities committed by the police as they rounded up radicals of every hue, of how they ripped up her house, stole her few valuables, and asked her little boy, "Where's your dad? We're going to hang him." She accused the prosecution of rejecting every Knight or trades unionist in assembling its "packed jury."[23]

Her delivery grew more impassioned as she warned of the revolution ahead, the "rumblings of a change." She cried out: "Heed them." The audience was enraptured, according to *Labor Leaf.* Resolutions by Labadie condemning the verdict and demanding justice were approved. Contributions and the sale of Parsons's photograph and Haymarket Square speech brought in nearly $80. There were more donations when Lucy spoke to the Henry George assembly of the Knights of Labor, of which Labadie was master workman. They were collected in defiance of Powderly's order banning contributions by Knights for the anarchists' defense.[24]

By this time, the Knights' national leader had embarked on a campaign of anarchist- and radical-baiting calculated to prevent any identification of his organization with the Haymarket anarchists. He believed, as he later wrote, that the bomb "did more injury to the good name of labor than all the strikes of that year." Initially, Labadie chose to disbelieve newspaper accounts of what the general master workman was doing. He ridiculed the idea that "Mr. Powderly is teetotally and fanatically opposed to socialism" and recollected publicly the time when Powderly was an SLP member and held a card "as red as the reddest card . . . and . . . he made no bones about it either." Labadie later claimed he revealed this information "never for a moment thinking Mr. Powderly cared to deny his connection with the socialist party."[25]

Labadie's charges created a nationwide scandal. They were so widely reported that a year later, in September 1887, Powderly finally felt called on to repudiate them. Obsessed with washing away all traces of red taint, he instructed his Detroit confidante John Devlin to publicize a twelve-page letter, characteristically self-serving and self-pitying, which began: "For the past two years every utterance of mine has been garbled and misconstrued. . . . The arguments of selfish politicians, weak-hearted friends or the threats of sniveling Anarchists have had and will have no effect on me." Socialists had "crowded into [our order] and attempted to force their opinions down our throats." He stated emphatically, "I am not and never was a Socialist." Indeed, he prided himself with never having performed "a single act that brings a blush to my cheek."[26]

By then, Labadie had realized the full extent of Powderly's red-baiting and repudiation of the Haymarket men. He turned into Powderly's bitter foe. Doubtless with relish, he blazoned across *Advance and Labor Leaf* (the paper's new name) a refutation of Powderly's anti-socialist claim based on the recollections of Grenell, E. W. Simpson, and other former SLP officials in Detroit. They recalled that Philip Van Patten told them he had issued a "red card" to Powderly after the 1880 Greenback-Labor convention, and received his dues for the next two years. Labadie snidely claimed he wanted to "refresh Mr. Powderly's memory" and was sure the Knights' leader "will not hesitate a moment in acknowledging their correctness." Although the new revelations by no means convicted Powderly of radicalism, they served to uphold Labadie's veracity.[27]

At the Knights' Richmond convention in October 1886, five months after the Haymarket affair, Powderly had angrily opposed a resolution expressing sympathy and requesting mercy for the doomed men. Not "morbid" sympathy, but "a debt of hatred" was due them, he asserted, for "cast[ing] a stain upon the name of labor which will take years to wipe out." The Order should do nothing that could "even by implication be interpreted as identification with the Anarchist element."[28]

An even more significant dispute erupted that fed Labadie's misgivings about Knights' leadership and its chance of fulfilling the promise of one big union. The battle with the trade unions came to a head when the delegates voted to expel all members of the Cigar Makers' International Union, with which it had a long-standing antagonism. The anti-unionists were "jubilant," but by forcing workers to choose between membership in their trade union or the Knights, they inflicted a "mortal wound" on the Order, as one observer recalled.[29] This wound became increasingly deadly in a swirl of charges of malfeasance, as well as the controversy over Haymarket.

Labadie initially tried to minimize the seriousness of the rift. He fulminated against the "capitalist" press and its "feigned concern" for differences between labor organizations, which it exploited in an attempt to destroy them.[30] Like many, he was slow to pit himself against Powderly in this tempestuous period, only a few months after Haymarket. Even Thomas Barry (whom Powderly hated and privately called "canine or bovine") wrote Labadie from the Order's Philadelphia headquarters, where he served on the General Executive Board, that he believed Powderly would declare the cigarmaker expulsion order unconstitutional. A few months later, Barry was still waiting, confused by the inaction of "Bro Powderly." Wherever he traveled, Barry found dissension rife among the Knights. He lamented to Labadie that "Kicking in Labor circles seems to be the order of the day . . . if we would kick against Capitalistic oppression we would have kicking enough."[31]

Labadie's tune changed dramatically when officials of the Knights ordered an enforcement of the cigar union expulsion order in early 1887. He spoke out vehemently in "Cranky Notions" against this "great injustice" to his cigarmaker comrades. The mandate of the Richmond convention was unconstitutional, he charged. Nowhere in the Knights' constitution was there a clause denying membership to anyone for belonging to a trade union. The resolution retroactively targeted those who had done no wrong. He called on the Executive Board to nullify the ruling.[32]

Never before had Labadie spoken out against Knights' policies with such passion. He did not relish the thought of undermining the organization he had worked so hard to build, but was indignant at those who suggested that "if I did not like the way things were done, I could get out of the Order."

As one of the pioneer Michigan Knights, he felt it his duty to protest "the usurpation of power . . . that has now grown unbearable."[33]

Liberty publisher Benjamin Tucker, meanwhile, did not share Labadie's concerns. He was gloating over "the ashes of the Knights of Labor." *Liberty* proclaimed—somewhat prematurely—that the organization had "subsided like a penny candle and is seized in its final flickerings." After Powderly's annual salary was raised from $2,000 to $5,000, Tucker gleefully detailed the contents of the $50,000 Philadelphia "mansion" bought for the Order's "high-salaried officials," which was "so elegantly fitted out with Wilton carpets, stained-glass windows, mirror-lined walls, old gold satin hangings, plate-glass windows, solid marble wainscoting, etc. that John Swinton calls it 'a palace for the rulers of the order.' "[34]

Tucker had never had any use for the Knights of Labor. He scoffed at its Declaration of Principles, full of demands for taxation, labor laws, and other "tyrannical measures" from the state. "Think of an Anarchist demanding anything of the State except its death!" Although he never confronted Labadie directly, his reproach was clear. If any "real Anarchist" belonged to the Order, he had written in *Liberty* in February 1886, he either did not know what anarchism meant or was false to his principles. Stung, Labadie twice inquired of Powderly just before Haymarket if one could be a conscientious Knight and not accept every plank in the organization's platform.[35] But after the bomb exploded that day in May, Powderly abruptly terminated their once-lively correspondence and never gave an answer.

The cigarmakers' expulsion order the following October shattered whatever harmony remained among Detroit Knights. This national resolution forced them to take sides, to choose between trade union or Knights membership, where previously they had lived comfortably with both. They divided into clear-cut factions: the pro-administration group, unsympathetic to union grievances, and those increasingly hostile to Powderly and his tactics. Nearly a decade of comradeship ended. "That unfortunate order" created "bad blood—miserably bad," John Devlin wrote Powderly.[36]

Everyone felt strongly about the issue. Thomas Dolan, former minute-taker of the Knights in its guise as the "Washington Literary Society," and a cigarmaker facing expulsion, protested that he had always been a loyal Knight but was compelled to go with the union: "My living is there." Henry Robinson, an official of Detroit's district assembly, asserted that the directive was unconstitutional. Powderly cohort Devlin, now U.S. consul in Windsor, proclaimed it legal. Grenell waffled. He thought Detroiters were not "proper judges of its constitutionality," but suggested that the district assembly refrain from enforcing it.[37]

Amid the general turmoil, there was a mysterious shakeup at the *Labor Leaf* in February 1887. Burton inexplicably relinquished the editorship and was replaced by occasional columnist and former lake vessel captain John Murray McGregor. The suspicion that this was a power play by the pro-Powderly forces in the district assembly is borne out by the complete turn-around thereafter in editorial position. McGregor compared the cigarmaker expulsion order favorably with Lincoln's Civil War emancipation proclamation. "The Captain," who had turned to journalism in his forties after being blacklisted for organizing Great Lakes pilots into the Order, announced his intention of supporting the principles of "the grandest labor organization yet known to history . . . the Noble Order of the Knights of Labor of the World."[38] He renamed the paper *Advance and Labor Leaf,* and, to Labadie's dismay, took off the Thomas Paine slogan, "The world is my country; to do good my religion."

"Let the *Labor Leaf* die or even go to the enemy, but let Joe Labadie and all his work be Anarchistic and be *known* as Anarchistic first, last and all the time," Tucker advised Labadie cryptically in a letter from Boston. Labadie stayed on, but he and McGregor were at loggerheads. The new editor accused Labadie of endeavoring to tear down the Knights because, as an anarchist, it was his nature to tear down constitutional bodies, although it was the directive's unconstitutionality Labadie was protesting. In a May article, McGregor called Labadie "selfish" for charging that using tax money to provide free school books for the poor would constitute "highway robbery under cover of 'law.' " (Labadie considered compulsory taxes government robbery regardless of what they were used for, and believed poverty was largely caused by government-supported monopoly). They clashed over Henry George's single tax, a cause McGregor—like nearly all Labadie's associates except the anarchists—delighted in.[39]

But McGregor's wrath was editorial, not personal. "Like Jo, he gives all the right to think as they like," Grenell said. Indeed, the new editor went so far as to include Tucker's *Liberty* among labor papers readers could subscribe to jointly with the *Advance.* Forty years later, McGregor and Labadie were still friends, still lamenting economic injustice together.[40] Here, as in other cases of personal friendship, a vehement argument never stood in the way of Labadie's affections.

If Burton had been ousted from the paper by the pro-Powderly forces in February, the tables were turned by July. A group calling itself the Michigan

Cooperative Publishing Company bought the paper, offered stock for sale, and appointed Labadie editor.[41] They could not have been oblivious to what a bombshell they were getting. Clearly, the opposing faction had gained control. Labadie immediately announced an aggressive new policy—to "drag before the bar of public opinion every industrial tyrant . . . to lash unmercifully those . . . who seek to use the voting laborers to advance their own political schemes . . . to expose the political corruption that rots and stinks in the heart of the town . . . and to criticize fairly and fearlessly the actions of labor leaders." He castigated Knights' national officers for remaining silent when their organizer H. F. Hoover was "shot like a dog by the 'best citizens of South Carolina' because he was organizing the laborers, negroes as well as whites." It was time for the rank and file to step in, he wrote, when their leaders allowed organizers to be "butchered in cold blood."[42]

Labadie assailed Powderly for weakness, lack of leadership, autocracy, and susceptibility to capitalist flattery. He enumerated his blunders as Knights' leader: undermining the eight-hour movement, sanctioning the cigarmaker expulsion order, interfering with the Southwest strike, and condemning the Haymarket men. The "scramble for power" in the organization "should bring heartaches to those who strive for the good and the true," Labadie wrote.[43]

Temperamentally a man of action, Labadie was not satisfied just to attack the ruling clique editorially. Amid seething dissension in the Detroit Knights, he decided to run for delegate to the October 1887 general assembly, the Knights' highest tribunal, on a strong anti-Powderly slate. For District Assembly 50 to elect such a ferocious opponent ("the most *anti* anti-Powderly candidate possible," as Richard Oestreicher has pointed out) would be widely viewed as a severe condemnation of the Knights' leadership, having significance far beyond Detroit. Labadie was both the most controversial and most influential labor leader in Michigan, well known in labor circles nationwide. D.A. 50—despite the opposition of pro-Powderly officials J. D. Long, its master workman, Devlin, and MacGregor—elected Labadie by an astonishing two-thirds majority. The vote reinforced its public image as a maverick in the Knights' herd, a reputation largely due to Labadie's rebellious influence. His victory was sweetened when a proposal to direct his vote on key issues at the coming convention in Minneapolis was defeated and he was given free rein.[44] By this move, Detroit clearly stated its position in the coming battle over the future of the Knights of Labor.

★ 11 ★

The Showdown

When men refuse to war with men,
When men will not their fellows rule,
When men decline to yield to reign,
When men give up the role of fool—
Then will the world have justice.

—FROM "WHEN," *DOGGEREL FOR THE UNDERDOG*

Terence Powderly was worried about the hell-raising delegate from Detroit as the Knights' national convention approached in 1887. His informant, John Devlin, tried to be reassuring. Admitting that "Bro. Labadie of late has manifested a disposition of opposition to you and your policy" and might "fall in and act with the extremists" in Minneapolis, Devlin nonetheless considered Labadie "a fair-minded man" who would not knowingly do the Knights' leader an injustice, he wrote in September.

He surmised that Labadie was listening to false tales of impropriety at the Philadelphia headquarters from Thomas Barry, whom Powderly had denounced to Devlin for going about the country "breeding discord," doing "the work of the Anarchist," engaging in "TREASON." Devlin advised that Labadie planned to investigate the charges himself, but assured Powderly that "if you greet him cordially and kindly and . . . personally explain any matter on which he desires light in a friendly way . . . he will return from the G[eneral] A[ssembly] your friend." Then, "the disgruntled element in this district would be forever silenced so far as you are concerned."[1] Labadie was scarcely recognizable in the amenable portrait sketched by Devlin, his former bureau of labor associate. Rather, triggered for an explosion, he set off for Minneapolis, determined to challenge Powderly's autocratic policies head on. Nearly a decade ago, he had introduced the Order to Michigan; he now found himself a leader of the demolition crew.

In Chicago, he visited the Haymarket prisoners in the Cook County jail. Their appeal had just been denied. Execution was re-scheduled for November 11, five weeks hence. In a section known as "murderer's row," Labadie found the seven men condemned to death in stone cells, side by side—Albert Parsons, Adolph Fischer, Samuel Fielden, Michael Schwab, August Spies, George Engel and Louis Lingg. Proceeding down the narrow footway, he shook hands with each by putting his little finger through the iron grating. Despite their imminent deaths, they were in good spirits, with no signs of weakening, although the caged canary in Spies's cell had died.[2]

Several of the wives visited daily, bringing *wurst,* herring, and cigars. Labadie arranged to dine with Nina Van Zandt, who had fallen in love with Spies while a spectator at the trial. The genteel, twenty-four-year-old Vassar graduate was convinced of the men's innocence and had taken up their cause with a passion, especially that of the handsome and dashing Spies. Denied visits because she was not a family member, she and Spies got married by proxy on January 29, 1887. This symbolic merging of a socially promi-nent young American girl with the fiery German revolutionary offended nearly everyone. She and her father, a well-to-do Chicago pharmaceuticals manufacturer, complained bitterly to Labadie that they were hounded by sensation-seeking reporters, who besieged them at all hours, hungry for scurrilous tidbits. The press impugned Spies as an opportunist, wangling for a reprieve and Nina's inheritance. Nina was ridiculed as a silly, mentally unstable publicity-seeker. A hostile mob attacked the Van Zandt home while Nina and her mother cowered within. Even on the defense side, Nina was denounced by some as a tool of the prosecution.

It was probably the competitiveness of yellow journalism rather than personal antipathy that drove most of the reporters. Labadie had the impres-sion that these aggressive journalists were in sympathy with the condemned men, but had to please their publishers. Public feeling in the past seventeen months had shifted dramatically away from the hysteria-driven antagonism surrounding the affair. It was now widely accepted that the anarchists had not had a fair trial. Even those who once loudly clamored for blood were signing clemency petitions. Hundreds of rallies and processions worldwide protested the upcoming "judicial murder."[3]

Once in Minneapolis, Labadie turned his attention to the immediate business at hand—the battle over leadership of the Knights. He found the 225 delegates to the general assembly anticipating sensational developments

and geared for what the *Chicago Tribune* called "a life and death struggle."
The lines between the "administrationists" and the "antis" were so sharply
drawn that they stayed in different hotels. Battle strategy reportedly had been
worked out in advance at secret caucuses. The "Kickers" were said to have
made their plans in Chicago; if so, Labadie was no doubt among them.[4]

During October 3 opening ceremonies at the Washington Rink, delegates whispered rumors among themselves of misappropriation of funds and
political machinations, while Knights' officials, including Michigan's em-
inent eight-hour activist Richard Trevellick, uttered platitudes about peace
and harmony. They stood before a backdrop displaying the Knighthood's
inspirational motto, "An Injury to One Is the Concern of All," and portraits
of founder Uriah Stevens and Powderly. At an evening reception for the
Irish revolutionist and Land League leader Michael Davitt, members rose to
express support for the Irish cause on behalf of their ethnic groups. Labadie
rather fancifully stood to join them as a representative of "the original Americans," who once roamed the country "bedecked in war-paint . . . and emitted
blood-curdling war whoops." "And they are whooping yet," Powderly joked
amiably, possibly hoping that Devlin's recommended cordiality toward the
rogue Knight from Detroit could save the day.[5]

Instead, discord prevailed from the start. Most of the first two days
were consumed in heated debate over credentials, centering around the
seating of Joseph R. Buchanan. The volatile and pugnacious "Kicker from
the Rockies," who rivaled his friend Labadie as one of the nation's most
radical labor journalists, had led the Knights to victory in great railroad
strikes and served as one of the high-ranking officers on its general executive
board. Buchanan's developing hostility to Powderly's blundering policies,
however, had caused him to be branded a traitor by the administrationists. As
an associate of Burnette Haskell (Powderly's bête noire) in the International
Workmen's Association, the Marxian-socialist "Red International," as well
as a leading champion of the Haymarket prisoners, Buchanan was regarded
by the Powderly forces as a formidable foe. He had even moved from Denver
to Chicago to assist the Haymarket prisoners, selling his *Denver Labor
Enquirer* and starting up a new version in Chicago, where he published
articles that Parsons and Spies sent from their cells.

Buchanan was barred from the convention on grounds that his local
assembly had been suspended for non-payment of dues. He and Labadie
were convinced this was a scheme engineered by Powderly and his machine
to keep a known enemy away.[6] The fight continued as Thomas Barry and
William Bailey, the "antis" on the seven-member executive board, accused

Powderly and other officers of circumventing it, of using the Order's money illegally and extravagantly for political campaigns and personal expenses, and of hiring staffers who were not Knights. The Powderly faction retaliated by trying to get all general officers to resign, confident that the convention, packed as it was with pro-administration delegates, would not re-elect the two.[7]

Amid reports that Labadie and others planned to raise the embarrassing "red card" issue (the claim that Powderly became an SLP member in 1880 and paid dues for two years), the distressed Powderly attempted to clear his name of socialist taint by claiming that Philip Van Patten had sent him only a complimentary membership, with dues paid up, which he had accepted as a "memento" of their work together as Knights' officers. Since the over-stressed former SLP leader had faked suicide in 1883 and disappeared, he was not available to dispute Powderly's claim.[8]

The convention comprised sixteen corrosive days of shouting matches, fist-shaking, and claims of lying and slander. Delegates plotted in secret meetings; rumors abounded. As charges of dishonesty, incompetence, malice, and conniving disrupted the gathering, "the endearing term 'brother' sounded strange and out of place," Labadie later observed.[9] The bitterest dissent arose over the issue of clemency for the seven Haymarket men awaiting the gallows. James E. Quinn of New York asked the assembly to go on record as believing that capital punishment was "a relic of barbarism," expressing sorrow over the death sentences, and endeavoring to secure commutation. This provoked an uproar. Powderly, who had warned Quinn not to introduce the resolution, ruled it out of order. He was sustained on appeal by a vote of 121 to 53. A motion to reconsider was followed by a half-day's impassioned debate. Labadie was one of fourteen delegates rising to oppose Powderly. In arguing for the clemency resolutions, he had available a detailed thirty-five page account of the travesty of the Haymarket trial and an exoneration of the defendants, prepared for him by William Holmes, who had hidden Parsons after the bombing. Holmes told Labadie he was counting on "the very best results of your effort in Minneapolis to save our comrades," expecting his presentation at least to "raise a great hue and cry among the enemy."[10]

As his antagonists spoke out, Powderly was beside himself with anger. He launched into a spluttering tirade. The day had come to stamp anarchism out of the Knighthood "root and branch," he thundered. It was a "festering, putrid sore," a "hell-infected association that stands as a foe of the most malignant stamp to the honest laborer of this land." Anarchists, "blatant, shallow-pated men . . . snivelling . . . pretending to be advanced thinkers," were driving men from the labor movement "by their wild and foolish mouthings wherever they congregate, and they usually congregate where beer flows freely. . . . They shout for the blood of the aristocracy but will turn from blood to beer in a twinkling."[11]

Labadie could not have been prepared for the vindictiveness of the outburst: "I hate the name of anarchy," Powderly shouted. "If I could, I would wipe from the face of the earth the last vestige of its double-damned presence . . . I have no use for any of the brood . . . no act of the anarchists ever laid a stone upon a stone in the building of this order." As for the condemned men, "it were better that seven times seven men hang than to hang the millstone of odium around the standard of this order in affiliating in any way with this element of destruction."

He threatened that passing the clemency resolution would destroy the Order. Whatever the vote, he would not feel bound to carry out any decision harmful to the Knights. Carried away with what sounded like paranoid delusions, he described diabolical schemes to do away with the general (formerly grand) master workman. A man had tried to shove him off a ferryboat between New York City and Hoboken; someone resembling the first "assassin" had attempted to push him off a train platform; a bomb was concealed in the pocket of the man seated next to him at a secret meeting in Denver he was lured to by Burnette Haskell. The accounts reminded Labadie of "a dime novel."[12]

Powderly was not always so hysterical. He was an intelligent man, who, in calmer moments, was able to outline the philosophy underlying anarchism well enough. But he seemed suffused with a fatherly protectiveness over his organization, seeing anarchists only as those injuring his "child." Those seeking commutation should have the "manhood" to sign a petition as individuals "instead of sneaking behind the reputation and character of this great order," he proclaimed.[13]

Thus the Knighthood's vaunted principles of the solidarity of all workers degenerated into an orgy of anarchist- and red-bashing. In the eyes of the hard-core administrationists, the assembly was riddled with an anarchist clique, including Barry and Buchanan, although Labadie was probably the only declared anarchist present. As Labadie sat there, with a red flag reportedly perched on his table, Powderly delivered the final drastic blow: every anarchist should be obliged to withdraw from the Order or be expelled.[14]

The fervid pleas that the convention go on record favoring clemency for the Haymarket condemned had been to no avail. On a final vote,

Powderly's position was sustained. It was a cruel disappointment for those who believed an appeal by the nation's foremost labor organization might induce Illinois Governor Richard Oglesby to commute the sentences to life imprisonment. After the final roll call on the Haymarket resolution, Powderly's opponents stormed from the hall. Nearly fifty delegates then signed a petition to the governor; Spies had sent word that no one should be solicited who had voted against the resolution.[15]

Vowing open warfare, the outraged dissenters met in Chicago two days later with the intention of reorganizing the Order or even overthrowing it and setting up a replacement. By this time, carpenters were at work on the sevenfold scaffold in the courtyard of the Cook County jail as thirty-five rebels, including Labadie, organized a provisional committee. They issued a manifesto charging that the Order was no longer "the Jerusalem of the humble and honest Knight" but "a machine to fill the coffers of designing and unscrupulous men." Local assemblies were asked to stop paying dues.[16]

The "kickers" were seceding, Labadie reported in *Advance and Labor Leaf,* to arouse the membership against "incompetent management" and "autocratic methods," against the extravagance of a labor leader who paid himself $5,000 a year when there were women earning a meager $1 to $3 a week. "Think of Garrison, Phillips, John Brown taking a salary of $5,000 a year to abolish slavery!" he wrote in a December 17 "Cranky Notions" column. He predicted the defection of 100,000 members. Although the provisional committee plans fizzled out, in the next months the Order, which had lost tens of thousands of members in the previous crisis-ridden year, suffered even more disastrous losses. The administration chose to view the secessionist movement in a positive light as "the last expiring gasp of the anarchistic element," and a "boon" if it drained off anarchistic sympathizers.[17]

Before leaving Chicago, Labadie visited the prisoners once more. By now, the execution was less than three weeks away. Returning to Detroit around October 22 in a fury, he hastened to organize mass meetings, raise funds, and distribute pamphlets denouncing the impending executions. Other long-time comrades joined him in an anarchists' defense committee—John Burton, E. W. Simpson, Henry Robinson, Charles Erb, Gustav Herzig, and Samuel Goldwater. Similar efforts were underway throughout the nation and the world. Governor Oglesby was swamped with clemency petitions from ordinary citizens and from prominent lawyers, businessmen, politicians, and literary figures, including William Dean Howells, Oscar Wilde, and George Bernard Shaw.[18]

It did not escape Labadie's notice that one of the most ardent workers in this cause was Samuel Gompers, president of the newly born AFL and a person much reviled by Knights' officials. (Powderly even stooped to jeering at the Jewish labor leader as one of "those Christ sluggers.") His shaky, year-old organization was willing to risk the public denunciation that the Knights of Labor dodged and adopted a resolution appealing for leniency. Gompers declared that labor must "stand for a fair trial for the underdog," no matter how radical he be. His hope "to maintain the dignity and honor of our organization, and withal to be manly and uncringing," impelled him to join several hundred petitioners at the State House in Springfield two days before the execution, seeking a last-minute reprieve. He warned Oglesby that if the men were hanged, they would be viewed by labor as martyrs who stood up for free speech and free assemblage.

Buchanan presented Oglesby with the petition from the dissident Minneapolis convention delegates. He read a letter from Spies requesting that he alone be executed to satisfy public anger and that his comrades be spared. He also read a letter from Parsons, ironically suggesting that since he was to be hanged simply for being present at the Haymarket rally, his wife and two children, who had been there as well, ought to be hanged with him.[19]

On November 10, two hours after Lingg blew himself up with a dynamite capsule concealed in his mouth, the governor commuted the sentences of Fielden and Schwab (the only ones who had requested mercy) to life imprisonment. Oglesby stated that he was prevented from considering commutation for the others because they had not asked for it, as required by law. Whatever his personal feeling, he believed, possibly correctly, that the majority of Americans felt the prisoners deserved to be hanged. The following morning, November 11, 1887, with the city under heavy guard in anticipation of a rescue attempt, Spies, Parsons, Engel and Fischer were led to the gallows. Their ankles were bound, ropes slipped around their throats and white caps fastened over their heads. From under his hood, Spies cried out the prophetic words: "The time will come when our silence will be more powerful than the voices you strangle today." The trap was sprung, the bodies plunged downward, the nooses tightened, and the men writhed in agony for several minutes as they slowly strangled, the *Chicago Tribune* reported.[20]

It was over. In an act condemned to the present day as "judicial murder"—to Labadie, "the crime preeminent of the century"—four men were hanged because a bomb was thrown by an unknown person for an unknown reason at an otherwise peaceful protest meeting. Labadie was heavy with rage, bitterness, and sorrow. He had never believed the authorities would be so foolish as to carry out the execution. He had warned that "These men dead are a hundred times more dangerous than living to the existing order of things." His grief was assuaged only by his consuming hatred of Powderly and a vow made to Barry "to drive him [Powderly] out of the labor movement in disgrace."[21]

Four days later, he delivered a scathing indictment in the form of a delegate's report to the Detroit district assembly of the Knights of Labor. D.A. 50 officials were understandably uneasy about its explosive potential and tried to keep it quiet by barring the public. Exasperated with such timidity, L.A. 901 (the original Detroit assembly Labadie had founded eight years before) advertised a mass meeting to circulate the charges. Labadie also passed a copy of the incendiary message to the *Detroit Evening News,* which published it practically verbatim, thereby gaining the report wide readership and national prominence.[22]

He did not mince words. He accused the Knights' leaders of gross abuse of power and recounted in detail the convention infighting and time spent "washing dirty linen." He said he had been persuaded that Barry and Bailey's charges of extravagance and misuse of funds were accurate. He cited a treasurer's report that showed total expenses in 1886, when the Order gained nearly 600,000 members, of $106,000, and four times as much the following year, when the Knights' fortunes were reversed, with a loss of over 217,000 members. "And these are the men who talk of reforming the financial and tax systems of the governments of the world," he sneered.

He was incensed by the delegates who seemed to agree that the Haymarket men had not had a fair trial, yet refused to "raise their voices" as representatives of the Knights of Labor. But the "most illogical, cowardly, brutal and violent speeches" were made by Powderly himself, Labadie charged. His denunciation was scathing: "I hold him as much responsible for the murder committed in Chicago last Friday as anyone connected with that most unfortunate affair. . . . He can now take what consolation he can in knowing that he helped to hang better men than he ever was or ever can be."

Money and power had corrupted the Knights' officers; they had to go. They were developing a strong centralized system, "and the labor movement cannot develop on that line." Powderly had become "autocratic, opinionated and unfair . . . spoiled by the flattery of sycophants and overzealous friends." These men could not lead a labor movement successfully; the decline of the Order was certain. As for himself, Powderly had said that an anarchist could not be a Knight of Labor. So, Labadie concluded, "whether I shall quietly take my leave of you or put you to the test of expelling me . . . I will determine before long."[23]

Labadie's indictment provoked heated controversy in D.A. 50. Alarmed administration supporters struggled to have it rejected, but they were overruled, and it was ordered printed and distributed among the Michigan assemblies. Repercussions were swift. Powderly vowed to "get even." He informed Devlin he intended to "tear off every veil of hypocrisy, deceit, false assumption of virtue and friendship for me personally" of the "knave" (Labadie) he once thought "honest, though radical." He even made the implausible claim that Labadie had come to him in Minneapolis after what Powderly euphemistically termed "the discussion on Anarchy" and begged him not to resign.[24]

A trusted Powderly minion in Detroit, Adelbert M. Dewey, launched the attack. In Minneapolis, he had apparently been Powderly's lobbyist, assigned to spread slurs against Barry and Bailey and suggest they be removed from office. Powderly now asked him to get the "good men" in Detroit who disapproved of Labadie's actions to "bestir themselves and . . . demonstrate their power in the coming year." Dewey was also reportedly directed to travel around Michigan, impugning Labadie's report.[25] Dewey began by castigating it in a letter to the *Detroit News*. He bragged to Powderly on November 25 that "hundreds of people . . . have congratulated me upon my defence of yourself and the Order from the attack of that blood-thirsty element." Devlin, who was on the Executive Board of D.A. 50, urged Powderly to come to Detroit to defend himself. "Something must be done and that soon to counteract the influence of Bro Labadie," he wrote.[26]

Within days of launching his attack, Dewey was forced to leave town, complaining to Powderly that the "Labadie gang" had made it "hot" for him and he could not get work as a printer in local shops. In search of a job, he suggested he had "some claim to consideration" as future manager of the *Journal of United Labor,* official publication of the Knights of Labor. Powderly rewarded his loyalty the following May by appointing him editor, although Dewey was a printer with no previous connection to labor papers.[27]

Dewey was the sort of man that "antis" in the provisional committee had in mind when they accused officers of using "secret channels and funds of the order to manufacture sentiment for certain members and against others." Powderly had appointed Dewey a Michigan organizer against the wishes of the state assemblies because he was satisfied, as he told Dewey, "that you will do good work and that it will be all K. of L. work and not Anarchistic or International Workingmen's work." Powderly then directed him to stay on the job despite opposition.[28]

Soon John M. Decker, the Minneapolis convention delegate from the Michigan State Assembly, issued his own vituperative, pro-administration report. Decker, reputedly "A Powderly man first, last and all the time," accused Labadie of "a disgraceful and untruthful fabrication of the facts." He suggested Labadie was gloating over the loss of members and engaging in "nasty kicking" in an effort to destroy the Order. As for Buchanan, who ran an "anarchist hotbed" in Denver, he was "one of the vilest and worst falsifiers in the Order for his own personal aggrandizement." Barry was part of a "band of conspirators . . . an anarchistic element" who had made Powderly's life "a perfect hell" for the last year. Decker's report concluded that Powderly had "fully explained away" all the charges made against him at the convention.[29]

The once-noble Knighthood was quickly disintegrating in an atmosphere of back-stabbing and intrigue. Both emotionally and professionally, Labadie's life was in turmoil. He lost his position as editor of *Advance and Labor Leaf* soon after his return from Minneapolis. Perhaps his notoriety at the convention and Powderly's tirade against anarchists made the paper's board of directors question the value of this divisive firebrand. Grenell, who replaced him, did his best to calm the waters by giving all factions access to its pages.[30]

The ousted Labadie got a job setting type at the Sunday *Detroit Sun*. Dyer Lum tried to lure him to Chicago for a "permanent 'sit' " on *The Alarm*, Parsons's paper, which Lum had revived after Parsons's imprisonment.[31] Apart from the fact that "permanent" had a certain nebulous quality when applied to a radical publication, this was not a very tempting proposal, and Labadie did not accept it. The journal and its editor were certainly too extreme for Labadie. Not only would he have had to uproot his family and leave his beloved Detroit, but he also knew Lum was hardly a secure port in a storm. Although the activities of this New York–born anarchist and abolitionist outwardly paralleled Labadie's more closely than that of any other labor radical of the time, Lum was captivated by visions of the violent drama in which he might play a heroic role.

A comparison of the careers of Lum and Labadie reveals a certain logical progression in an assortment of sometimes contradictory causes. A bookbinder of Puritan descent eleven years older than Labadie, Lum had been a ranking official of the Greenback-Labor party at its 1880 convention and fought hard to have the SLP delegates—Labadie among them—

admitted. Seeking a more radical course of action, he joined the SLP. Like Labadie, he then lost his faith in legislation and state control, and, along with his friend Parsons, formed the revolutionary anarchist IWPA, the group with which the Haymarket defendants identified. At the same time, Lum was attracted to the opposing individualist anarchist camp and began contributing to Benjamin Tucker's *Liberty*. He hoped, like Burnette Haskell, to unify all anarchist and socialist groups into one movement. He also joined the Knights of Labor, until, disenchanted, he allied himself with Samuel Gompers and the AFL. There, like Labadie, he was influential in forming its anti-political strategies.[32]

But underneath his calm exterior smoldered a revolutionary infatuation with dynamite plots and secret codes, with the use of terrorism as a weapon against tyranny, and with the yearning to die in the cause of human emancipation. Five days before the Haymarket executions, Lum had smuggled four pipe bombs into Lingg's cell concealed in cigar casings. Meant for self-destruction, they were discovered the next day. "Only terrorism . . . will now save them," he informed Labadie at the time. He began plotting to dynamite the jail and free the prisoners on the eve of the hangings. The condemned men, however, squelched the plan, preferring to die as martyrs and thereby immortalize their ideals.[33]

The agony of the executions combined with the continuing discord in the Knights of Labor left Labadie deeply dispirited. He was worn out psychically by his efforts and never fully recovered. After delivering his report on the turbulent Minneapolis convention, he could scarcely rouse himself to make decisions, to write, speak in public, or take part in labor activities. None of his letters from the weeks after the executions survive, but those written by others betray their concern. "I worry the Chicago tradgedy [*sic*] is disqualifying you for solid work," wrote his good friend, Chicago labor agitator George Schilling. Lum wrote to Labadie, "I am very sorry you take their deaths so hard—can't you realize that it was nothing but an episode in our work? I do."[34]

Intensifying his depression was the questionable behavior of Henry George, whom Labadie had greatly admired despite his objections to the single tax solution to economic woes. George believed the Haymarket defendants were guilty and justly sentenced. Although he tried to convince Labadie later that he had sought to prevent their hanging, George had refused to sign petitions for executive clemency. His claim that he was motivated "solely by conscience" would have been more plausible had he not been energetically campaigning for secretary of state of New York. The suspicion of political expediency crossed many minds. Considered a turncoat by workers and radicals, he was humiliatingly defeated in the November 1887 state elections.[35]

In Detroit, as the turmoil continued, Labadie was torn about his next move. His first impulse was to resign from the Knights as soon as his report was circulated, but Schilling advised him to "compel the gang to prefer charges against you and try to expell [sic] you." If he forced a showdown, Schilling argued, his influence would be far greater than if he simply faded away: "[It] will be but a short time when the revolt will begin on the inside." Tucker also advised him to stay, but used the opportunity to point out loftily that "for my own part, I never at any time would have had anything to do with the K. of L." Buchanan was taking the opposing view. He assailed those who stayed in the order believing that "the assassin has a better chance to use the knife when on the inside." The "honest protestor," in contrast, "comes right out with his protest and takes the consequences, even if expulsion results," Buchanan maintained.[36]

Labadie contemplated the possibility of decisively establishing the Knights in Detroit as an anti-administration camp by becoming master workman of D.A. 50 himself. The Order's highest post in Detroit, it now represented some 2,500 workers (down from over 4,600 eighteen months previously). Schilling, Lum, and Charles Seib, the Chicago leader of the provisional committee, all recommended that he gain control by that route. Labadie had good reason to believe he could win. D.A. 50 had just been applauded by the *Evening News* (where Grenell was a staffer) as a group that refused to give "servile acquiescence to every beck and nod" of the ruling faction, and whose "crowning act" had been sending Labadie to the Minneapolis assembly.[37] By now, however, his heart was not in it. His vision of a new age of labor solidarity lay shattered in an mess of power struggles, plotting, and bitter strife.

Health problems, which were to plague Labadie for the rest of his life, also began. His report on the Minneapolis general assembly had been delayed two weeks because of illness; for three months afterward he claimed he suffered "all of the known and a few of the unknown diseases," including "bilious fever" and boils. He referred later to having endured a siege of "nervous prostration" lasting more than two years; it may have begun at this time. It did not help that he worked fifty-seven hours a week as a printer in a poorly ventilated room, alternately enduring hot, polluted air and cold draughts, not to mention possible poisoning from the lead type. Conditions such as those helped explain printers' high rate of tuberculosis.[38]

Ironically, his nemesis Powderly also was ill for weeks after the Minneapolis convention. Powderly moaned, in a typically self-dramatizing fashion to John W. Hayes, his closest associate: "I fear the worst and must prepare for it." His mercurial emotions are reflected in letters to his associates. On the day of the executions, Powderly claimed that he had "never felt so stirred" as when "the poor fellows walked the plank." Yet a few days later, furious at Labadie's report, he poured out his wrath to his secretary: "He charges me with hanging the Anarchists . . . I am sorry I cannot hang them all for they are susceptible to no other argument. I was sorry for them but do not feel so now." Labadie was "no different from any other anarchist and will lie when it suits his convenience."[39]

Meanwhile, his energy sapped, Labadie decided not to run for master workman. It seems he had no heart for the politicking and scheming it would entail. Instead, he nominated the dedicated Thomas Dolan, who had begun organizing cigarmakers before the Civil War, and was known for giving "freely of his time and effort" in every attempt to benefit labor while earning small wages for a local cigar company. Dolan, "for countless years always among those present and always forgotten when rewards were handed out," as a fellow cigarmaker later observed, was well liked.[40] Despite his many years as an unsung lieutenant in labor's assaults, he was apparently not yet battle-weary.

Dolan was pitted against A. W. Vicars, also British born, a thirty-seven-year-old cracker baker nominated by Devlin as the pro-Powderly choice. The forces were almost evenly divided in the January 1888, contest; tension was high. Dolan was ahead on the first ballot, but with the candidates narrowed to two, Vicars was elected 45–43. Devlin, who became treasurer, wrote Powderly triumphantly that "Labadie & Co. were completely routed." He crowed that notwithstanding "the cry that this D.A. belong to the 'throttle the Law' Element . . . it is a Powderly District and is likely to remain so." Powderly confided to Devlin a bizarre-sounding plan to keep the Order under control. With a baby, you "just daub its hand with molasses, and give it . . . a feather; the time consumed in picking . . . the feather from one hand to the other . . . will keep [it] out of mischief." His enigmatic intention, he wrote, was to give "the babies in the order . . . lots of feathers and molasses for the next few months."[41] Devlin did not tell Powderly that the sole oppositionist among the newly elected chief officers was the most formidable "anti" himself. Labadie was chosen statistician in what seems a kind of consolation prize. Perhaps to show he harbored no ill will, he accepted the post.

But almost simultaneously, Labadie finally lashed out at Decker's report defending Powderly with a brutality that betrayed his anguished state of mind. The geniality for which he was so often commended disappeared in an *ad hominem* barrage against the state assembly delegate from Flint. He had heard that Decker was elected as a "representative 'day laborer,' " he commented sarcastically. If the characteristics of that class were "ignorance, illiteracy and boorishness," he continued contemptuously, then Decker was "a representative par excellence." As a delegate, he had been "presumptuous and officious," just the kind of man who would be a "blind supporter of men in power." Where Decker's report was "intelligible at all," Labadie charged, it was written by others.[42]

It appeared to be his final volley in the battle. After this cathartic outburst, Labadie was scarcely heard from for months. He had vowed in his column that "The men who are in the labor movement for place and power and money must be unmasked and I shall not shrink from the duty of unmasking them when I find them out." Yet the fire had gone out of him. He transferred "Cranky Notions" to Tucker's *Liberty,* and no longer wrote for *Advance and Labor Leaf.* He was replaced as master workman of the ideologically oriented Henry George local assembly. He faithfully carried out his duties as statistician of D.A. 50 by documenting the working conditions of Detroit printers, but otherwise was little heard from in Knights of Labor circles. There was no dramatic expulsion from the Order, nor did he resign in protest. Yet that was only a formality. His prominent role in the organization ended. As one of the most influential labor organizations in American history disintegrated, Labadie quietly dropped out.[43]

Powderly retained his position as Knights leader until finally driven from office in 1893. By then, the membership had fallen to 75,000; in 1900 the organization was barely a memory to most American workers. It is interesting to speculate on whether the Knights of Labor, under better leadership and minus the Haymarket bombing, might have evolved and endured. Or did its type of structure and vague but grand goals doom it from the start? In any case, an all-inclusive, non-trade-based form of unionization was not successfully put in place again until the Congress of Industrial Organizations (CIO) was formed in 1938, five years after Labadie's death.

★ 12 ★

Working with Gompers

You cannot freedom win alone,
You cannot wrongs aright:
Together we must each defend
Or wage a losing fight!
FROM "FREEDOM THRU ORGANIZATION,"
DOGGEREL FOR THE UNDERDOG

When Samuel Gompers arrived in Detroit in February 1888, he was greeted with considerably more enthusiasm than he had been two years before. Local Knights then had "painted Mr. Gompers in the most hideous colors," disparaging both his intellect and personal appearance, the *Evening News* recalled. It found that "he is not so black as he is painted." The paper thought he "evinced the gentleman," that his dark eyes "flash with intelligence," and concluded that "he is one of the great labor leaders of this country."[1]

Gompers visited Detroit during an arduous 20,000-mile, thirty-three-city tour. Its purpose was to convince workers that only through trade unionism and the AFL would they gain their fair share of the nation's wealth. He stressed that unions that joined his fledgling organization would not be dictated to by some central authority, as the Knights' assemblies were. They would be allowed to run their own affairs. They would band together to solve their common problems without asking for government help. So loose was the federation he outlined that Bolshevik leader Lenin later scoffed at it as "a rope of sand." Gompers retorted that that rope would prove more powerful than chains of steel.[2]

His stirring address in Foresters' Temple, sponsored by the Detroit Trades Council, was well attended. Eloquently, and with a flair for the dramatic metaphor, he disparaged the industrialists—"bees," who "are sucking the honey, but producing none." Dressed in fancy garments, they "care not that in every stitch and bead . . . there is a drop of blood from the heart of some poor workgirl." He spoke of children dragged into factories and mines by "monster greed." Only organization could oppose this tyranny, he proclaimed; the "natural organization" of labor was trade unions. All should join under the banner of the AFL.[3]

Gompers's plan for worker unification was far from the "noble and holy" aspirations of the evangelical Knights of Labor. He dismissed the Order as an organization "with high ideals but purely sentimental and bereft of all practical thought and action." If one were to place Gompers in the categories of reformers set out by John Stuart Mill, this rising labor leader would be the type who focused on the "immediately useful and practically attainable," rather than one of those who hoped to attain "the highest ideals of human life." The AFL was not to be one big union of the downtrodden, but a businesslike amalgamation of trade unionists for mutual protection. It represented practical-minded "bread-and-butter" unionism, seeking higher wages, shorter hours, and other tangible improvements of the craft worker's lot.[4]

Gompers's visit may have been the catalyst that shook Labadie out of the doldrums he had fallen into after the bitter losing fight over leadership of the Knights. Now thirty-eight, he appears to have decided to abandon his search for labor's Holy Grail and to join the more narrowly focused pragmatists. Trade unionism was not the stuff of his dreams; he had scorned its limitations in the past. But the Knighthood was in shambles. At least the new labor concept offered a field of agitation for his grander mission of furthering a stateless society. He was convinced that by "hammer[ing] away" at the doctrine of anarchism and the laissez faire principle while involved in the labor movement, he already had weakened the faith of many Detroit workers in government control.[5]

In those early days of the AFL, Gompers pretty much was the organization. He had little staff apart from the occasional services of his young son. He wrote official letters by hand. Sometimes there were no funds available to pay his $1,000 annual salary (less than he could earn as a cigarmaker); he returned from some of his lengthy speaking tours out of pocket. His large family—which eventually included a dozen children—suffered many privations. Throughout the formidable task of building the AFL and fighting the Knights of Labor, however, he mustered astounding vigor and tenacity of purpose.[6]

Gompers's custom, after his appearances, was to gather with labor figures in a tavern, black cigar between his teeth, discussing local problems over a beer or whiskey. His fellow unionists found him a jovial extrovert. Short and stocky, his large craggy head was covered with a thick growth of black hair, his large, drooping mustache overshadowing a small "imperial" goatee. Labadie enjoyed an occasional drink, and it may have been in such a locale that Gompers and Labadie renewed the acquaintance begun six years earlier, when Labadie had tried to persuade the FOTLU, precursor of the AFL, to merge with the Knights of Labor.

The two men seem to have liked each other from the start. It may be that Gompers's character, rather than his brand of "business unionism," most appealed to Labadie. The AFL leader's friendly and easy-going manner was in sharp contrast to the prim, puritanical Powderly, who condemned drink as the workingman's poison, and once sniffed that the Knights' executive board had "never had the pleasure of seeing Mr. Gompers sober."[7]

Probably none of the AFL president's policies was so impressive to Labadie at that troubled moment in his life as Gompers's spirited and courageous defense of the now-executed anarchists. Although often denounced as an opportunist, Gompers had rushed to Governor Oglesby's office to plead for clemency, seemingly without heed for the unfavorable impact this stand might have on his newly formed organization.

Gompers and Labadie had much in common. The same age, with little formal schooling, both had entered a trade as children (Gompers was indentured to a cigarmaker in his native England at age ten). Both had developed into self-educated worker-intellectuals and strong individualists. They both had flirted with socialism as young men, Gompers going so far as to learn German so he could read *Das Kapital* in the original. Like Labadie, Gompers later clashed with the socialists, but he acknowledged Marx as the father of trade unionism and greatly admired Engels. He called the socialist comrades of his early days "as high-minded a group of idealists as could be found." Both he and Labadie distrusted churches and considered their "religion" to be the brotherhood of man. Coincidentally, both had loyal, devoted wives named Sophie (Mrs. Gompers was "Sophia"), whom they lovingly called "Mamma," pillars of support waiting uncomplainingly in the background.[8]

They discovered they shared a passion for liberty, an abhorrence of compulsion, and an abiding distrust of government. When Gompers wrote "I believe that restrictions dwarf personality, and that the largest usefulness comes through the greatest personal freedom," it could have been Labadie speaking. Voluntary methods were the core of Gompers's credo. Even in the cause of improved working conditions, he feared government intervention. No minimum wage or hour laws, no compulsory arbitration, no state-run unemployment or health insurance, no social security (so favored by organized labor in later years). Workers had to be self-reliant. They should look after their own interests, not give up their freedom for the sake of government guardianship. A mighty labor movement could achieve the eight-hour day, fair wages, pensions, and all the benefits, through collective bargaining. Labadie could not have expressed his aversion to government more strongly than Gompers did: "There never was a government in the history of the world . . . that when a critical moment came, did not exercise tyranny over the people." His successor as AFL president, William Green, went so far as to call Gompers a philosophical anarchist.[9]

Four years before Gompers's 1888 arrival in Detroit, Labadie had hoped to consolidate all Michigan labor organizations into one central body, to include farmers, trade unionists, and "industrial societies" like the Knights. Now he was willing to pare down his vision. A state federation—even one restricted to trade unions—could be a powerful force. He began planning to form one with another Detroit labor leader of an anarchist bent, Samuel Goldwater, who often shared the stage with Labadie at radical gatherings.

Goldwater, a Polish-born Jewish cigarmaker, had been a close associate of the executed Parsons and Spies, and other anarchists in their circle. Fearing arrest himself, he fled Chicago after the Haymarket bombing and eventually opened a cigar business in Detroit. He joined Labadie as a fierce opponent of the Knights and an activist on the anarchists' defense committee. After pleading for clemency before Governor Oglesby, Goldwater had wandered the streets of Chicago with his close friend Gompers, "depressed . . . beyond words" at the impending executions, Gompers recalled.[10]

Goldwater quickly made a name for himself in Detroit labor circles, and was lauded as a man of principle. Honesty, selflessness, and identification with the workers' plight were enough to ensure widespread support for labor radicals in those days and gain them election to positions of trust, as Richard Oestreicher has pointed out, in commenting on Tom Barry. The Trades Council chose Goldwater as its delegate to the AFL convention in Baltimore at the end of 1887; he was elected Trades Council president a few months later. Soon the "two heavy-weight anarchists," as the mainstream *Detroit Tribune* called Goldwater and Labadie in apparent admiration, persuaded the Trades Council to call a convention for the purpose of setting up a state labor federation.[11] There was no plan initially to affiliate with the AFL.

Thirty-five delegates from twenty-seven Michigan trade unions and citywide labor bodies met at Pioneer Hall in Lansing in February 1889. Labadie represented Detroit's typographical union. One delegate recalled it fifty years later as a disparate group, representing "all the 'isms'," including "straight-out trades unionists, Knights of Labor, Socialists, dynamite anarchists . . single taxers on every hand," and a "nihilist" who shouted down the Lansing mayor during his welcoming address. Labadie was apparently in a restrained mood, since the chronicler remembered him as "so gentle that I'm sure he wouldn't have stepped on a fly or slapped a mosquito."[12]

Goldwater counseled the delegates, as they had been told by many labor leaders before, that to counteract the gigantic monopolies and trusts of the capitalists, labor must set up larger combinations of its own. Echoing Gompers, he maintained that the only "natural" form of labor union was one organized by trades. Mixed organizations, like the Knights, failed because decisions were made by those unfamiliar with each trade. He noted picturesquely that a horse-shoer would be as ill-equipped to negotiate a printers' strike "as would be the devil as an appraiser of the influence of holy mass on an expired soul."[13]

Organized as the Michigan Federation of Labor (MFL), this motley assemblage came up with resolutions that ranged far and wide. Labadie, who was elected its first president, predictably wanted to fight for a shorter day so workers would have time to study the "sound principles of social life and industry." One delegate opposed a Sunday rest bill then before the state legislature because it would establish a national religion. Proposals were made for vegetables to be sold by weight instead of measure, for wages to be paid weekly, for a two-cent per mile train fare, for children under fourteen to be obliged to attend school full time and for the anti-union Baker Conspiracy Law to be repealed. The German-born unionists wanted the federation's constitution printed in German. Demands that Oklahoma and Indian Territory lands be opened to homesteaders, that the only tax be on land, and that MFL officers be prohibited from holding political appointments were voted down.[14]

The Declaration of Principles, written by Labadie and adopted unanimously, was an ethereal mix of socialist, anarchist, and single-tax tenets. It stated that labor is the producer of all wealth, that "right and justice demand that the product shall belong to the producer," that only what labor produces should rightfully be owned, and that "personal occupancy and use" is the only rightful title to land. Labadie could not get the delegates to oppose the patenting of inventions, although they did agree that "the present patent laws are unjust."[15]

This declaration of high-blown principles was not much vaguer than those put forth by other labor organizations of the day. The editor of the typographical union journal *The Craftsman* pronounced it "a step in advance of any labor platform yet adopted." Labadie crowed over its anarchistic elements. "What do you think of Michigan trades unions that will pass such a declaration of principles?" he gloated to Reverend Hugh O. Pentecost, anarchist publisher of *Twentieth Century,* and one-time Congregational minister. He had to concede that no methods of bringing about these impressive objectives had been agreed on due to "the wide difference of opinion as to the best method." Michigan Deputy Commissioner of Labor Charles E. Barnes sternly reminded Labadie that the problem was "how can the working masses be . . . made to realise what these principles mean."[16]

That Michigan's unions went along with these head-in-the-clouds dreams reveals their lack of understanding of the revolutionary implications of Labadie's goals as well as a trustfulness that would not be sustained over time. (His cherished declaration of principles was watered down at an annual convention six years later, and after 1911, MFL conventions dispensed altogether with a statement of visionary reforms.) Labadie inaugurated his presidency by seeking to put into practice grand, but unworkable, ideas for expanding the Michigan federation. Gompers was appalled to learn that he planned to stimulate the formation of new unions in Michigan that would join the MFL and be issued charters, thereby putting it in competition with AFL organizing efforts. That was the AFL's job, Gompers protested; new unions should affiliate directly with his organization. "You assume the generally conceded functions of the AFL . . . and then assure me that there will be no conflict between the MFL and the AFL unless, of course, the latter body attempts to abridge the former's right. If the above does not constitute an assumption of prerogatives calculated to provoke a conflict I am at a loss to understand what would," he admonished Labadie. Gompers wrote in exasperation to Michigan organizer Robert Ogg: "It seems to me that our friend Labadie holds very peculiar views of the relations between the MFL and the AFL."[17]

By the time of the MFL's second convention in February 1890, Labadie's fervor was dampened. He had reluctantly agreed not to "usurp" the AFL and only to encourage existing Michigan unions to join the new state federation. He wanted it to focus on education and proposed that conventions spend a half day reading essays and discussing workers' rights. Now that the public generally supported the wage-earning class, he told delegates, it was time to abandon the "crude methods . . . of force and intimidation" (presumably strikes and violence) that had been used in trade unionism's early days and study how to replace them with "firm, dignified and reasonable" ones. He did not suggest what those might be.[18]

A few months before, he and Gompers had forged their friendship at the AFL's December 1889, convention in Boston, where Labadie represented the Detroit Trades Council. Gompers developed a fondness for the Detroit delegate, who may have been somewhat fuzzy-minded compared to the pragmatic Gompers, but was equally self-sacrificing in his endeavors to create a powerful labor force. He later called Labadie one of the "gentlest, most spiritual men" he had known. Labadie took seriously Gompers's flattering suggestion that they write frequently to "make suggestions to each other." When Labadie complained that he heard from Gompers only when the AFL president wanted to make use of him, Gompers curtly reminded him of the "difference in the opportunities for [correspondence] between Joe. Labadie and Sam. Gompers . . . who has certain responsibilities . . . to the world of labor, and must fulfill them." At the convention, Gompers showed he understood Labadie by letting him preside during the half-hour devoted to discussion.[19]

Held at Well's Memorial Hall, the Boston convention was a historic one. Excitement was generated by a massive new campaign to achieve the eight-hour day. Three years after the Haymarket catastrophe had nearly demolished the eight-hour movement, Gompers was breathing new life into the fight. May 1, 1890, was fixed as the date for a great general strike. Gompers was unanimously re-elected AFL president. Labadie was nominated for first vice-president, but declined. His suggestion of Detroit as the site for the next annual convention was approved. At the convention banquet, replete with toasts, Labadie raised his glass, appropriately, to "Labor Cranks."[20]

In preparation for the mighty May 1 strike, the AFL planned nationwide mass meetings and began issuing more than a half million circulars, pamphlets, and proclamations. The Second Labor and Socialist International had agreed at its founding meeting in Paris in July 1889, to help organize a great international demonstration in sympathy. Gompers then concluded that instead of a general strike for the eight-hour day it would be better strategy for one strong union to lead the way. The United Brotherhood of

Carpenters and Joiners, which had amassed a large strike fund and was the most successful AFL union, was chosen to go first.

On the appointed day, a massive, worldwide workers demonstration—the greatest ever seen—encouraged Gompers to foresee "The Federation of the World." The chosen union struck as arranged. Tens of thousands of unionists marched in solidarity in Chicago, New York, and other American industrial centers, as well as throughout the industrialized world. The success achieved by the United Brotherhood of Carpenters and Joiners was far greater than even the most optimistic estimates. The union claimed it had won an eight- or nine-hour day for over 76,000 of its members. Hundreds of thousands of other workers gained pay raises or shorter days. The AFL's well-organized militancy reaped enormous esteem for that organization; at the same time, the rival Knights of Labor, which had tried to torpedo the eight-hour movement, continued to lose ground.[21] Henceforth, May Day was celebrated as a workers' holiday in most of the world. Ironically, the United States, where the effort was conceived, kept Labor Day in September, a date with no socialist overtones.

Meanwhile, the MFL had not made much of a stir in its first year. Labadie pleaded frequent illnesses. He admitted to a lack of the "hustling" qualities essential to the presidency. Many of the unions that did join failed to pay their dues of one-half cent per month per member. There was no money to carry out the founding convention's resolution to print the constitution in German or the forms for the collection of statistics.[22]

Labadie was more successful in counteracting rustlings toward lobbying, a position that put him philosophically in tune with Gompers. He had managed to keep all mention of pro-labor legislation out of the original MFL constitution (although by 1912 it was listed as a primary objective). Even though at its 1886 founding, the AFL had expressed an intention to secure laws favorable to labor, Gompers's own conviction was "that which we do for ourselves, individually and collectively, is done best." His distrust of state action and stress on workers' looking to their own organizations to defend their interests was called "voluntarism." This anti-political stance resonated well with Labadie's anarchism. Labadie was adamant that the MFL not "wander from the paths of trades unionism after the political will o' the wisps that have so often led the working people into the mire of disappointment and destruction." Even discussing questions of a political nature would bring "discord and disunion," he maintained, preventing unionists with differing political allegiances from concentrating on mutually advantageous actions involving conciliation, arbitration, boycotts, and strikes.[23]

Labor historians are fond of questioning why the United States, uniquely among Western industrialized nations, failed to develop a successful labor or socialist party. This absence of an influential working-class political movement is often explained as part of America's "exceptionalism." Socialist and other third-party reform movements have never been able to loosen the hold of the two major parties for long. One historian suggests that after the collapse of the Knights of Labor and its replacement by the more conservative, craft-based AFL, the opportunity for the broad working-class solidarity that might have resulted in a European-style labor party was lost.[24]

In explaining American "exceptionalism," however, Gompers's distrust of the state along with that of others in his midst played a significant role. There were a number of anarchists active in the early AFL who were eager to keep it out of politics and with whom his "voluntarism" resonated. These included, in addition to Labadie, Dyer Lum, once Gompers's speechwriter and possibly his secretary; August McCraith, AFL secretary for a time; Henry Weismann; and others, like Peter J. McGuire and Frank K. Foster, who seemed to have anarchist leanings.[25]

Labadie's resistance to MFL involvement in politics was quickly attacked, and it was conservatism, not radicalism, he was accused of pursuing. Old buddies Henry Robinson and John Burton took him to task in a back-and-forth that consumed an exhausting twenty columns over two months in *The Workman,* the MFL's official organ. What should delegates talk about during the half-day's discussion if politics were taboo, asked Robinson, Michigan's future state commissioner of labor. Obviously they could not grapple with a solution of the land problem, "the real remedy," since that was certainly a political question. Robinson jeered that "our protean friend" had always been a champion of free discussion; why was he ready to suppress it now for the sake of peace and "nostrums" like strikes and boycotts?

"How the mighty have fallen!" Burton chimed in. "Ten years ago Joe Labadie was one of the radical men in Detroit." Now, he implied, Labadie was echoing "the parrot cry 'organize' " (Gompers's clarion call), the cry of men with "no idea of progress." There was "not a single question which affects the condition of the worker but is political," Burton wrote.[26]

The two well knew Labadie's anti-government stance, the basis of his antipathy toward politics. What seemed to be agitating them was the suspicion that in joining Gompers's camp, Labadie had sold out, that he was abandoning great schemes for social reform and a "brotherhood of toil" in favor of more bread and butter for the tables of skilled craft unionists alone.

Indeed, there was truth to their accusations. Ten years earlier Labadie had disparaged the trade union as "nothing but a monopoly of labor formed to counteract a monopoly of capital, and the sooner both are swept away the better it will be for all." "The Genial Frenchman," as *The Workman*'s editor called him, acknowledged that "it is no secret that I have changed my mind several times . . . as to the best methods to be pursued by the trades unions." He had scaled down his vision. At age forty and seasoned by years of struggle, he now believed that "more people can be organized for the accomplishment of one or two things in a well defined . . . way than can be organized for the accomplishment of a dozen or more objects in a dozen or more ways." Furthermore, how could a "heterogenous mass" of Democrats, Republicans, socialists, anarchists, free traders, protectionists, prohibitionists, woman suffragists, and more, find a common political position without committing the minority to principles they opposed? He argued that he was following the "law of progress" outlined by Herbert Spencer (one of his favorite authors), which describes evolution as moving from simplicity to complexity. Applying it to the labor movement, he concluded that unions had evolved to the point where they had to specialize. By attempting to reform the whole society, he maintained, they would violate the law of progress and bring about their downfall. It was certainly a sharp about-face from the broad goals of his younger days.[27]

Despite what many unionists must have viewed as the vagueness of its leader and founding delegates, by the time of its second annual convention in February 1890, the MFL had eclipsed the waning Knights of Labor in Michigan. Delegates of "the strongest labor organization in the State" were warmly received by the mayor of East Saginaw and the town offered the municipal council chambers as a convention site.

Soon after the seating of delegates, Thomas Barry, hero of the Saginaw Valley strike and declared enemy of Powderly, unexpectedly appeared in the chambers. He asked to be admitted as a delegate, presenting credentials from a new movement he had formed, the Brotherhood of United Labor. He had embarked on a strange, quixotic venture. His brotherhood—with its socialist principles and vague organizational structure—was hardly a trade union. Solely on that basis, the delegates had every reason to reject Barry. More significant, the brotherhood was a bitter rival of the Knights of Labor, and Barry and Powderly were engaged in a personal feud. The MFL would reap no benefit from antagonizing the Knights' leadership. Admission of the brotherhood into the new federation would bring it nothing but trouble.[28]

After the tumultuous Minneapolis convention of the Knights, Barry had vowed "to fight the gang . . . regardless of consiquences [*sic*]." Where Labadie gradually dropped out of the fray, Barry, a man of fiery intensity, planned to challenge the general master workman and his cronies at the next general assembly in Indianapolis in 1888. He confided to Labadie that there was a "dark plot" to keep him away, although he was still a member of the Knights' general executive board.[29]

Powderly forces contrived to force him out of office, then summarily expelled Barry from membership in the organization in apparent violation of its constitution. Ignoring the edict, Barry tried to take a seat in Indianapolis that fall. Efforts to have his expulsion declared unconstitutional failed. Powderly refused to begin the proceedings until Barry left. Like the previous convention, this one was torn by clashes, "not that Barry was loved but that Powderly was hated with a venomous hate born of jealousy and nursed in wrath," as even a Powderly man recognized.[30]

The Order had lost 300,000 members in 1888, but Powderly gloated over burying an enemy, especially one who, in his words, "was warmly associated with the anarchistic element." He told his lieutenant, John W. Hayes, "We have slipped off the snake's skin—its other name is Barry."[31] "Poor Tom," as Barry was sympathetically viewed, then launched a vitriolic attack on Powderly and the "gang in the palace." Blazoned in leading labor papers, it charged misappropriation of funds, deceit, favoritism, and extravagance. "I have got that Deception gang on the run and I want to Drive the band wagon over them it has been a big fight with the odds against me but being right I had the courage to go ahead," Barry wrote Labadie in his unschooled scrawl. He claimed to have more than three hundred letters asking him to start a new movement. In forming his brotherhood, he aimed to place the labor movement on a decentralized basis, "which will make it forever almost impossible for cliques and rings to be formed." Open to all, skilled and unskilled, it planned to remove power from the "usurers," "shylocks," "stock gamblers," and "speculators," and make its primary objectives "Land, Currency and Transportation reform."[32]

Widely respected for his courage, honesty, and steadfast devotion to labor's cause, Barry was able to attract some dissident Knights of Labor assemblies; in Michigan, the brotherhood had a brief local success. Labadie, however, did not join the ranks. Perhaps he was leery of another grand, amorphous scheme to solve all society's problems. "Gee," Barry pleaded, "cant you give me the Name of some good kicker in detroit that I could get to organize a branch of the Brotherhood."[33] Barry did not try to conceal

his disappointment with Labadie's inaction in the continuing battle against
Powderly. He reminded his old friend that after the Haymarket executions
Labadie had sworn to drive the Knights' leader out of the labor movement
in disgrace. "Joe," he remonstrated, "what are you doing to keep that swar
[swear]."[34]

At the MFL convention, Labadie could do little to help Barry. Several
unions threatened to secede if he were admitted as a representative of the
brotherhood, although they would accept him as a representative of his
ax- and toolmakers' union. It was a sad moment for many when this lone
warrior was sent away. The brotherhood failed to recover from its founder's
rejection. The victim of well-organized obstructionism by pro-Powderly
forces, its only hope for becoming an organization of national importance
was affiliation with an established body, in this case, the MFL. Unable to
compete with a rising AFL, the Brotherhood of United Labor expired after
only two years of existence.[35]

Although the founding members of the MFL may have represented
a range of extremists, delegates at its second convention were the voice of
moderation. Strikes were to be avoided, conciliation encouraged, and the
boycott to be exercised "only in a quiet way." They were in favor of such
reasonable reforms as free textbooks and secret ballots, and opposed prison-
made cigars and cigar vending machines. They advocated "mild but earnest
means" for the great eight-hour day effort to be launched the following
May 1, including "respectfully" asking employers to join in. In his annual
report, Labadie pointed out that the shorter day might not raise the wages of
all workers, that it would not change the industrial system, and ominously
suggested that it was possible "that some of us will suffer persecution, and
maybe death, at the hands of that class who are responsible for the judicial
murders that occurred at Chicago." His reference to Haymarket was not
well received and delegates voted to dissociate the convention from it. A
resolution to affiliate with the AFL lost by a vote of 14 to 18.[36]

Given this direction of the MFL, Labadie was torn over whether he
should try to hold onto the presidency. Gompers had encouraged him to
remain another year. Perhaps too trustingly, the AFL leader wrote that a
"level-headed man" should be at the head of the MFL, "and I have great
confidence in your judgment." A puzzling letter from Goldwater suggests
that Labadie himself, in addition to suffering ill health, was besieged by self-
doubt, stung by criticism from former comrades, and considered resigning,
possibly asking Goldwater to replace him. "Your reasons are shallow,"
Goldwater declared; Labadie should ignore the criticism of "our enemies."[37]

For whatever reason, Labadie did not run again. Almost as soon as he was replaced as president by L. E. Tossy, the MFL appeared to repudiate his advice by moving "to besiege the legislature in the interest of labor laws" and took credit for many victories. Soon ten hours was declared a legal day's work in Michigan (although many employees were forced to sign away this right), the Baker Conspiracy Law was abolished, free textbooks were provided, and the secret ballot was instituted. By 1893, the MFL represented an estimated 14,000 workers. Meanwhile, the last Michigan assemblies of the Knights of Labor shut down and Powderly was ousted from the organization's helm. Soon, all that remained of what was once the most potent organization of workers in America was a shell holding a few thousand hangers-on.[38]

Though out of office and not actively involved, Labadie continued his interest in the fortunes of the Michigan federation he had helped found. When the MFL and Detroit Trades Council jointly started a new labor paper in 1894, he was invited to contribute his "Cranky Notions" column. The editors of the *Industrial Gazette* clearly knew what they were bargaining for. Labadie remained his old provocative self. Even in the eyes of conservative forces, his unquestioned dedication to labor's cause and his personal charm often seemed to outweigh objections to his radicalism. In the five months the paper lasted, Labadie generated a predictable surge of apopletic rebuttal, answered by testimonials from admirers. He opposed a law to close theaters on Sundays because theaters provided "more humanity and good sense than . . . the majority of churches." He reflected on the Post Office deficit (government inefficiency); self-help (the best kind); smoking in public (no one has a right to pollute others' air); labor bills (none has benefitted the masses); and free trade (anarchism in commerce).[39]

Such polemics were what he excelled at. He was not cut out to head a large organization. Personal power did not drive him and he lacked the requisite inclination to mediate, compromise, and politic. His forte was as a catalyst, a gadfly, a controversialist. "I guess the machine was too much for you," Agnes Inglis speculated many years later. "One sees . . . that you kept pushing the movement every way you could, but you never cared for 'power' for yourself."[40]

Labadie had undertaken the creation of the MFL with verve and energy, but soon lost interest in the mundane task of running it and in its prosaic objectives. Although as late as 1910 he called the AFL "the greatest force in society today for the social and economic betterment of the masses," he was emotionally uncomfortable in the camp of "business unionism." Sticking to specific, concrete gains for the skilled might be a "scientific" tactic, per Spencer, but it did not excite him. The trouble with Gompers's brand of unionism, in Labadie's view, was what it did not address—the vast humanitarian goals, revolutionary ideals, abstract theories, utopian visions. It offered bread and butter while he craved champagne. He tried to embrace the cause, but the spark was not there and his attentions cooled. He had lost his true love. In his last years, it was the early Knights of Labor that he spoke of longingly and of his poignant wish that it could be resurrected.[41]

☆ 13 ☆

Pet Radical

In the regal realm of Me
I am rightful sovereign there;
None should question my decree,
None my wishes justly dare.
        ---"THE TRUE SOVEREIGN," *WORKSHOP RIMES*

Labadie always believed that if people could only see how thoroughly home-grown his kind of anarchism was, their terrors would be allayed. He thought if he could show that it sprouted from native soil and that its seed was the American love of liberty, he could persuade others to tolerate or even welcome it. Sometimes, to make the doctrine more palatable, he called it "philosophical" anarchism (to his mind, as silly as saying "philosophical philosophy") just so the word would not "strike the puny mind with so much force as to knock it out in the first round."[1] Labadie could, of course, have called his philosophy "libertarianism," as many did (and do) and avoided the commotion. Perhaps he saw that as being dishonest, or perhaps he enjoyed the commotion.

Partly because its best-known anarchist was considered to be peace-loving and law-abiding, Detroit had escaped much of the frenzy that convulsed other cities after the Haymarket bombing. The influence of the large and well-respected German socialist community probably also played a role. Detroit's radicals generally were tolerated as well-meaning reformers or impractical dreamers, no threat to the good burghers. But the affection Labadie enjoyed personally did not lessen his distress at the popular view of anarchists as "an ignorant, vicious, whisky-drinking gang, dirty in personal habits, careless of the rights of others, and ever ready to kill and burn," the portrayal Powderly hysterically painted at the 1887 Minneapolis convention.[2]

Labadie felt driven to tell the nation about its anarchists—who they were, what they looked like, what they thought and why. For most of his life, he operated on a naive faith that once people were presented with the logic of a case, their innate rationality would lead them to fair-minded conclusions. If interested persons could be shown that anarchists were well-behaved, honest, and just, "a good deal like other folks," they would be likely to examine the philosophy without prejudice.[3]

He first proposed that a conference of anarchists be held in Detroit in the summer of 1888, where they would issue to the world a clarifying "anarchistic manifesto." Anarchists of all stripes could become acquainted and possibly reach harmony between the individualist and the collectivist branches. He expected it to be well covered by the press and attract widespread attention. His anarchist mentor Tucker scoffed at the idea as an excuse for an expensive junket with no clear purpose. He thought Labadie "surprisingly ignorant of the nature of the beast known as a capitalistic newspaper" if he thought a declaration of principles would stop malicious reporting.[4]

Rebuffed by American anarchism's guru, Labadie shifted his attention to a book. No outline of the views of America's anarchists had ever been published. In late 1888 and early 1889, he sent out forty or fifty letters to leading anarchists, asking them to define the philosophy, why it was desirable, and how it should be attained. They were to include a biographical sketch and picture. Labadie hoped that Tucker would publish the study, adding it to the long list of works offered by "Liberty's Library." But seeking a consensus was never one of Tucker's priorities, nor was he prone to help others in their enterprises. He replied only that "I really cannot" publish it, a curt dismissal for one of the few of his circle with whom Tucker was on friendly terms.[5]

Labadie's grand scheme ran into other problems. The anarchists he approached proved very individualistic, indeed. Many found something to complain or quibble about in the proposed project. One female anarchist felt the plan was not worth the trouble. "Do you care for the opinions of the average man and woman? I do not," she sniffed. Another recipient grumbled that no one would be impressed by "the testimonials of good behavior that we may be pleased to give ourselves."[6] In the end, only fifteen of those approached appear to have sent useful material.

Charles Fowler, publisher of a Kansas City, Missouri, anarchist periodical, was serene in the belief that publicity was unnecessary because anarchism would come about naturally. E. W. Barber, former supervisor of internal revenue and assistant postmaster general, objected that he "most thoroughly dislike[d] the word Anarchists" to describe those who believed in "Individualism as against Socialism." Chicago labor organizer George A. Schilling, who had worked closely with the Haymarket anarchists, declined to say if he was an anarchist. He thought it misguided to use such a "confusing" term, and later scoffed that Tucker was foolish to insist on a name that to the average citizen meant "hell and damnation." Archibald H. Simpson, a Boston printer, refused to participate because he thought the cause of anarchy was hopeless. Maurice A. Bachman thought it impossible to make anarchism "fashionable, or at least not objectionable" without excluding Johann Most and those who advocated "propaganda of the deed," and he questioned how Labadie proposed to do this.[7]

Labadie did contact one exponent of the Kropotkin/Most doctrine, which looked to a society of decentralized communes. William Holmes, who had hidden Parsons after the Haymarket explosion and been a pallbearer at his funeral, assured Labadie that while their collectivist anarchist ideology foresaw possible violence during the overthrow of the existing system, they expected the resulting anarchy to bring peace, order, and local self-government—without force of any kind. Labadie had met with Holmes in 1887 while visiting the Haymarket prisoners in Chicago and they reached a meeting of the minds. The two agreed that anarchism did not deny the right of free contract, and thus the right to contract with others to live together communistically or by any other arrangement. Labadie thereafter emphasized that anarchism was totally planless, except for insisting on "a fair field and no favors." It permitted any kind of organization, including government, so long as membership was not compulsory.[8]

Those who responded to Labadie's appeal ranged from Buffalo day laborer Augustine Leroy Ballou, who had never met a single soul who sympathized with his belief, to prominent New York City architect John Beverley Robinson, later a professor at Washington University in St. Louis. Most were from the East Coast and several could trace their lineage back to the Puritans or colonists. Joshua K. Ingalls, born in Massachusetts in 1816, had already devoted some forty-five years to the cause of land reform and was weary. He confessed that he had been identified with so many "societies, orders, sects and parties, and to so little purpose, that I am tired of organizations. . . . Have we not enough of isms?"[9]

The contributions omitted any discussion of how anarchism could work in practice. Radicals of that era were roused by theories, not demanding the specifics of a later, more pragmatic age. The tomes of Karl Marx, for example, presented no clear strategy for realizing the classless society he forecast emerging through class struggle. Furthermore, mapping out an anarchistic society was a contradiction in terms. To systematize it would be to impose structure, when the idea was to let society develop freely. Without government interjecting itself to disturb the natural process, people would work out whatever society seemed best. They would choose to live together harmoniously because it would be in their self-interest to do so. These radicals were "abolitionists, not institution-builders, prophets, not priests; anarchists, not administrators."[10]

The material Labadie collected was never published. Perhaps the results seemed too sparse and inconsistent. Yet his desire to distill the essence of anarchist doctrine for public consumption kept nagging him. Bearing in mind the vast area of disagreement documented in the responses, he figured that by throwing out all disputed statements among the anarchists, he could arrive at the essence of the philosophy. His eventual synthesis of the beliefs of "anarchists everywhere" was simplicity itself, with many salient questions left unanswered. Although composed before 1900, it exists only in a 1908 leaflet, "Anarchism, What It Is and What It Is Not," printed and distributed in the thousands by Labadie's "Jewish comrades" in the International Anarchist Group of Detroit.[11]

Labadie postulated that anarchism was not a utopian chimera, but "a practical philosophy" and did not seek to establish the impossible—absolute freedom. Its aim was equal rights for all to land and natural resources. With anarchism, what was produced would belong to the producer, to be exchanged in any manner desired. Occupancy and use would be the sole claim to land. Anyone could issue money. Patents, copyrights, and other monopolies would be abolished. All taxation would be voluntary. There would be no restrictions on personal behavior that did not interfere with the rights of others. Crime would be eliminated, with crime defined as doing injury to another by aggression. There would be no killing, except in self-defense, because that would be an invasion of another's equal right to live. Happiness was the goal; freedom in every walk of life was the best way to achieve it.[12]

The pamphlet made no mention of morality, natural law, or natural rights, which Labadie had previously cited as the bases for his philosophy. Going along with Tucker, he now rejected such quasi-religious "myths," replacing them with the concept of "egoism." This shift to "egotistical anarchism" was derived from the views of German philosopher Max Stirner, who stated: "I am neither good nor evil. Neither has any meaning for me. . . .

For me there is nothing above myself."[13] As Labadie expressed it in the opening verse to this chapter, "In the regal realm of Me, I am rightful sovereign there."

Self-interest was the only motivating force in human conduct—so went the argument accepted by Labadie and Tucker. There was no absolute "right" or "wrong." Individuals were free to seek happiness however they liked, but since they would bear the social consequences of their acts, they were likely to find it useful to live in harmony with others and enter into contracts or cooperative arrangements to safeguard their own interests. Labadie declared: "To me there is no such thing as altruism—that is, the doing of anything wholly for the good of others. We do things for self-satisfaction."[14]

Although this point of view does not differ markedly from the central assumptions of classical laissez-faire economics, Tucker's deviation to egoism sent shock waves through the individualist anarchist community. In this rarefied intellectual world, where disputes could turn bitter over whether "anarchism" had its root in the Greek *archos* (leader) or *arche* (to be first, to rule), the new value-free dogma provoked widespread defections. Charging that abandoning a morality based on natural principles turned anarchism into a selfish, might-is-right philosophy, not unlike that of rapacious capitalism, many of Tucker's earlier associates deserted his camp and transferred their allegiance to radical movements that concentrated on practical social reform.[15]

Meanwhile, back in Detroit, while Labadie was employing sweet reasonableness to plead anarchism's case to the masses, a far more fanatical anarchist was lashing out at the world's injustices from a tiny, littered loft on Champlain Street. Little noticed by English speakers, but famous in German communities worldwide, editor Robert Reitzel was a violent revolutionist at heart, despairing of the moderation of American reformers. His weekly, *Der arme Teufel* (The Poor Devil), which he began in December 1884, expressed his pessimistic view that people were all poor devils in the end. Reitzel was the consummate iconoclast, negligent in dress, with a large head of tousled blond hair and small piercing eyes. His incendiary zeal often alienated those who had befriended him. The city's bourgeois Germans reviled him as a "blasphemer." Yet, a friend observed, he had "a quality sweet and mild, and sometimes he dipped his pen in gall and wormwood, and again he wrote with an Easter lily."

A one-time Lutheran minister who had become an agnostic, Reitzel never worked for wages. His improvidence caused his wife and eight children to suffer intense privation. When he was not fighting inhumanity and injustice, he penned essays on Shakespeare, Heine, Goethe, Thoreau, Whitman, and others. His paper, with a circulation of perhaps four thousand, was read by German radicals throughout the world and many cities had *Arme Teufel Klubs*. Reitzel occasionally printed translations of excerpts from Labadie's columns. Labadie, who believed that inside most German radicals "was that fox of the insuperable and infallible state eating out their vitals," valued Reitzel as one of the few Germans who had "any tolerably clear notion of freedom."[16]

A close friend of August Spies, Reitzel had yearned to play a noble role in the Haymarket drama. He was shocked that most of his fellow journalists refused to support the condemned men. After reading one of Labadie's "Cranky Notions" columns defending them, he wrote, "I despair no more about the Americans." As the fateful day of the executions approached in 1887, he met in Chicago with Dyer Lum. Together, they hatched a scheme to blow up the jail and free the doomed men on the eve of their execution. But the plot had been foiled by the prisoners themselves. They believed it would result in violent and bloody reprisals that would set back the cause of liberty and workers' rights for years to come. Reitzel and Lum had vainly awaited the signal to set off their bomb.[17]

At the burial of the four in Chicago's Waldheim Cemetery, Reitzel gave an impassioned eulogy in German. He called for vengeance, blood for blood. "We have loved long enough; now we are going to hate." But his hatred did not find release in action. Until his death of spinal tuberculosis in 1898 at fifty, his bitterness was confined to vitriolic writings and emotional memorial meetings honoring the "Chicago Martyrs," as they were now called.[18]

On the first anniversary of the executions, Reitzel and George Schilling arranged for Labadie to give the English-language memorial address at Waldheim Cemetery. Three thousand people stood by the resting place of the hanged men as crowds attended similar ceremonies throughout the United States and Europe. At the last minute, illness prevented Labadie from making the trip. But the following year and years afterward, when November 11 was observed as a revolutionary milepost throughout the world, he and Reitzel shared the podium at Detroit memorials for the "martyrs."[19]

As Detroit entered the 1890s, it was not an opportune time to be "agin the government." One of the nation's great reform mayors was running the city. A group of influential Republicans had picked Hazen S. Pingree as candidate in the 1889 election because they wanted a malleable, conservative businessman who could oust the Democrats. To their horror, Pingree used the mayoral position to embark on all sorts of crusades against civic abuses. He exposed widespread political graft, cracked down on election fraud, fought for city ownership of the overpriced and badly run streetcar monopoly, and cut the excessive gas, light, and tax rates. He even wanted the city to provide free water to promote cleanliness. He boasted that he had the support of "all classes, except what are called the best citizens." For refusing to call out the militia during the 1891 streetcar strike and advocating arbitration to settle the dispute, he was denounced as an "anarchist" by the company's officers—the most scurrilous accusation they could think up.[20]

When he took office in 1890 at the age of fifty, Pingree was a political novice. He was known as a harsh boss at his prosperous boot and shoe factory. Its repressive practices had caused the Knights of Labor to target it for a national boycott five years earlier. The firm of Pingree and Smith, the largest shoe factory west of New York City, had hired Pinkertons as spies and fired the employees they fingered as Knights. But Pingree was transformed after reading Richard Ely's books on the labor movement in the late 1880s. He became convinced of the justice and benefits in business negotiating contracts with trade unions.[21]

Once in office, Pingree began repaving the city's rutted streets, maintaining that well-paved roads were the key to a city's prosperity. He threatened to revoke a ferry company's license if it refused to lower its rates from ten to five cents. He reconstructed the sewer system, set up a free public bath, and forced the street railways to abandon horse cars and adopt an electrified rapid-transit system. There was little that escaped Pingree's attention as he established the first significant social-reform administration of any large city in the United States.[22]. Pingree's late-blooming compassion for the poor and suffering endeared him to the people. It ensured his election to four terms as mayor (1890–97) and two as governor (1897–1901), although he was viewed by Theodore Roosevelt and other Republicans as a traitor to his party. He chose as chief lieutenant and taxation expert the avid "single taxer" and labor sympathizer Robert Oakman, publisher of *The Spectator* when Labadie and Grenell wrote for it.[23]

By 1890 Detroit, considered one of the most beautiful cities of the "West," had catapulted from 116,000 residents ten years earlier to over 200,000. More than a third were foreign-born, nearly half of those German-Americans, who could choose from eight German-language newspapers, including three dailies. Its nationally known industries—stoves, tobacco, drugs and paint—were prospering. In 1896, both Henry Ford, a machinist with the Edison Company, and Ransom Eli Olds created the first gasoline-powered cars. Within a decade, both had founded automotive companies that made Detroit the center of the nation's automobile industry.

On Sundays, workers from all over Detroit flocked to the many beautiful parks, especially the 700-acre Belle Isle in the Detroit River, designed by the great landscape artist Frederick Law Olmstead. In summer, outdoor band concerts were plentiful. There were all sorts of amusements to choose from: vaudeville acts at the Wonderland, melodrama at the Whitney Opera House, and traveling stock companies at the Lyceum; the Detroit Symphony Orchestra was well established. Detroiters saw their first electric advertising signs. Like the rest of America, they were reading Edward Bellamy's 1888 novel, *Looking Backward,* which told them that by the year 2000 there would be no rich, no poor, no social divisions, and no war anywhere in the world.[24]

Modern bicycles replaced the precarious high-wheelers. Horse-drawn streetcars became a thing of the past as trolleys powered by copper wires strung down the middle of the streets were put into service. But strolling remained a sociable mode of transport; the city was still small enough that many recognized Labadie as he sauntered down the wide avenues, a striking figure in black and flowing tie, his wide felt hat slouched jauntily over his collar-length dark hair. The city's pet anarchist was sufficiently legendary that mail from Gompers addressed only to "Joseph A. Labadie, Detroit, Mich.," was promptly delivered.[25]

As the decade of the 1890s dawned, things were looking up for the Labadies. A stroke of enormous good fortune had befallen them. Jo and his sister-in-law, Mary June, had been struggling with the bureaucracy for years to obtain a government disability pension for Sophie's father. Once again, he saw no conflict between agitating for an ideal anarchist future and reaping government benefits in the here and now. Blinded by a mine explosion at Vicksburg during the Civil War, Joseph Archambeau was living in the Government Insane Asylum in Washington, D.C. Shortly before dying in 1890, he was granted the astonishing sum of more than $11,000 as back pension. Sophie and her two sisters each received over $2,500 from his estate. Their mother, divorced for thirty-four years, was not a legal heir according to court documents.[26]

Jo and Sophie paid off a $880 mortgage on the cottage they built in 1886 using the eight-hour day system. They were living there in cramped quarters with four-year-old Laura Euphrosyne, one-year-old Charlotte An-toinette, Sophie's mother, and an elderly aunt. They began plans for building a two-story house on the front part of the lot at 74 (later 2306) Buchanan Street, near Fourteenth Street, in the northwest section of the city populated mainly by Americans and British Americans. Its design provided for six small bedrooms, thought necessary by Labadie in order to be "sufficiently commodious to accommodate any of the family whom misfortune might overtake." Predictably, many needy relatives were lured by this provision. Sophie's mother, a demanding and domineering woman, was ensconced for ten years. "All my little spare time that I want to myself I must spend running my legs off to gratify her whims," Sophie sighed.[27] In planning the house, Labadie followed his exhortation to workers, "The best the world affords is none too good for you" (the motto was on cards he passed out). It was an impressive abode for a working-class family, costing more than $1,500. The Labadies had to borrow money to complete it. Over subsequent years, the large parlor with sliding dividing doors resounded to lively debate by a long procession of the nation's radicals. Perhaps the most significant space for the purposes of history was the attic, where Sophie conscientiously stored all the labor or radical materials that came into Jo's hands.

Joseph Archambeau had died at a most convenient time for his daughter and son-in-law. Now forty, with a household of six to support, Labadie lost his job at the *Sun*. Joseph Buchanan, working for the American Press Association in New York City in 1890, tried to get him a job as news editor in Buffalo. This once-militant Knights' official and labor publisher had been forced to give up the Chicago *Labor Enquirer* for lack of funds. He, too, had been profoundly shaken by the Haymarket executions and continuing disintegration of the Order. As with Labadie, these upheavals had knocked much of the fight out of him. He now declared himself an "opportunist" and, asking the impossible, solicited articles from Jo which would "give offense to none—save, probably, the ultra monopolist." In time, Buchanan and Powderly, once bitter enemies, reconciled and Powderly dismissed the ugly showdown that had shaken the Minneapolis convention as the result of a "misunderstanding."[28]

Sometime around 1890, Labadie was hired by the *Detroit News,* where he worked his way up from typesetter to labor news and general assignment reporter. He called it the "most congenial" job he ever had. The *News,* which treated labor and radical movements with commendable objectivity, not only allowed him an occasional editorial, but even let him loose with "Cranky Notions" columns, which, as always, he did not tone down for the market.[29]

Increasingly, Detroiters were coming to regard Labadie as a sort of charming eccentric, cantankerous and irreverent, but venerable. Commonly referred to as "The Gentle Anarchist," he favored calling himself "Injun Jo" or the "Ole Ojibway" and was slow to correct those who mistook him for a genuine half-breed. He enjoyed his status as a town character, one of Detroit's municipal attractions. He liked to be liked. It was "getting to be a fad here to have me at fashionable churches and clubs to talk radical social questions," he glowed to George Schilling in 1895. One of the first invitations came in 1892 from his friend, Robert Y. Ogg, an AFL activist and former state legislator, who asked him to give a speech titled "No Government" to the Civic Club of the Plymouth Congregational Church, which was involved in the Social Gospel movement of the era. It was intended to balance a previous lecture on "The Science of Government." But when some "pillars of the church" protested against an anarchist speaking in the chapel, the young pastor, Reverend L. Morgan Wood, got cold feet. Labadie showed up anyway to say he had no hard feelings, and all three Detroit papers thought that was nice.[30]

The church-goers reaction was extraordinarily mild, considering the unfortunate timing of the invitation. Only four months before, on July 23, 1892, anarchist Alexander Berkman had attempted to assassinate Henry Clay Frick, chairman of the Carnegie Steel Company, and ignited another Red Scare. The twenty-two-year-old Russian-born revolutionary planned the deed in revenge for Frick's brutal crushing of a massive strike that month at the company's Homestead, Pennsylvania, plant. Berkman's accomplice and lover was Emma Goldman, a young seamstress from Lithuania and a protégée of the infamous Johann Most. In one of the nation's most ferocious confrontations between capital and labor, Frick had hired three hundred Pinkerton agents to protect non-union strikebreakers. Both workers and Pinkertons were killed in a raging riverfront battle. As a result, Frick persuaded the governor to send in eight thousand National Guardsmen to impose martial law so he could re-open the factory.

Frick's use of the Pinkertons and his determination to smash the union at any cost evoked much public support for the strikers. Berkman's attempt to kill Frick was, however, nearly universally condemned, even by the Homestead strikers. Johann Most, of all people, repudiated Berkman's violent tactics and even suggested the would-be assassin might have been Frick's man, staging the attack to win sympathy. But Most's motives themselves were suspect. He not only fancied himself Berkman's rival for the affections of Emma Goldman, who was half his age (Most was forty-six), but was himself in danger of being arrested as Berkman's accomplice. Outraged by the perfidy of her one-time mentor, the volatile Goldman challenged Most at one of his lectures to prove his accusations. When he mumbled some comment about a "hysterical woman," she pulled a horsewhip from under her long, gray cloak, lashed him repeatedly across the face and neck, then broke the lash over her knee and threw the pieces at him. The incident, understandably, created a huge sensation.[31]

Labadie, iconoclastic as ever, challenged the public sympathy in support of the strikers. In a *Detroit News* "Cranky Notions" column on July 17, he condemned the strikers who greeted Pinkertons with a volley of shots, poured oil around their barges and set them ablaze, then stoned and clubbed the agents after their surrender. He saw the violence as a simple riot. It did not challenge the great monopolies, the special privileges, tariffs, patent system, or property in land that enriched Andrew Carnegie and his lieutenant, Frick. The violence represented no protest against injustice such as that mounted by the Haymarket anarchists. Its origin was a demand for higher wages by the unionized workers at the plant, an already well-paid minority. The Chicago anarchists had been within their legal rights in organizing a demonstration in support of the eight-hour day, yet were hanged. The Homestead strikers were being glorified for defying the law. Yet "Have not men the right to hire whomever they can as watchmen? Is not one citizen as much entitled as another to employment whether he be non-union or Pinkerton?" he remonstrated—a view that must have horrified many of Labadie's labor comrades.[32]

Berkman, on the other hand, who was widely condemned for his assassination attempt, Labadie saw as the prototypical idealistic revolutionary: "the likes of him are the John Browns of the proletarian class." His rash act was a futile reaction against the laws that benefitted "czar Frick." "To kill off the Fricks will no more prevent the robbery of the masses than the killing of the Berkmans will prevent violence and assassination. . . . Where there are Fricks there will be Berkmans," he wrote in a second *News* column. Gompers also spoke up on Berkman's behalf, campaigning for his pardon as he had campaigned on behalf of the Haymarket anarchists.[33]

Even though by then most American anarchists, like Labadie, had repudiated acts of violence, the public's well-established dread of anarchism was escalating. Berkman's attack lit a fuse of public indignation. Then alarming news from Europe brought anti-anarchist rhetoric to an explosion. A series of terrorist attacks attributed to anarchists began with a bomb thrown in a Barcelona theater in 1893 which killed thirty people. French President Sadi Carnot was assassinated in 1894 after a wave of bombings in Paris. The premier of Spain, Canovas del Castillo, was murdered in 1897, and

Empress Elizabeth of Austria the following year. Italian King Humbert I was assassinated in 1900 by an Italian anarchist who hatched the plot in Paterson, New Jersey. That same year, anarchists fired on the Prince of Wales and the Shah of Persia. Attempting to justify public revulsion with scientific "fact," Italian criminologist Cesare Lombroso lumped anarchists with other "born" criminals, who could be recognized by such "atavistic" traits as large ears and jaws, thin upper lips and "a ferocious look."[34]

The tide of blood-letting reached America when Detroit-born Leon Czolgosz, an avowed anarchist, shot President William McKinley in 1901, just six months after his second inauguration. By now, few doubted that anarchists were by nature murderous monsters—not at all, as Labadie wanted them to think, "like other folks." The individualist anarchists, who shunned dramatic acts, had no way to distinguish themselves from the assassins and terrorists. Their still, small voices, rarely raised except in cerebral debates, were utterly drowned out by practitioners of the "propaganda of the deed." While Labadie and his colleagues argued in ivory towers about egoism versus natural rights, their action-prone competitors, mostly Europeans, were making headlines and history. Public outrage prodded Congress to pass its first anti-anarchist law, prohibiting anyone "who disbelieves in or who is opposed to all organized governments" from entering the United States. Republican Senator Joseph Roswell Hawley offered a thousand dollars for a "good shot at an anarchist." Senators George Graham Vest, a Democrat, and George Frisbee Hoar, a Republican, proposed that all anarchists be imprisoned on some island.[35]

Despite the nation's continuing alarm, Detroit accepted Labadie, Robert Reitzel, Sam Goldwater (Democratic mayoral candidate in 1895) and other declared anarchists in its midst with no hint of physical threat against them. When the *Evening News* approached "Detroit's Representative Anarchist" for comment on Senator Hoar's bill, Labadie jocularly suggested Belle Isle, Detroit's playground, for the anarchist penal colony. Witty retorts, however, could not squelch public dismay. Labadie had carved a niche in the city's heart, but his sweet reasonableness exacted a price. Audiences in respectable venues might listen calmly to his expositions, nod a few times in assent, and then comment that, of course, Jo Labadie was not a real anarchist. Gompers, in his autobiography, tells of one listener, who commented, after Labadie opposed overthrow of the government by force in a speech at New York's Cooper Union, "You are a hell of an anarchist." "Yes, that's the kind of an anarchist I am," Labadie calmly replied.[36]

Reporters may have thought they were doing Labadie a favor by describing him as a "mild-mannered parlor anarchist," "not a practicing anarchist," or "an imposter," but being thought quaint and quirky made the middle-aged rebel uneasy. When his friends John Burton and Henry Robinson questioned his degree of radicalism, he asked plaintively, "What in the world am I anyway? It is generally supposed that an anarchist is a radical among radicals."[37]

★ 14 ★

A Humbling Job

Try to learn, my comrade true,
Hear the other side.
There're lots that may be new to you,
There're lots that's good you may taboo,
There're lots you may now misconstrue
Or not discern, my comrade true;
Hear the other side.

FROM "HEAR THE OTHER SIDE," DOGGEREL FOR THE
UNDERDOG

The prosperity of the early 1890s was short-lived. Grover Cleveland's election on a progressive Democratic ticket in 1892 seemed to promise better times ahead, but the stock market crash the following year plunged the nation into a long and terrible depression, worse than those of 1873 and 1882. The series of panics, crashes, and depressions was beginning to seem as inevitable as natural disasters like floods or tornadoes.

Millions were jobless. On Easter Sunday 1894, Jacob Coxey's ragtag "army" of the unemployed began a march from Ohio to Washington, D.C., to demand that the federal government create work building roads. Most of Detroit's big industries shut down. The city's poor fund was exhausted. One-third of the workers were unemployed, many roaming the streets carrying their own picks and shovels in a desperate search for jobs.[1] Alarmed by the misery and suffering, Mayor Hazen Pingree begged owners of vacant land to allow the jobless to grow food crops there. He set up a charity fund for seed and plows, with Labadie's pal Judson Grenell as treasurer. He even auctioned off his favorite Kentucky driving horse to raise money. The mayor's "potato patch" crusade was a huge success, hailed throughout the nation for its originality, and imitated by other hard-hit cities. Becoming increasingly radical, Pingree attacked those with vast accumulations of wealth as "more dangerous to the liberties of our republic than if all the Anarchists, Socialists, and Nihilists of Europe were let loose on our shores."[2]

In the midst of this severe depression, Labadie, now forty-four, suffered another setback in his long battle with illness and lost his job at the *News*. He believed the foul air in printing plants played a role in his poor health. "Times are very hard and I cannot make enough money to keep myself going," he lamented to George Schilling. All of Sophie's legacy, and more, had been spent on the house.[3]

Unemployed and pressured by precarious financial straits, Labadie accepted what he could get—a job as foreman over a gang of men laying pipe for the water commission, a civil service position. This tidbit of security was probably wangled by friends in the city administration like Grenell and Robert Oakman. Although desperate for cash, Labadie had hesitated. He was already squirming in the role of pet radical, and loath "to put myself in any way subject to petty politicians who would presume to tie a little red ribbon about my neck and lead me around like a French poodle," he later maintained. He foresaw that working for the government would be a serious embarrassment for an anarchist. Anarchist leader Benjamin Tucker, however, saw no harm in it and noted that "I make it a point to get all that I can out of my oppressors, provided I do not thereby too seriously impair my power of struggle against them."[4] The job, which Labadie accepted in 1893, lacked prestige and stimulation, but it was steady, not too hard, and relatively healthy. He ended up being employed by the water department for the next thirty years, never again working full-time as a printer or reporter.

Being accused of compromising his convictions was only part of the humiliation Labadie endured while working for the water board into his seventies. The Detroit typographical union withdrew his membership on the grounds that he was no longer working in the trade.[5] Although the action was logical, it was a sad blow for Labadie to have his twenty-six-year formal affiliation with unions so abruptly severed.

A bloody labor confrontation involving Polish ditch diggers in the spring of 1894 compounded the ambiguity of Labadie's water board employment. Three hundred strikers, mostly Poles, tried to prevent excavation for a water main because they believed a new piece-rate system would provide them less than half their previous wages. Some strikers attacked the project foreman with a shovel and, in the melee that ensued, three laborers were fatally shot by police and a score of persons were seriously injured, including the foreman and the sheriff. The Detroit press castigated these often-scorned new immigrants as "riotous Poles" for their attack on law and order. It was alleged that they had been incited to riot by anarchist agitators. At mass meetings of sympathy by the Trades Council and German Central Labor Union the piece-rate system was denounced, but the digging continued with non-Polish workers protected by two hundred armed guards until the job was completed, after which the water commission voted to revert to the old pay policy.[6]

As Labadie was supervising a gang of Polish ditch diggers on Monroe Avenue that summer, trousers splashed with clay, shirt collar unbuttoned, hat disreputably askew, a roving reporter from the *News* took the opportunity to taunt him. Remarking on the change from Labadie's once-immaculate appearance in the newsroom, he inquired how an anarchist could reconcile his convictions with becoming "a minion of the government." With a "genial smile" and the disingenuous reply that "government has nothing to do with digging a ditch," Labadie terminated the discussion by jumping into the excavation and demonstrating the proper way to pound sand. But he still had to deal with those who accused him of selling out. A socialist candidate for mayor, Meiko Meyer, sneered that this "fake labor leader" had been bought up by Pingree.[7]

By the 1890s, most of the old guard of radical activists, including Grenell, had dropped out of the labor movement. The discord leading to the slow disintegration of the Knights of Labor had disillusioned many. Strike failures and the long depression begun in 1893 further discouraged workers from looking to unions for social remedies. A declining proportion of Detroit workers held union membership. Those who remained active were looking for the kind of tangible economic gains the AFL offered, not the visionary transformation of society its predecessors had sought.[8]

Although he regretted the loss of his old labor comradeship in Detroit, Labadie was heartened that he remained highly respected in national labor circles. Neither the involuntary divorce from his union nor his self-appointed role as controversialist of the first order stopped labor editors from seeking him out; it may even have increased his attractiveness as a colorful and provocative contributor. P. J. McGuire, the rabble-rousing head of the United Brotherhood of Carpenters and Joiners of America, a power in the AFL and quite a radical himself, asked Labadie to write for *The Carpenter* on "cranky carpenters," "the danger of too much state power," and why unions should stay away from politics. Labadie's long-time verbal sparring partner Henry Robinson, now Michigan Commissioner of Labor, had him contribute a nine-page section for the Bureau of Labor's 1893 annual report outlining "the different 'isms' in sociology"—Georgeism (the single tax), socialism, communism, and anarchism. As a frequent columnist for Frank K. Foster's influential *Labor Leader,* Labadie inveighed against the powers of the state and blamed the poor for supporting a system that allowed the rich to rob them. He continued to urge workers to cultivate the selfish principle of life— "When every individual is so selfish that he will not let any one impose upon him, the laboring man will be respected."[9]

When Gompers began publishing the *American Federationist* in 1894, he commissioned an article from Labadie, "Trades Unionism as I Understand It." As Gompers knew he would, Labadie expressed complete harmony with the AFL principle that unions should stick to matters peculiar to their own trade—especially how to increase wages—and not involve themselves in the problems of other trades or political issues. At the time, many unionists were panting to officially support the Populist party or create an independent party. Gompers confided to Labadie that he considered the pressure, which was dividing the labor movement, "not an unmixed evil." He hoped the political squabbling would bring matters to a head and finally be resolved to his liking, thereby saving the AFL from future involvement in partisan politics.[10]

The following year, the *American Federationist* was the forum for a lively debate on political action and socialism, in which Labadie had his say. It came just after an upheaval in the organization in which Gompers ended up both winner and loser. Daniel De Leon, who had assumed leadership of the fading SLP in 1890 and brought it new vigor, launched an all-out attack against the AFL, which he called "at best a cross between a windbag and a rope of sand." Any labor organization that did not struggle exclusively for the overthrow of capitalism was, in De Leon's view, reactionary. At union meetings, flare-ups between AFL loyalists and De Leon followers who wanted to break away were frequent. Tempers were running hot.[11]

The radical mood prevalent during the economic crisis of 1893 was pervasive enough to enable the socialists to score a tremendous victory at the AFL convention in Chicago that year and gain acceptance of a plank calling for "collective ownership by the people of all means of production and distribution." Gompers was clever enough not to oppose publicly the so-called Plank 10, but by a series of cunning maneuvers the AFL leadership managed to get it repealed at the following year's convention. It was replaced in 1894 by a resolution offered by Labadie's friend and fellow anarchist, August McCraith, calling for the abolition of monopoly land ownership and for property title to be based entirely on "occupancy and use." The term was straight out of an anarchist textbook. Convinced that the AFL leader had plotted to defeat Plank 10, infuriated socialists exacted their revenge by persuading delegates to oust Gompers from the presidency for the only time in thirty-nine years (he was reelected in 1895). McCraith was appointed AFL secretary, a high official position, and made sure Labadie's thoughts continued to be aired in its journal.[12]

Though not directly engaged in union activities, Labadie had no shortage of vehicles for his views. He expounded them in a parade of Detroit labor papers that sprang up and blossomed briefly before withering when cash nourishment ran out: the *Industrial Gazette, Citizen, Sentinel, Printer,* and *Street Railway Employee's Gazette.* Outdoor work and exercise had reduced his weight, improved his sleep, and restored his health. During the cold months, he worked inside as clerk of the leak and storage yard section of the water commission. He earned a modest but dependable $900 a year.[13]

One day in August 1897, the daily routine at the water works was interrupted by a visit from Prince Peter Kropotkin, the legendary Russian geographer and revolutionary anarchist. The fifty-five-year-old Kropotkin, in Detroit to attend the annual meeting of the American Association for the Advancement of Science, wanted to meet the forty-seven-year-old author of "Cranky Notions," which he had read in *Liberty.* Speaking in fluent English, he told Labadie about his special mission in North America—to gather data for a great papier-mâché globe of the world, one hundred twenty feet in diameter, with rivers, lakes, oceans, mountains, and cities, on a scale of five miles to the inch, which he and fellow geographer/anarchist Élisée Reclus were constructing for the Paris Exposition of 1900.

As Labadie conducted Kropotkin through the engine room, he noted that his visitor—"a most engaging man"—was small, but had "a large head, big whiskers, smiling eyes." Kropotkin seemed nervous, making jerky, surprised movements, "as is an animal that is always hunted." The behavior was consistent with his hounded life. As a young man, Kropotkin had advocated the formation of armed peasant bands, been arrested in 1874 for "nihilistic" activities, and imprisoned in the fortress of Ss. Peter and Paul in St. Petersburg. Russian prison officials nevertheless permitted him to complete a scientific work on the glaciers of Finland. He made a dramatic escape from a military hospital, fled to England, then Switzerland, was expelled, and then was imprisoned by the French. By the time of his release in 1886, he had turned into a respectable and scholarly theorist, who believed that he could further the revolution more effectively with the printed word than by violent acts.[14]

As the foremost anarchist philosopher of his time, Kropotkin was keenly interested in how the doctrine was developing in America. He called himself an anarcho-communist, but read and had written for libertarian journals of all persuasions, including Tucker's *Liberty,* Albert Parsons's *Alarm,* and Johann Most's *Freiheit.* He was eager to meet his fellow contributors. Soon after chatting with Labadie, he called on Most in Buffalo. Tucker, who disparaged the communist anarchists as authoritarians, and contended that Kropotkin had no business calling himself an anarchist, nevertheless visited the Russian nobleman in New York.[15]

Like Labadie, Kropotkin had sought to base his philosophy on the principles of natural science. His observations of animal life and village communities, however, led him to the conclusion that mutual aid, not the Darwinian struggle for existence, had the greatest impact on the survival of the species and its evolution. Where Labadie saw egoism and competitiveness as the driving forces in the natural world, Kropotkin found solidarity and cooperation. Humankind would recognize that it was through helping each other that all would survive and prosper. In his idealized society of the future, there would be no private property or poverty; no one would be compelled to work but nearly everyone would choose to; and goods and services would be distributed freely by self-governing communes according to need, even to those who had contributed no share of the labor. Kropotkin himself was so ethical, benevolent, and unegotistical that it was said that if all were like him, no government or restraint would be necessary and anarchism would be the only possible system.[16]

Kropotkin's first visit to the United States and Canada was a huge success. He delivered papers at the Toronto meeting of the British Association for the Advancement of Science and the National Geographic Society in Washington, D.C., and spoke on both science and anarchism in crowded halls seating thousands. The communist anarchist movement was growing, due largely to his influence, and prominent liberals flocked to meet him, as well as such unlikely candidates as Andrew Carnegie (Kropotkin declined the opportunity) and the widow of Confederate leader Jefferson Davis. As he traveled from coast to coast during his four-month trip, the anarchist prince was everywhere lauded as a mild and gentle man, with the manners of a "polished gentleman." Predictably, he was described as "anything but the typical anarchist."[17]

As the century came to a close, even the well-to-do and well connected began to involve themselves in "constant discussion" of the ills of society, as Jane Addams chronicled in *Twenty Years at Hull House.* She recalled the many Chicago clubs of the 1890s whose members enthusiastically debated the "new social science," rejecting as unworthy all discussion except that which "went to the root of things."[18] Their membership included many prominent citizens, who, shaken by fears of worker unrest engendered by the 1886 Haymarket riot and 1892 Homestead strike, had concluded that the way to avert revolution was to exchange views openly with all shades of radicals.

Detroit was lively with similar gatherings. Labadie, always keen to study, debate, and propagandize, was in his element. With no other outlet for his leadership qualities, he threw himself into promoting a profusion of these discussion groups that arose in the late 1890s—the Social Science Club, Qui Vive Club, Fellowcraft Club, Mohawk Bimetallic Club (advocating both gold and silver as a monetary standard), and the Labor Exchange Association.[19]

Although Labadie always identified himself with the working people, he rejected the concept of class struggle so essential to Marxist ideology. Because a man was an industrialist did not necessarily make him an enemy. Labadie could even bring himself to refer to "our capitalistic brothers," as he did when defending the participation of Gompers, John Mitchell, and other labor leaders in the controversial National Civic Federation. Organized in 1900, it sought to settle industrial disputes by means of discussions among prominent labor, business, and public figures, a previously untried cooperative policy. Some workers were outraged that their leaders would consort with the likes of Cyrus McCormick, J. Ogden Armour or Louis F. Swift, capitalists whose companies were notoriously anti-union. They saw the federation as collaborating with the enemy. Labadie, with his unshakable faith in the power of discussion to bring about a just consensus, responded that the labor movement should be represented "in every possible place where delegates can get a foothold. . . . If we have words of justice and mercy and humanity don't our capitalistic brothers need them as much as our brothers and sisters of toil?"[20]

Many Detroit businessmen, politicians, and clergymen, too, began grappling with the questions of social injustice and the legitimacy of working-class grievances by means of discussion groups. With the progressive Mayor Pingree in the vanguard, they now saw the advantage of negotiating with union leaders and backing liberal reforms. Meanwhile, few of the old guard still held office in any of the local unions. A loyal core of craft unionists retained their membership even through the severe mid 1890s depression, but they represented an ever-decreasing percentage of the work force. One-fifth of Detroit's workers had been members of either the Knights of Labor or craft unions, or both, in the peak year of 1886. Six years later, the figure had dropped to 8.2 percent, and was to continue its decline in subsequent years.[21]

The labor activists of the 1880s who had turned away from the labor movement in disillusionment, joined by many of the rank and file, increasingly put their hopes for social reconstruction in the new coterie of enlightened civic leaders. In late 1895, Labadie's parlor resounded with the give-and-take of one such discussion group, assembled for the earnest purpose of collecting facts on economic matters. Members divided themselves into three sections—assigned to land, machinery, or money. From this informal get-together, Labadie soon founded the Social Science Club, so successful that it began with a membership of more than one hundred and met weekly at the St. James Hotel on the corner of Bates Street and Cadillac Square, with *The People* as its official organ. He promoted joining it as a matter of self-interest for all who wanted to avert "a social cataclysm." At a time when "the hungry social outcast and the rich glare with hatred into each others' faces" and "violence of every description" abounded, businessmen, professionals, civic leaders, and workers would find it useful to study the laws of social harmony and economic equity, club president Labadie urged.[22]

With social problems newly fashionable, Labadie was able to enlist for his board of managers such prominent personages as Levi Barbour, a regent of the University of Michigan, and Homer Warren, later United States postmaster general. Debates at club meetings were so animated that hotel residents complained of the noise. Members heard such speeches as "How Would You Uplift the Masses?" "The Main Error of the State Socialists," "What Can We Do for the Criminal?" "Free Water: Is It Just and Equitable?" and "Should Women Be Allowed to Vote?" Ten women attended the latter event; to Labadie's disappointment, none spoke up. Some working-class members complained about the "dilettante" aspect of the club, peopled as it was with lawyers, ministers, and the occasional "dress suit and display of diamonds." There was muttering when the elegantly attired Homer Warren stopped by on his way to a charity ball to read a paper, "How to Procure Work for the Unemployed." Disputing that there were in fact 25,000 jobless at the moment in Detroit, he noted smugly that possessions were in any case a burden and the rich were no happier than the poor.[23]

Labadie was joined in the endeavor by Judson Grenell, Captain John M. McGregor, and other former labor activists. By 1897, he initiated intriguing proposals to set up a labor exchange system as a substitute for money and a voluntary court where disputes could be settled without recourse to the government courts. But it was a tame comedown from the grander endeavors of his past. Middle age had found his youthful idealism severely tested by reality. Nearing fifty, Labadie was no longer willing to be thought "a kind of mild lunatic." He had come to the conclusion, as he told club members, that "You cannot reach people's reason except by mild manners, earnestness and a clear presentation of your own case."[24]

He intended to be pragmatic and proclaimed himself ready to join any group striving for greater freedom. He had supported Cleveland in 1888, as he wrote in *Liberty,* because Cleveland ran on a program of tariff reduction, and free trade was "anarchy in the exchange of products." He joined Richard Trevellick and Social Gospel preacher Reverend L. Morgan Wood in speaking on behalf of Mayor Pingree in his 1893 campaign. When William Jennings Bryan fought an anti-imperialism campaign against McKinley in 1900, Labadie considered stumping for him. Tucker and *Liberty*'s "plumb line" anarchists were horrified at his compromise with the ballot. Tucker caustically pointed out that with Labadie campaigning for him, Bryan's chance of election would be diminished.[25]

Faced with heavy topics and the requirement to study them, some Social Science Club members lost interest and stopped paying their dues. The group disbanded in 1897 and was quickly replaced by the Qui Vive Club, featuring judges, doctors, professors, and legislators as speakers. Meeting in Bamlet Hall at Grand River and Rowland Street every Monday evening, its objectives were to discuss questions of the day, promote truth, justice, and liberty, encourage tolerance for the opinions of others, and "cement members in bonds of fellowship." Dues were four dollars a year. Chairman Labadie advertised the club as "no ritual, no flummery; no flapdoodleism. . . . Just trying to get at the truth." At his insistence, women were now eligible and could "talk and smoke and swear and put their feet upon the chairs" just like the men.[26]

Even at the classier clubs, attended by society ladies and the elite, it became fashionable to invite Labadie and other radicals to speak. He told *Liberty* readers his reception was always "most respectful . . . and cordial." By 1895, trustees of the progressive Plymouth Congregational Church had a change of heart and invited Labadie to give the lecture on anarchism they had canceled three years before. Although the *Detroit Evening Press* suggested the church be draped with red bunting while it aired "this poisonous mental disease," sixty parishioners showed up on December 23 to hear Labadie deliver an hour-long disquisition on the ideas of Spencer, Warren, Tucker, Proudhon, Kropotkin, and, of course, Labadie. He explained that anarchism was "a purely negative philosophy," with "no cut and dried rules for the guidance of society outside of that embraced in the word liberty." He compared the Christian ideal to the anarchistic ideal; both envisioned a perfect society where prisons and other restrictive institutions would wither away. The audience listened attentively and Labadie recorded that his address received "hearty applause."[27]

Working closely with Labadie in several of his discussion club ventures was John Shillady, a traveling salesman in millinery, then in his early twenties. He became a protégé of sorts and was elected Qui Vive president in 1897. Over the next twenty years, he aimed a barrage of letters at his Detroit friend, some two hundred in all, from various hotels. As a New York social worker in 1918, he was hired by the ten-year-old National Association for the Advancement of Colored People (NAACP) as its executive secretary. Like most of the organization's early officers, Shillady was white. He participated in an intensive anti-lynching drive in 1918, and the following year in Texas was attacked and severely beaten by what the local deputy sheriff called "red-blooded white men." The attack left him psychologically unable to continue his duties, and he resigned in 1920.[28]

Shillady's attraction to the middle-aged Detroit radical was doubtless deepened by Labadie's outspoken hatred of race prejudice, a not-so-common phenomenon even in labor and reform movements. Although blacks had joined the Knights of Labor nationwide in numbers approximately equal to their share of the total population, they were commonly organized into "colored locals," and Terence Powderly tolerated discriminatory practices in fear of alienating Southern Knights. By the late 1890s, Gompers, too, refused to fight Jim Crow unionism because trade unions might shun the AFL if forced to eliminate discrimination.[29]

By his own testimony, Labadie challenged segregated unionism, organized black workers, fought to get their jobs back when they were discharged for racial reasons, served as pallbearer for a black shoemaker, and considered a black "Mammy" one of his best friends. He was unusual in his frequency of association with blacks, who in 1894 represented less than 1 percent of the state's inhabitants. Wayne County, which included Detroit, had only 4,150 blacks, most of them descendants of escaped slaves. Excluded from most industrial jobs, they had been denied schooling with white children until 1869 and only permitted to vote since 1870.[30]

By the standards of the period, Labadie was devoid of bigotry. Yet he held the view that blacks were "down on organized labor," a common belief among unionists, especially because they were often recruited as strikebreakers. He also betrayed a certain patronizing quality, reflective of the times, in a story he told of coming upon a black teamster, overcome by the heat, sitting on the curb. A crowd of people had collected, gawking, yet no one moved to help. Labadie rubbed alcohol on his head, washed his face with cold water, and, when the man had recovered, helped him on his wagon. A classic Good Samaritan act, one would conclude, until his concluding remark: "I felt no humiliation."[31]

Soon after Michigan troops left for Cuba after the outbreak of the "splendid little" Spanish-American War in 1898, which ushered in the era of American imperialism, the Labadies finally had their third child, a son. Sophie was forty-seven; Jo, forty-eight. They named him Laurance Cleophis, after Sophie's mother and Jo's father. Sophie wanted to consecrate him "to the service of God" and asked her childhood priest to pray that Laurance would become "A worker in God's vineyard." Consistent with Jo's beliefs, however, Laurance was allowed the utmost freedom. His parents never told him "do this" or "do that."[32] As a result, he did pretty much what he liked throughout life and bitterly disappointed both parents. Yet it was Laurance Labadie who, after his father's death, harbored the flickering flame of individualist anarchism and carried it into the modern age.

⋆ 15 ⋆

Jabs from Right and Left

You who pretended friendship and hurt my heart with
insult;
You who loved me with a wealth of words and hated me
in your heart; . . .
Think you I clutter my heart with trashy hate and gloat in
it? . . .
Think you I do not know that more than ever you need
the good that I can do? . . .
Unload yourselves, beloved ones! . . .
I'm wistfully waiting word from you that all is well.
    FROM "TO THOSE WHO HAVE DONE ME HURT,"
    SING SONGS AND SOME THAT DON'T

In 1897, the infamous Emma Goldman, co-conspirator and
lover of would-be assassin Alexander Berkman, arrived in Detroit. Denounced in the press as a monster and a menace, the "Anarchist Queen"
was on a cross-country lecture tour preaching Kropotkin-style communist
anarchism and "free love." Her tour was hugely successful. The sensation-
alism surrounding her, the sarcastic, "sledgehammer" speaking style and
inflammatory topics, plus the exciting possibility that police would break up
the meeting, guaranteed large audiences.[1]

Berkman was now incarcerated in a Pennsylvania prison, serving
fourteen years for his attempt to assassinate Henry Clay Frick. Goldman had
not been implicated as his accomplice. In the intervening five years, she had
developed into a skilled agitator and orator, an organizer of mass meetings
and hunger demonstrations, and had served a year in the penitentiary for
"inciting to riot."[2] In a few years, she was to become the leading figure in

the American anarchist movement. Robert Reitzel, the German anarchist and editor in Detroit, bedridden with spinal tuberculosis and near death, had invited his dear friend Goldman to appear before the city's Central Labor Union. She would speak to this organization of German-born workers at its annual November 11 Haymarket memorial meeting.

Although the young Goldman was a Johann Most protégé, Labadie must have greeted the arrival of America's most renowned anarchist with as much anticipation as he had the visit of Most fourteen years before. Reverend H. S. McCowan, the young pastor of the Plymouth Tabernacle, where Labadie had lectured on anarchism two years before, told Labadie and Robert Ogg that he was eager to "take in the spirit of the whole affair." The three agreed to attend together. Like his predecessor, Reverend L. Morgan Wood, McGowan was caught up in the Social Gospel movement, determined to keep abreast of all manner of social-reform efforts. New in the post, he already had invited trade unionists to discuss social and economic questions at the Friday evening prayer meetings. Only the week before, the prominent Christian Socialist George D. Herron had spoken to the congregation.[3]

When the three arrived, they were disappointed to learn that Goldman was going to speak in German, which she had learned in her childhood as a Lithuanian Jew, and which none of them understood. Turner Hall was packed, the audience soon intent on the dramatic oratory of the fiery twenty-eight-year-old revolutionist. Small of stature, she looked almost girlish in her shirtwaist, except for hair severely knotted in back, penetrating blue eyes, and her signature pince-nez hanging on a cord. The Socialist *Maennerchor* (men's singing group) had refused to perform for an anarchist, but it was replaced by a children's chorus and the reading of a revolutionary poem honoring the Chicago martyrs.[4]

When Goldman learned the forty-seven-year-old Labadie, a comrade of sorts, was in the audience, she had him sent for and asked him to arrange a Detroit appearance for her in English. McCowan wanted to have her at the Tabernacle. Labadie took him to meet Goldman. Surprised to learn that she would be speaking from a pulpit, Goldman joked that she might "roast" McCowan in his own church. He said he could take it, she was free to say what she liked. He expected his parishioners, as good Christians, to be charitable to her.[5]

When word got out of this invitation, the papers reacted with sensational headlines, as Goldman remembered it: FREE LOVER IN A DETROIT PULPIT---CONGREGATIONAL CHURCH TO BE TURNED INTO HOTBED OF ANARCHY AND FREE LOVE. There were warnings of a revolt by church members.

Although Goldman delighted in mocking religion, she offered McCowan a chance to renege. He said he was determined to uphold free expression. The meeting duly took place on November 19, 1897. Initially, the audience of 1,500 listened respectfully while Goldman explained the "economic side of anarchism," avoiding religious and sexual matters out of concern for the pastor. But once the questions began, she pulled no punches. If God existed, he had botched the job. It was commendable to kill the Russian czar although not an "ineffectual" American president. The right to love whomever one pleased should replace the coercion of marriage laws.[6]

The congregation erupted in shocked outrage, Goldman recorded. Press accounts termed it a "lurid spectacle." The resulting uproar became national news. Famous agnostic orator Robert G. Ingersoll proclaimed all anarchists insane and called McCowan foolish for letting one share his pulpit. Some parishioners complained that the sanctity of the church had been violated. Three deacons resigned and church trustees censured McCowan. Goldman, in her autobiography written many years later, claimed McCowan resigned and ended up preaching in a mining town; for his part, Labadie reported at the time that only eleven people left the church and the pastor was expecting an increase in membership.[7]

An admirer of forceful and outspoken women, Labadie found Goldman's frankness refreshing, as he wrote in the *Detroit Sentinel.* He commended her audacity in denouncing "usurers . . . land grabbers . . . profit mongers face to face," for exposing hypocrisy and bringing bigots out into the open. He credited her with staying away from "the marriage question" until asked by a parishioner, and having only good words to say of Christ.[8]

A "very interesting person indeed," Labadie pronounced her, generous, knowledgeable, and engaged in valuable work. But he disagreed with her philosophically and probably squirmed in the face of her enthusiasm for sexual liberation and view of marriage as a form of prostitution. Labadie objected to coercion in all human relationships, but as a devoted husband and family man, he chose not to embroil himself in the "free love" crusade. He also acknowledged that Goldman was not his "ideal woman," and that he found her "as naive as a child." It is amusing to note that Goldman criticized Kropotkin for his naiveté, and that many made the same comment about Labadie himself.[9]

Goldman soon proved the accuracy of Labadie's judgment of naiveté. After self-professed anarchist Leon Czolgosz shot President McKinley in Buffalo on September 6, 1901, she passionately rushed to the assassin's defense. The country was hysterical over the murder, yet she idealized the unstable twenty-eight-year-old as a hero with a "beautiful soul." By then opposed to violence, she did not uphold his act, yet said she sympathized with "the poor unfortunate"—as she did also with the dying McKinley, whom she offered to nurse. Goldman was enraged when the majority of American anarchists, who now deplored such acts of violence, insisted that Czolgosz was simply mentally ill and totally ignorant of their philosophy. Even Johann Most and Lucy Parsons, Albert Parsons's widow, condemned the assassination. When Berkman wrote Goldman from prison that the deed lacked "social necessity" compared to his own attempt against a true "enemy of the people," Goldman broke down in sobs.[10]

Labadie, who joined in condemning the killing, was certain Czolgosz was not an anarchist. Indeed, the assassin, born in Detroit of Polish immigrant parents, seemed to know little of anarchism except that one of Goldman's lectures in Cleveland had thrilled him. He had followed her to Chicago, but behaved so strangely there that her comrades put out word that he was a spy. Doctors later concluded he was delusional, if not insane. But Goldman, like her former teacher Most, was a romantic rebel, tuned to the voice of feeling, not of reason. That she was damaging the entire anarchist movement by expressing sympathy for a terrorist, that radicals everywhere were in danger of being arrested or set upon by mobs, that she herself might be imprisoned did not deter her. Perhaps her emotional reaction was a form of misplaced maternalism. The "poor boy, condemned and deserted by all" must be taken under her protective wing. The "poor boy," in fact, was only four years her junior.[11]

The public, still reeling from the inflammatory publicity generated by the series of violent acts involving anarchists—the 1886 Haymarket bombing, the attack on Frick in 1892, and the wave of European assassinations at the end of the century—was once again plagued with fear and wrath, more convinced than ever that anarchism and terrorism went hand-in-hand. The assassin was thought to be the harbinger of a widespread anarchist conspiracy. The courageous, but impolitic, stand of anarchism's self-styled high priestess reinforced the apprehension. There were rumors that Czolgosz had acted as an agent of Kropotkin and Goldman. The new president, Theodore Roosevelt, dealt with the peril in his first message to Congress. He called for a war "not only against anarchists, but against all active and passive sympathizers with anarchists," all of whom were "morally accessory to murder before the fact." The anti-anarchist immigration legislation enacted in 1903, the first statute in United States history to exclude persons from entering the country because of their political beliefs, would not, however, have applied to the Detroit-born Czolgosz. It also did not distinguish between the philosophical anarchists like Labadie and those who advocated terrorism. Goldman and Berkman were deported in 1919 under this legislation.[12]

Despite Labadie's doubts about Goldman's modus operandi, he continued to support and defend her and to praise her self-sacrifice and courage in protesting social wrongs. He even compared her to Christ as "the butt for the ridicule, vituperation and brutality of every upholder of things as they are" in a letter to the *Windsor Record*. During the nearly three decades that she outraged the nation, no woman was more hounded and vilified. As antagonism to Goldman's message grew, police increasingly suppressed her lectures and were in turn denounced by free-speech advocates throughout the nation.[13]

When police prevented her from addressing Detroit's Central Labor Union in 1907, Labadie protested in the *Detroit News* that the police action not only deprived Goldman of her right to speak, but also violated the rights of hundreds of citizens who wanted to hear her. What especially shamed him, he wrote, was that he had bragged to comrades in more repressive cities that Detroit's police force was humane and liberal. Following Labadie's lead, the Detroit Federation of Labor declared the police conduct a menace to free speech. To the conservative *Windsor Evening Record,* however, Labadie was a "paradox," seemingly mild-mannered, yet ready to listen "with infantile enjoyment to the murderous fulminations of this hyena."[14]

As the century came to a close, the labor movement in Detroit continued losing ground. The depression of the 1890s was over and prosperity shone on the horizon. The new generation of labor leaders was increasingly leery of anything that smacked of radicalism and did not attend labor reform discussions by such speakers as Christian socialist George D. Herron, not to mention radicals like Goldman. With most union organizers confining themselves to the narrowest of economic aims, and little worker enthusiasm for the movement, the daily press stopped regular coverage of labor news.[15]

A last attempt was made to revive the labor press. The Building Trades Council, undeterred by the failure of other labor papers, started up the *Detroit Sentinel* as its official organ in May 1897, with Labadie as editor. Naturally, he welcomed the new weekly as a bully pulpit, a stimulating counterpoise to the water department ledgers of his workplace. Front-page articles by American anarchists ran alongside science, fashion, and cooking news. Department store ads jostled tributes to Thomas Jefferson ("Greatest of all Democrats; Enemy of Centralized Power"), Herbert Spencer, and John Stuart Mill. Labor news was augmented by columns promoting currency and land reform, the single tax, and enfranchisement of the Chinese, as well as Detroit's new Labor Exchange, where shirt collars, lamps, meal tickets, honey, and salmon were being exchanged for other goods with no money involved.[16]

"Cranky Notions" again had a temporary home. Labadie lost no time in hammering out his libertarian credo of untrammeled individual rights: the right to enough of the earth's bounties to make a living, to own what one produced, to exchange it without tariffs or the need for legal currency, to be free from taxes, patent fees, compulsory schooling, and laws concerning moral, physical, or intellectual behavior. He still believed that as civilization progressed, greater individual freedom would come about by orderly, peaceable means. He made clear, however, that he was not a Tolstoyan non-resister and "there is a time when a smash in the jaw is the most convincing of arguments."[17]

Complaints about the editorial slant were curiously almost nonexistent; the professional-looking paper lasted until May 1899. Labadie was looked on as a good fellow, "not an Anarchist of the Anarchists, but an Anarchist of his own kind."[18] He was easy to tolerate now that his activism was confined to the pen or groups like the Qui Vive Club, where civic leaders grappled only conversationally with unemployment, state socialism, municipal reform, taxation, and the boycott. He was not lumped in with the Goldman-Most contingent.

Public expression of anti-anarchist vitriol was markedly lower in Detroit than in most of the nation. Among the handful of journals that rejected the popular hysteria was the *Detroit News,* not surprisingly, since Labadie was its former reporter and had many friends among its staffers.[19] Nevertheless, Labadie did not entirely escape the long-lasting McKinley assassination backlash that had driven many anarchists underground.

Detroit's first attempt to repress Labadie's right of free speech occurred in April 1908, when he began adorning his letters with little anarchist stickers purchased from Tucker. Quotations he pasted on the envelopes included sentiments by George Bernard Shaw ("Liberty means responsibility. That is why most men dread it."), Lao-Tze ("The more mandates and laws are enacted the more there will be thieves and robbers."), and Spencer ("The ultimate result of shielding men from the effects of folly is to fill the world with fools."). When this new mode of anarchist advertising came to the attention of Post Office Inspector J. J. Larmour, he pronounced the thoughts "bloodthirsty," and unmailable. Labadie was told he could complain to Washington if he liked.[20]

The inspector vastly underestimated public support for "harmless Joe." Newspapers rallied to his defense and ridiculed "sleuth Larmour." "ARE WE TO HAVE A PRESS CENSORSHIP?" the *Detroit Journal* challenged, accusing postal authorities of "seeking despotic power" and "some new bogey to scare ourselves with." Labadie reveled in the attention. He wrote Tucker that nearly all the townspeople were "in a glorious state of excitement." Confidently, he continued gluing the slogans on his letters. He gloated that the papers were printing excerpts from his pamphlet, "Anarchism, What It Is and What It Is Not," because it was contained in the envelopes. "They are doing more to disseminate Anarchy than we are," he crowed. Labadie also got support from his friend Eugene Debs, leader of the Socialist party, then numbering 41,000 dues-paying members. Debs wrote Labadie he could count on him to join the fight if things became serious, but he viewed the flap in a positive light because it gave Labadie "fresh credentials."[21]

Response to the stickers incident was mild compared to the sensation in Detroit in May when another unwitting bureaucrat, Water Board Commissioner James Pound, a former trade unionist and supposed friend, insisted that Labadie be fired from his $70-a-month job at the water board. "I am teetotally opposed to an employee of this department, enjoying municipal pap, who attacks the government," Pound declared with what the *Detroit News* described as "a red, white and blue glare." He argued that it brought the water board notoriety to have an employee whose mail was being stopped and who did not believe in property rights. Labadie (a firm supporter of property rights) expressed surprise at Pound's remarks, but he told the reporter playfully he welcomed the "advertising . . . just when this post office trouble was being forgotten. . . . Persecution keeps us going."[22]

Two weeks later, water board officials had to reinstate Labadie after being swamped with a deluge of letters, petitions, telephone calls, and personal visits on his behalf. The case was the talk of the town; the papers were full of the affair for weeks. Pound was widely labeled an "ass" and lampooned in newspaper cartoons. Some called for his resignation. Labadie found he had powerful friends in town. Clothing store magnate J. L. Hudson, pharmaceutical manufacturer J. F. Ingram, leather factory owner Carl E. Schmidt, and the Bishop of Michigan, Charles D. Williams, signed petitions for his reinstatement. "One would think this was a question of national importance by the way they're coming at us," complained one water board commissioner. In the decision to rehire Labadie, the three Republicans on the board overrode the two Democrats who wanted him out. Years later the *Detroit News* reminisced that "to hear the conversations on the streets, a stranger might have thought Detroit the world capital of anarchism."[23]

Labadie chose not to say a word in his own defense. Touched by the outpouring of indignation over his discharge, he wanted to convince himself that he was admired as a prophetic voice, not merely an engaging personality. "May it not be that my tactics have won the day?" he suggested to Tucker. "I have not been asleep in this community . . . everywhere . . . I have been persistently, kindly, and practically trying to show what Anarchy is and its practicability here and now. . . . Maybe it DID do good."[24] He could not, or preferred not to, recognize that he was regarded mainly as a harmless fifty-eight-year-old "parlor anarchist" of eccentric ideas, a charming character who strolled picturesquely through town in flowing necktie, goatee, and Buffalo Bill slouch hat and disturbed no one's peace of mind.

Ironically, the affair was for him the most gratifying of his life. His finest moment, when he courageously denounced Powderly and defended the Haymarket martyrs two decades earlier had brought him bitter denunciation. This time, he could sit back calmly and relish his admiring supporters. It was delicious to have one's persecutors publicly proclaimed fools. It was "glorious," this "Anarchist war."[25]

Tucker told Labadie he was holding up publication of *Liberty* to await newspaper clippings of the controversy, but his own fortunes were in peril. Fire had wiped out his printing office and storeroom in New York City, destroying an estimated $10,000 worth of anarchist literature and nearly all his publishing plates. He had no insurance, an omission Labadie tactlessly termed "inexcusable carelessness." Tucker was eager to make contact with a wealthy friend of Labadie's, since he astutely perceived that "a few rich men will come in handy." Further jeopardizing his financial status was the fact that his "sweetheart," Pearl Johnson, twenty-five years his junior, the daughter of a free-thought lecturer and the manager of Tucker's book shop, was expecting their baby. After the birth, they were going to pull up stakes and move to Paris.[26]

In advising Labadie of his devastating loss, Tucker was unemotional, even casual. It was not like him to betray whatever anguish he felt. An aristocratic-like reticence that came across as coldness of spirit was the image he habitually cloaked himself in. A friend of Labadie's who dropped in at Benj. R. Tucker's Unique Book-Shop on Sixth Avenue after the fire described its proprietor as repellently self-absorbed and "cold-blooded," with a hollow "candy-apple smile."[27]

Labadie was appalled by Tucker's impending departure. How could he abandon the movement he had dominated for nearly thirty years? Who was competent to take his place? Tucker assured him he was not giving up. Another copy of *Liberty* was imminent; thereafter he would issue it from Europe. Water would be no barrier to furthering the cause. Labadie, however, was becoming disenchanted with his hero, especially after Tucker lost one of Sophie's precious scrapbooks of clippings and then tried to squirm out of responsibility. When Labadie wrote that he was sick over Tucker's carelessness, Tucker argued that if his memory was deteriorating with age, he should be pitied, not blamed. "Yet you are 'genial Joe' and I am 'that brute of a Tucker'," he complained.[28]

Tucker, Pearl Johnson, and their baby daughter, Oriole, moved to France at the end of 1908 as planned, never to return. Along with the scrapbook, Tucker also had misplaced the newspaper clippings concerning the anarchist stickers. He never published the promised issue of *Liberty,* which was to expose the attempt to censor Labadie's envelopes, nor, indeed, any further issues. He simply abdicated his post as chief promoter of individualist anarchism. Perhaps, at the age of fifty-four, Tucker was exhausted by his long effort. Government was, if anything, bigger than ever. Gripped by pessimism, the once-aggressive anarchist advocate no longer believed the anarchist solution of free competition could destroy the might of the huge monopolies that had developed. Like so many others, he seemed to have lost faith in a movement that had become sterile and hide-bound and was going nowhere.[29]

Without the "pope's" dogma (and dogmatism) as stimulus, the little band of anarchist disciples who had not already fallen out with Tucker looked elsewhere for salvation. There had never been much they could do to hasten the hoped-for non-violent evolution to anarchism except disseminate its precepts. Those who were action-oriented now turned to other, more practical movements. "How dead the movement seems now," Labadie wrote Tucker soon after he arrived in Europe. Three years earlier, in 1906, he had reported forty "Russians, Jews, and Germans" claiming to be anarchists in Detroit's Liberty Club. Only Labadie still called himself one. By 1910, Carl Nold, a Detroit anarchist who had been imprisoned for complicity with Berkman in the attack on Frick, considered Emma Goldman and Ben Reitman, her then comrade-lover, the only two remaining anarchists of any significance. (He ignored Berkman, released from prison in 1906 after serving fourteen years, who had taken over editorship of Goldman's *Mother Earth.*) "We are no longer in it," he lamented to Labadie. Johann Most had died in 1906, a bitter sixty-year-old, overtaken by Goldman, his former protégé.[30]

The damage Czolgosz had done the anarchist cause forever rankled Labadie. Years after the assassin was executed in the electric chair—his head then sliced open to look for signs of insanity, his body dissolved in a bath of sulfuric acid—the argument over him raged on. Annoyed that some persisted in adulating a "common murderer," Labadie determined to settle the matter once and for all. He recalled that former Illinois Governor John Peter Altgeld, who in 1893 earned the reverence of radicals (and committed political suicide) by pardoning the remaining Haymarket prisoners, had maintained Czolgosz was not an anarchist and had never subscribed to the cause. He asked Altgeld the source of his information and was referred to Clarence Darrow, who had represented the first anarchist deported under the new immigration law. Through Darrow, Labadie got in touch with the city clerk in Cleveland, who verified that Czolgosz was a registered Republican and had voted in the Republican primaries for years. Labadie offered this as "proof" that Czolgosz could not have been an anarchist, conveniently forgetting that he himself had supported Cleveland and Bryan, although perhaps not actually voting for them.[31]

Goldman erupted in fury when she read Labadie's "ravings" in the *Firebrand,* an anarchist periodical, in 1909. Her contempt was unbounded. She sneered that he was "stupid," "superficial," and "getting old." She dismissed him as one of those in "snug, bourgeois positions, making of our propaganda, not a life issue, but a mere pleasant pastime that costs nothing." Czolgosz may have voted the Republican ticket, but she knew that he belonged to the SLP. Even if he was not an anarchist, he had the right to resist invasion, and McKinley "was the father of American invasion against all liberty." Moreover, Czolgosz was "the most pathetic and dramatic figure in revolutionary history. . . . Not since the death of Christ was a man so absolutely forsaken by foe and friend."[32]

It was Goldman's habit to vilify and belittle others and quickly forget about it. She had a "genius for hurting people," Berkman said. A year later, the attack was out of mind and she did not hesitate to approach Labadie to sell tickets for her 1911 Detroit lecture series and raise money for an ailing comrade. Labadie took the opportunity to accuse her of being "boorish, discourteous, and unjust." He questioned why it was necessary "to spit fire at every one one meets, especially at those who have grown gray in the movement and . . . stood faithfully by their guns, even long before you knew there was a social movement."[33] Goldman was not in the least dismayed. She purported to be baffled as to why her brutal frankness had wounded Labadie. Since he believed in free speech, why should he be angry with her for expressing her opinions? "I am so glad i [*sic*] gave you an opportunity to get rid of your gall . . . Old Man," she twitted, then shamelessly asked him to arrange another lecture.[34]

Others' opinions of her mattered little to Goldman; she had no use for social diplomacy. "I do not consider myself at fault when people speak ill of me," she once told Labadie, "nor do I think myself virtues [*sic*] if they say kind things. In either case they are following their own desires, why should I then express thanks, or sorrow."[35] As the front-line general, she felt justified in riding roughshod over all who did not meet her standards of activism and purity of principles.

But "Red Emma" brought dynamism and glamour to an otherwise faltering movement. Her controversial persona was ever in the public eye, rallying both American and foreign-born leftists to her cause. She succeeded in bringing her own brand of non-violent communist anarchism, strongly colored by overtones of the individualist anarchist wing espoused by Labadie, into the mainstream of American life. When she was thrown out of the country after the world war, the lifeblood was drained from American anarchism and it was reduced to yesterday's dream.[36]

Soon the anarchist press was dead. The repressive anti-anarchist laws had silenced many old-time radicals. Communism was becoming the new bogeyman. By 1923, Labadie began to think of himself as America's only remaining anarchist. "It seems I am pretty well alone in the movement," he mused sadly to Tucker, far away on the Riviera.[37] It was close enough to the truth to dishearten the seventy-three-year-old.

☆ 16 ☆

A Millionaire Patron

Far from the crazy city's strife,
Away from its wretchedness and woe,
I cogitate for a saner life
And hopefully dream in the ingle's glow.
                    INTRODUCTION TO "*SONGS OF THE SPOILED,*" 1922

Frustrated in his other efforts yet still driven by passionate yearnings to be heard, Labadie turned to verse at age fifty. It was fitting. For most of his life, his practical side dominated, but by nature he was a romantic. From 1900 to 1920, he composed more than five hundred poems. Their quality was uneven, but they were widely printed in the daily press as well as in radical journals.[1] He attempted all manner of styles. At his most literary, he emulated Walt Whitman's wild and impassioned free verse. He also favored sing-song rhymes like the sentimental and well-known ditties of his fellow Detroiter and friend, Edgar Guest. In tribute to the "common man," he indulged in homespun vernacular pieces ("An when he got hiz skinny pay/He guv it all fer fambly needs"), a type popularized by Joel Chandler Harris in his Uncle Remus stories and Mark Twain. His love of alliteration reminded one critic of the early English "Piers Plowman," but it could carry him to such abominations as "The millions of moiling, maudlin men/ Mean in mawkish meekness to a merciless monarch."[2]

The struggle for social justice inspired most of the poems. Labadie addressed his "doggerel" to the underdog, the wage worker, the hired hand, the washerwoman. He reviled "the idle rich," the Russian czar, the coal baron, and the politician. He implored workers to unite, to strike, and to buy union-made cigars. His tender side produced love poems, lullabies, and tributes to friendship. Sometimes he dreamed of the wild woods, of a

                    211

kiss, of "A' Floating Down the Manistee." Among his paeans to liberty, free speech, and equal rights was a glorification of the self, the ego, the "I." The influence of the champions of individualism—Whitman, Emerson, and Thoreau—was clear.

Critical judgments were mixed. Benjamin Tucker, admitting to a prejudice against the "Whitmanian no-form," declined to publish Labadie's poetry in *Liberty* or even offer helpful criticism. H. L Mencken, a libertarian himself, told a friend, "Say what you will, Labadie has the gift. Who has ever written nobler American?" Proletarian author and editor Jack Conroy credited Labadie with the ability to "transmute the dross of the workaday world into the pure gold of poetry." He compared some poems with "the best efforts of Whitman." Another objected that his propaganda poems were "brutal" and made him sound angry.[3] Although often rough-hewn, his output brimmed with vitality and sincerity, and included some poetic gems.

Labadie often disparaged his verse as "bum stuff." Yet he bragged to Tucker in 1923 that it had brought in more than $3,000. He was keen on its propaganda value. Poetry had a regular place in the popular press of the time; printed verses often were clipped and pasted into scrapbooks. Labadie chose the doggerel style with an eye to reaching a wider audience. He yearned to be included in an anthology, and he lived to see it happen.[4]

In the spirit of British utopian socialist William Morris's nineteenth-century handicraft movement, Labadie bought an old printing setup like those he had worked on in his tramp printing days and around 1906 began publishing unique and artistic booklets of his verse at home. The archaic Washington Jobber press on which he painstakingly hand-set the type was older than he was. Many of the hand-sized booklets were printed on stationery samples. Sophie bound them in covers made from wallpaper sample books or scraps that others would find useless—of leather, linen, velvet, even birch bark. They were hand-sewn and tied with leftover pieces of ribbon. No two copies were alike.[5]

Sales practices at the Labadie Shop at Fifteenth and Buchanan Streets were as out of touch with the new age of mass production as its manufacturing methods. The booklets were made "principally for love," their advertisements announced. They served as recreation from the "demnition grind" of getting food and shelter. Those who wished to could pay what they chose. Labadie soon discovered that most of the profit turned out to be in "love and gratitude" only. To supplement his seventy-dollar monthly wages from the water commission, Jo used the press for job printing, made leather handbags, and created baskets from cardboard, old calendars, twigs, and raffia. Sophie and the girls did their share by painting chinaware and doing fancy sewing.[6] In spirit, Labadie was a throwback to the early nineteenth century. His shop symbolized his desire to return to the simpler, pre-industrialized world of his childhood. His love affair with anarchism had a similar origin—a craving to go back to the voluntary communities of the Indians or the Old West, when the individual seemed unfettered and self-sufficient.

Between 1910 and 1911, the little press was kept busy churning out collections of his verse: *Doggerel for the Under Dog, The Red Flag and Other Verses, I Welcome Disorder, What Is Love? and Other Fancies, Workshop Rimes,* and a volume called *Essays.* Labadie also printed *Jesus Was an Anarchist* by Elbert Hubbard, whose Roycrofters in East Aurora, New York, were creating an American version of the British arts and crafts movement and producing exquisite handmade books and furniture.

Throughout his life, Labadie never lacked prominent supporters in Detroit's business and civic community. One of the influential leaders who forced the water board to reinstate him in 1908 was millionaire tanner, civic leader, and philanthropist, Carl E. Schmidt. Soon afterward, Schmidt began contributing leather for the handbags and bindings, in time becoming a lavish benefactor. In accepting the leather scraps, Labadie quipped, he salved Schmidt's conscience and saved him the trouble of disposing of the leather commercially instead of for love and friendship.

Schmidt, six years Labadie's junior, was a curious patron. A leading Republican, he had served in various positions during Hazen Pingree's terms as mayor and governor. He fancied himself something of an anarchist, to the extent that he wanted a hands-off government. Fond of social rebels, he sought out the friendship of criminal lawyer Clarence Darrow, a Tolstoyian non-resister and libertarian, and Socialist party leader Eugene Debs, as well as the iconoclastic Detroit anarchist Robert Reitzel, the most famous radical in the German community.[7] As time went by, a strange, symbiotic relationship developed between this rich and powerful capitalist, whose every venture prospered, and Labadie, the radical struggling to get by. Schmidt became Labadie's friend as well as benefactor, and sustained him in his later years.

Schimdt was no self-made man. He inherited vast wealth and a prosperous leather-tanning business from his father, Traugott Schmidt. Born in Detroit but educated in Germany, the son maintained close ties to Detroit's German community and its many leftists. Labadie encountered this "American Midas" at Alt Heidelberg and at Conrad Beutler's famous tavern in the Randolph Hotel, which was frequented by anarchists Carl Nold, Tobias

Sigel (a promoter of Esperanto), Reitzel, and, when she was in town, Emma Goldman.[8]

As a staunch defender of civil liberties, Schmidt had taken the lead in the campaign to protect Labadie from the water commission. The story as told by Agnes Inglis goes that he told the water board he would have no objections if they were discharging Labadie because of poor work, but if it was on account of his opinions, "I shall see to it that the right to do so is taken away from you, and, gentlemen, I guess you know I can do it." Later, when the police threatened to bar Emma Goldman from speaking in Detroit in 1910, Labadie persuaded Schmidt to intercede with the police commissioner, although Schmidt was no Goldman enthusiast. This female firebrand was in character when she reciprocated by attacking the Detroit radicals as "backsliders" because they did not attend her lectures, reserving special contempt for Schmidt—"an ordinary exploiter" who pretended to be a humanitarian.[9]

In the first decades of the twentieth century, Detroit was rapidly exploding into a booming "Motor City" and putting America on wheels. Ransom E. Olds had begun turning out one or two "horseless carriages" a day in his "Oldsmobile" factory on East Jefferson Street in 1899. By 1908, Michigan's burgeoning automotive industry was producing 65,000 cars a year, including the first Model Ts from Henry Ford's Highland Park assembly plant. Reports of the growing need for workers in the new mass production factories lured the skilled and unskilled from all over the country and the world. Polish immigrants also came for jobs in cigar-making, the city's fourth largest industry, eventually replacing Germans as Detroit's single largest ethnic group.[10] The 1900 population of 285,000 had soared to nearly a half million a decade later and reached 1,720,000 by 1930. Charming old boulevards were widened to accommodate honking autos. Hordes of new assembly-line workers jammed the available housing. Old social patterns were disrupted. Urban life was crowding Labadie, and he grew eager to flee it.

As early as 1905, he had toyed with the idea of setting up a sort of "art-craftsmen" colony like the ones springing up across America in reaction to the congestion of the modern metropolis. These utopian communes, tucked away in lovely sylvan settings, were populated by artists and artisans, writers, dancers, actors, and leftists of all hues. Inspired by the medievalist spirit of William Morris and John Ruskin, their denizens sought to escape the machine age, go back to pre-industrial times, and create the perfect society in microcosm. The settlers lived in rustic cottages and tried to earn their living making practical and beautiful things by using the simple craftsmanship of a bygone age.

Labadie saw some of these experimental colonies while visiting his brother, Francis, in Philadelphia in 1905. He found the single-tax colony of nearby Rose Valley, then four years old, "quaint and lovely," bustling with workshops producing handsome furniture and high-quality pottery. He considered moving his family there, setting up shop, and supplementing their income through lecture tours his brother, proprietor of the Labadie Lecture and Amusement Bureau, would arrange. Friend Eugene Debs, who knew the lecture game well, attempted to dissuade him. Since Labadie was neither "a quack revivalist, or sensationalist or fantastic humbug," his chances of success were minimal, Debs counseled. In nearby Delaware, Labadie visited Arden, another single-tax community. In this settlement of twelve unique and artistic cottages, one could rent up to four acres and "live one's own life in one's own way" for six dollars a year. He came home via East Aurora, New York, so he could make the acquaintance of author and publisher Elbert Hubbard and see his Roycrofters at work in their idyllic setting.[11]

Despite the happy outcome of the water board affair, Labadie recognized that an anarchist in a municipal clerkship always faced possible dismissal. The establishment of the Labadie Shop in 1910 again prompted him to dream of forming a colony like Rose Valley. Schmidt decided to play benefactor. He owned thousands of acres of once-poor land some two hundred miles north on Michigan's Lake Huron shore in Iosco County, where he had developed a prosperous estate and built a vacation villa, Walhalla. He deeded Labadie eighty acres of it.[12]

Labadie's land, however, proved a disappointment to him. He knew nothing of farming nor how to start up a colony so far from his home. Schmidt again came to the rescue. In 1912, he let Labadie choose a site more suited to his abilities and desires. It turned out to be forty acres of farmland in Wixom, about thirty-five miles from Detroit, near Kent Lake in Livingstone County.[13] This bucolic spot, with meadows, rolling fields, brooks, bubbling springs, lakes, and miles of woods, was a tranquil haven. The nearest neighbor was a half-mile away. The Labadies named it Bubbling Waters and began spending their summers there, moving back to Detroit for the colder months.

Labadie was not embarrassed to accept the capitalist's largesse. Plutocrats should be allowed to unload their millions "as a means of squaring themselves." He maintained quite generously it was not their fault the system allowed them to amass riches; they could then make partial restitution by giving to the needy. For his part, he resolved not to ask Schmidt for favors, and showed his appreciation by means of flattering poems and all manner of testimonials to the nobility of his patron's character.[14]

Just as he justified working for the government, since there was one, he apparently had no qualms about owning two plots of land he could not "occupy and use" at the same time in apparent violation of the anarchist canon. Never an anarchist purist, he excused these anomalies on the grounds that anarchism represented the ideal society of the future; in the here and now, it was necessary to accommodate oneself to what existed. "None of us are really anarchists," he rationalized, "only believers in anarchism," because there was no place in the world where its doctrines prevailed.[15]

Full of optimism and enthusiasm for the new project, Labadie in 1913 gave up his job at the water works, which he had held through all the ups and downs of the past two decades. With his teenage son, Laurance, he started building simple wooden structures at Bubbling Waters—a cabin, barn, henhouse and outhouse. He intended to erect a group of rustic cabins for friends and poor people who could not afford summer resorts. Sophie, who seems to have entered enthusiastically into all of Jo's ventures, began cooking such delights as acorn bread, squirrel stew, woodchuck, rabbits, chipmunks, and frogs, which Laurance caught (a delicacy selling in Detroit for forty to sixty cents a dozen, with factory wages as little as $2.50 per day). They plowed and planted seed. They found a plentiful supply of watercress in a spring brook and drove it to market by horse and wagon.

Labadie's romantic flight from the city symbolized a return to nature. Now he could work in his own time and own way, not under an employer's thumb. But country life for a city family was harder than anticipated. Hawks, owls, skunks, foxes, and weasels ate the chickens. A brood sow Schmidt gave them ran wild. Their crops withered from lack of rain. What with "poor seed, bugs, worms, varmints and droughts," Labadie found the lot of a farmer a frustrating one.[16]

He was now in his mid sixties. His health was far from robust. "Grippe," pneumonia, rheumatism, lumbago, and other ailments laid him low, sometimes for weeks at a time. He complained frequently of "disordered nerves," without explaining the symptoms. With medicine as with society, he turned to a radical remedy, the fasting cure and "no breakfast plan" of Dr. Edward Hooker Dewey, of Pennsylvania. Labadie believed most diseases were caused by gluttony, and that long fasts were the cure. On one thirty-nine-day fast he lost twenty-eight pounds. Sophie and daughter Laura also took up fasting under the care of Detroit homeopathic physician and anarchist Dr. Urban Hartung.[17]

Labadie's health nostrum involved him in a sensational episode. A Boston friend, Frank Pickett, was eager to try the Dr. Dewey fasting cure, and the Labadies invited him to take it in their home. For forty days, Pickett, who was suffering from "catarrh of the stomach," took nothing but hot distilled water. The *Detroit Times,* reporting regularly on the regimen with banner headlines, marveled that this appeared to "loosen the foul matter that his stomach is drawing from all parts of his body" and enabled him to vomit it.

Dr. Dewey himself visited on the forty-fifth day, found the patient "aglow with new life" and predicted that he would recover completely. On the fifty-first day, Pickett inconveniently died, leaving behind a letter absolving the Labadies of any responsibility for his chosen regimen. The autopsy surgeons determined that he was suffering from chronic Bright's disease (a kidney disorder) and that Pickett's stomach was several times the normal size due to overeating. They also stated that he could have lived another month without starving to death, and without fasting, he would have died sooner. The Labadies were thus publicly exonerated and the *Detroit Times* lauded them for their compassion. Undeterred by Pickett's demise, they continued engaging in periodic long fasts.[18]

Progress in setting up their Bubbling Waters retreat was slow. Money was tight, but many well-wishers were happy to contribute their discards. The Labadies, inveterate string savers and nail straighteners, threw nothing away. The Detroit police commissioner "pensioned" an old horse, Blanche, to the farm. Despite this assistance, Labadie was forced to sell a gift from another wealthy admirer in order to buy lumber. It was a bungalow in Coral Gables, Florida, which anarchist Henry Bool, an Ithaca, New York, businessman, had intended for Labadie's old age. Jo also had to return to his water department clerkship during the winter months, when the family lived together on Buchanan Street to escape the unheated quarters at Bubbling Waters.[19]

From the outset, however, Labadie's actor brothers were delighted with Bubbling Waters. They found it an ideal spot to make movies. Oliver, who had been touring in comedy farces and cabaret acts since 1899, and Hubert, known since the 1880s as an interpreter of Mephisto in "Faust," bought more than three hundred acres adjoining Jo's property, called it Labadie Island, and set up a film colony around 1914. They began with one-reel comedies starring Henry Russell, a popular Detroit comedian. *The Three Bad Men,* their first feature film in 1915, was produced with established Chicago filmmaker Harry F. Ross and starred Oliver, Hubert, and scriptwriter L. Andrew Castle, with Jo as leader of the pioneers and Blanche as his horse. When the wind blew fiercely, a farmer's plowed field made a nice desert for the horsemen to gallop over. They reined in at the "Wells Fargo office" of the Wild West set erected by the Labadies on the shores of Kent Lake.[20]

By 1921, the Labadie-Detroit Motion Picture Company was turning out five- and six-reelers and attracting some of the big Hollywood names to Labadie Island. Such stars as Romaine Fielding, Mabel Taliaferro, Mildred Harris (recently divorced from Charlie Chaplin), Percy Marmont, Frank Mayo, and Cullen Landis could be seen lolling in Western apparel in the picturesque surroundings, where they were housed in quaint log cabins and fed at the Labadie brothers' BuckHorn Hotel.[21]

Labadie's dream of creating a utopian community at Bubbling Waters never materialized. Of the twelve structures he eventually erected, most were little huts intended to provide "poor devils" a country vacation. He anticipated a cooperative enterprise, with everyone helping out in exchange for free housing. Although this goal reflected Labadie's "beautiful heart and soul," commented Nina van Zandt, widow of the executed August Spies, "you will have a splendid collection of bums, tramps, dead-beats and so on living with you," she correctly predicted. Visitors flocked to the locale, some Sundays as many as forty-five. Woods and fields were filled with campers. Eventually, Labadie had to admit that not all vacationers were imbued with the cooperative spirit and began to charge rent for the cabins.[22]

The printing press was moved from Detroit to the stone "Den," where he could run the Labadie Shop comfortably warmed by a great cobblestone fireplace. A suitcase full of poems and essays stood ready to be put into booklets, but farming chores and the joys of outdoor living continually seduced him. It was nearly ten years before he produced *Songs of the Spoiled, Sing Songs and Some That Don't, Anarchism: Genuine and Asinine,* and other 1920s collections of verse and prose.[23]

A lavish correspondence with far-flung radicals emanated from Bubbling Waters, but Labadie found no market for his essays. The last of his "Cranky Notions" appeared in Ross Winn's *Firebrand* in 1910. Within a few years, the nation's English-language anarchist press had virtually disappeared. Younger reformers were turning to Eugene Debs and his Socialist party, the unifying center of Progressive-era leftists. Labadie's views were too extreme for conservative publications and too out of step with radical ones—to the extent that radical papers existed after the postmaster general crushed those that criticized the war or the Allies.[24]

He felt alone as an anarchist and isolated from the twentieth-century labor movement. Only Samuel Gompers still solicited his articles for the

AFL's *American Federationist*. When labor papers rejected his contributions on the grounds that he was behind the times, he responded angrily: the movement could use more "mossbacks" in place of labor leaders who exploited the movement for their own financial interests, "who eat the seed rather than wait for the harvest when all can eat." At the same time he was lamenting the anarchist creed as a dying cause, he sadly watched Detroit's union movement losing ground. The majority of wage earners worked in the auto industry, automotive industrialists like Henry Ford wanted no part of unions, and the high wages they paid discouraged unionism. By 1906, less than 6 percent of the work force belonged to a union. Detroit was the least unionized major city in America.[25]

When Eugene Debs helped form the IWW in 1905, Labadie asked him for information on the revolutionary new organization that hoped to unionize whole industries and overthrow capitalism and had just set up a Detroit local. Its promise of "One Big Union" of all workers—unskilled as well as skilled—appeared to echo the ideals of the Knights of Labor. But the IWW soon descended into factionalism, with those advocating "sabotage and direct action" winning out. It set itself as a rival to the AFL, which the IWW leadership viewed as elitist traitors to the working class. The IWW sought to organize the least skilled and worst paid, those it viewed as victims of exploitation by capitalist bosses, but its extremist, ends-justify-the-means tactics were denounced by Debs himself, who left the group.[26]

In 1913, buoyed by successful strikes just conducted among Lawrence, Massachusetts, textile workers and Paterson, New Jersey, silk workers, the "Wobblies," as IWW members were popularly called, launched a major Detroit autoworkers strike. Leaders mustered a walk-out of 3,500 non-unionized workers at a Studebaker plant and attempted to mobilize the entire auto industry before being arrested. Henry Ford not only was determined to keep unions out, but also, like other Detroit business and community leaders, saw himself as a reformer. To stave off future organizing efforts and assuage worker discontent, he quickly made a promise to pay every worker the staggering sum of five dollars for an eight-hour day, more than double the salary of his unskilled factory hands. This five-dollar day "profit-sharing plan" became the most famous labor-management reform program in American history and shattered the hope of organizing his auto workers. The IWW, meanwhile, could not maintain its momentum in the auto industry. Wobblies continued to run a Detroit soup kitchen and overnight shelter known as the IWW Flop, but never represented more than a few hundred Detroiters. Labadie did not join them. He was not lured by the IWW's rather muddy brand of anarcho-syndicalism, which called for abolishing government and replacing it with union control of each industry. Nevertheless, he spoke occasionally at IWW meetings and allowed that "if these chaps had as much good sense as courage they in time might do some worthwhile thing."[27]

Nor could he ally himself with his longtime friend Debs, the tall, balding founder of the Socialist party and its perennial presidential candidate. They were enormously fond of each other, but ideologically irreconcilable. Labadie revered the evangelical reformer for "the sweetness of his character and loyalty to his principles," as he wrote daughter, Charlotte, in 1912, when she was about to nominate Debs in a mock presidential convention at the University of Michigan. The election marked the high point of Socialist party strength. Fifty-six cities had socialist mayors and Debs polled nearly one million votes. Averring that Debs had "devoted his life to the cause of his fellows," Labadie nevertheless considered him an authoritarian, like all socialists. On his side, Debs publicly equated anarchists with lawlessness and sabotage. Yet he assured Labadie that he wanted no fights with anyone who was opposed to capitalism, and wished to extend the old anarchist his friendship "regardless of your philosophy or tactics for I know your great heart is always dead right."[28]

It was unfortunate that Debs was ideologically on the wrong side of Labadie's fence. Here, finally, was the hero of courage, commitment, and compassion that Labadie had sought in Powderly and Tucker. Debs's whole life was a fight for the underdog. Always opposed to force and violence, he was described by those who knew him as kind, gentle, and brave. First imprisoned in 1894 for defying a federal court injunction in the Pullman strike, Debs was convicted under the Espionage Act in 1918 for speaking out against the war. This draconian act prohibited, during wartime, "any disloyal, profane, scurrilous or abusive" language about the United States, or its government, Constitution, armed forces, or flag, with possible imprisonment of twenty years. He received a ten-year sentence. "Those who hound you will be remembered only as the hounds who hounded you," Labadie predicted correctly in a 1920 letter. He assured Debs's brother, Theodore, that "It is a mark of merit to have been imprisoned for love's sake, even tho this love does include the whole human family." Debs responded effusively from prison, asking his brother to tell Labadie that "I have him in my arms and can feel his great, loving heart beat next to mine."[29]

While in prison, Debs polled over a million votes during the 1920 presidential election, the highest level ever attained by a national socialist

candidate (although the electorate was greatly increased due to the enfranchisement of women). He was released the following year, broken in
health. He died in 1926, aged seventy-one. Labadie kept Debs's picture
hung prominently in his print shop, surrounded by the images of others who
were vilified and hounded but whom he was sure would be glorified in time.[30]

Every year Jo and Sophie sojourned at Bubbling Waters from early
spring until the chill forced them back to the radiators and hot water of their
Detroit home. Sophie occasionally mailed boiled muskrats or other edible
wildlife to the two daughters and their younger brother in Detroit. Laurance
spent summers helping his father build cabins and amusing himself shooting
rabbits and woodchucks, the girls coming out weekends when they could
get a ride.

Charlotte had graduated and was teaching school in Detroit. Laurance
was an undistinguished student at Cass Technical High School, under the
thumb of the domineering Laura, twelve years his senior. All three children
greatly loved and admired their father, yet none took after him. In contrast to
his hearty gregariousness, dynamism, and flair, they tended to withdraw from
society. They betrayed a certain wariness of the world outside the parental
doors. It was a curious development, inasmuch as Labadie was no repressive
patriarch, but granted his children the utmost freedom.[31]

Laura never had a profession, nor married. She developed no liberal
interests and spent her life puttering around her childhood home. Charlotte,
possessed of Sophie's quiet, obliging disposition, also lived at home until
she married in her late thirties. Laurance, the indulged child of his parents'
middle age, turned into something of a lost soul, constantly changing jobs,
unable to strike out on his own, suffused with a deep pessimism.

"Papa's dearly beloved boy" was the apple of his father's eye. Jo
Labadie hoped his only son would attain a high position in the world
and exceed what he considered his own meager accomplishments. At six,
Laurance was a beautiful child, with large dark eyes and foot-long blond
corkscrew curls, not unusual for boys in those days. He was pictured in
a Detroit paper in 1904 as "The Boy Who Has Never Eaten Breakfast,"
a flourishing example of Labadie's health fad at the time. Labadie took
Laurance along on speaking engagements and let him distribute anarchist
literature. In 1911, when the boy was thirteen, and Labadie sixty-one, they
spent several glorious months on a houseboat that his actor-brothers used as
their base while giving performances between Wisconsin and Louisiana.[32]

Laurance became a machinist at seventeen, finishing high school in
Detroit at night. From his country retreat at Bubbling Waters, Labadie sent a

Polonius-like barrage of advice and admonition to a son he was uneasy about. Laurance should be a "manly man . . . fair and square . . . brave without bravado . . . polite without obsequiousness." He should be careful not to lose his job or antagonize his co-workers or boss. It was a pity he did not want to go into business or agriculture, where he could get away from wage earning and "the dominion of others." Yet he confessed that the day his son left home to "battle with the world" would be for him "a day of heartache and grief." Labadie's anarchistic principle of live and let live was quite overwhelmed by old-fashioned fatherly concern for a son who seemed troubled and purposeless.[33]

When nineteen-year-old Laurance entered the University of Michigan in early 1918, his father was reassured. He hoped the boy would soon figure out "the line of your endeavors," but feared he might have to fight the war first. Although Jo's sleep was disturbed by thoughts of a "murderously insane" world in conflict, Laurance was thinking of enlisting. He thought military discipline might be good for him. His father was appalled and advised that for Laurance to become "a professional murderer . . . would be the end of your mother as well as a great grief to us all."[34] After one semester of failing grades, Laurance dropped out. His ability to conform to requirements of the classroom, not his intellect, was deficient. The rebellious spirit that fired him, unlike his father's, was bitter and self-destructive, and he lacked his father's impulse to compromise when necessary. When Labadie received the dean's last warning about his son's failing performance, he was crushed. "My heart was set on you as it has been on nothing else in the world," he reproached Laurance. He did not comprehend why his son behaved in a way that led to "broken hearts and disaster" or what had distorted him and turned him from "the path of rectitude."[35]

Approaching seventy, Jo needed the support of his son, but Laurance could not provide it. The elder Labadie felt his energies weakening and his mood darkening. Rheumatism and lumbago made it difficult for him to struggle with the unending farm chores. His "nerves" prevented him from sleeping. He was tormented by the horrors of the war in which America was engaged and the Wilson administration's savage repression of civil liberties in the name of patriotism. The Federal Espionage Act of June 1917, and the Sedition Act the following year, made it traitorous to speak for peace. The "saturnalia" of American-style "Prussianism" was wiping out the radical press, free speech, and individual rights, he wrote Henry Bool in England in 1917. Letters were censored. Publications were suppressed. The doctrine of hate was rampant. In such an insane world, he was losing interest in the future, he wrote. It was breeding in him a "pessimism that is dark and foreboding, and I don't like to be pessimistic."[36]

In the patriotic mania, even Henry Ford was targeted. A bitter anti-war protester, the automotive king was accused of anarchism by the *Chicago Tribune*. He countered with a million-dollar libel suit. When it came to trial in 1919, the *Tribune* called Labadie as an expert witness. After being interrogated by its lawyers for a week, he was never put on the stand. He also was never paid the promised $500 fee for travel and hotel expenses, despite his direct appeal to *Tribune* publisher Robert McCormick to "do the fair thing."[37]

Labadie had not heard from Benjamin Tucker for years, and missed him acutely. No one else seemed so brilliant, so intellectually stimulating, so on the mark. He craved Tucker's judgment of the world predicament. He was told that Tucker "has burnt all his bridges and doesn't care to have his old American friends to bother him." When he learned that Tucker had abandoned his pacifist, anti-government stand to become an enthusiastic supporter of the Allies in the war against Germany, he was shocked and disappointed, as were most of the former anarchist icon's other old comrades. Since Tucker did not answer his letters, Labadie asked Henry Bool in England—where the Tucker family had taken refuge—if he could find out why. In response to this inquiry, Tucker broke his six-year silence with a terse note: "I favor the Allies because I pity the Belgian people, because I admire the British influences that make for liberty, because I feel some (though I regret to say a declining) concern for the future of the American people, because I have a considerable sympathy for the people of Russia, and because I hate and fear the German people as a nation of domineering brutes bent on turning the whole world into a police-ridden paradise on the Prussian pattern." When faced with "permanent annihilation of our liberties" at Germany's hands, he was even willing to cooperate temporarily with the state in such an "evil" as conscription, he wrote another friend.[38]

Labadie was not. He spoke out against the war, even after peace talk was deemed treasonous. Although he had always upheld the right of those invaded to strike back, he viewed war as "a species of insanity" that never brought lasting good to mankind, but served only as a lesson in the fruitlessness of the rulership of man by man. In 1917, the local civil service commission asked the water board to fire its anarchist clerk because he refused to sign a loyalty pledge, but it refused to do so. Expecting (possibly hoping) to be arrested for anti-war talk, Labadie was chagrined that a local Justice Department official characterized him as "harmless." Had he known that an agent from the Bureau of Investigation (later the FBI) made notes on his speech before the Detroit Labor Forum in 1920 and reported back to Washington, he would have been pleased.[39]

As the war ended and business briefly boomed, consumers could once more buy goods that had been in short supply. Then prices skyrocketed. Between 1919 and 1922, a massive strike wave jolted the country, widely viewed as proof that radical agitators were fomenting social disorder. Then came a precipitous economic decline. Unemployment soared. Like so many in those stressful times, Labadie was overwhelmed by a sense of dread and foreboding. Government repression intensified. A rash of bombings in the East and Midwest by Italian-born anarchists, culminating in the prosecution of anarchists Nicola Sacco and Bartolomeo Vanzetti for killing two men in a payroll robbery, terrified the public and revived the stereotype of anarchists as madmen carrying a bomb in one hand and a pistol in the other. Reports of the "atrocities" of the Russian Revolution contributed to an anti-Red hysteria unmatched since the Haymarket bombing. Radicals, socialists, foreigners, and those viewed as "Bolsheviks" were hounded in a tyrannical crackdown.

In his infamous "Palmer Raids" of 1919 and 1920, the new attorney general A. Mitchell Palmer (assisted by a recent law school graduate, J. Edgar Hoover) dealt with the "red menace" by jailing thousands of leftists, dissidents, and foreigners with little regard for their constitutional rights. Jails were crammed with political prisoners. Aliens were deported en masse, including Emma Goldman and Alexander Berkman. Labadie recklessly denounced America as the most reactionary place in the world, and suggested that everyone in labor's ranks carry "a good Colt hanging to his side" to deter the bullies.[40]

In early 1920, Justice Department agents broke into homes and meeting halls in thirty-three cities, rounding up everyone they found. In Detroit, on January 2 and 4, some eight hundred suspected radicals were imprisoned incommunicado for days in a windowless corridor of the city's antiquated Federal Building. Agents grabbed several hundred attending meetings at the House of the Masses on Gratiot and St. Aubin, a socialist and labor headquarters. Nearly 51,000 other "Bolsheviks" were arrested the same night in other cities. Many were deported as "undesirable" without criminal charges or trial. The Wobblies, in particular, were pursued with a merciless vengeance. Nearly two hundred of the country's IWW leaders were found guilty of sedition and conspiracy and sentenced to harsh prison terms. With so many of his comrades denounced, persecuted, and imprisoned, Labadie wondered to Gompers if he had been "derelict in some duty" for having escaped jail. He considered starting an anarchist monthly to test if the authorities would stamp it out.[41]

In the labor movement, anti-capitalist militants had clashed with conservatives, like Gompers, who were eager to prove their patriotism during the war years. The AFL head had abandoned his lifelong pacifism to become an enthusiastic supporter of President Wilson and the war. Determined to dissociate AFL members from Bolshevik sympathizers, he turned into a rabid red-baiter in a move reminiscent of Powderly's efforts to protect the Knights of Labor during the Red Scare three decades earlier. Gompers even expressed willingness to supply the Justice Department with information on anarchists, IWW members, and other seditious people in labor's ranks.[42]

Somehow none of this shook the personal affection Gompers and Labadie shared. As Gompers, in his later years, became increasingly identified with the respectable and powerful, Labadie took the liberty of notifying his "dear Old-Time Friend Sam" that many in labor's ranks "hooted" when his name was mentioned. Mentioning that there were few friendly enough to the AFL leader to tell him his reputation, he wrote in 1919 that he wanted to guide him "into less stormy environments." He warned that diatribes against "frowzy bolshevists and wild-eyed radicals" in the AFL's *American Federationist* were giving aid and comfort to the enemy, an enemy with Machievellian schemes to trap Gompers and his associates and destroy the labor movement. The "Junkers" wanted labor engaged in violent warfare "so they can kill the leaders and leave the workers in confusion, the more easily to subdue them." It was solidarity that labor needed, Labadie counseled, and its most powerful weapon was passive resistance in the form of the general strike. Gompers quickly acknowledged receipt of the "interesting personal letter," but apparently never commented on it further.[43]

In those tumultuous years, the one encouraging development Labadie saw was the Russian Revolution. Exulting over a program that seemed to promise a more righteous society, he was prepared to suppress any doubts about Bolshevik tactics. He thought the Russian communists were "making headway against the hosts of darkness," and that once Russia got on its economic feet, its revolution would be repeated worldwide. Calling Lenin and Trotsky "mere pikers" compared to the Christian communists of the early church, he told the Detroit Labor Forum that the soviet, or local council, was simply the logical outcome of the trade union movement. He wanted to believe the Russian Revolution's anarchist influences would prevail over the authoritarian governmentalism of the new "dictatorship of the proletariat." Like so many, he saw "the red in the east [giving] hope of a brighter day."[44]

★ 17 ★

A Pack Rat's Hoard

If you have flowers for me, dear,
Wait not to place them on my bier,
But let their fragrance soothe me here.
Oh, if you love me tell me so
In velvet words with accents low,
And do the things that make me know.
—From "Tell Me If You Love Me," *What Is Love?
and Other Fancies*

Before the turn of the century, the materials Sophie was so faithfully storing in the Buchanan Street attic were recognized as a historical treasure trove. Every issue of every publication Jo wrote for or subscribed to was piled into its dark corners. Many existed nowhere else; even their publishers had not saved them. Sophie bundled flyers, tracts, pamphlets, circulars, handbills, union constitutions and initiation ceremonies, badges, copies of resolutions, programs, poems, newspaper clippings, even menus, and toted them upstairs. Thousands of letters from radicals of every stripe had their niche. It seems that no scrap escaped "Mamma." Anything connected with "the struggle of the underdog for a fair field" that had come into Jo's hands was stowed away with no idea of who might ever use it or for what purpose.[1] Preserving them was the only active role Sophie played in Jo's reform efforts, but it was a major one.

In 1897, economist Richard T. Ely wrote Labadie requesting "a favor." He had sent the Wisconsin State Historical Society a collection of labor literature and asked Labadie to do the same. He had an idea of the range of Labadie's materials from having borrowed some for his pioneering study, *The Labor Movement in America,* a decade earlier. Now director of the school of economics, political science, and history at the University of Wisconsin, Ely hoped to make Madison the national center for labor scholarship.[2]

A few years later, Ely teamed up with his former student, John R. Commons, and Commons's student, John B. Andrews, to form a powerhouse of researchers in labor studies. Commons and his associates, the nation's first labor historians, were scouring the country for source material for their groundbreaking ten-volume *Documentary History of American Industrial Society*. During an intense five-year courtship of Labadie beginning in 1906, they tried to entice him to sell his collection to the University of Wisconsin, "where more work along the line of social movements is being done than anywhere else in the country."[3] It may be that the value of Labadie's mass of materials first became apparent to him because of the steadily intensifying interest of academia.

Commons came to Detroit in mid 1906 to examine the contents of the attic; Andrews later stayed a week trying to persuade Labadie. They offered only $500, no more than Labadie's estimate of the original cost. Loath to part with the treasured hoard, Labadie turned to his mentor, Benjamin Tucker for advice. Hold onto them, Tucker urged, unless there was a "very attractive" offer and money was needed. He was convinced their worth would increase. America's reigning individualist anarchist did not share the disdain for money matters characteristic of his Detroit comrade.[4]

Labadie, nearing sixty, was torn between a sentimental desire to keep near him the tangible evidence of his life's work and the recognition that making it available to the public would serve to promulgate it. In making a preliminary catalog of the papers, he had paused to re-read many. "This makes me live my life over again," he told Andrews. Observing the development of his thinking over the years gave him satisfaction. To let the documents go so far away as Wisconsin, where he would probably never see them again, seemed like burying them. He began to think of offering the collection to the University of Michigan, where he could "look it over when the mood prompted."[5]

Andrews tried to prevent this train of thought. Wisconsin was amassing the largest library of such material in America. "Where one student of labor problems will visit Michigan library . . . fifty will come to Wisconsin," he argued to Labadie. Ely added his voice. With due respect for Labadie's state loyalty, and his own "great admiration for Michigan," he wrote, it would be a mistake to let the collection go where it would be "comparatively isolated, not forming part of any large collection." Michigan had done so little to collect such materials that it was impossible that institution could ever cover the entire field, Ely maintained. Students doing thorough research would have to visit both universities. Ely enlisted professors at other universities to lobby Labadie in favor of Wisconsin. Even some of Labadie's friends warned that the Michigan faculty was not sufficiently advanced concerning the principles of freedom to value the collection and that "it might be stowed away in some garret and lost, probably forever."[6]

Perversely, Labadie approached the University of Michigan in 1907 himself, sending a list of part of his holdings and offering them for sale. The response was less than enthusiastic. An investigator was sent to cull through the contents of the attic. He apparently returned to Ann Arbor unimpressed. When Labadie inquired about the matter two years later, he was told that the material must be properly cataloged and arranged before the university could evaluate it. In the meantime, he was approached by two new suitors, a professor from Johns Hopkins University in Baltimore and the acting commissioner of the United States Bureau of Labor, who wanted the collection for their respective institutions.[7]

By 1912, however, Labadie had decided to send it "where it was most needed—old moss-back Michigan,—conservative, reactionary, and positively crass in some things," as he told Commons. He knew "you Wisconsin folk" would have done well with it, but was sure they would recognize what "a light it will be to the U. of M."[8]

Several personal circumstances played a role in convincing him. Michigan had been the cherished home of his ancestors for five generations; additionally, his daughter, Charlotte, was at the point of graduation from the university. He had been pleased at the response by students and professors there to two speeches he gave on anarchism. A philosophy professor, who included anarchist writers in his lectures, was enthusiastic about obtaining Labadie's collection for the university and had inquired the year before what price he would put on it.[9]

In exchange for what he now recognized as probably the best private collection of such literature in the country, Labadie asked very little. He told the board of regents in 1911 all he wanted was a guarantee that his accumulation of forty years would be put into good shape and placed where students could get data at first hand "instead of taking their information from interpreters who might not have entered into the real spirit of the struggle." He was poor and getting old and could not afford to donate it outright, he explained. Rather than requesting payment from the university, he offered to seek the money to recompense him directly from public-spirited persons.[10]

University president Harry Burns Hutchins was not keen on the whole idea. He was "not a very ardent believer in the utility of any radical movements," a history instructor had confided to Labadie. Also, the university librarian objected that it would be difficult to preserve the newspapers. Nevertheless, two faculty members sent to look over the collection gave Hutchins a glowing report, and on November 17, 1911, four years after it was offered to them, the board of regents voted to accept Labadie's gift, which, of course, was going to cost them nothing.[11]

Labadie now had the job of finding the requisite public-spirited citizens to recompense him; their names were to be memorialized on the bookplate of donors. Admitting that he found personal solicitation distasteful and knew few people of means, he nevertheless immediately sent a printed appeal to likely prospects, explaining that once fifteen persons had sent him $100 each, the collection would be forwarded to the university. He suggested that in no other way could they have their names commemorated at the university "in so laudable a purpose and with so little outlay of effort."[12]

Carl Schmidt and Henry Bool responded promptly, as did real estate developer Robert Oakman, whose labor paper, *The Spectator,* Labadie had written for thirty years earlier. Six other business or professional men, not all of whom were sympathetic to the contents of the collection, donated, making a total of only $900. Schmidt pointed out to Labadie in February 1912, that if he did not receive $1,500 he could return the monies and call off the deal. Commons made one last plea in April, asking Labadie to name a price. But money had ceased to be the decisive factor. Labadie had set his heart on Michigan, while recognizing that it would "have to do some hustling" to compete with Wisconsin in the "sociological literature department."[13]

In September, with only the $900 in hand, he sent twenty boxfuls of the precious documents to Ann Arbor. They were unpacked and the bundles piled in their shipping wrappers on distant shelves of the library. There they remained for years, unorganized, uncataloged, unusable, gathering dust. The university made no effort to fulfill its part of the bargain to arrange the material, or to make it available to students, although President Hutchins generously allowed Labadie's son Laurance a free nose operation at the university hospital.[14]

Once again, as often occurred in Labadie's time of need, a sympathetic figure of wealth and privilege eventually came to the rescue. Agnes Inglis, a beneficiary of the capitalist system, had spent her inheritance on behalf of anarchism, atheism, the IWW, and infamous radicals, especially Emma Goldman. Through her labors, not her money, she became the catalyst that enabled the Labadie Collection to expand into one of the best-known and most important archives of its kind in the world.

The youngest child of a prominent physician who died in 1874 when she was four, the sister of influential bankers and manufacturers, Inglis was raised in a rigidly ordered, conservative, socially prominent Detroit family. She was a shy and introverted "model child," acutely fearful of seeming ridiculous. In adulthood, Inglis regarded herself as "a daughter of Mrs. Grundy" (a prudish literary figure), scarred by her Scottish Presbyterian upbringing. "I knew I was born in sin, and my body was dirty and not to be looked at or thought about." Looking back over these early years, she regretted that much of her "love life" had gone into loving Jesus.[15]

Inglis took refuge in a closely circumscribed home life until 1898, when she was twenty-eight. Around that time her sister, whom she had been nursing, died. Her mother died soon afterwards, leaving her an heiress with nothing to do and no worldly experience. In her early thirties, in an effort to "reach out into the world," Inglis moved to Ann Arbor, began studying the history of the Middle Ages at the university, and joined the Alpha Phi sorority. A year later she turned to social work, first in Detroit at the Franklin Street Settlement House and later at settlement houses in Chicago and East London, England. Exposed daily to the degradation of the poor, she found radical ideas edging out the "do-goodism" of the typical social worker. Social settlements began to seem mere palliatives for poverty in a society divided into exploiters and the exploited. Initially, she thought socialism the answer.

Inglis still appeared a genteel and proper "maiden lady" of forty-two, an Ann Arbor Presbyterian Sunday school teacher, when, in March 1912, a little booklet by Emma Goldman titled "What I Believe" came into her hands. "I have to say it burned my fingers to hold the book. I thought Emma Goldman was a bad, terrible woman," she relates in her unpublished autobiography. But the pamphlet's message—that "this world could be beautiful and without poverty or hate or cruelty or disease"—along with its author, transformed her life. At one of Goldman's lectures, she was awed by the courage of the stocky woman with steely blue eyes who faced a roomful of boys jeering at her every mention of sex or free love.

After Goldman's next appearance in Ann Arbor, in the summer of 1913, Inglis dared invite her for dinner, tentatively offering future help (which she anticipated would be minor). To her surprise, she found herself enthusiastically embraced as Goldman's Ann Arbor representative and a major financial supporter. The militant anarchist's forceful style impelled Inglis to overcome her own natural reserve and face public scorn. She arranged lectures for Goldman on Nietzsche and birth control, handed out anti-war literature, organized a meeting for Alexander Berkman to protest the arrest of labor organizer Thomas Mooney for the Preparedness Day parade bombing in San Francisco, and wrote generous checks. She even risked arrest by passing out explicit information on contraceptive methods. "I don't suppose there ever was a more audacious deed done in staid Ann Arbor," she wrote in her autobiography. "Never once did she fail me," Goldman commended. Yet in time Inglis harbored a certain resentment, a suspicion she was being used. "Being Emma's friend meant never relaxing," she noted. If Goldman wanted a thing done, "you had to do it." She also came to the realization that Goldman cherished her less in true friendship than "based on my activity for her work and on money that I gave so willingly."[16]

By 1916, Inglis, now forty-six, was identifying herself as an anarchist and atheist. That year she met Labadie, although she knew of him already through her older brother, David, who had been a member of Labadie's old Social Science Club. He must have complained about the neglect of his collection at the University of Michigan because she quickly went to have a look at it and started discussing plans to get it into usable shape. She also was interested to hear about Sophie, asking with the naiveté that never left her, "Does your wife ever strike? I'm encouraging all women to strike."[17]

Inglis was befriended by the Labadies and, in 1919, invited to Bubbling Waters, but it was not until 1924 that she began working intermittently in the library stacks. In the intervening years, she scandalized her family by agitating for the IWW, holding meetings at her house (duly monitored by the Bureau of Investigation), putting up bail money for fellow Wobblies and other political prisoners, and purportedly fomenting a strike. She recounts in her autobiography how a patriotic ex-sorority sister once kidnapped her and handed her over to local officials of the Justice Department. Militant radicals, however, continued to view her as a rich, bourgeois woman, valuable because she could solicit money from others. They urged her to raise money for bail, trials, propaganda, prisoner defense, strike assistance, anti-conscription efforts, deportations, Sacco and Vanzetti, Alexander Berkman, Tom Mooney, "Big Bill" Haywood, Union of Russian Workers prisoners, and, especially, Emma Goldman. She used her two houses in Detroit and Ann Arbor as security for the bail of IWW activists she had never seen, renting a room for her own use in someone else's house. This lavish generosity and self-sacrifice helped dissipate her sense of guilt for living off unearned income from family investments. She found, however, that "you could be pretty sure you would be called counter-revolutionist if you stopped paying out to a particular revolutionary specialty."

Although personally frugal, she eventually ran out of money and had to live off an allowance from another brother, James, a wealthy businessman. She seemed relieved to be rid of the constant appeals for funds. "I did not like being thought of as a woman who had money," she admitted. "If you havent [*sic*] any money you might as well drop out of the radical movement."[18] About this time, in the mid 1920s, she removed herself from the revolutionary fray and began to immerse herself in the Labadie Collection. In the remotest corner of the library stacks she found it piled neatly, exactly as Labadie had shipped it twelve years before. She perceived that it needed "fixing" and volunteered to whip it into shape without charge. What she anticipated as a job of weeks or months became her life.[19] When she died in 1952, she was still at work.

With boundless enthusiasm and curiosity, but no library skills, Inglis concocted an idiosyncratic card cataloging system, without cross references or call numbers, that only she understood. Items were placed in boxes, unalphabetized, with no guide or index but her own memory. For the few researchers who learned of the existence of the materials and confronted the disarray, only she could solve the enigma. She delighted in fitting together the jigsaw of facts that documented the radical past and scrawled her notes haphazardly on little cards. Anecdotes concerning radical and labor figures were carelessly typed on slips of paper she tucked away among the manuscripts. She believed in letting researchers browse in open stacks. Sometimes she let them take items home, not all of which were returned.[20]

Literature that had been stashed away by Labadie's friends and associates continually arrived to be added to the collection. Labadie himself added boxfuls in his last years and urged others to do the same. Inglis was indefatigable in enticing radicals and scholars from all over the world to send materials.

In lonely silence, Inglis spent her days exploring the labyrinth of materials. At night, she worked on them in the room she shared with a woman friend a few blocks from campus. She found her solitude alleviated by the thrill of discovering "this! that! and this!" as she exclaimed to Labadie. Vicariously, she experienced the revolutionary activities she had cut herself off from, especially vivid because they often concerned people, events, or ideas well known to her. But sometimes she was depressed at absorbing herself so wholly in the past and longed for "present day heart beats."[21]

The dire predictions of the Wisconsin professors about Michigan's disregard for labor and radical history proved all too accurate. For the most part, the university administration neither interfered with Inglis's activities nor supported them. She was unable to procure even a few hundred dollars for steel files. She craved the coming of a prominent researcher who would demand better facilities. Yet she rationalized that the collection's continuing obscurity protected it "until the years sort of relieve it of any danger of anger on the part of the D.A.R. or such!" Labadie also feared it might be destroyed when the authorities caught on to what it contained.[22]

In 1928, Inglis took over more or less officially as curator of the neglected archives then known as the Labadie Collection of Sociological Literature. Her new title did not represent either salary or clerical help. For a brief period, Judson Grenell's second wife, Margaret, volunteered to help paste clippings in scrapbooks on subjects like the Knights of Labor, the Saginaw strike, and the Haymarket bombing.[23]

Although Labadie had insisted that his collection go to Michigan so it would not be forever lost to him, he did not visit it once the boxes were sent off in 1912. Without a car, the aging couple found it too difficult to journey to Ann Arbor from Detroit or Bubbling Waters. An opportunity finally presented itself in the form of a joint birthday celebration for Labadie and Judson Grenell in Ann Arbor in April 1926. As Inglis guided Jo and Sophie past a stack of Benjamin Tucker's *Liberty,* they saw on the cover page of the first issue the image of Sophie Perovskaia, who was hanged for the murder of Czar Alexander II. The sheet was torn, fading and very dusty. "Gently Mrs. Labadie's hand passed over the picture, stroking it and wiping off the dust. 'Ah! Sophie!' said Mrs. Labadie with lingering tenderness. And she took the sheet and turned it over so the page would not face the weathering any more," Inglis recalled. The act endeared Sophie Labadie to her forevermore.[24]

Long after Labadie's death, Inglis, by then a white-haired, fragile-looking eighty-one-year-old, was still at work. Adored by the handful of graduate students who frequented her secluded nook in the bookstack area, she was a familiar character as she crossed the campus, a stooped old lady in antiquated clothing, quaint hats, and shapeless shoes. By the time of her own death in 1952, she had increased the holdings of the Labadie Collection perhaps twenty-fold. Many items she donated herself. She coaxed rare and valuable items from the "trunks and attics" of her former comrades and a wide circle of radicals, rebels, and revolutionaries of her acquaintance. She sent out mass mailings and put notices in likely publications worldwide soliciting contributions. She subscribed to obscure publications with her own money.[25]

Agnes Inglis deserves the most credit for enormously expanding the nucleus of the collection safeguarded by Sophie Labadie into the invaluable resource it has become. From a core literature of the early labor movement and anarchism, the scope and depth of this "library of protest," as it has been called, continued to expand to the present day to include a wide array of out-of-the-mainstream social protest and reform movements and constitute the most comprehensive collection of radical literature in the United States.

Inglis never married but had many close friends. Labadie was exceedingly fond of her, certainly because of her loyalty and zeal on behalf of the collection, but also due to her warm, supportive nature. She took pains to reassure the aging rebel that he had played a big part, had stood true to his ideals, and would live forever through his collection. Her deep affection and admiration for Labadie was not diminished by her perception that he was an "egoist." But she seemed especially to love the quiet, self-effacing "Mamma" for having preserved the records of a radical golden age with such meticulous care.[26]

☆ 18 ☆

Looking Back on It All

When I am dead
Waste not yourself in either grief or joy because of so,
As I'll not know,
And recompense, the spur to all we do,
Will never come to you,
Except as one in sounding glen bewails or sings
And echo brings on airy wings
The messages himself sent out.
PUBLISHED IN *MAN*, NOVEMBER 1933

D riven by automobile manufacturing, Detroit in 1920 was zooming into the top rank of American cities in both industrial production and population. It soon outranked all but New York and Chicago in dollar value of industrial output. As the fourth most populous city, it burst into the suburbs, expanding from 28 square miles in 1900 to 139 by 1925. Along with fabulous wealth generated by the assembly lines—soaring skyscrapers, mansions, new factories—came social upheaval, crowded housing, ghettos, poverty, and disease.

Prohibition was laxly enforced, which encouraged widespread disrespect for the law. As a "wide open booze town," Detroit became a magnet for bootleggers, whose payoffs corrupted the police force. It experienced gang warfare and a rash of underworld killings. European immigration, reduced to a trickle during the war and after the 1921 Emergency Immigration Act, was replaced by the migration of Southern blacks. They began streaming into the city to fill the ever-increasing number of factory jobs. The 100,000 black migrants who were transported by the trainload to Detroit in the 1920s encountered resentment and even violence when they moved into a city with scarce housing. By 1924, the Ku Klux Klan, which flourished nationwide after World War I, claimed a Detroit membership of 32,000.[1]

The auto industry remained substantially unorganized. Efforts by industrial unions like the IWW had failed in the face of implacable opposition from the employers; the craft-oriented AFL had little interest in organizing less-skilled workers who held mass production jobs. Indeed, the nation's strike wave and Red Scare after the war had engendered such anti-labor sentiment that AFL membership fell to under three million by 1924. Most of the auto strikes attempted in the 1920s ended in defeat for the workers.[2]

Disillusionment and bitterness, those frequent companions of old age, were common among Labadie and his old comrades as they watched organized labor going downhill. Throughout the nation, once-militant labor activists were eager to come to terms with the existing society. The AFL had turned into big business unionism. Labadie castigated what remained of the labor press as timid and worthless, shunning, as it did, mention of socialism, anarchism, the single tax, or anything tinged with radical ideas. He sneered to labor historian John B. Andrews that the much fought-for labor bureaus were "simply places for political henchmen who don't care a dam [sic] about getting the facts." Labor men elected to political offices were in his eyes largely "tools of political rascals, and capitalistic crooks."[3]

Despite the dejection that often clouded his normally jovial disposition, and his half-humorous gripe that after all these years of helping the underdog it was "about time the underdog did something for himself," Labadie kept on "pushing whenever I get the chance," as he assured Benjamin Tucker in one of his unanswered communications. By the 1920s, his chances were few. Manuscripts were returned with a comment either that he was thirty years behind the times or three hundred years ahead, he told friend Henry Bool. The "Dean of Detroit's Bohemia," as the *Detroit Free Press* dubbed the seventy-two-year-old, gave the occasional speech, possibly scheduled more in his role as living legend than because the public was avid for his views. He continued to publish revolutionary verse, and kept up a voluminous correspondence with the handful of libertarians who still absorbed themselves in splitting hairs over such esoteric matters as the definition of terms used in their writings.[4]

Labadie often mused "About What It Is All About," as he titled one of the last of his speeches. Looking back on it all, he wondered: Did we do any good? Was it all worthwhile?[5] It was a question he frequently pondered with his old comrades. Some had grown bitter and cynical; others were more philosophical; some were even upbeat as they approached the end of their lives. In their summings up, they offered contrasting historical assessments of the causes they strove for and also revealed much about their own characters.

Judson Grenell, Labadie's dearest crony and his associate on the old labor papers, reviewed his swath of history cheerily. Easy-going, prone to compromise, Grenell was satisfied to see himself as a drop of water or a grain of sand, a contributor to the whole. He pointed with satisfaction to the gains in his lifetime—a shorter working day, equal pay for equal work for both sexes, improved factory sanitation, an increasing wage rate. He saw progress toward the curbing of monopolies, ballot reform, women's rights, and the single tax. "I have had my hour," he rejoiced. Now editor of the *Washtenaw Post* after twenty-five years as labor editor at the *Detroit News,* he decided by 1923 that he had outgrown the study of sociology and turned over to Labadie nearly three hundred books on the subject.[6]

John Burton, the former *Labor Leaf* publisher, stood at the opposite pole. Seventy-two in 1922, he was disillusioned and cynical. An adventurous spirit had taken the tolerant, high-principled, single-tax enthusiast into many strange byways. Experience had taught him "the fallacies underlying our pet schemes of reform." Despondent after the 1890 failure of his paper, *Onward,* which promoted the Henry George tax scheme, he had become a spiritualist and "healing medium" in San Francisco. After a brief sojourn in a socialist colony in Seattle around 1898, where he was reproved for not being a socialist, he joined the anarchist Home Colony near Tacoma, Washington, where he was told he was not an anarchist. He found the supposedly authority-hating settlers of the state's utopian communities to be "cranks" and "tyrants." Whether "Free Lovers, Anarchists, Socialists, Communists, I.W.W. . . . all wanted their own way . . . to do as they please and make others please likewise," he informed Labadie.

Wherever Burton journeyed, he discovered as much greed and disregard for the rights of others in the "little homesteader" as in the "big capitalist." Those who objected to rent, interest, and profit had nothing to rent or loan, he observed, and desired other people's profits. Only George's proposal to tax just land still seemed valid. "Enlightened despotism" now appeared to him the best form of government. Burton did not think death would end his role as a reformer, however, since he expected to be reincarnated as a guide "to help others on their way."[7]

Captain J. M. McGregor, one-time Great Lakes boat captain and Burton's successor on *Advance and Labor Leaf,* still had to work for the Detroit health department to support himself at age eighty-six. He told Labadie he was overwhelmed with pessimism and saw America inescapably headed for the fate of the old Roman Republic. McGregor found the numbers of the "disinherited" multiplying and the capitalist system "more strongly enthroned than when we first began protesting more than forty years ago." A long-lasting industrial depression lay just ahead, he correctly predicted in 1927, two years before it occurred; he wrongly believed it would culminate in a revolution.

McGregor's feud over Labadie's anarchist writings was long forgotten. Instead, he recalled with nostalgia their camaraderie in the old Henry George assembly of the Knights of Labor back in the mid 1880s. The years had gone so fast, they had accomplished so little, he mourned two years before his death in 1929. Yet this old comrade-in-memory of Labadie's expected they would "keep on protesting because it is a part of us."[8]

Thomas Barry, the charismatic leader of the 1885 Saginaw Valley strike and Powderly's most influential critic, was loud in the chorus of disillusioned one-time labor activists when he pronounced Samuel Gompers "as big a grafter as Powderly was." Disgusted with the trade union movement, Barry had joined the Socialist party and devoted his spare time to "the Socialist work." When he died in 1909 at age fifty-seven, labor's one-time hero was largely a forgotten man. Long blacklisted by the National Association of Manufacturers for his unionizing efforts, Barry had been unable to work as an ax maker since 1883. He earned a living running the Lyceum Specialty Company in his hometown of Saginaw. Its function was "Introducing High Class Specialties with the Latest Illustrated Song Hits."[9]

Samuel Gompers, by contrast, seemed quite pleased with himself at age seventy, not long before he completed his autobiography, *Seventy Years of Life and Labor.* Although widely accused of rank conservatism and rabid Red-baiting, the AFL leader exulted to Labadie in 1920, four years before his death, that he had lost none of the "hopes and aspirations that animated me in youth." His desire to help others was "an inspiration that keeps me young both in mind and body." He felt like a forty-year-old, he maintained, spent all his time working, often until late at night, and was convinced "work is the greatest medicine known to man." He assured Labadie that his mind was untroubled by thoughts of old age or death.[10]

Socialist leader Eugene Debs had returned to his native Terre Haute in poor health and depressed spirits after his ten year sentence for violation of the 1918 Espionage Law was commuted by President Warren Harding in 1921. His Socialist party was torn by factional disputes and losing ground rapidly. Tempted to join with the Communist party in a united labor front, Debs instead endorsed the 1924 presidential bid of U.S. Senator Robert La

Follette, the Progressive candidate. The disappointing results of the election brought the collapse of the entire third-party movement and speeded the disintegration of the Socialist party. Ailing, no longer able to rouse audiences with his past fervor, Debs wrote Labadie wistfully soon after the election: "You and I can do our little utmost and then drop away to make room for others to do the same, and all the reward, all the honor, all the satisfaction we ever want is the knowledge that we have given all and done our best without expecting anything in return." He died two years later, at age seventy.[11]

The much-reviled Terence Powderly, of course, did not share any ruminations on the meaning of it all with his friend-turned-foe in Detroit, although his later career was often remarked on in Labadie's circle. The once grand master workman had done well for himself after being driven from office in 1893 and expelled from the Knights of Labor. Blackballed because of his reputation when he sought work as a machinist, Powderly turned to law, then politics. His energetic efforts in 1896 for the election of President McKinley, a notorious foe of labor, gained him an appointment as commissioner general of immigration in 1897. Many former labor colleagues denounced him for supporting McKinley against the liberal William Jennings Bryan. Gompers protested the appointment as an insult to the labor movement.[12]

"You sized Powderly up years ago . . . a d—d scoundrel . . . a soldier of fortune," Henry Robinson assured Labadie from Washington in 1896. The former Greenbacker and Detroit Knight had been appointed statistician of the Department of Agriculture by President Cleveland after his term as Michigan's labor commissioner.[13] Whatever Powderly's personal shortcomings in the eyes of some, he was a survivor, still thriving as a high-ranking bureaucrat in the immigration bureau into his seventies.

Even after the brutal repressions carried out by the new Soviet dictatorship became well known, Labadie clung to the belief that the Bolsheviks were making "laudable efforts to at least try some way out of the hell of industrial slavery." In March 1921, the same month that hundreds of striking sailors at the Kronstadt naval base were slaughtered by the Soviet military, Labadie maintained that even a dictatorship dedicated to economic reform was better than continued exploitation of the workers by the czarist regime. Speaking at a memorial meeting for Russian anarchist Peter Kropotkin, he condemned the "little dogs barking at the heels of this Bolshevik elephant" who were doing nothing to change the system themselves.[14]

Labadie soon heard that Emma Goldman and Alexander Berkman had fled Russia in horror and that the admired Kropotkin, an implacable foe of

Bolshevism, had died that February "of a broken heart." Labadie's exhilaration over the revolution and hope that it would develop a strong anarchist influence was fast ebbing. Although the aging anarchist was still trying to keep an open mind, Detroit's Bolshevik sympathizers were denouncing him as a counter-revolutionary. As Goldman and Berkman embarked on their long search for a congenial refuge in December 1921, Labadie forgot his previous differences with the vexatious Emma. He tried to get her address so he could commiserate with her and let her know that "she is not forgotten by the old guard, even tho we did not wholly agree with her."[15]

Labadie also did not forget Benjamin Tucker, nor reconcile himself to the cleavage from Tucker's intellectual leadership. He finally acknowledged that America's foremost agitator for individualist anarchism had "cut the bridges behind him" after leaving the United States in 1908 and settling in France. Years of futile efforts could not entice Tucker into a correspondence. "While I miss him greatly I refrain from intruding upon his privacy and hug my disappointment and my loss," he revealed to a friend in 1924.[16]

Despite declining health and hearing, and a heart often "torn to shreds by the awfulness" of the world, the "old injun," as Labadie fancied himself, was no pitiable figure in old age. Summers were idylls at Bubbling Waters, where Jo and Sophie were at one in their delight in the primitive life. Undisturbed in their rural paradise except by the warbling of birds perched in the towering oak, white ash, and tamarack trees, and the annual visit of the tax assessor, they reveled in a panoply of meandering streams, marshes studded with cattails, water lily–filled ponds, spouting bubbling springs, and an array of rue anemones, marsh marigolds, forget-me-nots, wild phlox, lilies of the valley, buttercups, and May apples. On hot days, the elderly couple splashed unclothed in an icy pool, untroubled that "our nakedness . . . ain't the nicest in the world." Weekends often brought scores of visitors, friends of Jo and his brothers, but few rented the rude cabins originally erected for poor people.

November's chill, the need for cash, and a longing for his comrades lured Labadie each winter from his Arcadian hideaway back to the "toils and tribulations of the tarting town," which by 1930 had swollen to a cacophonous metropolis of a million and a half souls, more than thirty-five times as large as the golden city of his youth. Lacking a pension, he spent winters clerking for the water board for seventy-five dollars a month until he was discharged in 1920.[17]

In his seventies, Labadie delved into the long-ignored suitcase of manuscripts, set aside a decade before in the den at Bubbling Waters.

He began publishing new booklets of verse and essays. He reveled in the painstaking process of running the century-old press by foot power, plucking the type, letter by letter from a font drawer, setting a single page at a time because of shortage of type. Valuing the little homemade products of the Labadie Shop as charmingly archaic, others begged him to publish their works as well.[18]

A proposal in 1927 from a University of Michigan professor to compile an anthology of his poems intrigued Labadie for a time. Lawrence H. Conrad, a teacher of rhetoric, described himself as a great admirer of Labadie's for living "fearlessly and without compromise . . . a splendid example for a young man like myself to follow." He offered to select a group of Labadie's "literary" works and write an appreciative introduction. His idea was to omit poems "with hate in them" as well as the doggerel. Confessing that he found much of the verse "brutal" and "bitter," he mentioned that it would have been nicer if Labadie had handled anarchy "sweetly," in the manner of Ruskin and Thoreau. Conrad tried for a year to convince Labadie that what he had done "in the sounder tradition of poetry" would outlive his anarchist teachings, and for a time Labadie seemed elated over the anthology idea. But it never materialized. It seems likely that Labadie eventually realized that Conrad's judgments, as Grenell noted, were calculated to "please the bourgeois[ie]," and that was what the old anarchist had spent his life avoiding.[19]

Near-poverty conditions during the cold months in their Buchanan Street house were relieved by brushes with a millionaire's life for the elderly Labadies. Carl Schmidt invited them for weeks and even months to his vacation villa, Walhalla, two hundred miles north of Detroit on the Lake Huron shore. At this seven-thousand-acre estate romantically named after the mythological gathering place of dead warriors, they were lavished with the utmost luxury, waited upon by servants, sometimes joined by fellow guests like Clarence Darrow, Eugene Debs, or other kindred spirits. Here Jo and Carl, ignoring their divergent social standings, rode horses, sailed on a hundred-foot yacht, rambled through the woods, and exchanged off-beat ideas in front of the fireplace until early morning. Schmidt liked to think of them as "two contrary, unconventional damn fools."[20]

Sophie also was welcomed warmly at Walhalla, but not for her progressive views. After observing her for a half century, Grenell noted that she "never utters a think [*sic*] that is not built on the most orthodox and conservative lines." A lifetime catering to a stormy petrel had not altered her outlook in the slightest. Her Catholic faith was steadfast. Although Jo maintained that he did not know if there was a God, or care much, he did believe in a paradise to come.[21] His quasi-religious devotion to the canons of anarchism remained as unwavering as he approached eighty as at his conversion nearly fifty years before.

The real pain of his last years was disappointment in his children. Neither Laura nor Laurance achieved worldly success, nor provided an extension of the devotion and harmony he enjoyed with his beloved "Mamma." He wanted them to make their mark, while at the same time, as an elderly parent, he craved them always around him. They did stick around, unwilling or unable to forge out on their own, but there was little harmony.

Laura, who spent her entire life in the parental homestead, clashed constantly with her brother. She complained frequently that the household chores and burden of caring for her aged parents fell unfairly on her. Laurance regarded her as a bitter and suspicious nag. Jo could not have been pleased that Laura chose, as lifelong companion, a businessman of unenlightened views, with no discernible interest in social reform. After Jo's death, this Fred Saxby moved into the Labadie house and spent the rest of his life with Laura, but never married her. Her sister, Charlotte, found him "an all around reactionary," who had influenced Laura contrary to her father's teachings, and unfairly deprived her of children and married life for unknown reasons.[22]

Charlotte agreed with her sister that Laurance was rude, lazy, and failed to do his share of the chores, but she tried to be a peacemaker. A schoolteacher, like her mother, she was finally married, at thirty-seven, to Fred Hauser, a Swiss-born engineer and socialist of sorts, whom friends had brought to Bubbling Waters to meet Jo. Offered a year's assignment teaching an experimental reading method in a Los Angeles primary school, Charlotte was sufficiently adventurous to drive across the country in a Model T Ford in 1926 with her fiancé and a fellow teacher, the three of them camping along the way. But when the couple decided to remain in California, Jo was disconsolate. He expressed his bitterness to Agnes Inglis: "Our Charlotte and her man have got as far west as they could without swimming, and then tell us how much they enjoy our letters!"[23] He saw them only once again, when they stopped en route to Switzerland in 1931, just before Sophie's death. (With them was the Labadies' two-year-old grandchild, author of this biography.)

What troubled Jo most, however, was the aimlessness and despondency of Laurance, the child of his middle age, and his favorite. What was the cause of his son's pessimism, misanthropy, and depression? Perhaps during his impressionable adolescent years he was infected by the virus of his father's disillusionment born of the war. If so, he wallowed in that negativism, but lacked his father's ability to bounce back with cheerfulness, a witty remark, and an abiding faith in the essential good judgment of humanity, if only it were liberated. Whatever demons tormented Laurance, he did not blame them on Jo. When he was himself advanced in years, he described his father as the only person he ever met who was completely lovable his whole life.[24]

After failing engineering studies in his one semester at the University of Michigan, Laurance turned to tool making and became expert at it, but flitted from job to job in the machine and automotive industries, often remaining only a few weeks. By his early thirties, he could list twenty-five workplaces where he had held short-term jobs. Jo was never hesitant to nag Laurance about career moves, but made no attempt to steer him toward anarchism. The young man turned to economics and philosophy on his own in his late twenties, beginning with his father's favorites, Herbert Spencer and Josiah Warren, and proceeding to Schopenhauer, Nietzsche, and H. L. Mencken. He announced to his elderly parents in 1927, at the age of twenty-nine, that "nothing means anything." He pronounced the "whole cosmic process . . . utter hopelessness and futility." His father's reproaches, "smug platitudes," infuriated him. He readily confessed to a lack of ambition and "hate of everything."[25]

But after Sophie's death in 1931, Laurance tended to his father lovingly, spending summers with him at Bubbling Waters. In 1932, he took Jo, then eighty-two, to Ann Arbor for one last nostalgic look at his precious papers. Although Labadie's memory was nearly gone, curator Agnes Inglis was cheered to see how attractive he still looked, with his neatly groomed white mustachio and "imperial" goatee.[26]

Laurance brought the printing press back from Bubbling Waters to their Detroit home and, in 1932, helped his father produce a last booklet, *Anarchism,* containing an excerpt from an earlier publication. Laurance organized and shipped some nine thousand items of his father's correspondence to the University of Michigan, making copies of those which particularly interested him. Mercifully oblivious to the miseries of the Great Depression and the family's poverty, Jo spent his last year wandering plaintively from room to room, searching for his beloved "Mamma."[27]

Jo Labadie died in Detroit's Receiving Hospital on October 7, 1933, at the age of eighty-three. He had instructed that his funeral be as simple as possible, with no music, sermon, or tears. Those present found it almost joyous. A remarkable number of old comrades, and the sons of dead ones, mingled with young radicals to exchange remembrances and pay last respects to this relic of bygone causes. A wreath from the Detroit Russian Anarchists' Group was placed on his casket. Carl Nold, who had been imprisoned for conspiring with Alexander Berkman in the attack on Henry Frick, added a paper rose.[28] Labadie was buried next to Sophie in Parkview Memorial Cemetery on Five Mile Road near Farmington. Only copper plates mark their graves.

Obituaries in the Detroit dailies were respectful and affectionate. "Gentle Anarchist Toiled for the Brotherhood of Man," the *Detroit News* summed up. Other articles remembered him as "a gentle Red," "inimitable," and "a picturesque figure" of whom it was once said that not to know him was not to know Detroit.

Except for the enduring legacy of his papers, it had been many years since Jo Labadie had made much of a difference in the world. The labor movement had passed him by. While he was longing for a revival of the early, idealistic Knights of Labor, a new breed of union leaders was cropping up. It included such stellar figures as Walter Reuther, soon to begin organizing Detroit auto workers into the UAW, but also men like Jimmy Hoffa, future Teamsters Union boss, labor racketeer, and the consort of mobsters, who around the time of Labadie's death was unionizing workers at Kroger's grocery warehouse in Detroit.[29]

In his last years, as he looked back on a lifetime's endeavors, Labadie felt that all his moral indignation and tireless activity had accomplished little. So few of the cherished goals of his youth had been realized. He saw the bulk of the laboring people still toiling in "wage slavery" in ever-larger industrial conglomerates. Their welfare was still threatened by the vagaries of monopolistic capitalism. "An injury to one is the concern of all," the Knights' motto, was as far from a reality as ever. The Michigan Federation of Labor (MFL), which he had founded, was solidly in place as an AFL affiliate and provided bargaining power to labor's aristocracy, the craft unionists, but most of the state's workers remained unorganized. The AFL was losing ground nationwide.

When Labadie died in 1933, the most devastating depression in the country's history had left some fifteen million Americans jobless, and many more with their wages drastically cut. With nearly half of Michigan's workers unemployed, more than six hundred thousand of the desperate went on relief. Barracks were filled with the homeless and an army of unemployed roamed from place to place seeking work. Starving people were found unconscious on Detroit streets. Thousands of families were evicted for non-payment of rent or had their utilities shut off.[30] The New Deal lay just ahead, but its government-run benefit system would not have been Labadie's idea of the solution.

Stifled by twentieth-century bureaucracy, there was probably less, not more, individual liberty in the country than when Labadie first began fighting for it. Few remained who would insist, as he had, that anarchism was not a "cloudland" movement. In his valiant uphill battle to convince the public of the beauty of the anarchist idea, he may have broken down "more prejudice against the word 'anarchist' than can ever be estimated," as Agnes Inglis insisted, but then, as now, it constituted only a drop in a cascade of anti-anarchist venom.[31]

When he was being honest with himself, Labadie acknowledged that his life had been "largely spent in the Land of Dreams." Although his accomplishments fell far short of his goals, he aimed high, struggled mightily, and risked denunciation for being true to himself. A memorialist commented in 1950 that he kept himself as free as a man ever could: "Many envied him who did not have his courage." Personal charm, a strong sense of identity, and an irrepressible rebelliousness enabled him to live pretty much as his fancy dictated. He was, an admirer summed up, "a genial, whimsical dreamer whom the gods love and to whom they have been kind."[32]

Yet the endeavors of Labadie and his comrades were not in vain. Unions today may be but a shadow of their promise of a century ago, but it was their demands and the threat of union action that produced improved working conditions for the majority of American workers today, even the unorganized. The Knights of Labor, though it failed, showed muscle that strongly affected industrial relations to come and the AFL/CIO is still a force to be reckoned with.

What Labadie believed in—from beginning to end—was the value of the individual. It defined everything he did. He strode through a somewhat quixotic career fueled by confidence in the ability of the unique individual standing alone, self-led, self-governed, to make a difference, and convinced many others that his ideas were worthy of consideration. By understanding the power of the press, he showed how a popular figure could mold public opinion. Through his impassioned protests he helped define the limits of government force and coercion. Indeed, Labadie might be heartened to know that at the end of the twentieth century disenchantment with government and its ability to ensure liberty and justice for all is rife in the land. Like others who fought lost causes, Jo Labadie nonetheless influenced the outcome of those causes that survived.

EPILOGUE

The Flame Is Passed

Shortly before Jo Labadie died in 1933, his son, Laurance, used the Labadie Shop's archaic printing press to publish a well-received speech Benjamin Tucker had given before the National Civic Federation conference on trusts in Chicago in 1899. Titled "The Attitude of Anarchism Toward Industrial Combinations," it opposed the anti-trust legislation favored by most of the nationally prominent speakers attending and impressed professor of labor history John R. Commons as "the most brilliant piece of pure logic" heard at the conference.[1]

Laurance, then thirty-five, sent a packet of the booklets to the seventy-nine-year-old Tucker in Monaco by way of introduction. Tucker pointed out the proofreading errors but otherwise seemed pleased. Over the next five years, Laurance wrote several adulatory letters to Tucker, describing himself as one interested in the propagation of anarchism, "while not an enthusiast," although he considered Proudhon the greatest philosopher he had ever read. He observed that the individualist school of anarchism seemed "quite dead." Tucker confirmed the observation by dedicating a photo presented to Laurance to "the only young person that I recall who, being the offspring of an avowed Anarchist, finds his greatest satisfaction in continuing the battle, even though the cause be lost."[2]

Laurance confided to Tucker that, unlike his father, he was "unsocial," egocentric, irritable, and solitary, and that "a despondent pessimism fastened on me about 15 years ago, when I was emersed [*sic*] in Schopenhauer."[3] At the same time, he greatly understated to Tucker his commitment to the individualist doctrine. Laurance devoted the rest of his lifetime to its promulgation. In 1933, the same year he originally contacted Tucker, he published an essay, "Anarchism Applied to Economics," the first of several hundred pieces he was to write in the next thirty-odd years. Originally concentrating on what he considered the evils resulting from the monopolization of money and banking, he went on to examine from the anarchist viewpoint education, racial problems, and religion—as well as issues unique to the twentieth century, such as the Vietnam conflict and the threat of nuclear war. Many of these sometimes brilliant expositions eventually found their way to obscure radical publications.[4]

Laurance thus became Jo's intellectual heir, and equally significant, Tucker's. He claimed that his father never attempted to convert him to anarchism; indeed, there is no evidence that, in his old age, Jo was even aware of his son's growing attachment to the doctrine or would have welcomed the development if he had. Acknowledged as the "keeper of the flame," Laurance, the last of Tucker's circle, carried the sputtering flicker of nineteenth-century "plumb line" individualist anarchism into the mid twentieth century.[5] There it was rekindled in a modified form in the early 1970s by the more mainstream libertarian movement, illustrating that yesterday's left-wing radicals and today's right-wing libertarians have more in common than generally thought. Indeed, American individualist anarchists are a puzzle for those who like to fit ideologies neatly into ready-made right-wing/left-wing, liberal/conservative, slots. They were "liberals" in their belief in the sanctity of individual rights, and "conservatives" in their calls for a free marketplace. Individualist anarchism and the theories of today's libertarians both descend from the laissez-faire principles of Adam Smith and John Locke, and accept that free competition does not bring equal outcomes for each individual, but do not see that as injustice. Although many who profess libertarianism simply resent government regulation of their enterprises, the Labadies focused on the disparity in wealth and power caused by state-created monopolies of land, money, trade (tariffs), ideas (patents/copyrights), and natural resources.

In 1937, finding no publication receptive to his writings, Laurance started his own. In the modest, mimeographed *Discussion—A Journal for*

Free Spirits, he engaged some of Benjamin Tucker's original associates and a few interested readers in the type of contentious discussion he and Tucker so much relished. Focused on the desirability of competing money systems and banking free of government control, the modest journal lasted for eight issues.[6]

Throughout these years, Laurance continued to co-exist discordantly with his sister, Laura, and her companion, Fred Saxby, in the family home at Fifteenth and Buchanan Streets, working, when necessary, as a highly skilled tool and die maker. He devoted his lonely hours to studying the old issues of *Liberty* and his father's correspondence, and developing his ability to think and write. Although Laurance adored his father, Tucker was his great intellectual ideal and model.[7]

At about fifty, in 1948, Laurance became interested in the decentralist School of Living movement founded by Ralph Borsodi. In its homesteading communities, far from urban blight, families under Borsodi's guidance sought security from unemployment and depressions by living communally and providing their own necessities from the land. Laurance began writing for the school's publications. Though afraid of traveling, he was persuaded to visit the Lane's End Homestead of John and Mildred Loomis in Brookville, Ohio, where a branch of the School of Living was located.[8]

By then, this self-taught, worker-intellectual had developed a "fiercely logical and precise style" of writing, clear and direct, that historian James J. Martin compared to Tucker's. Laurance is considered by some to have surpassed his father as thinker and essayist. His articles over the next twenty years and his argumentative and cantankerous presence had a profound effect on many of the decentralists, who had taken government for granted until he introduced them to the individualist viewpoint.[9]

Of short stature, like his father, with a strong nose and Indian-appearing physiognomy, Laurance also was given to romantically exaggerating the slight degree of Native American genetic material remaining in the Labadie blood line. Unlike his father, he dressed neglectfully and often slept in his clothes.

Whatever money Laurance earned, he saved whenever possible. Mildred Loomis remembered him washing socks at Lane's End Homestead in leftover suds and retrieving half-smoked cigarettes from the ashtray. In 1952, his frugality enabled him to buy Borsodi's old "Dogwood's Homestead" on beautifully wooded acreage in Suffern, New York. He derived income from renting out the three apartments in the stately stone house and converted the tool shed to quarters for himself and his extensive library. Here he worked at Tucker's massive rolltop desk, loaned to him by Tucker's daughter, Oriole Tucker Riché. In the former chicken coop, he ran a little mailing list business.[10]

Despite grossly deficient housekeeping skills, Laurance maintained precise files of his prodigious correspondence with still-living members of his father's circle, with latter-day libertarians, and with those involved in the Borsodi-Loomis back-to-the-land movement, which advocated Henry George's single tax on land. He thrived on controversy and his verbal tangles with correspondents could be insulting. "He would eat you alive at the faintest sign of wavering of intelligence," his friend James Martin remembered.[11] Many folders full of "Unsent Letters to Mildred Loomis" (Borsodi's chief lieutenant), plus copies of the ones Laurance actually sent, testify to his profound exasperation with what he considered her (and Borsodi's) muddle-headed thinking. Like his father, he exhibited particular scorn for most of the academic community.

Increasingly reclusive as time went on, Laurance would engage in interminable monologues with his few visitors, switching abruptly from subject to subject in a sort of stream of consciousness style. Sharp-tongued and irascible to some, slyly sarcastic, he was also often generous and kindly. He took special delight in children, with whom he felt a kinship; the children of former black neighbors in Detroit spent what must have been a couple of gloriously unstructured summer vacations with him in the 1960s in Suffern. To a few intimates, he revealed a delightfully acerbic wit, often telling jokes on himself. He claimed, for example, that he followed a well-balanced diet, eating carrots one year, spinach the next, and so on, a problem arising only if he did not live long enough to incorporate all the food groups.[12] To those few friends, he possessed an endearing vulnerability.

Laurance never married. He thought it a humorous irony that when, in his fifties, he finally asked a woman at the School of Living to marry him, even though he considered her unattractive because of "bad skin," she turned him down. He told a friend that he had tried sex a couple times and thought it highly overrated. Depicting himself as "psychically out of gear," Laurance felt the emotional side of his nature was undeveloped. "Probably thru fear, I kept it suppressed and never let my heart out to anyone," he wrote.[13]

Bedeviled by feelings of his own worthlessness, Laurance considered most of mankind pretty worthless as well. He concluded, toward the end of his life, that he had had no influence whatever. He attributed the destruction of his health and spirit mainly to "the frustration coming from lack of communication." His outlook became so cataclysmic that "it made even most editors of radical journals flinch and run," according to James Martin. In his last published work, *What Is Man's Destiny?* (1970), Laurance foresaw the impending doom of humanity and stated that "it is completely preposterous to expect that the general battle for power between governments (whose mere existence as mutual threats mutually support each other) could possibly eventuate in anything other than the mutual extermination of the human race." He concluded in his last years that the practical realization of anarchism was "a pipe dream."[14]

By the time Laurance died on August 12, 1975, at age seventy-six, of lymphosarcoma, America's present-day libertarian movement was well underway. Its basic theoretical underpinnings were those he and his father combined had been preaching for nearly one hundred years, and which in turn were inspired by the eighteenth-century classical liberalism of Smith, Locke, and the Founding Fathers. As outlined by libertarian leader Murray N. Rothbard in 1974, the doctrine holds that no person or government has the right to aggress against the person or property of another; people have the right to do whatever they wish so along as they do not invade the rights of others; war is mass murder; conscription is slavery; taxation is banditry; and that "throughout history, there has been one central, dominant, and overriding aggressor upon all of these rights: the State."[15]

Few of today's libertarians are aware of the role Laurance played in keeping the ideology alive, nor do most know much of Jo Labadie, Benjamin Tucker, and their circle. Laurance's unprepossessing, rumpled figure would have been a curious sight alongside these libertarians and "anarcho-capitalists" in dapper suits, who put no one in mind of the old-time stereotypical wild-eyed, bushy-haired anarchist. Although Jo and Laurance's sympathies lay with the poor and downtrodden, not those at the top of the heap, they were, nevertheless, philosophical ancestors of the new breed.

AFTERWORD

The Labadie Collection Today

EDWARD C. WEBER
Curator of the Labadie Collection

Agnes Inglis's familiarity with even small details of the Labadie Collection enabled her informal archival arrangement to serve users very well—better than anyone has since been able to do. To the trained librarian's eye Inglis's system appeared idiosyncratic. Her death in February 1952 removed the easy key to her arrangement, namely, herself.

The graduate (then general) library began official cataloging of the Labadie Collection that same year but we have no record of the procedures followed or the reasons advanced for them. Strangely, some periodicals and monographs, notably IWW materials, were transferred to the library stacks, and other parts of the collection—labor colleges, cooperatives, and WPA plays, for example—were judged no longer to be within its proper scope. A few of these were transferred to the Detroit Public Library; the fate of most of the others remains unknown.

Throughout the remainder of the 1950s, the collection remained behind chicken wire in an area on the eighth level of the stacks. Its distant location meant that those who wanted to use it were handed the key and could browse unsupervised. Cataloging ceased within a year after its start; the rearranged collection of books, serials, pamphlets, and vertical files without designation or records was just as bewildering as Inglis's own system. The general impression of the viewer was of confusion and neglect, aggravated by the piles of unshelved materials for whose place in the arrangement no clues could be found.

In 1960, I was assigned as full-time librarian and head of the Labadie Collection to create some system to provide ready access. There were thousands of uncataloged periodicals and pamphlets, the latter arranged only by large subject category without other clues. The 20,000 pamphlets were checked item by item to prepare a card index for personal author, group, significant title, and related subject entries, with cross references. The vertical file cases, containing a wealth of leaflets, flyers, newspaper clippings, and records of research, received a similar analysis for the necessary card index. After the periodical records were checked for verification of holdings and locations, card indexes for place of publication and for date by decade gave clues for many research questions. Toward the end of the 1960s the copious manuscript correspondence was examined for making indices of authors and subjects. Not everything had been in place. After searching for Emma Goldman's letters to Agnes Inglis, I came upon them in a cabinet of supplies in a box marked "Folders" that I was preparing to throw away.

Unfortunately, very little could be done with Agnes Inglis's handwritten cards. They had all been dumped into a cardboard box but fortunately not discarded. Attempting to reconstitute her files was a laborious, sometimes vain, task. The cards contain references not found elsewhere, but the location symbols were useless after the 1950s re-organization. Indeed, the footnotes of scholars who did their research while Inglis was in charge are tantalizing to today's historians, since the cited locations of many materials no longer exist.

In 1977, librarian Margaret Berg began to reconstitute the Labadie manuscript collections by donor and provide inventories, a task carried on by her successor, Kathryn Beam, from 1983. The work still goes on, although almost all the older manuscript collections were complete enough for Beam to edit a guide, *Manuscripts in the Labadie Collection,* in 1987.

Grave problems remained with the periodicals, whose official cataloging was piecemeal from 1960 on. It was estimated that of approximately 8,000 serial titles in the Labadie Collection, only 15 percent had been cataloged. In 1983, librarian R. Anne Okey secured a two-year grant from the National Endowment for the Humanities to establish a database for the periodicals and uncataloged pamphlets. All the serials and three-quarters of the pamphlets were entered before the funding ran out. A recent grant is making possible full cataloging of the periodicals, which are then to be entered on MIRLYN, the University of Michigan's on-line catalog, and on national databases.

The Labadie Collection does not have the single catalog, so often requested. Its holdings must be sought from a variety of sources: MIRLYN, for all officially cataloged materials, alphabetical card indexes for certain categories of pamphlets, 25 drawers of vertical files, 600 reels of microfilm, and 300 records, cassettes, and tapes, as well as sheet music and photographs. The 225 linear feet of manuscript holdings remain in varying states of processing. Some parts of the collection, such as posters, are still without precise guideposts except large subject designations.

As the lives of Jo Labadie and Agnes Inglis would suggest, the outstanding feature of the collection is the in-depth documentation of the anarchist movement, perhaps the most comprehensive in this hemisphere. Other notable strengths are in radical social protest and reform movements of the nineteenth and twentieth centuries, socialism, communism, early labor history (especially the Knights of Labor and the IWW), civil liberties, cooperatives, free thought, sexual freedom, colonialism and imperialism, the radical right, monetary reform, the single-tax movement, the Spanish Civil War, and youth and student protest, with the documents sometimes donated by the organizations concerned. The collection is also known for its ephemera, which Labadie and his wife, Sophie, were adept at collecting, and includes flyers, scrapbooks, buttons, badges, armbands, and bumper stickers.

The flood of acquisitions has always been much greater than the cataloging. From the 1960s, following Agnes Inglis's earlier example, I began corresponding with individuals, groups, and organizations active in publishing or disseminating radical literature. This gained the collection substantial holdings in the areas of civil rights, the student protest and anti-war movements, modern anarchist and socialist literature, gay liberation, radical feminism, pacifism, environmental concerns, and anti-nuclear movements. In 1964, the library director decided to add radical right materials to the radical left.

Since the collection burgeoned greatly in the 1930s and even more so in the 1960s and after, one may ask how significant today are the contributions by its founder and by its first curator. They are immensely valuable. Jo Labadie's printed materials are often unique, shedding light on radical and labor history beyond the Michigan locale, while his immense personal correspondence over decades serves to give perspective on a wide variety of political and social issues of the time. Agnes Inglis's bibliographies do not correspond to a dictionary definition but are repositories of factual information, just as her handwritten cards give clues to articles never analyzed elsewhere. Her personal correspondence is another mine of insightful comment.

It should not be overlooked that both Labadie and Inglis were pioneers in gathering radical materials when official institutions, among them libraries, frowned on the idea. They rescued what would otherwise have been lost, and the gratitude of subsequent researchers cannot be overstated.

NOTES

Abbreviations

AFL:SG	American Federation of Labor Records, Samuel Gompers Era
EVD	Eugene V. Debs Papers
GS	George Schilling Papers
J.L.	Joseph Labadie
LC	Labadie Collection
LC/AI	Agnes Inglis Papers, Labadie Collection
LC/HB	Henry Bool Papers, Labadie Collection
LC/JG	Judson Grenell Papers, Labadie Collection
LC/LL	Laurance Labadie Papers, Labadie Collection
MSBLS	Michigan State Bureau of Labor and Industrial Statistics
MSUAHC	Michigan State University Archives and Historical Collections
NYPL	New York Public Library
TVP	Terence V. Powderly Papers
SHSW	State Historical Society of Wisconsin

Preface

1. Emile Zola, *Germinal* (Aylesbury, Bucks., England: Penguin Books, 1984), 499.
2. Carl Nold, "Anarchists: Joseph A. Labadie," *Man!* 6, no. 69 (November 1933).
3. J.L., "Uncle Sam, the Real Culprit," *Liberty,* October 3, 1885.
4. Lee J. Smits, "Dean of Detroit's Bohemia," *Detroit Free Press,* October 29, 1922, J.L. Scrapbook I, 104, LC.
5. J.L. to "Friend Albertus" (Albert G. Wagner), February 8, 1927, LC.
6. Agnes Inglis, "Grenell—Judson," 5, LC/JG.

Chapter 1

1. Norman Ware, *The Labor Movement in the United States* (Gloucester: Peter Smith, 1959), 377, xiv; Foster Rhea Dulles and Melvyn Dubofsky, *Labor in America* (Arlington Heights, Ill.: Harlan Davidson, Inc., 1984), 121.
2. George E. McNeill, ed., *The Labor Movement: The Problem of Today* (Boston and New York: A. M. Bridgeman, 1887), 147.

3. J.L. to Richard T. Ely, August 8, 1885, Ely Papers, SHSW.

4. *Detroit Evening News,* October 5, 7, 1878.

5. George W. Stark, *City of Destiny* (Detroit: Arnold-Powers, Inc., 1943), 396, 394.

6. Judson Grenell, "Detroit News and Notes," *The Socialist* (Chicago), October 19, 1878; "Labor Day!" *Detroit Evening News,* September 5, 1887; Joseph A. Labadie, "How the Knights of Labor Came to Michigan," 1926, and two untitled typescripts dated April 1929, beginnning "Charles Litchman came to Detroit" and "The first move for the organization of the Knights of Labor," LC.

7. A. M. Dewey, *Industrial Leaders of Today* (Detroit: A. M. Dewey, 1888), 5; Gary M. Fink, ed., *Biographical Dictionary of American Labor* (Westport, Conn.: Greenwood Press, 1984), 358; Ware, *The Labor Movement in the United States,* 20–21.

8. *The Socialist* (Detroit), October 19, 1878.

9. Agnes Inglis, "Charles Joseph Anthony Labadie," three-page biographical sketch, LC.

10. Terence V. Powderly, *The Path I Trod* (New York: Columbia University Press, 1940), 49.

11. In his 1926 account Labadie identified this man only as "Miller." Contrary to some speculations, this could not have been Charles E. Miller, who, according to his profile in *Industrial Leaders of Today,* did not come to Detroit until 1885, and would, in any case, only have been seventeen years old at the time of the initiation.

12. Ware, *The Labor Movement,* 377–78; Philip S. Foner, *History of the Labor Movement in the United States* (New York: International Publishers, 1947), 1:434, 436.

13. *Adelphon Kruptos,* no title page, n.d., 6–7, 28, TVP, reel 67.

14. Ware, *The Labor Movement,* 20–21. Except for his fourteen years in the Knights of Labor, Litchman was active in the Republican party. M. B. Schnapper, *American Labor: A Pictoral Social History* (Washington, D.C.: Public Affairs Press, 1975), 137–138.

15. Schnapper, *American Labor,* 113.

16. Knights of Labor, *Record of Proceedings of the Second Regular Session of the General Assembly* (St. Louis, June 14–17, 1879), 64. Labadie often mistakenly said he joined the Knights in 1879, probably because his first commission from Powderly is dated December 13, 1879. He apparently forgot that his original commission from Uriah S. Stephens was recalled in September 1879, along with all the Knights of Labor commissions, and replaced with one signed by Powderly, the new grand master workman.

17. *The Haverhill Laborer,* clipping of letter from Labadie dated August 16, 1884, J.L. Scrapbook II, 92–93, LC; Foner, *History of the Labor Movement,* 1:509; Jonathan Garlock, *Guide to the Local Assemblies of the Knights of Labor* (Westport, Conn.: Greenwood Press, 1982), xix.

18. The references to the first meetings of Local Assembly 901 are based on the minutes of the Washington Literary Society, December 1, 1878 to March 3, 1879, LC.

19. David A. Boyd to A. Inglis, April 10, 1939, LC/AI; J.L. to Ely, December 16, 1885, SHSW; *Labor Leaf,* February 29, 1886, 2.

20. *Adelphon Kruptos,* 6–7; Schnapper, *American Labor,* 136–38; Ware, *The Labor Movement,* 26. For an extensive examination of the ritual and religiosity of the Knights, see Robert E. Weir, *Beyond Labor's Veil: The Culture of the Knights of Labor* (University Park: Pennsylvania State University Press, 1996), 19–66.

21. *Detroit Evening News,* September 5, 1887; D. Boyd to A. Inglis, April 10, 1939, LC/AI.

22. MSBLS, *First Annual Report* (Lansing), 1884, 68–71. In 1882, there were 659 Detroit children under age fourteen working in factories or as messenger boys, including one age seven. MSBLS, *Second Annual Report* (1885), 63.

23. Ware, *The Labor Movement,* xiii–xvi.

24. *Bay City Globe,* letter from J.L., n.d. (ca. 1881), J.L. Scrapbook II, 49–50, LC; J.L. Account Book, March 1879–March 1880, LC.

25. MSBLS, *First Annual Report,* 1884, 71; *Detroit Evening News,* July 16, 1884, J.L. Scrapbook II, 69, LC; Washington Literary Society minutes.

26. Ware, *The Labor Movement,* 75, 346–48; Weir, *Beyond Labor's Veil,* 46, 51; *Detroit Evening Journal,* interview with J.L., n.d., J.L. Scrapbook I, 51, LC.

27. *Detroit Evening News,* September 5, 1887. McClellan is sometimes spelled McClelland or McClellend.

28. Richard Jules Oestreicher, *Solidarity and Fragmentation: Working People and Class Consciousness in Detroit, 1875–1900* (Urbana: University of Illinois Press, 1986), 91–92.

29. Dewey, *Industrial Leaders of Today,* 17; *The Socialist* (Detroit), April 20, 1878; "Eccentric Characters," J.L. Scrapbook 1882–1929, 13–14, LC/LL.

30. [*Lansing Sentinel*], 1884, J.L. Scrapbook 1883–1901, 10, LC/LL.

31. J.L. to Powderly, December 7, 1879, February 24, 1880, TVP; Knights of Labor, *Record of Proceedings of the Fourth Regular Session of the General Assembly,* Pittsburgh, September 7–11, 1880, 213, TVP, reel 67; J.L., untitled typescript, beginning "The first move," April 1929, LC.

32. *Labor Review,* September 25, 1880.

33. Richard J. Oestreicher, "Terence Powderly, the Knights of Labor and Artisanal Republicanism," in *Labor Leaders of America,* ed. Melvyn Dubofsky and Warren Van Tine (Urbana: University of Illinois Press, 1987), 47–48; J. Grenell, untitled typescript, beginning "The order of the Knights of Labor," 1–2, LC/JG.

Chapter 2

1. Labadie's experiences living in the wilderness among the Indians of southern Michigan are described in his letters to Al G. Wagner, October 23, 1925; J. Grenell, January 15, 1928, February 27, 1930; A. Inglis, May 25, 1929; C. H. Engle, July 14, 1913; and in L. Labadie, "Jo Labadie," October 22, 1944, LC. See also J.L., three-page typescript, beginning "It has been my fate to be a worker all my life," n.d., LC; J.L. to "Dear Mrs. Bather," n.d., LC.

2. J.L. to Wagner, October 23, 1925, LC.

3. F. Clever Bald, *Michigan in Four Centuries* (New York: Harper and Brothers, 1961), 8–19.

4. Information about Anthony C. Labadie is found in J.L., "My Outings," n.d., LC; U.S. Army, "Discharge Certificate for Anthony C. Labadie," April 2, 1863, LC; U.S. Census, Lafayette (later Paw Paw), Michigan, 1840; L. Labadie, "Jo Labadie."

5. J.L., "The History of the Labadie Family," n.d., LC; J.L. to J. Grenell, February 27, 1930, LC; U.S. Census, Lafayette, August 11, 1850.

6. J.L. to Dr. William E. Gilroy, June 14, 1925, LC.

7. The French settlers often had more than one surname, connected by the word "dit," meaning "alias" or "also known as." Descomptes is variously spelled Descomps, De Combs, Descompte, and Descom. Labadie is also spelled Labodie, de la Badie, and la Bady in early records. Larry Emery, "The Story of Marie Sauvagesse and Antoine 'Badichon' Labadie," July 1997, 30p. ts., 2, LC. Labadie family genealogical data is found in the following: Clarence M. Burton, "The Labadie Family in Detroit," LC; idem, *The City of Detroit, 1701–1922* (Detroit: Clarke, 1922), 1382–84; Fr. Christian Denissen, *Genealogy of the French Families of the Detroit River Region, 1701–1936* (Detroit: Detroit Society for Genealogical Research, 1987) 616–23; "The Labadies of Windsor, Ontario," n.d., LC; A. Philippe E. Panet, "The Labadie Family in the County of Essex, Ontario," *Essex Historical Society* 1 (1905): 12–27, 38–55; Antoine Descomptes dit Labadie's will, English translation, May 26, 1806, LC; J.L., *Detroit News* questionnaire, February 20, 1920, *Detroit News* files; General Friend Palmer, *Early Days in Detroit* (Detroit: Hunt and June, 1906), 370–72, 623–25; *Border Cities Star* (Windsor, Ont.), December 10, 1932; Francis X. Chauvin, *Hiram Walker: His Life, His Work* (Windsor: Hiram Walker Distillery, n.d. [1925]). The earliest known map of Detroit, dated 1752, reproduced in the *Detroit News,* December 7, 1930, shows members of the family settled on both sides of the Detroit River. An extended account of the early Labadies is found in Carlotta Anderson, "The Ancestors of Jo Labadie (Charles Joseph Antoine Labadie) Detroit Labor Leader and Anarchist, 1850–1933," 1995, LC.

8. Chauvin, *Hiram Walker,* 5, chap. 9; J.L., "Backward Look, Vanishing Vision," n.d., LC.

9. J.L. to Clarence Burton, March 18, 1917, LC.

10. J.L. to A. Inglis, May 25, 1929; U.S. Census, Lafayette, 1840; Antoine Descomptes dit Labadie will, LC. Marie was, more specifically, a Sauteuse. The home ground of the Ojibway tribe was around the Sault Sainte Marie. The French called these Indians Saulteurs, which, corrupted a bit and applied to a female, would be Sauteuse. For an examination of data regarding Marie, see Emery, "Marie Sauvagesse and Antoine 'Badichon' Labadie," 11–17. Even in Michigan, some British subjects, but not Americans, were permitted to own slaves after 1796. Bald, *Michigan in Four Centuries,* 98. Slavery in Canada continued until it was abolished by the 1833 Imperial Act, and in Michigan until the state's first constitution came into effect in 1837. David M. Katzman, *Before the Ghetto: Black Detroit in the Nineteenth Century* (Urbana: University of Illinois Press, 1973), 5–6.

11. The East Sandwich period and the development of Walkerville are described in J.L. to Burton, March 18, 1917, LC; Chauvin, *Hiram Walker;* J.L., "Backward Look, Vanishing Vision"; "The Labadies of Windsor, Ontario"; "Labadie Heirs," [*Detroit Evening News*], January 16, 1886, J.L. Scrapbook I, 65, LC; "Labadies are Likely to be Millionaires," *The Show World,* April 10, 1909, LC; "Obituary" and "An Old Resident Dies," n.s., March 6, 1886, J.L. Scrapbook II, 1, LC; J.L. to A. Inglis, May 25, 1929, LC; J.L. to J. Grenell, February 27, 1930, LC; J.L. to *Detroit News,* February 25, 1924, LC.

12. Obituary of Felice Montreuil Chapoton, newspaper clipping, n.s., 1899, LC.

13. J.L. to Grenell, February 27, 1930, LC.

14. The Pottawatomi were Indians of the Algonquian stock, who at one time formed a confederacy with the Ojibway and the Ottawa. They settled in lower Michigan and lived chiefly by hunting and fishing. In 1838, the U.S. government moved most of them West, but the band led by Leopold Pokagen was allowed to remain. Leopold's son, Simon, the last of the Pottawatomi chiefs, attended Notre Dame University and Oberlin College, and made several trips to Washington, D.C., to obtain payments due the tribe and to demand the fulfillment of treaty promises. E. F. Greenman, "Indian Chiefs of Michigan," *Michigan History* 23, no. 3 (summer 1938): 229–32.

15. J.L., "It has been my fate . . . ," LC.

16. J.L., "To the Editor of the Michigan Catholic," LC.

17. *The Ledger,* similar to *Harper's Weekly* or *Vanity Fair,* was designed for Sunday reading and featured reports and pictures from the Civil War battlefields, as well as popular romances and useful information.

18. J.L., "What Is Love?" *What Is Love? and Other Fancies* (Detroit: The Labadie Shop, 1910), LC.

19. Information on Anthony Labadie is found in J.L., "My Outings"; Anthony Labadie's U.S. Army discharge certificate; *Record of Service of Michigan Volunteers in the Civil War, 1861–1865* (Kalamazoo: State of Michigan, 1905), 41:110; "Declaration for the Increase of an Invalid Pension" (Clerk of the Circuit Court, State of Michigan, County of Kalkaska), September 8, 1877, LC; L. Labadie, "Jo Labadie," LC.

Chapter 3

1. *Michigan Federation of Labor Yearbook,* 1896, 16, LC; George Stark, "Letter to a Friend," *Detroit News,* July 21, 1939; J.L. to "Dear Aunt," February 7, 1866, LC.

2. J.L. to Clarence Burton, March 18, 1917, LC.

3. L. Labadie, "Jo Labadie"; Stark, "Letter to a Friend."

4. Judson Grenell, "Autobiography" (Clearwater, Fla.: n.p., 1930), 17–19, MSUAHC.

5. Ibid.

6. Schnapper, *American Labor,* 88; Foner, *History of the Labor Movement,* 1:365.

7. Dulles and Dubofsky, *Labor in America,* 101–2; Melvyn Dubofsky, *Industrialism*

    and the American Worker, 1865–1920 (Arlington Heights, Ill.: Harlan Davidson, 1985), 121.

8. Stark, "Letter to a Friend"; J.L. to International Typographical Union, August 9, 1925, LC.

9. *Typographical Journal,* July 15, 1889, Communications Workers of America, Washington, D.C., 6.

10. Labadie's working cards issued by local typographical unions, LC. For an overview of tramping in America by both skilled artisans and the wandering poor, see Eric H. Monkkonen, ed., *Tramping to Work: Tramps in America, 1790–1935* (Lincoln: University of Nebraska Press, 1984).

11. *Typographical Journal,* July 15, 1889, 6; J.L. to "My Dear Brother Devine," January 8, 1915, LC.

12. J.L. to Richard T. Ely, July 4, 1885, Ely Papers, SHSW.

13. J.L. to Paul J. Maas, n.d., LC; J.L. to Burton, March 18, 1917, LC; Labadie, "When the writer came into Detroit," n.d., LC; Stark, "Letter to a Friend."

14. Melvin G. Holli, ed., *Detroit* (New York: New Viewpoints, 1976), 59, 82–86, 269, 275; Olivier Zunz, *The Changing Face of Inequality: Urbanization, Industrial Development, and Immigrants in Detroit, 1880–1920* (Chicago: University of Chicago Press, 1982), 16–18.

15. Holli, *Detroit,* 62; Leon Fink, *Workingmen's Democracy: The Knights of Labor and American Politics* (Urbana: University of Illinois Press, 1983), 178, 182; Zunz, *Changing Face of Inequality,* 32, 35; Oestreicher, *Solidarity and Fragmentation,* 10, 34–35, 53.

16. *Detroit Evening News,* January 1, 1880.

17. MSBLS, *First Annual Report,* 1884, 187.

18. "Old Labor Movements," *Detroit Evening News,* 1890 (with notation by A. Inglis, "written by Joe"), LC.

19. Anthony C. Labadie to "dere brother," February 1875, LC; J.L., "My Outings," n.d., LC.

20. J.L., "My Outings"; Anthony C. Labadie to "well joseph," July 9, 1886, LC; Anthony C. Labadie Discharge Papers, April 2, 1863, LC.

21. J.L. to Sophie Archambeau, November 12, 1876, LC.

22. J.L., "To the Editor of the *Evening News,*" *Detroit Evening News,* May 6, 1876, J.L. Scrapbook II, 2, LC; J.L. to "Father," May 4, 1876, LC.

23. Ibid.

24. J.L. to Myra Weller, September 23, 1925, LC.

25. There are ten letters from J.L. to Sophie Archambeau, 1870 to 1876, and six letters from Sophie Archambeau to J.L., all written in 1876, LC.

26. J.L. to Sophie Archambeau, n.d. ("Wednesday, 12 o'clock"), and September 3 and 13, November 12, 1876, LC.

27. Sophie Archambeau to J.L., October 15, November 26, 1876, LC; J.L. to Sophie Archambeau, n.d. ("Tuesday night, 8½ o'clock"), LC.

28. J.L. to Sophie Archambeau, September 3, November 12, 1876, LC.

29. Catholic Information Center, Washington, D.C.

30. J.L. to Sophie Archambeau, September 3, 1876, LC.

31. J.L. to Sophie Archambeau, n.d. ("Tuesday night, 8½ o'clock"), and September 3, 1876, LC.
32. A. Inglis, "Jo and 'Mamma' Labadie," September 12, 1948, LC; J.L., "Cranky Notions (The spirit moves me . . .)," ca. 1899, LC.
33. J.L., "What Is Love?"
34. J.L. to Weller, September 23, 1925, LC.

Chapter 4

1. Foner, *History of the Labor Movement,* 1:413.
2. In 1880, there were 23,769 Germans in a total Detroit population of 116,340. Holli, *Detroit,* 62, 269–270; Oestreicher, *Solidarity and Fragmentation,* 37, 44–52; *Detroit Evening News,* September 5, 1887.
3. Holli, *Detroit,* 82; Patricia A. Cooper, *Once a Cigar Maker: Men, Women, and Work Culture in American Cigar Factories, 1900–1916* (Urbana: University of Illinois Press, 1987), 170; Judson Grenell, "Rubbing Elbows With People Worthwhile: XXVI. Charles Erb," *Detroit News,* ca. 1916, Detroit Labor Leaders File, LC; *Detroit Evening News,* September 5, 1887.
4. J. Grenell, "Rubbing Elbows With People Worthwhile: XXVI. Charles Erb"; idem, "Autobiography," 29.
5. J.L. to Henry Ford, unsent, 1914, LC.
6. J. Grenell, "Autobiography," 30.
7. J. Grenell, "Autobiography," 1, 21, 23, 26–27.
8. Ibid., 27, 34; Judson Grenell, "Rubbing Elbows With People Worthwhile: V. Joe Labadie," *Detroit News,* September 11, 1916.
9. J. Grenell to A. Inglis, October 28, 1929; J. Grenell, "Autobiography," 29; *The Socialist* (Detroit), December 8, 1877; Siegfried E. Rolland, "The Detroit Labor Press, 1839–89" (master's thesis, Wayne State University, 1946), 13. The first issue of *The Socialist* was dated October 13, 1877.
10. *The Socialist* (Detroit), December 8, 1877, January 5, 1878; *The Socialist* (Chicago), November 16, 1878; D. Boyd to A. Inglis, November 29, 1938, LC.
11. J. Grenell, "Autobiography," 31, 33. Although no editor was named and most of the articles were unsigned, Grenell stated in his autobiography that he was the editor. Frank Hirth, who became editor of the Chicago *Socialist,* could not have been editor of the Detroit *Socialist,* as some historians have written, because the issue of June 1, 1878, stated that the editor was unable to read German and Hirth was German.
12. Oestreicher, *Solidarity and Fragmentation,* 83–84; J. Grenell, "Autobiography," 32–33.
13. *The Socialist* (Detroit), December 8, 1877; Labadie Account Book, January 1878, LC; J. Grenell, "Autobiography," 81.
14. The number of members claimed was probably fanciful. Morris Hillquit, in his *History of Socialism in the United States* (New York: Dover Publications, 1971), 206, estimates SLP membership at the beginning of 1879 as 10,000. *The Socialist* (Detroit), January 5, 12, and May 11, 25, 1878.

15. J. Grenell, "Autobiography," 32; Daniel Bell, "The Problem of Idealogical Rigidity," in *Failure of a Dream: Essays in the History of American Socialism*, ed. John H. M. Laslett and Seymour Martin Lipset (Berkeley: University of California Press, 1974), 7.

16. *The Socialist* (Detroit), January 12, February 16, March 16, 1878; J.L., "Eight Hours a Day," *The Socialist* (Chicago), October 19, 1878.

17. Richard Oestreicher, "Socialism and the Knights of Labor in Detroit, 1877–1886," *Labor History* 22 (1981): 12. *The Socialist* (Chicago), January 18, April 20, 1878; J.L., "Pauper Labor," *Labor Enquirer* (Denver), October 14, [1884], J.L. Scrapbook II, 89–90, LC.

18. *The Socialist* (Detroit), May 18, 1878 (quoting from a *Detroit Evening News* article).

19. *The Socialist* (Detroit), January 12, February 9, 23, and May 25, 1878.

20. Labadie Account Book, 1878; MSBLS, *First Annual Report*, 1884, 86–87.

21. Sidney Glazer, "Labor and Agrarian Movements in Michigan, 1876–1896" (Ph.D. diss., University of Michigan, 1932), 38. The typographical union was the first trade union in Michigan. It originated in March 1839, when Detroit printers and employers banded together to form a Typographical Society "in the interest of both the employing and the employed." When the ITU was founded thirteen years later, the Detroit printers' group was chartered as T.U. 18. For many years, it was the sole labor organization in the city. *Detroit Evening News*, September 5, 1887.

22. Dulles and Dubofsky, *Labor in America*, 106. The Typographical Union had only 4,260 members in 1878. Ware, *The Labor Movement*, 51.

23. J.L. to Richard T. Ely, August 30, 1885, Ely Papers, SHSW; J.L., Letters to the Editor, *Our Organette*, July 29, 1882; August 11, 1883.

24. International Typographical Union, *Report of Proceedings of the Twenty-sixth Annual Session of the International Typographical Union*, Detroit, June 3–7, 1878, 19, 48, 54–56, Microfilm Misc. #60, American Labor Union Constitution and Proceedings, 1836–1974, ITU Constitution and Proceedings, University Microfilm, Inc., Ann Arbor, Michigan; *Detroit Evening News*, June 5, 6, 7, 1878.

25. Labadie Account Book, June 1878.

26. Socialist Labor Party, *Proceedings of the Second National Convention*, December 26, 1879–January 1, 1880, Records of the Socialistic Labor Party of America, microfilm edition, SHSW, 1970, 7–8.

27. J. Grenell, "Autobiography," 34; Fink, *Workingmen's Democracy*, 194; Bruce C. Nelson, *Beyond the Martyrs: A Social History of Chicago's Anarchists, 1870–1900* (New Brunswick, N.J.: Rutgers University Press, 1988), 203.

28. Oestreicher, *Solidarity and Fragmentation*, 130; Foner, *History of the Labor Movement*, 2:29–31.

Chapter 5

1. *The Socialist* (Chicago), January 4, 1879.

2. J.L. to Paul J. Maas, n.d., LC; *The Socialist* (Chicago), January 4, May 10, 1879.

3. J.L., untitled two-page typescript, beginning "Some of the comrades say . . . ," LC; J. Grenell, "Rubbing Elbows With People Worthwhile: V. Joe Labadie"; idem, "These socialist tracts . . . ," note, summer 1929, attached to copy of *Labor Review,* July 1880, LC; *The Socialist* (Chicago), May 10, June 14, 1879.

4. *The Socialist* (Chicago), May 10, 1879; Karl Marx, *Poverty of Philosophy* (New York: International Publishers, 1936), 60, cited in Rolland, "The Detroit Labor Press," 70–75; "John F. Bray," *Detroit Evening Journal,* reprinted in the *Labor Leaf,* June 30, 1886. Born in Washington, D.C., but taken to England at the age of twelve, Bray was a fascinating man. According to Rolland, his parents were actors, dancers, and singers in England and the United States. Bray worked as a printer and daguerrotype artist, edited the Pontiac *Jacksonian,* and wrote on aerial navigation, perpetual motion, and farmers, as well as utopian socialism. In his 1840 *Aerial Navigation,* he maintained that the advent of the steam engine had made flight in heavier-than-air machines possible. He even designed a crude airplane that resembled a box car with rotating wings at the side and stern and a steam engine with a system of screws and shafts for transmitting power.

5. "What Is Socialism?" Socialistic Tract Association, Tract no. 1, LC.

6. Ibid.

7. *The Socialist* (Chicago), May 10, 1879; *Labor Review,* July 1880; J. Grenell, "Autobiography," 31–32; *Detroit News,* November 21, 1878.

8. J.L., "Some of the comrades say," LC.

9. *The Socialist* (Chicago), January 18, February 1, 1879.

10. "Greenbacks! Greenbacks!" speech by Moses W. Field, reprinted from *Detroit Daily Sun,* 1875, clipping, Greenback folder, LC.

11. Foner, *History of the Labor Movement,* 1:476–79; Glazer, "Labor and Agrarian Movements in Michigan," 189–92; *The Socialist* (Detroit), January 19, May 11, 1878; *The Socialist* (Chicago), October 5, 19, 1878; J. Grenell, "Autobiography," 31; J.L. to Maas, n.d., LC.

12. Foner, *History of the Labor Movement,* 1:484.

13. *Detroit Evening News,* October 25, 27, 1879.

14. "City Politics," [October 27, 1879], n.s., J.L. Scrapbook III, 11, LC.

15. Ibid.; *Detroit Evening News,* October 27, 1879; "To the Voters of Detroit," handbill, Political Activities folder, LC.

16. J.L., "Taxation," [*Bay City Globe*], ca. 1881–82, J.L. Scrapbook II, 53, LC.

17. Ibid.; *Detroit Evening News,* October 30, November 5, 1879; J.L. to Powderly, December 7, 1879, TVP.

18. *Detroit City Directory for 1880* (Detroit: J. W. Weeks, 1880), 514–15, Burton Collection, Detroit Public Library, Detroit, Michigan; Labadie Account Book, 1878–79; *Labor Leaf,* April 7, 1886.

19. Labadie Account Book, 1879–80; "The No-Rent Manifesto," [*Bay City Globe*], November 10, 1881, J.L. Scrapbook II, 45, LC.

20. J.L., "Stop the Leak," *Our Organette,* September 9, 1882; J.L., "Almost an Anarchist," *Liberty* (Boston), June 9, 1883.

21. Henry George to J.L., March 10, 1881, LC.

22. J.L. to Frederick F. Ingram, October 29, 1919, LC. Interest in George's ideas,

which nearly died out after his death, has been growing in recent years. There are a number of Henry George schools in the United States and Canada and a modified form of his land-value tax is practiced in Australia.

23. *Labor Review,* February, April, and September 18, 1880; Oestreicher, *Solidarity and Fragmentation,* 5.

24. Beecher quoted in *Labor Leaf,* September 29, 1886; *Labor Review,* March 1880; Sophie Labadie quoted in A. Inglis, "Charles Joseph Antoine Labadie," three-page biographical sketch, 1, LC; idem, "Charles Joseph Antoine Labadie," ten-page biographical sketch, 2, LC.

25. *Labor Review,* May 1880; Labadie Account Book, June 1880.

26. Philip Van Patten to Powderly, July 15, 1880, TVP; *The Socialist* (Chicago), May 10, 1879; J. Grenell, "Autobiography," 34–35.

27. *Labor Review,* May 1880.

28. *Advance and Labor Leaf,* September 17, 1887.

29. J.L. to E. A. Stephens, published letter, n.s., June 1, 1880, J.L. Scrapbook II, LC. This is probably the E. A. Stevens who was one of the earliest members of the Knights of Labor in Detroit and who was living in Chicago in 1880.

30. Hillquit, *History of Socialism in the United States,* 244–45; Convention report, *Labor Review,* June 1880; J. Grenell, "Autobiography," 35.

31. *Labor Review,* June 1880; Paul Avrich, *The Haymarket Tragedy* (Princeton: Princeton University Press, 1984), 47–48.

32. *Labor Review,* June 1880, August 28, 1880 (platform).

33. Ibid., August 7, 21, 1880.

34. Ibid., September 11, 1880; J.L., "Who is a Socialist?" in *Doggerel for the Underdog* (Detroit: The Labadie Shop, 1910), LC. For an account of local German opposition to SLP involvement in the Greenback campaign, see Oestreicher, *Solidarity and Fragmentation,* 93–96.

35. *Labor Review,* October 2, 1880. Weaver polled more than one million votes in 1892 as presidential candidate of the Populist party. In 1882, Josiah W. Begole was elected governor of Michigan on a Democrat-Greenback fusion ticket.

36. Hillquit, *History of Socialism in the United States,* 217; *Labor Review,* November 1881.

37. J.L., "Almost an Anarchist," *Liberty,* June 9, 1883. See *Truth,* September 1884, for the last mention of Labadie as an SLP official. One-time state socialists who turned to anarchism in this period include Dyer Lum, whose intellectual development most closely parallels Labadie's, and Moritz A. Bachmann, in the individualist camp, as well as William Holmes, and all the Haymarket defendants in the collectivist camp.

Chapter 6

1. *The Unionist,* September 4, 1882.

2. *Detroit Evening News,* September 5, 1887.

3. MSBLS, *First Annual Report,* 1884, 74. This report incorrectly gives the founding date of the Detroit Trades Assembly as 1865. The population of Detroit in 1860 was 45,619.

4. *The Socialist* (Detroit), January 12, 19, 1878.

5. Ibid., January 19, 1878; Ware, *The Labor Movement,* 60, 377.

6. Oestreicher, *Solidarity and Fragmentation,* 78.

7. *** (Detroit), February 1880; *Labor Review,* March 1880.

8. *Labor Review,* March 1880; *Detroit Times,* April 17, 1881; MSBLS, *First Annual Report,* 1884, 75; D. Boyd to A. Inglis, July 22, 1938 (re: Strigel), LC; *Detroit News,* July 21, 1880.

9. MSBLS, *First Annual Report,* 75; *Detroit Times,* April 10, 1881; D. Boyd to A. Inglis, November 29, 1938, LC.

10. *Labor Review,* October 23, 1880.

11. Ibid., October 9, 23, 1880; Labadie Account Book, October 1880, LC.

12. *Labor Review,* September 18, 1880.

13. *Detroit Times,* April 17, 1881.

14. Ibid., April 10, 1881; Hillquit, *History of Socialism in the United States,* 208.

15. *Detroit Times,* April 10, 1881. The Trades Council reported a drop of one-third in the circulation of the paper's Sunday edition as a result of the boycott. Oestreicher, *Solidarity and Fragmentation,* 109. The concept of a boycott, of course, had been employed by American colonials who refused to buy British goods after the passage of the Stamp Act in 1765. But the term itself was not used until after 1880, when local people in Ireland refused to cooperate with Captain Charles Cunningham Boycott, an English land agent, because of his ruthlessness in evicting tenants.

16. *Detroit Times,* April 17, 24, and May 8, 14, 1881. Oestreicher estimates the city's industrial workers in 1880 as 14,500 (*Solidarity and Fragmentation,* 4).

17. Labadie Account Book, May 1881; J.L., "The Law of Wages," *Labor Star,* n.d., J.L. Scrapbook II, 61–62, LC; J.L., "Two Kinds of Slavery—Chattel and Wages," *Labor Star,* n.d., J.L. Scrapbook II, 74–75, LC.

18. J. Grenell, "Autobiography," 32; Margaret Grenell to A. Inglis, June 22, 1946, LC.

19. Silas Farmer, *History of Detroit and Wayne County* (Detroit, 1890), 681; *Labor Review,* September 1881. The *Herald* folded shortly thereafter.

20. Labadie was editor of the revived *Labor Review.* See John Swinton to J.L., July 26, 1881, LC.

21. *Labor Review,* August and September 1881; Richard O. Boyer and Herbert M. Morais, *Labor's Untold Story* (Pittsburgh: United Electrical, Radio, and Machine Workers of America, 1988), 82–84; *Truth,* May 1884, 11–12.

22. William H. Foster to J.L., May 4, 1885, LC; Emma Goldman, *Living My Life* (New York: Dover Publications, 1970), 1:140; Boyer and Morais, *Labor's Untold Story,* 80–82; Foner, *History of the Labor Movement,* 2:30; J.L., "Labadie's Lessons," *Labor Enquirer* (Denver), February 15, 1884, J.L. Scrapbook II, 97–98, LC.

23. Swinton to J.L., December 24, 1889, LC. Labadie later tried to obtain missing copies of *John Swinton's Paper* for his collection, but Swinton himself could not supply them.

24. A. Inglis, Labadie character sketch beginning, "In a letter to me dated 1929," 1, LC.

25. J.L. to Richard T. Ely, July 4, 1885, SHSW; A. Inglis, "Jo and 'Mamma' "; idem, notes on Labadie's 1926 Ann Arbor visit, n.d., written underneath a picture of Labadie; idem, "Charles Joseph Antoine Labadie," three-page biographical sketch, 1.

26. They included *The Exponent* (Cincinnati), *The Trades* (Philadelphia), *Labor Star* (Cleveland), *The Voice* (New York), *Our Organette* (Philadelphia), *Truth* (San Francisco), *Journal of United Labor* (Pittsburgh), *Labor Herald* (Pittsburgh), *The Crisis* (Indianapolis), *Labor Enquirer* (Denver), *John Swinton's Paper* (New York), *The Craftsman* (Washington, D.C.), and *Liberty* (Boston), as well as the *Detroit National* (Greenback), *Bay City Globe, Flint Labor News Echo,* and *Grand Rapids Daily Democrat.*

27. *Detroit Times,* May 8, 1881; "A Socialist Replies," *Detroit Evening News,* n.d., J.L. Scrapbook II, 36, LC.

28. J.L., "How the Knights of Labor Came to Michigan," 1926, LC; Knights of Labor, *Record of Proceedings,* 1880, 213–14.

29. Ware, *The Labor Movement,* 75, 92.

30. Ibid., 66, 93; J.L. to Richard T. Ely, December 16, 1885, SHSW.

31. Powderly to J.L., June 8, 1882, TVP; J.L. to Rev. Dr. Rexford, November 12, 1882, LC.

32. J.L., untitled typescript beginning, "The first move . . . ," LC; Knights of Labor, *Record of Proceedings of the Sixth Regular Session of the General Assembly,* New York City, September 5–12, 1882, 389; Ware, *The Labor Movement,* 96.

33. *Detroit Evening News,* September 5, 1887; *The Unionist,* September 18, 1882; Fink, *Workingmen's Democracy,* 9.

34. *The Unionist,* January 22, 1883; *Detroit Evening News,* September 5, 1887; Oestreicher, *Solidarity and Fragmentation,* 188.

35. *The Unionist,* April 30, 1883; Foner, *History of the Labor Movement,* 2:58–59; Carolyn Ashbaugh, *Lucy Parsons: American Revolutionary* (Chicago: Charles H. Kerr Publishing Co., 1976), 26; Bernard Mandel, *Samuel Gompers* (Yellow Springs: The Antioch Press, 1963), 186; *John Swinton's Paper,* September 27, 1885; Joseph Buchanan, *The Story of a Labor Agitator* (New York: The Outlook Co., 1903), 276–78.

36. *The Unionist,* April 21, 1882; October 2, 16, 1882. Lord was not re-elected. Rolland, "The Detroit Labor Press," 107.

37. Foner, *History of the Labor Movement,* 2:361–64.

38. J.L., "Uncle Sam, the Real Culprit," *Liberty,* October 3, 1885.

39. Foner, *History of the Labor Movement,* 2:75–76; Boyer and Morais, *Labor's Untold Story,* 80; J. Grenell, "A Foreword" (March 1928), LC; *Our Organette,* July 29, 1882.

40. J.L., "What Is a Workingman?" August 3, 1881, [*Detroit National*], LC; J.L., "Political Economy," *Bay City Globe,* n.d., both J.L. Scrapbook II, 49–50, LC.

41. *Our Organette,* September 9, 1882; J.L., "Citizens of the Republic . . . ," *Bay City Globe,* May 5, 1882, J.L. Scrapbook II, 50–51, LC; J.L., "The Labor Problem," *The Unionist,* June 12, 1882. To the modern reader, the idea of eliminating interest may seem curious, but payments for the use of money were forbidden in Biblical

times and during the Roman Republic. In general, people regarded interest and usury as synonymous until the late Middle Ages. Marx thought it "a crime against humanity." Islamic law still bans interest.

42. Fink, *Workingmen's Democracy,* 6; J.L., "The Benefit Working People Would Derive from Free Land," *Labor Star,* April 23, 1883, J.L. Scrapbook II, 74, LC; *Our Organette,* August 5, 1882.

43. J.L., "Letter from Michigan," n.s., November 1, [1884], J.L. Scrapbook II, 94, LC. Powderly was also equivocal on the issue of political action, ruling that it must not be discussed in local assemblies, while maintaining that "wise legislation" would eliminate the necessity of strikes. Foner, *History of the Labor Movement,* 2:80–81.

44. Editor's note, *Bay City Globe,* n.d. [1882], J.L. Scrapbook II, 51, LC.

45. Editor's note, *Labor Star,* n.d., J.L. Scrapbook II, 58, LC; "Mass Meeting," *Labor Star,* [October 6, 1882], J.L. Scrapbook II, 55–57, LC.

46. Ware, *The Labor Movement,* 251.

47. Ibid., 248; J.L., "An Open Letter," *Labor Star,* November 17, 1882, J.L. Scrapbook II, 58–59, LC. The FOTLU wanted legislation for the incorporation of trade unions, enforcement of the eight-hour day, repeal of the conspiracy laws used to prosecute strikers, abolition of child labor and contract convict labor, compulsory education, uniform apprentice laws, bureaus of labor, and the exclusion of Chinese coolies—demands similar to those of the Knights.

48. J.L., "An Open Letter," *Labor Star,* November 17, 1882; J.L., "To the Editor," *Our Organette,* November 18, December 16, 1882.

49. *Labor Star,* [November 1882], J.L. Scrapbook II, 59, 61–62, LC.

50. Ibid.; International Typographical Union, *Report of Proceedings of the Thirty-first Annual Session of the International Typographical Union,* Cincinnati, [1883], 41 (report on the 1882 convention of the FOTLU), Microfilm Misc. #60, American Labor Unions Constitutions and Proceedings, 1826–1974, ITU Constitution and Proceedings, University Microfilms, Inc., Ann Arbor, Michigan.

51. "Banquet and Dance," *Labor Star,* [November 1882], J.L. Scrapbook II, 61, LC.

52. *Our Organette,* December 16, 1882.

53. J.L. to Powderly, August 27, 1884, TVP; *Our Organette,* November 18, December 23, 1882.

54. ITU, *Report of Proceedings,* [1883], 13; J.L., "Labadie's Logic," *Labor Enquirer* (Denver), March 12, 1883, J.L. Scrapbook II, 67–69, LC; *Our Organette,* February 24, 1883.

55. International Typographical Union, *Report of Proceedings of the Thirty-second Annual Session of the International Typographical Union,* New Orleans, [1884], 92, Microfilm Misc. #60, American Labor Unions Constitutions and Proceedings, 1826–1974, ITU Constitution and Proceedings, University Microfilms, Inc., Ann Arbor, Michigan; J.L., "Magnificent Michigan," *Labor Enquirer* (Denver), June 15, [1884], J.L. Scrapbook II, 81–82, LC; J.L. to Powderly, August 6, 27, 1884, TVP.

56. Ware, *The Labor Movement,* 238; ITU, *Report of Proceedings,* [1884], 12; *Labor Leaf,* June 16, 1886.

Chapter 7

1. *The Unionist,* May 13, 1883; *Detroit Evening News,* [May 1883], J.L. Scrapbook II, 64, LC.
2. Avrich, *The Haymarket Tragedy,* 61, 64, 66.
3. Ibid., 164–68; *The Alarm* (Chicago), December 27, 1884.
4. *Detroit Evening News,* [May 1883], J.L. Scrapbook II, 64, LC; Avrich, *The Haymarket Tragedy,* 61–62, 65.
5. Avrich, *The Haymarket Tragedy,* 64.
6. *Detroit Evening News,* [May 1883], J.L. Scrapbook II, 64, LC; "Reformers," [*The Unionist*], [June 1883], J.L. Scrapbook II, 65, LC.
7. Avrich, *The Haymarket Tragedy,* 60, 67.
8. Samuel Gompers, *Seventy Years of Life and Labor* (New York: Augustus M. Kelley, 1967), 2:177.
9. Ashbaugh, *Lucy Parsons,* 45; Avrich, *The Haymarket Tragedy,* 133; Nelson, *Beyond the Martyrs,* 154–55.
10. J.L., "The Duty of Reformers," *Lansing Sentinel,* n.d., J.L. Scrapbook II, 91, LC; J.L., "Labor's Only Hope," *Detroit Spectator,* November 22, 1883, J.L. Scrapbook 1883–1901, 101a, LC/LL.
11. J.L., "Labor's Only Hope," 101a.
12. J.L., "Cranky Notions," *Liberty,* December 15, 1888; J.L, "The Anarchistic View of the Expansion Question," *Liberty,* February 1905.
13. Rudolf Rocker, *Pioneers of American Freedom: Origins of Liberal and Radical Thought in America* (Los Angeles: Rocker Publications Committee, 1949), 238–40; David DeLeon, *The American as Anarchist* (Baltimore: Johns Hopkins University Press, 1978), 3–4.
14. J.L. to Dr. William E. Gilroy, June 14, 1925, LC; J.L., "Your interesting editorial . . . ," LC. William Lloyd Garrison, Adin Ballou, and other Christian abolitionists denounced all law and government and believed in a new order in which the individual would be guided only by a love of God. Corinne Jacker, *The Black Flag of Anarchy: Antistatism in the United States* (New York: Charles Scribner's Sons, 1968), 72–81.
15. J.L., "Almost an Anarchist"; *Detroit Free Press,* January 15, 1950 (J.L. on "Marxmanship").
16. J.L., "Almost an Anarchist," *Liberty,* June 9, 1883 and editor's note.
17. Benjamin Tucker to J.L., May 9, 1883, LC; Charles H. Hamilton, "Introduction: The Evolution of a Subversive Tradition," in Michael E. Coughlin et al., eds., *Benjamin R. Tucker and the Champions of Liberty* (St. Paul: Michael E. Coughlin, 1987), 4.
18. J.L., "Your interesting editorial . . . ," LC.
19. The account of Warren's activities is based on James J. Martin, *Men Against the State: The Expositors of Individualist Anarchism in America, 1827–1908* (Colorado Springs: Ralph Myles Publisher, Inc., 1970), 1–102. See also Rocker, *Pioneers of American Freedom,* 50–69; William O. Reichert, *Partisans of Freedom: A Study in American Anarchism* (Bowling Green: Bowling Green University Popular Press, 1976), 64–78.

20. Martin, *Men Against the State,* 13.
21. For extended discussions of Warren's associates and Lysander Spooner, see ibid., 105–53, 167–201. See also Martin Henry Blatt, *Free Love and Anarchism: The Biography of Ezra Heywood* (Urbana: University of Illinois Press, 1989).
22. Benjamin Tucker, *Instead of a Book* (New York: Haskell House Publishers, 1969), dedication page; Hamilton, "Introduction," 5. Woodhull was a co-founder of the Equal Rights Party in 1872 and became its presidential candidate. Tucker describes her seduction of him in Emmanie Sachs, *The Terrible Siren: Victoria Woodhull* (New York: Harper and Bros., 1928), 236–66.
23. J.L, "Plain Talks on Plain Subjects," *Labor Review,* January 1882, LC; J.L., "Labadie," *Labor Star,* March 7, 1883, J.L. Scrapbook II, 66–67, LC; J.L. to Professor George D. Herron, October 23, 1918, LC; J.L. to Richard T. Ely, July 4, 1885, SHSW; J.L., "Cranky Notions," *Labor Leaf,* April 23, 1887, LC.
24. *Detroit Evening News,* September 5, 1887; Foner, *History of the Labor Movement,* 2:41.
25. "Anarchy or Reason," [Illegible] *Movement* (SLP publication), n.d. (after June 9, 1883), J.L. Scrapbook II, 85, LC.
26. S. Robert Wilson to J.L., November 30, 1883, LC; Hillquit, *History of Socialism in the United States,* 219. Labadie was apparently still secretary of the SLP National Board of Supervision as late as September 1884, since members nationwide were instructed to send complaints and grievances to his 44 Canfield Street home until that date. *Truth,* September 1884.
27. Burnette G. Haskell to J.L. and August Spies, September 1, 1883, LC.
28. Avrich, *The Haymarket Tragedy,* 68–70; Haskell to J.L., September 12, 1883, LC.
29. For discussions of Haskell and the Pittsburgh Congress see Charles M. Destler, *American Radicalism* (Chicago: Quadrangle Books, 1966), 78–104; Avrich, *The Haymarket Tragedy,* 68–78; Reichert, *Partisans of Freedom,* 201–10; Martin, *Men Against the State,* 221, 223.
30. Buchanan, *The Story of a Labor Agitator,* 266; Haskell to J.L., February 2, 1885, LC.
31. Haskell to J.L. and Spies, September 1, 1883, LC.
32. *Liberty,* October 6, 1883. Detroit was not among the cities listed as having sent delegates to the Pittsburgh Congress in accounts published in *Vorbote,* October 13, 16, 1883, although it is possible Labadie was there representing San Francisco, Haskell's base.
33. Avrich, *The Haymarket Tragedy,* 74–75.
34. *Liberty,* September 6, 1884.
35. Haskell later joined the Kaweah Cooperative Colony near Mt. Whitney, California, a socialist society based on Edward Bellamy's 1888 utopian romance, *Looking Backward.* See Reichert, *Partisans of Freedom,* 209.
36. Tucker had joined the militants two years earlier in forming the Revolutionary Socialistic party in Chicago; *Liberty* had been chosen as their English-language organ. He later rejected the use of force, and declined to send a delegate to the congress.
37. J.L., "Is Tyranny a Necessity?" *Liberty,* February 23, 1895.

Chapter 8

1. J.L., "Labor Department," *Lansing Sentinel* [March 1885], J.L. Scrapbook 1883–1901, 30–31, LC/LL.
2. Quoted in DeLeon, *The American as Anarchist,* 5.
3. *The Unionist,* April 30, May 13, 1883.
4. *Labor Leaf,* November 15, 1884; *Detroit Spectator,* November 10, 17, 1883; J.L., "Labor Not a Commodity," *Detroit Spectator,* July 1883, J.L. Scrapbook 1883–1901, 99, LC/LL.
5. In December, Labadie's account book shows rent, $7.50; food, $13.55; one ton of coal, $7.00; dentist, $5.00; pew rent, $3.50.
6. *Detroit Spectator,* November 17, 1883; J.L., "Magnificent Michigan," *Labor Enquirer* (Denver), June 15, [1884], J.L. Scrapbook II, 81–82, LC; "The Trevellick Home Fund," *National Labor Tribune,* March–September 1884, J.L. Scrapbook III, 20, 24–25, LC; J.L. to Powderly, November 7, 1885, TVP.
7. *Labor Leaf,* May 19, 1886.
8. MSBLS, *First Annual Report,* February 1, 1884, 179–81.
9. Ibid., 67–81; Benjamin Tucker to J.L., January 6, 1883, LC. Labadie identified himself as the author of this section in a postcard to Richard T. Ely, June 18, 1885, SHSW.
10. *Progressive Cigarmakers' Journal,* August 1, 1884, J.L. Scrapbook 1883–1901, 70, LC/LL; J.L. to Powderly, November 28, 1885, TVP.
11. J.L., "Labor Department," *Lansing Sentinel,* n.d. [1884], J.L. Scrapbook 1883–1901, 17, 4–5, LC/LL; J.L., "Plain Talks on Plain Subjects," *Labor Review,* January 1882.
12. J.L., "Labor Department," *Lansing Sentinel,* 1884–85, J.L. Scrapbook 1883–1901, 2, 5, 18, 28, LC/LL.
13. *Labor Leaf,* January 14, 1885; Oestreicher, *Solidarity and Fragmentation,* 127, 181; *Detroit Evening News,* September 5, 1887.
14. J.L. to Ely, July 4, October 18, 1885, SHSW.
15. Oestreicher, *Solidarity and Fragmentation,* 123, 127.
16. Ibid., 114; J.L., "Wolverine K. of L.," *Labor Enquirer* (Denver) January 25, 1884, J.L. Scrapbook II, 80–81, LC. Accounts of this convention are also found in *John Swinton's Paper,* January 20, 1884; *The Crisis,* April 25, 1885, J.L. Scrapbook 1883–1901, 32–33, LC/LL; Michigan State Assembly of the Knights of Labor, *Record of Proceedings of the First Regular Session of the Michigan State Assembly,* Detroit, January 11–12, 1884; *Journal of United Labor,* June 25, 1884, 723–24.
17. J.L., "To the Editor," *John Swinton's Paper,* May 4, 1884; J.L., "Magnificent Michigan," 81.
18. J.L., "Labadie's Lines," n.s., n.d., J.L. Scrapbook II, 86–87, LC; "Lansing Knights of Labor Declare Against Millionaire Alger," n.s., n.d., J.L. Scrapbook II, 85, LC. Alger was Secretary of War during the Spanish-American War.
19. *Labor Leaf,* November 1, 1884, March 4, 1885; Oestreicher, *Solidarity and Fragmentation,* 127. Detroit had been without a labor paper since the *Detroit Spectator* went out of business a year earlier.

20. *Labor Leaf,* September 9, 1885.

21. Oestreicher, *Solidarity and Fragmentation,* 122; *Labor Leaf,* November 26, 1884.

22. *Labor Leaf,* December 31, 1884. See J.L. Account Book, May–June 1885.

23. J.L., "Labadie's Lessons," *Labor Enquirer* (Denver), February 15, 1884, J.L. Scrapbook II, 96–99, LC.

24. *Labor Leaf,* June 17, July 15, October 7, 1885; Bruce Laurie, *Artisans into Workers: Labor in Nineteenth-Century America* (New York: The Noonday Press, 1989), 161. One of the firm's founders was Hazen Pingree, who later became mayor of Detroit and governor of Michigan.

25. Powderly to J.L., January 22, 1883, LC; *Labor Leaf,* June 3, 1885; Boot and Shoe Cooperative Association of Detroit, Certificate no. 89, issued to Joseph A. Labadie; Labadie Account Book, December, 1885, LC.

26. D. Boyd to A. Inglis, September 25, 1938, LC; *Labor Leaf,* December 31, 1884; J.L., "Plain Talks on Plain Subjects," *Labor Review,* March 1, 1882.

27. J.L. to Ely, October 18, 1885, SHSW; J.L., "To the Editor," *Labor Star,* J.L. Scrapbook II, 82–83, LC.

28. The account of the Saginaw Valley strike is based on the following sources: Doris B. McLaughlin, *Michigan Labor: A Brief History from 1818 to the Present* (Ann Arbor: Institute of Labor and Industrial Relations, University of Michigan/Wayne State University, 1970), chap. 2; MSBLS, *Third Annual Report,* February 1886, 92–126; *Detroit Evening News,* August 15–22, 1885; *The Alarm* (Chicago), September 19, 1885; *John Swinton's Paper,* August 9, 1885; *Labor Leaf,* July–October 1885.

29. D. Boyd to A. Inglis, July 22, 1938, LC; *Labor Leaf,* October 7, 1885.

30. J.L., "Barry Defense Fund," *Labor Leaf,* September 23, 1885; J.L., "Cranky Notions," *Labor Leaf,* July 29, 1885.

31. Louis Adamic, *Dynamite: The Story of Class Violence in America* (New York: Chelsea House Publishers, n.d.), 57–59.

32. *Detroit Evening News,* September 5, 1887; *Labor Leaf,* July 15, 1885; J.L., "Cranky Notions," *Labor Leaf,* July 22, 1885.

33. J.L., "To the Editor," *John Swinton's Paper,* October 12, 1884; J.L. to Ely, July 4, 1885, SHSW.

34. *Labor Leaf,* February 25, 1885, February 3, 1886; J.L., "Cranky Notions," *Liberty,* January 14, 1888; John Swinton to J.L., July 17, 1895, LC.

35. *Labor Leaf,* May 20, 1885, February 3, 1886; J.L., "Cranky Notions," *Labor Leaf,* June 24, 1885; J.L., "Cranky Notions," *Labor Leaf,* September 2, 1885.

36. J.L. to Ely, June 18, December 20, 1885, SHSW; Ely to J.L., June 30, August 4, 1885, LC. For an examination of the correspondence between J.L. and Ely, see Sidney Fine, "The Ely-Labadie Letters," *Michigan History* (March 1952): 1–32.

37. J.L., "Information Wanted," *Labor Leaf,* August 12, 1885; J.L. to Ely, August 8, 1885, SHSW.

38. Ely to J.L., August 14, 1885, LC. It is interesting to note that Ely did not mention his New York experience in his 1938 autobiography. Fine, "The Ely-Labadie Letters," 17n. 43.

39. Ely to J.L., September 28, November 17, 1885, LC; J.L. to Ely, October 18,

December 16, 1885, SHSW; "Report of Joseph A. Labadie, Delegate to the General Assembly, K. of L., Minneapolis, 1887" (Detroit: John R. Burton, n.d.), 14.

40. *Liberty,* July 3, 1886, July 30, 1887; Tucker to J.L., September 21, 1885, October 1, 1886, LC. See also Fine, "The Ely-Labadie Letters," 8n. 23.

41. Richard T. Ely, *The Labor Movement in America* (New York: Thomas Y. Crowell and Co., 1886), vii, 125; *Liberty,* December 29, 1894. In his book, Ely also refers to Labadie's letter of July 4, 1885, without identifying him, on 245–46 and in a note on 236.

42. J.L., "Our Bitter Foes," *Labor Leaf,* October 7, 1885; J.L., "Labor Department," *Lansing Sentinel,* [1885], J.L. Scrapbook 1883–1901, 30, 16, LC/LL.

43. *Labor Leaf,* February 25, March 4, August 19, September 2, 1885.

44. A. Inglis, "Charles Joseph Antoine Labadie," ten-page biographical sketch, 4, LC.

Chapter 9

1. Foner, *History of the Labor Movement,* 1:369; Avrich, *The Haymarket Tragedy,* 181.

2. McLaughlin, *Michigan Labor,* 15–16.

3. J.L., "To the Editor of the *Detroit Journal,*" *Detroit Journal,* September 11, 1885, J.L. Scrapbook I, 55, LC.

4. Ware, *The Labor Movement,* 252–53; Foner, *History of the Labor Movement,* 2:98–103.

5. *Labor Leaf,* December 10, 1884; J.L., "Cranky Notions," *Labor Leaf,* July 15, 1885.

6. *Labor Leaf,* February 17, April 28, 1886.

7. Ibid., February 17, March 17, 1886.

8. Oestreicher, *Solidarity and Fragmentation,* 135, 150.

9. *Labor Leaf,* March 24, 1886. This "Cranky Notions" column was republished in German in Johann Most's *Freiheit,* April 17, 1886.

10. Avrich, *The Haymarket Tragedy,* 186–87.

11. Oestreicher, *Solidarity and Fragmentation,* 150–55; *Labor Leaf,* May 12, 1886.

12. J.L., "Cranky Notions," *Labor Leaf,* May 5, 1886.

13. *Detroit News,* May 5, 1886; *Labor Leaf,* September 2, 1885, February 17, 1886; Avrich, *The Haymarket Tragedy,* 122–24.

14. Avrich, *The Haymarket Tragedy,* 6–11; J.L., "Labadie's Advice to the 'Alarm,' " *Liberty,* January 3, 1885; J.L., "Cranky Notions," *Labor Leaf,* October 13, 1886.

15. Avrich, *The Haymarket Tragedy,* 215–19.

16. Dulles and Dubofsky, *Labor in America,* 138; Avrich, *The Haymarket Tragedy,* 184, 186.

17. The account of the Haymarket incident is based on Avrich, *The Haymarket Tragedy,* 188–214; Sidney Lens, "The Bomb at Haymarket," in *Haymarket Scrapbook,* ed. Dave Roediger and Franklin Rosemont (Chicago: Charles H. Kerr Publishing Co., 1986), 17–18.

18. J.L., "Cranky Notions," *Labor Leaf,* May 12, 1886.

19. Avrich, *The Haymarket Tragedy,* 220–21; J.L., "Cranky Notions," *Labor Leaf,* May 19 1886; *Labor Leaf,* June 16, 1886. For extensive excerpts from Labadie's writings on the Haymarket episode, see Carlotta Anderson, "Joseph A. Labadie (1850–1933): 'Cranky Notions' on Haymarket," *Haymarket Scrapbook,* ed. Dave Roediger and Franklin Rosemont (Chicago: Charles H. Kerr Publishing Co., 1986), 123–24.

20. Avrich, *The Haymarket Tragedy,* 220.

21. J.L. to Powderly, March 25, 1886, TVP.

22. Powderly to J.L., June 8, 1882. LC. The article was printed in the *Journal of United Labor,* June 1882, 244.

23. *John Swinton's Paper,* quoted in Ware, *The Labor Movement,* 83.

24. J.L. to Powderly, January 6, 1886, TVP; Powderly to J.L., January 25, 1886, LC; J.L. to Powderly, August 5, 1884, TVP; Powderly to J.L. August 7, 1884, LC.

25. Ware, *The Labor Movement,* 86; Knights of Labor, *Record of Proceedings from the Eighth Regular Session of the General Assembly,* Philadelphia, September 1–10, 1884, 572–73.

26. Powderly to J.L., November 13, 1882, January 22, 1883, LC.

27. *Labor Leaf,* June 30, 1886; "He Would Throw It," *Detroit Tribune,* June 29, 1886, LC.

28. *Labor Leaf,* July 7, 1886, Labadie Account Book, June 1886, LC.

29. J.L., "Cranky Notions," *Labor Leaf,* December 9, 1885, April 28, 1886.

30. Ibid., June 16, 1886; International Typographical Union, *Report of Proceedings of the Thirty-fourth Annual Session of the International Typographical Union,* Pittsburgh, June 7–11, 1886, 83, 90–94, 112; "ITU Convention," *John Swinton's Paper,* June 13, 1886; Ware, *The Labor Movement,* 237–39.

31. *Detroit Evening News,* quoted in A. Inglis, "Charles Joseph Antoine Labadie," ten-page biographical sketch, 4, LC; *Detroit News,* October 8, 1933; Oestreicher, *Solidarity and Fragmentation,* 24.

32. Leo Donatus was buried in Mt. Elliott Cemetery on February 2, 1880. See Burial Records, Mt. Elliott Cemetery, Detroit.

33. Laurie, *Artisans into Workers,* 161; Susan Levine, *Labor's True Woman: Carpet Weavers, Industrialization and Labor Reform in the Gilded Age* (Philadelphia: Temple University Press, 1984), 59, 104–5, 111–12; Gregory S. Kealey and Bryan D. Palmer, *Dreaming of What Might Be: The Knights of Labor in Ontario, 1880–1900* (Cambridge: Cambridge University Press, 1982), 324; J.L., "Editorial," *Advance and Labor Leaf,* September 10, 1887.

34. A. Inglis, "Charles Joseph Antoine Labadie," three-page biographical sketch, 1–2, LC.

35. *Labor Leaf,* August 12, 1885, February 3, September 8, 1886.

36. J.L., "My Outings"; Anthony Cleophis Labadie to "well brother Joseph," April 20, 1883, both LC; Betty J. Dunham, *Oliver Township History* (Kalkaska: Rowell Printing, 1985), 19, 29.

37. "Declaration for the Increase of an Invalid Pension," State of Michigan, County of Kalkaska, September 8, 1877 (Veterans Records, St. Louis); Anthony Cleophis Labadie to "Well Joseph," April 13, 1885, July 9, 1886, LC.

38. J.L. to Powderly, January 6, 1886, TVP; *Detroit Evening News,* January 4, 1887, J.L. Scrapbook II, 99, LC.

39. *Labor Leaf,* February 24, June 9, 1886; J.L. "To the Editor: The present disturbance . . . ," n.d., LC.

40. *Labor Leaf,* April 21, 1886; Henry George to J.L., May 21, 1886, LC; *Labor Leaf,* January 20, 1886; J.L., "Almost an Anarchist," *Liberty,* June 9, 1883; Peter J. McGuire to J.L., February 26, 1895, LC.

41. J.L., untitled manuscript written on backs of envelopes dated 1921, beginning, "A few days ago . . . ," LC; J.L., "Cranky Notions," *Labor Leaf,* June 24, 1885. In 1891 the streetcar workers in a newly electrified system were organized into the AFL by Robert Y. Ogg. See MSBLS, *Ninth Annual Report, 1892,* 344–45.

42. J.L., "Cranky Notions," *Labor Leaf,* March 31, 1886; Ware, *The Labor Movement,* 66; Oestreicher, *Solidarity and Fragmentation,* 109, 242.

43. *Labor Leaf,* August 4 and 18, 1886.

44. Ibid., September 8, 1886; Detroit Council of Trades and Labor Unions, *Columbian Labor Day Souvenir* (Detroit: The Jefferson Press, 1893), 25–26; J.L., "Cranky Notions," *Labor Leaf,* September 8, 1886; "Labor Day," ibid.

Chapter 10

1. Dulles and Dubofsky, *Labor in America,* 133–37; J.L., "Cranky Notions," *Labor Leaf,* August 4, 1886.

2. Ware, *The Labor Movement,* 152–53.

3. *Labor Leaf,* May 26, June 23, 1886; Oestreicher, *Solidarity and Fragmentation,* 189.

4. Oestreicher, *Solidarity and Fragmentation,* 189–90; Foner, *History of the Labor Movement,* 2:133–36.

5. *Labor Leaf,* September 8, October 13, 1886. For an extensive treatment of the role of the ILP in the 1886 election, see Oestreicher, *Solidarity and Fragmentation,* 180–87.

6. *Labor Leaf,* September 8, 1886.

7. Oestreicher, *Solidarity and Fragmentation,* 182–83.

8. J.L., "Cranky Notions," *Labor Leaf,* September 22, 1886; *Labor Leaf,* October 6, 1886.

9. J.L., "Cranky Notions," *Labor Leaf,* January 6, October 13, 1886.

10. A. Inglis, "Charles Joseph Antoine Labadie," ten-page biographical sketch, LC; J. Grenell, "Autobiography," 45; Oestreicher, *Solidarity and Fragmentation,* 183; Rolland, "The Detroit Labor Press," 44, 81.

11. *Labor Leaf,* August 5, October 14, 1885, September 29, December 8, 1886; J. Grenell, "Autobiography," 34.

12. J.L., "The politicians of the world," note on scrap of paper, LC; A. Inglis, "Charles Joseph Antoine Labadie," ten-page biographical sketch, 3, LC; idem, "Grenell-Judson," 5, LC.

13. J. Grenell, "Autobiography," 44–45. That year George was mayoral candidate of the United Labor party in New York City, receiving 68,000 votes, more than Theodore Roosevelt, who came in third.

14. *Liberty,* May 22, June 19, 1886; Benjamin Tucker to J.L., June 5, 1886, LC. Tucker had previously accused Most's followers of setting fire to several dwellings they owned, in which six residents burned to death, for the insurance money. No evidence was ever presented to connect Most with the arsonists. See Avrich, *The Haymarket Tragedy,* 174; *Liberty,* August 18, 1886. Tucker later changed his tune. After the executions, he called the men the "John Browns of America's industrial revolution," and branded Henry George a "vile sinner who betrayed the cause of liberty for refusing to defend the condemned men." *Liberty,* November 19, 1887, January 5, 1889.

15. *Liberty,* July 31, 1886.

16. Avrich, *The Haymarket Tragedy,* 277.

17. *Labor Leaf,* August 25, 1886.

18. Ibid.; J.L., "Cranky Notions," *Labor Leaf,* August 25, 1886, and July 21, 1886 (quoting Wallaceburg, Ontario, *Herald Record;* August Spies to J.L., September 7, 1886, LC.

19. Avrich, *The Haymarket Tragedy,* 290–93.

20. Ashbaugh, *Lucy Parsons,* 104; Avrich, *The Haymarket Tragedy,* 297–98.

21. Lucy Parsons to J.L., October 11, 1886, LC; Avrich, *The Haymarket Tragedy,* 300–301.

22. Avrich, *The Haymarket Tragedy,* 298; Ashbaugh, *Lucy Parsons,* 56, 109.

23. *Labor Leaf,* December 8, 1886, January 26, 1887.

24. *Labor Leaf,* January 26, 1887; *Detroit News,* January 26, 1887; Ashbaugh, *Lucy Parsons,* 110.

25. Avrich, *The Haymarket Tragedy,* 429; J.L., "Cranky Notions," *Labor Leaf,* August 25, 1886; J.L., "Has Mr. Powderly Ever Been a Socialist?" *Advance and Labor Leaf,* September 17, 1887, also published in the *Detroit Evening News,* same date.

26. Powderly to John Devlin, August 30, 1887, published in the *Detroit Free Press* and reprinted in *Advance and Labor Leaf,* September 17, 1887.

27. J.L., "Has Mr. Powderly Ever Been a Socialist?"

28. Terence V. Powderly, *Thirty Years of Labor* (Columbus: Excelsior Publishing House, 1890), 544.

29. Buchanan, *The Story of a Labor Agitator,* 314–15.

30. J.L., "Cranky Notions," *Labor Leaf,* December 29, 1886.

31. Ware, *The Labor Movement,* 87; Thomas B. Barry to J.L., February 24, June 14, 1887, LC.

32. J.L., "Cranky Notions," *Labor Leaf,* February 9, 1887.

33. Ibid.

34. *Liberty,* March 12, 1887.

35. Ibid., February 20, 1886; J.L. to Powderly, January 6, March 25, 1886, TVP.

36. Devlin to Powderly, January 31, 1888, TVP. For the dispute between the Knights of Labor and AFL unions, see Elizabeth and Kenneth Fones-Wolf, "Knights versus the Trade Unionists: The Case of the Washington, D.C., Carpenters, 1881–1896," *Labor History* 22 (spring 1981): 192–212.

37. *Advance and Labor Leaf,* February 19 and 26, 1887.

38. For the significance of the change of editors, see Oestreicher, *Solidarity and Fragmentation,* 217n. 34. *Advance and Labor Leaf,* February 19, 1887; J. Grenell, "Autobiography," 58. Burton began publishing a new journal, *Onward,* in September 1888. Devoted principally to the single tax movement, it lasted until October 1890.

39. Tucker to J.L., February 6, 1887, LC; *Advance and Labor Leaf,* February 19, May 14, 1887; J.L., "Cranky Notions," *Advance and Labor Leaf,* May 5, 1887. Labadie's letters to Tucker prior to 1905 are lost.

40. J. Grenell, "A Foreword," March 1928, LC; *Advance and Labor Leaf,* February 19, 1887; John M. McGregor to J.L., March 1, 1922, February 17, 1927, LC.

41. *Advance and Labor Leaf,* June 11, July 16, 1887. McGregor, Grenell, and Robinson were among the stockholders.

42. J.L., "This Paper, Its Policy," *Advance and Labor Leaf,* July 16, 1887; J.L., editorial, *Advance and Labor Leaf,* July 23, 1887.

43. J.L., editorials, *Advance and Labor Leaf,* August 6 and 20, 1887.

44. Oestreicher, *Solidarity and Fragmentation,* 203; *Advance and Labor Leaf,* August 13, September 17, 1887; Devlin to Powderly, September 21, 1887, TVP.

Chapter 11

1. Devlin to Powderly, September 21, 1887, TVP; Powderly to Devlin, December 4, 1886, TVP. Devlin had been deputy labor commissioner when Labadie worked in the Michigan Bureau of Labor, had served as a Democratic state legislator, and was now U.S. consul in Windsor, as well as a member of the executive board of D.A. 50.

2. "Working for the Reds," *Detroit Tribune,* October 27, 1887, J.L. Scrapbook I, 45, LC; Avrich, *The Haymarket Tragedy,* 314–15; *Freedom,* November 1933.

3. "Working for the Reds," 45; Avrich, *The Haymarket Tragedy,* 314, 323–26, 338–39, 348.

4. *Chicago Tribune,* October 1, 1887; *Minneapolis Journal,* October 3 and 15, 1887, LC.

5. *Minneapolis Journal,* October 3, 1887, LC; *Report of Proceedings of the Eleventh Regular Session of the General Assembly,* Minneapolis, October 3–19, 1887, p. 1842.

6. Buchanan, *Story of a Labor Agitator,* 325, 363–68; Avrich, *The Haymarket Tragedy,* 308; *Minneapolis Journal,* October 6, 1887, LC. Buchanan was head of the Rocky Mountain Division of the IWA.

7. "Report of Joseph A. Labadie, Delegate to the General Assembly, Knights of Labor, Minneapolis, 1887" (Detroit: John R. Burton, November 14, 1887), 10–11, LC; Knights of Labor, *Record of Proceedings of the Eleventh Regular Session of the General Assembly,* Minneapolis, October 3–19, 1887, 1791; Foner, *History of the Labor Movement,* 2:162.

8. "Powderly's Socialism," *Advance and Labor Leaf,* October 15, 1887. Van Patten wrote Powderly on August 13, 1880, two months after the Chicago Greenback-Labor convention, "From your letter I judge that you wish to remain a member," with instructions on sending quarterly SLP dues.

9. *Minneapolis Journal,* October 15, 1887, LC; J.L., "Report," 11, LC.

10. Avrich, *The Haymarket Tragedy,* 241, 349; Powderly to Annie Wright, October 27, 1887, TVP; Knights of Labor, *Record of Proceedings,* 1887, 123–25; William Holmes to J.L., October 3, 1887, TVP. The document and accompanying letter from Holmes were apparently sent to Labadie in Minneapolis or Chicago. They mysteriously ended up in the Powderly papers.

11. Powderly, *Thirty Years of Labor,* 548–58.

12. Ibid., 551–53; *Ohio Valley Budget Weekly* (Wheeling, W. Va.), November 5, 1887; J.L, *Report,* 5.

13. Powderly, *Thirty Years of Labor,* 529, 553.

14. "Report of John M. Decker, Delegate to the General Assembly, Knights of Labor, Minneapolis, 1887" (Detroit: John R. Burton, n.d.), 3; Knights of Labor, *Record of Proceedings,* 1887, 1513.

15. Ibid., 1723–25; Oestreicher, "Terence Powderly," 54; Avrich, *The Haymarket Tragedy,* 374, 350.

16. "Now the Battle Is On," clipping regarding dissenters, n.s., October 23, 1887, LC.

17. J.L., "Cranky Notions," *Advance and Labor Leaf,* December 17, 1887; *Advance and Labor Leaf,* October 29, November 12, 1887.

18. "Working for the Reds," *Detroit Tribune,* October 27, 1887; *Advance and Labor Leaf,* October 22, November 5, 1887; Avrich, *The Haymarket Tragedy,* 338–39, 350–53.

19. Ware, *The Labor Movement,* 87; Avrich, *The Haymarket Tragedy,* 346–47, 373–74.

20. Avrich, *The Haymarket Tragedy,* 378, 392–93, 401.

21. J.L., "A Revolutionary Milepost," *Mother Earth* 7, no. 9 (November 1912), LC; J.L., "Cranky Notions," *Labor Leaf,* October 13, 1886; Thomas B. Barry to J.L., February 5, 1889, LC.

22. *Advance and Labor Leaf,* October 29, 1887; "Powderly Belabored," *Detroit Evening News,* November 16, 1887.

23. J.L., *Report,* 7–15.

24. *Detroit Evening News,* November 16, 1887; Powderly to Emma Fichenscher, November 23, 1887; Powderly to Devlin, November 29, 1887, TVP.

25. *Minneapolis Evening Journal,* October 15, 1887, LC; *Advance and Labor Leaf,* October 22, November 26, 1887; Powderly to A. M. Dewey, October 23, 1887, TVP. Dewey was not a delegate to the convention.

26. *Advance and Labor Leaf,* November 26, 1887; Dewey to Powderly, November 25, 1887, TVP; Devlin to Powderly, November 16, 1887, TVP.

27. Dewey to Powderly, November 25, 1887, TVP; *Advance and Labor Leaf,* June 2, 1888. After less than a year as editor, Dewey was forced out by other Knights of Labor officials, who complained of his work habits, writing style, and editorial judgment. Weir, *Beyond Labor's Veil,* 154.

28. "Now the Battle Is On," n.s., October 23, 1887, LC; Powderly to Dewey, April 27, 1887, TVP.

29. Decker, "Report," 1–4, 8, 10. The state assembly, unlike Detroit's free-wheeling district assembly, tended to tow the administration line and had adopted a res-

olution condemning "anarchy and revolutionary schemes." *Advance and Labor Leaf,* August 6, 1887.

30. Dyer Lum wrote to Labadie on November 6, 1887, "I understand that you 'have stepped down and out' from the *Advance.*" Tucker wrote on January 16, 1888, "I was sorry that circumstances compelled you to leave the *Advance*" (both LC).

31. Lum to J.L., December 31, 1887, LC.

32. Frank H. Brooks, "Ideology, Strategy and Organization: Dyer Lum and the American Anarchist Movement," *Labor History* 34, no. 1 (winter 1993): 57–83; Avrich, *The Haymarket Tragedy,* 317–21.

33. Avrich, *The Haymarket Tragedy,* 368. As the years went by, frustrated in his yearning to avenge the tragedy or die for the cause of human freedom, Lum sank into depression and alcoholism, and eventually poisoned himself. Ibid., 408–9.

34. George A. Schilling to J.L., December 26, 1887, LC; Lum to J.L., December 26, 1887, LC.

35. Henry George to J.L., August 19, 1889, LC; George to Mr. Gutshow, November 25, 1887, NYPL; Avrich, *The Haymarket Tragedy,* 343–45.

36. Schilling to J.L., November 24, December 12, December 26, 1887, LC; Benjamin Tucker to J.L., December 11, 1887, LC; *Solidarity* (New York), December 31, 1887, quoting the *Labor Enquirer* (Chicago).

37. Oestreicher, *Solidarity and Fragmentation,* 220nn. 88, 89; *Detroit Evening News,* September 5, 1887. Labadie was master workman of Henry George Assembly 2697 at the time.

38. *Advance and Labor Leaf,* February 4, March 10, 1888; J.L., "Seek Good Health," n.s., n.d., J.L. Scrapbook IV, 38–310, LC; J.L. "Cranky Notions," *Liberty,* March 16, 1889; Oestreicher, *Solidarity and Fragmentation,* 28n. 36.

39. Powderly to John W. Hayes, November 12, December 12, 1887, TVP; Powderly to Emma Fichenscher, November 23, 1887, TVP.

40. "Men Who Make Your Cigars," [*Detroit News*], July 28, 1889, Labor Leaders folder, LC; D. Boyd to A. Inglis, July 22, 1938, LC.

41. *Advance and Labor Leaf,* January 14 and 21, 1888; Devlin to Powderly, January 20, 1888, TVP; Powderly to Devlin, February 3, 1888, TVP.

42. J.L., "Cranky Notions," *Advance and Labor Leaf,* January 14, 1888.

43. *Advance and Labor Leaf,* December 17, 1887, April 28, June 23, 1888; J.L. to Schilling, January 25, 1895, GS. By June 1888, Grenell, Burton, and McGregor had all severed their connection with the paper as well.

Chapter 12

1. *Detroit Evening News,* February 27, 1888.

2. Philip Taft, *The AFL in the Time of Gompers* (New York: Harper and Bros., 1957), 44, 45; Gompers, *Seventy Years of Life and Labor,* ed. Philip Taft and John A. Sessions (New York: E. P. Dutton, 1957), 6.

3. *Advance and Labor Leaf,* March 3, 1888.

4. Gompers, *Seventy Years of Life and Labor,* ed. Taft and Sessions, 169. Mill is quoted in Jane Addams, *Twenty Years at Hull House* (New York: MacMillan, 1912), 189.

5. J.L., "Cranky Notions," *Liberty,* November 10, 1888.

6. Gompers, *Seventy Years of Life and Labor,* ed. Taft and Sessions, 18–20, 191, 161–62; Mandel, *Samuel Gompers,* 87, 92.

7. Gompers, *Seventy Years of Life and Labor,* ed. Taft and Sessions, 178, 157–58.

8. Ibid., 25, 50–51, 74, 77, 214; Mandel, *Samuel Gompers,* 11, 167.

9. Gompers, *Seventy Years of Life and Labor,* ed. Taft and Sessions, 35, 51; Taft, *The AFL in the Time of Gompers,* 147; Charles A. Madison, *American Labor Leaders* (New York: Frederick Ungar Publishing Co., 1950), 98, 110.

10. "Men Who Make Your Cigars," clipping, n.s., July 28, 1889, Detroit Labor Leaders file, LC; Gompers, *Seventy Years of Life and Labor,* ed. Taft and Sessions, 239. Goldwater, whose career paralleled Labadie's in many respects, played a prominent role in Detroit labor and radical activities as well as Democratic politics. See Robert Rockaway, "The Laboring Man's Champion: Samuel Goldwater," *Detroit Historical Society Bulletin* (November 1970): 4–9.

11. Richard J. Oestreicher, "The Limits of Labor Radicalism: Tom Barry and the Knights of Labor," unpublished paper, 1981, 19; Oestreicher, *Solidarity and Fragmentation,* 209; "Working for the Reds," *Detroit Tribune,* October 27, 1887, J.L. Scrapbook I, 45, LC.

12. George W. Stark, "We Old Timers," *Detroit News,* January 28, 1939.

13. Michigan Federation of Labor (MFL), *First Annual Convention of the Michigan Federation of Labor, 1889. Record of Proceedings.* Lansing, February 19–21, 1889, 6–7, LC.

14. Ibid., 9–11; MFL, *Resolutions,* February 1889, LC. Conspiracy laws, which had their origin in eighteenth-century English law, held that by combining to improve working conditions or strike, workers were engaging in conspiracy.

15. MFL, *First Annual Convention,* 3.

16. *The Craftsman,* April 13, 1889; *Twentieth Century,* January 16, 1890, clipping attached to copy of Michigan Federation of Labor, *Second Annual Convention of the Michigan Federation of Labor, 1890. Record of Proceedings,* East Saginaw, February 4–7, 1890, 12; Charles E. Barnes to J.L., April 2, 1889, LC.

17. Gompers to J.L., April 1, 1889, LC; Gompers to Robert Ogg, May 20, 1889, AFL:SG. Although the MFL used the AFL title on its letterhead and worked closely with that organization, it did not immediately affiliate. Delegates at the 1894 convention balked at the per capita tax. AFL records indicate the MFL did not formally affiliate until January 31, 1901.

18. MFL, *Second Annual Convention,* 10.

19. Gompers, *Seventy Years of Life and Labor,* ed. Taft and Sessions, 236; Gompers to J.L., January 14, 1890, February 12, 1894, LC; AFL, *Record of Proceedings of the Ninth Annual Convention of the American Federation of Labor,* Boston, December 10–14, 1889, 17.

20. Ibid., 15, 35, 39, 43.

21. Foner, *History of the Labor Movement,* 2:178–83.

22. MFL, *Second Annual Convention,* 9–10, 13.

23. Gompers quoted in Madison, *American Labor Leaders,* 99; *The Workman,* January 11, 1890, J.L. Scrapbook 1883–1901, 35, LC/LL. Only some years later

did the AFL use the slogan, "Stand faithfully by our friends and elect them; oppose our enemies and defeat them." Gompers's voluntarism is extensively treated in Michael Rogin, "Voluntarism: The Political Functions of an Antipolitical Doctrine," in *Labor and American Politics,* ed. Charles M. Rehmus and Doris B. McLaughlin (Ann Arbor: University of Michigan Press, 1967), 108–28.

24. Kim Voss, *The Making of American Exceptionalism: The Knights of Labor and Class Formation in the Nineteenth Century* (Ithaca: Cornell University Press, 1993) 1, 248–49. See also Fink, *Workingmen's Democracy,* 228–29.

25. Philip Taft speculates that anarchists in the AFL played a role in preventing the development of a labor party (*The AFL in the Time of Gompers,* xvi). Frank Brooks discusses anti-state contributors to AFL "voluntarism" in "Ideology, Strategy and Organization: Dyer Lum and the American Anarchist Movement," *Labor History* 34, no. 1 (winter 1993): 79–80. See also George B. Cotkin, "The Spencerian and Comtian Nexus in Gompers' Labor Philosophy: The Impact of Non-Marxian Evolutionary Thought," *Labor History* 20 (fall 1979): 510–23. Labadie claimed Peter J. McGuire "leaned considerably toward anarchism" (*Liberty,* June 9, 1883).

26. *The Workman,* January–March 1890, J.L. Scrapbook 1883–1901, 35–55, LC/LL.

27. J.L., "To the Editor," *The Exponent,* July 4, 1880, J.L. Scrapbook II, 76–77, LC; *The Workman,* January–March 1890.

28. "State Convention," *Saginaw Evening News,* February 4, 1890, LC; MFL, *Second Annual Convention,* 9.

29. Thomas Barry to J.L., June 25, September 6, 1888, LC.

30. *Advance and Labor Leaf,* October 20 and 27, 1888; Powderly, *Thirty Years of Labor,* 648; "Report of J. H. Morrow, Delegate to the Eleventh General Assembly of the American Federation of Labor," Indianapolis, 1888, 1, quoted in Maurice M. Ramsey, "The Knights of Labor in Michigan, 1878–1888" (master's thesis, College of the City of Detroit, 1932), 42–43.

31. Powderly, *Thirty Years of Labor,* 646; Powderly to John Hayes, December 8, 1888, quoted in Ware, *The Labor Movement,* 373.

32. Robert Ogg to J.L., December 11, 1888, LC; Barry to J.L., February 5, 1889, LC; *New York Sun,* October 5, and Brotherhood of United Labor, *Circular,* 1889, quoted in Ramsey, "The Knights of Labor in Michigan," 43–44; Oestreicher, "The Limits of Labor Radicalism," 5.

33. Barry to J.L., February 25, 1889, LC.

34. Ibid., February 5, 1889.

35. "State Convention."

36. MFL, *Second Annual Convention,* 9–11, 14–24. The eight-hour day was not common for decades. It was 1929 before the forty-hour work week was tried in Michigan. See *Michigan Federationist* 1, no. 7 (January 1929).

37. Gompers to J.L., January 14, 1890; Samuel Goldwater to J.L., August 25, 1889, LC.

38. *Michigan Federation of Labor Yearbook,* 1896, 3, LC; Sidney Glazer, "Origins and Early Development of the Michigan Federation of Labor," *American Federationist,* May 1934, 528–30.

39. J.L., "Cranky Notions," *Industrial Gazette,* December 1894–April 1895, LC. Detroit had been without a labor paper since *Advance and Labor Leaf* folded in November 1889.
40. A. Inglis to J.L., May 10, 1931, LC.
41. J.L., dedication to AFL, *Doggerel for the Under Dog* (Detroit: The Labadie Shop, 1910); J.L. to A. Inglis, December 10, 1929, LC.

Chapter 13

1. J.L., "Cranky Notions," *Liberty,* August 13, 1892, reprinted from the *Detroit News.*
2. The popular view is described in J.L., "Letter to Anarchists," March 16, 1889, LC.
3. Ibid.; J.L., "Cranky Notions," *Liberty,* June 8, 1889.
4. J.L., "Cranky Notions," *Liberty,* February 25, December 15, 1888.
5. J.L., "Letter to Anarchists"; Benjamin Tucker to J.L., August 12, 1888, December 20, 1891, LC. Only two books published in the United States at the time had titles that even suggested a general treatment of the subject: Albert Parsons, *Anarchism: Its Philosophy and Scientific Basis as Defined by Some of Its Apostles* (1887), issued after his death by his wife, Lucy; and *Anarchy and Anarchists* (1889) by Chicago police captain Michael J. Schaak, who rounded up and jailed hundreds of radicals after the Haymarket bombing. It was not until the 1931 publication of Eunice Schuster's *Native American Anarchism* that a systematic study of the subject became available.
6. J.L., "Cranky Notions," *Liberty,* June 8, 1889. Labadie's project is covered more extensively in Carlotta R. Anderson, "America's Anarchists: Who They Were and What They Stood For," *the dandelion* 22 (spring 1998).
7. Charles Fowler to J.L., n.d., LC; E. W. Barber to J.L., March 19, 1889, LC; George Schilling to J.L., January 25, 1889, April 4, 1894, LC; Archibald H. Simpson to J.L., January 20, 1889, LC; Maurice A. Bachman (Moritz A. Bachmann) to J.L., n.d., LC.
8. William Holmes to J.L., April 7, 1889, LC; J.L., "Cranky Notions," *Liberty,* January 28, April 14, 1888, May 24, 1890; William Holmes to *Liberty,* February 25, 1888.
9. Augustine Leroy Ballou to J.L., March 22, 1889, LC; John Beverley Robinson to J.L., n.d., LC; Joshua K. Ingalls to J.L., March 25, 1889, LC.
10. DeLeon, *The American as Anarchist,* xiii.
11. J.L., "Anarchism, What It Is and What It Is Not" (Detroit: The International Anarchist Group of Detroit, [1908]; J.L. to Tucker, May 21, 1908, NYPL. The International Anarchist Group of Detroit was associated with the Modern School Movement and was predominantly Jewish and German. See Paul Avrich, *The Modern School Movement* (Princeton: Princeton University Press, 1980), 314, 633–64.
12. J.L., "Anarchism: What It Is and What It Is Not." Even this barebones exposition did not please everyone. Tucker protested that one was an anarchist by virtue of belief, not actions. See Tucker to J.L., May 4, 1908, LC. Voltairine de Cleyre

objected that anarchists might commit crimes even though it would not be true to their beliefs. See de Cleyre to J.L., May 11, 1908, LC.

13. Charles A. Madison, *Critics and Crusaders* (New York: Henry Holt, 1947–1948), 159–60. Stirner's *Der Einzige und Sein Eigentum* (The Ego and His Own) was published in 1845.

14. J.L., "Cranky Notions," *Liberty,* May 26, 1888.

15. Martin, *Men Against the State,* 246, 250–54. See also Hamilton, "Introduction," 5–6, 15.

16. John Hubert Greusel, "The Poor Devil: A Memorial of Robert Reitzel" (Detroit: The Labadie Shop, 1909), LC; Oestreicher, *Solidarity and Fragmentation,* 47–48; J.L. to George Herron, October 23, 1918, LC. For a discussion of Robert Reitzel's literary influence, see Randall Paul Donaldson, "Robert Retizel (1849–1898) and his German-American Periodical *Der arme Teufel*" (Ph.D. diss., Johns Hopkins University, 1976).

17. Richard J. Oestreicher, "Robert Reitzel, Der arme Teufel," in *The German-American Radical Press: The Shaping of a Left Political Culture, 1850–1946,* ed. Elliott Shore et al. (Urbana: University of Illinois Press, 1992), 153, 165n. 12; Avrich, *The Haymarket Tragedy,* 384–85.

18. Avrich, *The Haymarket Tragedy,* 396–97.

19. Ibid., 411–12; Robert Reitzel to J.L., October 25, 1888, LC; Schilling to J.L., November 7, 1888, LC; *Chicago Tribune,* November 11–12, 1888; Agnes Inglis, "Robert Reitzel and the Haymarket Affair," LC.

20. Holli, *Detroit,* 110–16; Bald, *Michigan in Four Centuries,* 325–28.

21. Oestreicher, *Solidarity and Fragmentation,* 234–35.

22. Melvin G. Holli, *Reform in Detroit: Hazen S. Pingree and Urban Politics* (New York: Oxford University Press, 1969), 24, 30, 157, xiii.

23. Bald, *Michigan in Four Centuries,* 331; Stark, *City of Destiny,* 419.

24. Stark, *City of Destiny,* 431–32. By 1900, *Looking Backward* had sold more copies than any book written in the United States except *Uncle Tom's Cabin.*

25. Samuel Gompers to J.L., February 12, 1894.

26. August Donath to J.L., October 15, 1884, November 10, 1885; February 1, 1886; January 24, 1887; March 26, 1891, LC; State of Michigan, Circuit Court for the County of Wayne, "Bill of Exceptions, Mary J. June vs. Sophie Labadie and Joseph Labadie," July 1907, 20–21, LC. Mary J. June (née Archambeau) sued her sister, Sophie, and Jo Labadie for $142.04 plus interest, which she claimed was owed her. The suit was filed in 1899 and heard twice before the State Supreme Court before being decided in the Labadies' favor in 1907.

27. J.L. to "My Dear Molly," January 1891, and Sophie Labadie to "My dear Josia and Mary," January 21, 1895, State of Michigan, Circuit Court for the County of Wayne, "Bill of Exceptions," 2–3, 16, LC.

28. Joseph Buchanan to J.L., March 13, April 9, 1890, LC; Powderly, *The Path I Trod,* 161–62.

29. Labadie obituary, *Detroit News,* October 8, 1933; J.L., "Cranky Notions," *Liberty,* August 13, 1892, reprinted from the *Detroit News.*

30. J.L. to Schilling, December 27, 1895, GS; Robert Ogg to J.L., October 20, 1892,

LC; *Detroit Evening News,* November 28, 1892; *Detroit Journal,* November 29 and 30, 1892; "Plymouth Church Affair," *Detroit Tribune,* November 29, 1892, LC. The Social Gospel movement in American Protestantism during the latter half of the nineteenth century concerned itself with the application of Christianity to social problems.

31. Richard Drinnon, *Rebel in Paradise* (New York: Harper and Row, 1976), 52–54; Goldman, *Living My Life,* 1:97, 105.
32. J.L., "Cranky Notions," *Detroit Sunday News,* July 17, 1892, J.L. Scrapbook 1883–1901, 81, LC/LL.
33. *Detroit News,* reprinted in *Liberty,* August 13, 1892; Gompers, *Seventy Years of Life and Labor,* ed. Taft and Sessions, 33.
34. Cesare Lombroso, *Crime: Its Causes and Remedies* (Montclair: Patterson Smith, 1968; reprint of 1906), xxx, 434.
35. Drinnon, *Rebel in Paradise,* 90–91. See also Sidney Fine, "Anarchism and the Assassination of McKinley," in *The Underside of American History,* ed. Thomas R. Frazier (New York: Harcourt Brace Jovanovich, 1971), 61–83.
36. *Detroit Evening News,* September 11, 1901, J.L. Scrapbook IV, 45–46; Gompers, *Seventy Years of Life and Labor,* ed. Taft and Sessions, 235–36.
37. Labadie's anarchism was downplayed in "The Labadie Scrap Press," *Detroit News,* August 20, 1911; R. C. Stewart, "The Labadie Labor Collection," *Michigan Alumnus Quarterly Review,* May 10, 1947, 250; Lee J. Smits, "Dean of Detroit's Bohemia," *Detroit Free Press,* October 29, 1922, J.L. Scrapbook I, LC; J.L. to *The Workman,* February 13, 1890, J.L. Scrapbook 1883–1901, 45, LC/LL.

Chapter 14

1. Holli, *Reform in Detroit,* 63–64.
2. Stark, *City of Destiny,* 419–20; Holli, *Reform in Detroit,* 61–62.
3. J.L. to George A. Schilling, March 25, 1894, GS.
4. J.L. to Lester Clancy (water department official), April 12, 1917, LC; Benjamin Tucker to J.L., September 7, 1893, LC.
5. Peter J. McGuire to J.L., March 8, 1895, LC; Withdrawal notice for Labadie from Typographical Union No. 18, June 3, 1894, LC. Labadie was later granted honorary membership and paid dues until his death. "Typo Union Celebrates 100th Year," clipping, Detroit *Labor News,* 1939, LC.
6. Lawrence D. Orton, *Polish Detroit and the Kolasinski Affair* (Detroit: Wayne State University Press, 1981), 174–80.
7. *Detroit Evening News,* August 9, 1894, Labadie Scrapbook 1883–1901, 86–88, LC/LL; *The People* (New York), April 11, 1897.
8. Oestreicher, *Solidarity and Fragmentation,* 237–40.
9. McGuire to JL, May 7, 1892, March 8, 1895, February 26, 1896, LC; J.L., "The Danger of Too Much State Power," *The Carpenter,* June 1895; Henry Robinson to JL, February 8 and 17, 1893, LC; Michigan Bureau of Labor, *Tenth Annual Report,* 1893, xxxiii–ixl; J.L., "The State Fallacy," *Labor Leader,* April 7, 1894, J.L. Scrapbook 1883–1901, 85–86, LC/LL; J.L., "Anarchism," *Labor Leader,* March 21, 1896, J.L. Scrapbook 1883–1901, 89–90, LC/LL; J.L., "Where the

Blame Lies," *Labor Leader,* February 24, 1894, J.L. Scrapbook 1883–1901, 83–84, LC/LL; *The Workman,* March 1, 1890, J.L. Scrapbook 1883–1901, 56–57, LC/LL. Labadie's articles in the *Labor Leader* appeared from 1893 to 1896.

10. *American Federationist,* April 1894; Samuel Gompers to J.L., September 13, 1894, LC.

11. *American Federationist,* May 1895; Foner, *History of the Labor Movement,* 2:280, 286.

12. Mandel, *Samuel Gompers,* 152–55; Foner, *History of the Labor Movement,* 2:287–94; August McCraith to J.L., April 28, 1894, February 10, 1895, LC.

13. J.L. to Schilling, December 18, 1894, GS; "Big Increase," *Detroit News-Tribune,* June 13, 1897, LC.

14. *Detroit Sentinel,* August 21, 1897; J.L., "Address by Jo Labadie," Kropotkin Memorial Meeting, March 1921, LC; James Joll, *The Anarchists* (New York: Grosset and Dunlap, 1966), 126–27, 150.

15. Paul Avrich, *Anarchist Portraits* (Princeton: Princeton University Press, 1988), 81, 84, 88; "General Walker and the Anarchists," *Liberty,* November 19, 1887.

16. Avrich, *Anarchist Portraits,* 56, 59, 62, 65, 76.

17. Ibid., 82, 84, 85, 88, 97, 98.

18. Addams, *Twenty Years at Hull House,* 177–79.

19. J.L., membership cards and personal documents, LC.

20. J.L., "Cranky Notions," beginning "I have read 'Labor and the Civic Federation,' " n.d., LC. Labadie seemed devoid of the class consciousness emphasized by some historians in analyzing nineteenth-century labor activism.

21. Oestreicher, *Solidarity and Fragmentation,* 237–42.

22. J.L. to Schilling, November 19, 1895, GS. Reports on the Social Science Club are contained in newspaper clippings, December 23, 1896 to May 28, 1897, J.L. Scrapbook I, 1–34, in *The People* (Detroit) (1897–1899) and the *Detroit Sentinel* (1897–1899), LC.

23. Ibid.; "In a Dress Suit," *Detroit News,* December 30, 1896, J.L. Scrapbook I, 2.

24. *The People* (Detroit), January 28, April 23, 1897, J.L. Scrapbook I, 5, 30, LC.

25. J.L., "Cranky Notions," *Liberty,* November 10, 1888; Holli, *Reform in Detroit,* 141; Tucker to J.L., September 7, 1900, LC.

26. *The People* (Detroit), November 24, 1899.

27. J.L., "Anarchism in Detroit," *Liberty,* February 22, 1896; *Detroit Evening Press,* December 23, 1895, quoted in *Liberty,* January 11, 1896; J.L., "Anarchism," nine-page typescript, LC. Labadie published this speech in 1896. It was sold for five cents through E. H. Fulton's "Age of Thought" Library.

28. Charles Flint Kellogg, *NAACP: A History of the National Association for the Advancement of Colored People* (Baltimore: Johns Hopkins University Press, 1967), 1:114–15, 229–30, 239–41.

29. Mandel, *Samuel Gompers,* 236–39; Foner, *History of the Labor Movement,* 2:352–53. Gompers defended at length the AFL's practices related to black workers in letter to J.L., September 11, 1900, LC.

30. J.L., "My Dear Al [Weeks]," n.d. (after 1919), LC; MBLIS, Sixteenth Annual Report, 1899, 327; Bald, *Michigan in Four Centuries,* 264, 316.

31. J.L., "Cranky Notions," *Advance and Labor Leaf,* April 7, 1886; J.L. to Al [Weeks], n.d., LC.
32. P. P. Cooney to Sophie Labadie, May 13, June 8, 1898, LC; Paul Avrich, "Laurance Labadie," in *Anarchist Voices: An Oral History of Anarchism in America* (Princeton: Princeton University Press, 1995), 16.

Chapter 15

1. Alice Wexler, *Emma Goldman: An Intimate Life* (New York: Pantheon Books, 1984), 85–86.
2. Ibid., 74–77.
3. Goldman, *Living My Life,* 1:202–7; *Detroit Sentinel,* November 13, 1897, LC. The church was known variously as the People's Church, the Plymouth Congregational Church, and the People's or Plymouth Tabernacle.
4. *Detroit News,* November 15, 1897; Goldman, *Living My Life,* 1:203.
5. J.L., "Cranky Notions," *Detroit Sentinel,* November 27, 1897; Goldman, *Living My Life,* 1:206.
6. Goldman, *Living My Life,* 1:205–7; J.L., "Cranky Notions," *Detroit Sentinel,* December 11, 1897.
7. *Detroit News,* November 20–23, 1897; Goldman, *Living My Life,* 1:207; *Detroit Sentinel,* December 11, 1897.
8. J.L., "Cranky Notions," *Detroit Sentinel,* November 27, December 11, 1897.
9. Wexler, *Emma Goldman,* 48–49; J.L., "Cranky Notions," *Detroit Sentinel,* December 11, 1897.
10. Wexler, *Emma Goldman,* 108–9, 298n. 27; Richard Drinnon, *Rebel in Paradise* (New York: Harper and Row, 1976), 75; Goldman, *Living My Life,* 1:323–24.
11. Wexler, *Emma Goldman,* 103–7; Drinnon, *Rebel in Paradise,* 76–77; Goldman, *Living My Life,* 1:322.
12. Avrich, *Anarchist Portraits,* 103; Sidney Fine, "Anarchism and the Assassination of McKinley," in *The Underside of American History,* ed. Thomas R. Frazier (New York: Harcourt Brace Jovanovich, 1971), 2:72–74, 77, 82–83. See also Robert G. Scofield, "Anti-Anarchist Laws," *the dandelion* 5, no. 18 (spring–winter 1982): 3–11.
13. J.L., "To the Editor of the *Windsor Record,*" LC; Drinnon, *Rebel in Paradise,* 121–22.
14. J.L., "To the Editor," *Detroit News,* March 18, [1907], J.L. Scrapbook I, 40–41, LC; *Detroit Times,* March 24, 1907, J.L. Scrapbook I, 41, LC; *Windsor Evening Record,* March 23, 1907, J.L. Scrapbook I, 41, LC.
15. Henry A. Robinson to J.L, November 22, 1897, LC; Oestreicher, *Solidarity and Fragmentation,* 243–44.
16. *Detroit Sentinel,* September 25, 1897, 4. Labadie is never listed as editor, but his stewardship is referred to in letters from William Holmes, Henry Robinson, and other friends as well as in comments in the publication. Among the American anarchists who wrote for the paper were John William Lloyd, Lizzie Holmes, Stephen Byington, Victor Yarros, Voltairine de Cleyre, and Rafael Buck.
17. J.L., "Cranky Notions," *Detroit Sentinel,* November 6, 1897, May 7, 1898.

18. J.L., "Cranky Notions," *Detroit Sentinel,* November 6, 1897, quoting from the *American Craftsman.*

19. Fine, "Anarchism and the Assassination of McKinley," 74n. 55.

20. Anarchist stickers, LC; *Detroit Journal,* April 7, 1908, J.L. Scrapbook IV, 302, LC.

21. *Detroit Journal,* April 11, 1908, J.L. Scrapbook IV, 787–88, LC; J.L. to Benjamin Tucker, April 8, 1908, NYPL; Allan Benson to J.L., May 1, 1908, LC; E. Debs to J.L., May 5, 1908, LC. Tucker was also having troubles with the stickers. The assistant attorney general for the Post Office Department declared some of them unmailable and ruled that all mail bearing them would be discarded. See Tucker, "Article about Jo Labadie," Tucker Collection, NYPL; Tucker to J.L., May 4, 1908, LC.

22. *Detroit News,* May 13, 1908, J.L. Scrapbook I, 122–23, LC.

23. *Detroit Free Press,* May 13, 1908, J.L. Scrapbook I, 121, LC; ibid., May 20, 1908, J.L. Scrapbook I, 124, LC; *Detroit News,* November 9, 1933.

24. J.L. to Tucker, May 21, 1908, NYPL.

25. Ibid.

26. Tucker to J.L., January 15, June 11, 1908, LC; J.L. to Tucker, January 17, 1908, NYPL.

27. Avrich, *Anarchist Portraits,* 145–47; Benson to J.L., April 14, 1908, April 23, 1908, LC. Benson was the Socialist party candidate for president in 1916.

28. J.L. to Tucker, June 30, 1908, NYPL, Tucker to J.L., July 2, September 6 and 17, 1908, LC; J.L. to Tucker, September 13, 1908, NYPL.

29. Hamilton, "Introduction," 14–15; Martin, *Men Against the State,* 273.

30. J.L. to Tucker, August 15, 1906, February 8, March 28, 1909, NYPL; Carl Nold to J.L., April 17, 1910, LC.

31. Drinnon, *Rebel in Paradise,* 74; J.L., "Cranky Notions," *The Firebrand,* December 25, 1909; Fine, "Anarchism and the Assassination of McKinley," 80. Long after Altgeld's death in 1902, Labadie venerated him as a "Great Soul!" with "a red, red heart beating with justice and mercy" in "John P. Altgelt [*sic*]," *Sing Songs and Some That Don't.*

32. *The Firebrand,* January 5, 1910. Goldman considered Tucker and his circle cold, with "no depths, no passions, no intencities [*sic*]. Just sawdust." See Wexler, *Emma Goldman,* 290n. 13.

33. Wexler, *Emma Goldman,* 186; Goldman to J.L., January 16, July 27, 1911, LC; J.L. to Goldman, August 3, 1911, LC. The wife of Ross Winn, publisher of *The Firebrand* and *The Advance,* had appealed to Goldman for help. See Mrs. Ross Winn to Goldman, July 12, 1911, LC.

34. Goldman to J.L., September 30, 1911, LC.

35. Ibid., April 11, 1906, LC.

36. Wexler, *Emma Goldman,* 122, 281.

37. J.L. to Tucker, March 28, 1923, NYPL. Tucker did not reply. After World War I, there were still small groups of foreign-born anarchists in the United States, chiefly Italian, Spanish, and Russian. See Paul Avrich, *Sacco and Vanzetti: The Anarchist Background* (Princeton: Princeton University Press, 1991).

Chapter 16

1. *Detroit Journal,* July 1, 1901, J.L. Scrapbook I, 114, LC.

2. J.L., "Bob Hendrie, Teamster," *Doggerel for the Under Dog* (Detroit: The Labadie Shop, 1910), 49; Jack Conroy, "Jo Labadie, Craftsman and Poet," *Northern Light* 1, no. 7 (November–December 1927): 160; J.L., "The Russian Red Revolt," *Russian Verses* (Detroit: The Labadie Shop, 1932), 6, LC.

3. Benjamin Tucker to J.L., January 17, August 11, 1903, LC; Harry Rickel to J.L., September 10, 1919, LC; Conroy, "Jo Labadie, Craftsman and Poet"; Lawrence H. Conrad to J.L., January 24, May 5, 1927, LC. Ironically, Whitman was a great admirer of Tucker, who, in 1882, sold *Leaves of Grass* in defiance of Boston postal censorship. See Martin Blatt, "Ezra Heywood and Benjamin R. Tucker," in *Benjamin R. Tucker,* 35–37.

4. J.L. to Tucker, March 28, 1923, NYPL; Lawrence H. Conrad, "Jo Labadie—Poet," *Michigan History* 16, no. 2 (spring 1932): 223; *Haldeman-Julius Weekly* (Girard, Kansas), March 22, 1924, LC; J.L., "Freedom of Speech" in *Anthology of Revolutionary Poetry,* ed. Marcus Graham (New York: Active Press, 1927), 217–18.

5. J.L. to Dr. William E. Gilroy, June 14, 1925, LC; "The Labadie Scrap Press," *Detroit News,* August 20, 1911, J.L. Scrapbook I, 94–95, LC. The booklets generally measured three-and-a-half by five-and-a-half inches.

6. J.L., three-page manuscript beginning, "The demand for the products of the shop," LC; Loose advertisements for the Labadie Shop, LC.

7. Paul Leake, *History of Detroit* (Chicago: The Lewis Publishing Co., 1912), 976; J. Grenell, "Autobiography," 67–68; Reichert, *Partisans of Freedom,* 353–58. Schmidt was a member of the board of police commissioners, the state board of arbitration and mediation, and the state board of forest inquiry.

8. J.L. to Henry Bool, January 26, 1917, LC/HB; J.L., "While I put the taboo on no place . . . ," one-page manuscript, LC; Lee J. Smits, "Sidewalks of Detroit," [*Detroit Free Press*], August 7, 1928, J.L. Scrapbook V, 376, LC; Carl Nold to J.L., postcard, March 16, 1916, LC; Goldman, *Living My Life,* 1:203.

9. A. Inglis, "Charles Joseph Antoine Labadie," three-page biographical sketch, 2; J.L. to Carl Schmidt, "My dear Karl . . . ," [January 2, 1910], LC; Schmidt to J.L., February 4, 1910, LC; J.L. to Emma Goldman, August 3, 1911, LC; Goldman to J.L., August 10, 1911, LC.

10. Steve Babson, *Working Detroit: The Making of a Union Town* (New York: Adama Books, 1984), 18; David Montgomery, *The Fall of the House of Labor* (Cambridge: Cambridge University Press, 1987), 215; Cooper, *Once a Cigar Maker,* 190–92.

11. J.L. to "Papa's Dearest," September 9, 1905, LC; J.L. to "Ma chère" (Sophie Labadie), September 12, 1905, LC; J.L. to "Mamma and the Babies," Labor Day, 1905, LC; J.L., to "Dear Ones," September 6, 1905, LC; E. Debs to J.L., December 12, 1905, LC. Arden, founded in 1900, is still in existence. Hubbard told Labadie he was impressed with his definition of anarchy and proposed to use some of the ideas as his own, "for that is the way I get my original things." E. Hubbard to J.L., September 13, 1904, LC.

292 NOTES TO CHAPTER 16

12. J.L. to Tucker, February 8, 1909, NYPL; J.L. to Herman Kuehn, n.d., LC.
13. J.L. to Bool, July 14, 1913, LC/HB. The stone ruins of two Bubbling Waters buildings are located in Kensington Metropark, near Brighton. The land was deeded to the Huron-Clinton Metropolitan Authority by Labadie's children in 1948 for $1, possibly as a result of condemnation proceedings. See deed dated December 12, 1948, Oakland County Land Records. Labadie Road runs through what is now a Nature Area. An exhibit about the Labadies is housed in the Nature Center building.
14. J.L., "Cranky Notions," *The Firebrand,* November 1910; J.L. to "Dear Old George [Schilling]," May 6, 1925, LC.
15. J.L., "What Is Anarchism?" ten-page typescript, n.d., 8, LC.
16. J.L. to Bool, July 14, 1913, September 3, 1917, LC/HB. For descriptions of life at Bubbling Waters, see J.L. to Sophie, Laura, and Laurance Labadie, LC.
17. J.L. to Bool, August 20, 1914, LC/HB; J.L. to J. Grenell, October 19, 1929, LC/JG; "Dr. Urban Hartung's record of some of his fasting patients," LC. Labadie wrote many articles about good health for the *Detroit Times.* See J.L. Scrapbook IV, 286–310, LC.
18. Clippings from the *Detroit Times,* October 24, 1903, J.L. Scrapbook I, 116–17, LC; ibid., October 30, November 9 and 10, 1903, J.L. Scrapbook IV, 228, 250–52, LC.
19. "Police Horse Blanche, . . ." *Detroit Journal,* September 30, 1915; J.L. to J. Grenell, 1927, LC/JG. Bool was a financial supporter of Tucker and other anarchists. After President McKinley's assassination, he was threatened with violence and a boycott of his business. He returned to his native England in 1910 after his wife died, but continued to send Labadie money until his death in 1922. See Eunice Minette Schuster, *Native American Anarchism* (Port Townsend: Loompanics Unlimited, 1983; reprint of 1932), 155–56.
20. *The Vaudeville Breeze* (Chicago), June 18, 1915; "Motion Picture Ranch Is Filming Scenes Out in Wilds of Oakland County," *Detroit News,* June 18, 1916; "Staging Movies in the Wilds of Oakland County," *Detroit Free Press,* n.d. [1915], author's collection.
21. Gregg Sutter, "Making Movies in Michigan," *Detroit News Magazine,* November 1, 1981; "Motion Picture Ranch," *Detroit News,* June 18, 1916. Fielding and Taliaferro starred in "The Rich Slave" (1921); Harris, Marmont, and Hubert and Oliver Labadie in "The First Woman" (1922); and Mayo and Landis in "Then Came the Woman" (1926).
22. J.L. to Bool, December 18, 1915, July 9, 1921, LC/HB; Nina Van Zandt to J.L., January 10, 1913, LC; J.L., "An Explanation," leaflet, LC.
23. J.L. to Bool, August 17, 1916, LC/HB. Ruins of the fireplace are still visible in Kensington Metropark.
24. J.L. to "My good old friend" (Henry Bool), n.d., five-page letter, LC/HB. Labadie was a contributing editor of the Bowman, North Dakota, *Truth Seeker* in 1913. He wrote occasionally for *The Egoist* (1921–1925) and *The Mutualist* (1925–1926), both published in Clinton, Iowa.
25. Gompers wanted Labadie to discuss the labor provisions of the Clayton Anti-Trust Act of 1914, which he termed labor's "Magna Carta." He seems to have

forgotten that Labadie, who turned him down, had little use for labor laws. Gompers to J.L., July 13, 1915, September 3, 1915, LC. See also J.L., "Some of the comrades say . . . ," ms., LC; Oestreicher, *Solidarity and Fragmentation,* 244–45. In 1886, over 20 percent of the workers had been organized.

26. E. Debs to J.L., December 12, 1905, LC; Nick Salvatore, *Eugene V. Debs* (Urbana: University of Illinois Press, 1982) 254–56, 245.

27. Stephen Meyer III, *The Five Dollar Day: Labor Management and Social Control in the Ford Motor Company, 1908–1921* (Albany: State University of New York Press, 1981), 91, 93, 108; Babson, *Working Detroit,* 33; Joyce Shaw Peterson, *American Automobile Workers, 1900–1933* (Albany: State University of New York Press, 1987), 108–10; J.L. to Bool, August 7, 1918, LC/HB; J.L. to L. Labadie, September 4, 1917, LC.

28. J.L. to Charlotte Labadie, April 28, 1912, LC; E. Debs to J.L., May 5, 1908, March 13, 1909, LC.

29. J.L. to E. Debs, December 9, 1920, EVD; J.L. to T. Debs, December 9, 1920, EVD; T. Debs to J.L., December 24, 1920, LC.

30. J.L. to E. Debs, December 9, 1920, EVD.

31. J.L. to "Dearies" (his children), November 6, 1916, LC; J.L. to L. Labadie, November 11, 1918, LC.

32. *Detroit News Tribune,* July 31, 1904, J.L. Scrapbook IV, 802, LC; Clipping, *Portage Daily Democrat,* August 19, 1911, LC.

33. See correspondence between L. Labadie and J.L., 1915–17, LC.

34. Ibid., 1917–18, LC.

35. University of Michigan, transcript for L. Labadie, June 1918; J.L. to L. Labadie, July 2, 1918, LC.

36. J.L. to Bool, June 15, September 3, 1917, May 20, 1918, LC/HB.

37. Roger Burlingame, *Henry Ford* (New York: Alfred A. Knopf, 1955), 3–4; J.L. to Robert McCormick, n.d., LC.

38. George Schilling to J.L., n.d. (after 1914), LC; J.L. to "My dearly beloved brother Bool . . ." (Henry Bool), n.d. (before December 23, 1914), LC/HB; Tucker to J.L., December 23, 1914, bMS Am 1614 (218), by permission of the Houghton Library, Harvard University; Tucker to "an American friend," n.d., one-page typescript titled "Tucker's attitude during World War I," LC/LL.

39. J.L. to Schilling, February 23, 1925, LC; " 'Jo' Labadie's Job in Doubt," *Detroit Journal,* April 23, 1917, LC; Microfilm 1085, Investigative Case Files of the Bureau of Investigation, 1908–1922, Microfilm Reel 141-B, File Nos. 3253–3376, Entry 12B, March 20 and 27, 1920, National Archives, Washington, D.C.

40. Avrich, *Sacco and Vanzetti,* 165, 173–75; J.L. to William Kelsey, May 2, 1920, LC.

41. David H. Bennett, *The Party of Fear: From Nativist Movements to the New Right in American History* (New York: Vintage Books, 1990), 192; Babson, *Working Detroit,* 38–39; Joseph R. Conlin, "William D. 'Big Bill' Haywood: The Westerner as Labor Radical," in *Labor Leaders in America,* ed. Melvyn Dubofsky and Warren Van Tine (Urbana: University of Illinois Press, 1987), 114; J.L. to Gompers, November 15, 1919, AFL:SG; J.L. to Tucker, 1922, NYPL.

42. Mandel, *Samuel Gompers,* 351, 396–97, 437, 477–78.

43. J.L. to Gompers, November 15, 1919, AFL:SG; Gompers to J.L., December 5, 1919, LC.
44. J.L. to Allan Benson, February 25, 1920, LC; J.L. to Bool, January 20, November 9, 1919, LC/HB; *Detroit Times,* March 22, 1920, J.L. Scrapbook III, 49, LC; J.L. to Tucker, 1922, NYPL.

Chapter 17

1. J.L., "To the Board of Regents of the University of Michigan," July 28, 1911, LC. As early as the 1880s, Labadie was trying to get missing copies of such publications as *Our Organette, John Swinton's Paper,* and *The Craftsman.*
2. Richard T. Ely to J.L., April 10, 1897, LC. For an account of the origins of the collection and its first thirty years, see Arthur John, "A History of the Labadie Collection of Labor and Radical Literature in the University of Michigan Library," unpublished term paper, 1941–42, LC. The Labadie-Ely correspondence is reproduced and discussed in Fine, "The Ely-Labadie Letters," 30–32. Labadie's literature was of particular interest to Ely in 1897 because he was contemplating a revision of his book, *The Labor Movement in America.*
3. Richard T. Ely to J.L., November 7, 1906, LC.
4. J.L. to Benjamin Tucker, August 15, 1906, NYPL; Tucker to J.L., August 17, 1906, LC. Although Labadie regularly contributed unpaid articles to *Liberty,* Tucker charged him the full subscription price.
5. J.L. to John B. Andrews, August 14, 1906, LC.
6. Andrews to J.L., August 22, 1906, LC; Ely to J.L., November 7, 1906, LC; Graham Taylor to J.L., November 13, 1906, LC; Edward W. Bemis to J.L., November 14, 1906, LC; J.L. to Board of Regents, July 28, 1911, LC.
7. Henry Carter Adams to J.L., May 5, 1909, LC; George E. Barnett to J.L., May 2, 1910, LC; G. W. W. Hanger to J.L., November 23, 1910, LC. Labadie said he also was offered $3,000 for his collection by the Michigan State Librarian (J.L. to Henry Bool, December 1, 1913, LC/HB), although a letter dated April 20, 1914, from State Librarian Mary C. Spencer seems to indicate no money was available for this purpose.
8. J.L. to John R. Commons, April 4, 1912, quoted in "A Letter from Jo Labadie to John R. Commons," *Labor History* 2, no. 3 (summer 1970): 345.
9. J.L. to Tucker, March 28, 1909, NYPL; Robert Mark Wenley to J.L., February 22, 1911, LC.
10. J.L. to Board of Regents, July 28, 1911, LC.
11. Carl E. Parry to J.L., October 17, 1911, LC; A. Inglis, "The Labadie Collection," 1932, LC.
12. *Detroit Journal,* August 28, 1912, J.L. Scrapbook I, 119–20, LC; J.L., "The Labadie Collection of Sociological Literature," one-page printed leaflet, LC.
13. John, "A History of the Labadie Collection," 24–27; Carl Schmidt to J.L., February 24, 1912, LC; Commons to J.L., April 1, 1912, LC; *Detroit Journal,* August 28, 1912, J.L. Scrapbook I, 119, LC.
14. John, "A History of the Labadie Collection," 27–28; Harry Burns Hutchins to J.L., May 27, 1916, LC.

15. Material regarding Agnes Inglis's life is based primarily on her autobiography, "Reflections—Notes for a Book," two-part, 244-page typescript, LC/AI. See also Dione Miles, "Agnes Inglis: Librarian, Activist, Humanitarian," *the dandelion* 3, no. 12 (winter 1979): 7–15; James J. Martin, "Agnes Inglis: Recollections and Impressions," in *Laurance Labadie: Selected Essays* (Colorado Springs: Ralph Myles Publisher, Inc., 1978), 67–74; R. Anne Okey, "They All Knew Each Other: Agnes Inglis and the Labadie Collection," exhibit catalog, Special Collections Library, University of Michigan Library, 1992. See also Richard Drinnon, *Rebel in Paradise* (New York: Harper and Row, 1961), 138–39.
16. A. Inglis, "Reflections—Notes for a Book," part 1, 43–44, 88–89, LC/AI; Goldman, *Living My Life,* 2:666; Wexler, *Emma Goldman,* 184–85.
17. A. Inglis to J.L., April 13 and 18, November 5, 1916, LC.
18. A. Inglis, "Reflections—Notes for a Book," part 2, 12–14, 16, 86–87, LC/AI; A. Inglis to J.L., October 21, 1928, LC.
19. A. Inglis to J.L., February 11, 1924, LC; J. Grenell, "Autobiography," 82.
20. Edward C. Weber, "The Labadie Collection in the University of Michigan Library," *Labor History* 31, nos. 1–2 (winter–spring 1990): 157–59; Author's interviews with Edward C. Weber, May 1985; A. Inglis, one-page typescript, beginning "I have preserved in the Collection . . . ," December 12, 1938, LC.
21. A. Inglis, two-page typescript, beginning "I began work in the collection in 1924 . . . ," LC; A. Inglis to J.L., January 15, September 6, 1928, June 12, 1930, LC.
22. A. Inglis to J.L., September 6, 1928, LC; J.L. to A. Inglis, May 11, 1925, LC/AI.
23. A. Inglis to J.L., November 24, 1925, December 17, 1926, May 10, 1931, LC.
24. A. Inglis, two-page biographical sketch, "Item of interest in regard to Jo Labadie," December 11, 1932, 2, LC.
25. Miles, "Agnes Inglis: Librarian, Activist, Humanitarian," 8; Martin, "Agnes Inglis: Recollections and Impressions," 68, 71; Weber, "The Labadie Collection," 159; J.L., one-page typescript, "To Friends, who may be glad to hear about the Labadie Collection," n.d. [1927], LC; A. Inglis to J.L., January 21, February 12, 1928, LC.
26. A. Inglis to J.L., August 25, 1929, June 12, 1930, May 10, 1931, LC; A. Inglis, "Charles Joseph Antoine Labadie," three-page biographical sketch, 2, LC. Labadie did not deny his self-centeredness, but attributed the quality to everyone else as well. "What we do to the Collection is not for the other fellow so much as it is for ourselves," he wrote Inglis in August 1928. "No one does unselfish things, tho he may think he does . . . [and] others may get benefit to [*sic*]."

Chapter 18

1. Holli, *Detroit,* 125–26; Babson, *Working Detroit,* 41–44.
2. Babson, *Working Detroit,* 39–40; Ron Alpern et al., *Union Town: A Labor History Guide to Detroit* (Detroit: Workers Education Local 189, n.d.), 4.
3. J.L. to J. Grenell, 1927, LC/JG; J.L. to John B. Andrews, [1922], LC.
4. J.L. to A. Inglis, September 1928, LC/AI; J.L. to Benjamin Tucker, March 28, 1923, NYPL; J.L. to Henry Bool, January 20, 1920, LC/HB; "Dean of Detroit's

Bohemia," *Detroit Free Press,* October 29, 1922, J.L. Scrapbook I, 102–4, LC. Labadie exchanged hundreds of letters with money reformer Herman Kuehn and Albert G. Wagner, both former Tucker associates. Other radical correspondents of his last years included William C. Owen, John William Lloyd, Alexander Berkman, Edward H. Fulton, Allan Benson, Clarence Darrow, John Henry MacKay, Carl Nold, John Beverley Robinson, George Schilling, Myra Pepper Weller, Austin W. Wright, Hippolyte Havel, Leonard Abbott, Emile Armand, Henry Cohen, and Alfred B. Westrup.

5. Detroit Labor Forum flyer. The lecture was part of a 1920 series that included Roger Baldwin, founder of the American Civil Liberties Union, whose speech was titled, "The Revolt of Labor"; J.L. to J. Grenell, 1927, LC/JG.

6. J. Grenell, "Autobiography," 96–98; J.L. to Tucker, March 28, 1923, NYPL.

7. John Burton to J.L., July 10, 1912, January 16, 1922, LC. Burton established *Onward* in 1888 as a successor to *Advance and Labor Leaf.*

8. John M. McGregor to J.L., February 17, 1927, March 1927, LC; McGregor to J. Grenell, October 11, 1927, LC/JG.

9. Thomas Barry to J.L., September 2, 1907, LC; Oestreicher, "The Limits of Labor Radicalism," 16–17.

10. Gompers to J.L., January 27, 1920, LC.

11. Salvatore, *Eugene V. Debs,* 327–28, 334–38; E. Debs to J.L., January 5, 1925, LC.

12. Oestreicher, "Terence Powderly," 56; Madison, *American Labor Leaders,* 68.

13. Henry A. Robinson to J.L., September 12, 1896, LC.

14. J.L., "Address by Jo Labadie," Kropotkin Memorial Meeting, March 1921, LC.

15. J.L. to Tucker, 1922, NYPL; J.L. to "Dear George" (Schilling), February 23, 1925, LC. At the time of their 1919 deportation, Goldman and Berkman committed themselves to support the Bolsheviks. They fled Russia in despair two years later. Goldman, *Living My Life,* 2:927.

16. J.L. to William C. Owen, March 17, 1924, LC.

17. J.L. to J. Grenell, December 23, 1927, August 4, 1928, LC/JG; J.L. to Bool, November 9, 1919, LC/HB; J. Grenell, "Rubbing Elbows with People Worthwhile: V. Joe Labadie," *Detroit News,* September 11, 1916. See also "Joe Labadie Leads Simple Life," *Detroit Free Press,* June 27, 1915.

18. J.L. to Albert G. Wagner, August 31, September 10, 1925, LC. Labadie issued *What Is Love?* second edition (1921); *Songs of the Spoiled* (1922); *Windows* (1924); *Sing Songs and Some That Don't* (1925); *Anarchism: Genuine and Asinine* (1925), and *Holiday Sentiments,* n.d., a booklet of four short poems.

19. Lawrence H. Conrad to J.L., December 27, 1926, January 24, 1927, March 3 and 17, 1928, LC; J. Grenell to J.L., March 26, 1928, LC.

20. Carl Schmidt to J.L., November 15, 1919; J.L., "Walhalla and Its Host" (Detroit: The Labadie Shop, 1910), 10, LC.

21. J. Grenell to J.L., May 11, 1928, LC; J.L. to "Friend Albertus" (Albert Wagner), February 8, 1927, LC.

22. L. Labadie, unsent letter [to Charlotte Labadie Hauser], n.d. (after 1927), beginning "It is a deplorable circumstance," LC/LL; C. Labadie Hauser to L. Labadie, May 13, 1932, LC/LL, Family Papers, box 19.

23. J.L. to A. Inglis, September, 1928, LC/AI.
24. L. Labadie to author, May 29, 1965, LC/LL.
25. L. Labadie, "Places I have worked," n.d., LC/LL; Avrich, *Anarchist Voices,* 16; L. Labadie, "Dere foks," [1927], "Dear Fadder and Mudder," February 17, n.d. (after 1925), LC/LL. See also additional correspondence, L. Labadie with parents, 1921–24, LC/LL.
26. A. Inglis, note, beginning "April 23, 1932—Joe visited the Labadie Collection," J.L. biography and character sketches, and miscellaneous notes, LC.
27. L. Labadie to A. Inglis, December 21, 1932, LC/AI; "Jo Labadie's Only Funeral Is Goodbys [*sic*] of His Friends," *Detroit News,* October 10, 1933, J.L. Scrapbook V, 402, LC. *Anarchism* consisted of a single essay, "Anarchism and Crime," originally published in *Anarchism: Genuine and Asinine* (1925).
28. *Detroit News,* October 10, 1933, J.L. Scrapbook V, 402, LC.
29. Estelle James, "Jimmy Hoffa: Labor Hero or Labor's Own Foe?" in *Labor Leaders in America,* 304.
30. Bald, *Michigan in Four Centuries,* 404–5, 414–16, 423; Alpern et al., *Union Town,* 4.
31. A. Inglis, "Charles Joseph Antoine Labadie," three-page biographical sketch, 3, LC.
32. J.L. to Bool, undated fragment, beginning "Of course, what to me seems depressing," LC/HB; W. K. Kelsey, *Detroit News,* April 18, 1950, J.L. Scrapbook IV, 559, LC; Lee J. Smits, "Sidewalks of Detroit," *Detroit Free Press,* [after 1920], LC.

Epilogue

1. Benjamin Tucker, "The Attitude of Anarchism Toward Industrial Combinations" (Detroit: Laurance Labadie, 1933), LC, Anarchism 8019; Martin, *Men Against the State,* 271–73. In the speech, Tucker maintained that industrial combinations per se were simply a form of competition based on cooperation and that the "baneful" trusts of the time were "systems of a social disease" created by the state in the form of "land monopoly . . . idea monopoly . . . tariff monopoly and money monopoly." The only remedy was the establishment of "free access" in those areas. The success of the conference prompted the organization of the National Civic Federation, which sought to establish labor-capital cooperation and industrial peace. In 1934, Laurance Labadie reprinted Tucker's "Why I Am an Anarchist" (first published in the *Twentieth Century* in 1892).
2. Tucker to L. Labadie, June 3, 1933, bMS Am 1614 (220), by permission of the Houghton Library, Harvard University; L. Labadie to Tucker, March 30, September 17, 1936, LC/LL; Inscription on a photograph of Benjamin Tucker sent to L. Labadie, LC/LL. Tucker's assessment that the cause was lost was perhaps bleaker than warranted. There are, at this writing, several websites on the internet concerned with the American individualist anarchism represented by Tucker, Labadie, and others. Frank Brooks, speculating on the causes of the movement's decline, points to the extreme individualism that prevented the formation of any effective organization, to tactics that were gradualist,

individualist, and passive, and to a strategy limited to "conversion through preaching." Brooks, "American Individual Anarchism: What It Was and Why It Failed," *Journal of Political Ideologies* 1, no. 1 (1966): 75–95. Tucker died in Monaco on June 22, 1939, at the age of eighty-five.

3. L. Labadie to Tucker, July 9, September 17, 1936, LC/LL.

4. A selection of his essays was reprinted in 1978 in Martin, *Laurance Labadie: Selected Essays.* For an extensive treatment of L. Labadie's views, see two undergraduate papers by Fritz Ward, "Laurance Labadie and the Individualist Anarchist Critique of War" (1987), and "Laurance Labadie and the Origins of Modern Radical Libertarianism" (1988), LC.

5. Avrich, *Anarchist Voices,* 16; Mildred J. Loomis and Mark A. Sullivan, "Laurance Labadie: Keeper of the Flame," in *Benjamin R. Tucker,* 116–30.

6. Loomis and Sullivan, "Laurance Labadie," 119.

7. Martin, "Laurance Labadie," 5–6.

8. In *This Ugly Civilization* (1929) and *Flight from the City* (1933), Borsodi advocated homesteading as an alternative to the problems of urban industrialization. For a discussion of the decentralist movement and Lane's End Homestead, see Mildred J. Loomis, *Decentralism: Where It Came From; Where It Is Going* (York, Penn.: The School of Living Press, 1980). The school's publications included *Interpreter* (1947–1957), *Balanced Living* (1958–1961), and *A Way Out* (1962–1966).

9. Martin, "Laurance Labadie," 6, 8, 16. Among those writing for the School's publications at the time were Robert Anton Wilson, Paul Goodman, Murray Rothbard, S. E. Parker, Timothy Leary, Theodore Schroeder, Robert LeFevre, and Frank Chodorov.

10. Loomis and Sullivan, "Laurance Labadie," 121; L. Labadie to "Fred" (Saxby), May 16, 1952, LC/LL. On the Borsodi homesteading experiment at "Dogwoods," see Ralph Borsodi, *Flight from the City,* 3d ed. (Suffern: School of Living, 1947).

11. Martin, "Laurance Labadie," 10.

12. The neighborhood of the Labadie family home in Detroit was then almost all black.

13. Related to the author by Mark Sullivan, September 21, 1987; L. Labadie to author, December 12, 1948, LC/LL.

14. L. Labadie, "Published Articles by Laurance Labadie," April 4, 1964, two-page typescript, LC/LL; Martin, "Laurance Labadie," 17; L. Labadie, "What Is Man's Destiny," reprinted in Martin, "Laurance Labadie," 65; Avrich, *Anarchist Voices,* 16.

15. Murray N. Rothbard, *For a New Liberty* (New York: Macmillan, 1974), 8–10.

BIBLIOGRAPHY

Bibliographical Note

Most of the primary materials used for this book were saved by Jo and Sophie Labadie and may be found in the Labadie Collection at the University of Michigan in original, photocopied, or, in some cases, microfilmed form. They include letters received by Labadie from his many correspondents, along with his manuscripts, personal account book, publications of the Labadie Shop, family photographs, and eight family scrapbooks. Those sent to the collection during his lifetime, or recently by me, are found in the Joseph Labadie Papers. Materials I sent immediately after his son, Laurance, died in 1975, were placed with the Laurance Labadie Papers. Letters from Labadie to others are generally located with the papers of the recipient, either in the collection itself (e.g., the Agnes Inglis Papers, Judson Grenell Papers) or in another library.

Of particular interest are the eight scrapbooks consisting primarily of clippings from a wide range of publications, from both the popular press and obscure journals, of articles by or about Jo Labadie, his activities, or his associates. Five were photocopied from originals in my possession and are designated I–V for identification purposes. They are with the Joseph Labadie Papers. Three originals are housed with the Laurance Labadie Papers. They are referred to as scrapbook 1883–1901, scrapbook 1882–1929, and "Cranky Notions scrapbook" (mostly Labadie's published poems). Labadie's account book for the years 1878–86 contains many valuable details of the family's daily expenses and income.

I made extensive use of the valuable research notes written by Agnes Inglis, first curator of the Labadie Collection, about persons and events mentioned in the book. These are cited in the chapter notes but not included in the bibliography. She left two biographical sketches of Labadie titled "Charles Joseph Antoine Labadie." I have differentiated them by noting whether I refer to the three-page version or the ten-page one.

Jo Labadie's manuscripts and published writings (with the exception of those issued by the Labadie Shop) are too numerous to list. Details of many other documents not listed in the bibliography may be found in the notes. The periodicals listed are in the collection, some in microfilm versions. Carefully saved by the Labadies, they often represent the only extant full run.

Unpublished Documents

American Federation of Labor. Records. Samuel Gompers Era. Microfilm edition. Microfilming Corporation of America.

Debs, Eugene V. Papers. Cunningham Memorial Library, Indiana State University, Terre Haute, Indiana.

Ely, Richard T. Papers. State Historical Society of Wisconsin, Madison.

Grenell, Judson. Autobiography. Archives and Historical Collections, Michigan State University, East Lansing.

Joseph Ishill Collection. Manuscript Department, Houghton Library, Harvard University.

Labadie Collection. Special Collections Library, University of Michigan, Ann Arbor. Joseph A. Labadie Papers. Laurance Labadie Papers. Agnes Inglis Papers. Judson Grenell Papers. Henry Bool Papers.

Parsons, Albert R., Collection. State Historical Society of Wisconsin, Madison.

Powderly, Terence V. Papers. Catholic University of America, Washington, D.C. Microfilm edition. Microfilming Corporation of America, Glen Rock, New Jersey.

Schilling, George A. Papers. Illinois State Historical Society, Springfield, Illinois. Joseph Regenstein Library, University of Chicago.

Tucker, Benjamin R. Papers. Manuscripts and Archives Division, New York Public Library, Astor, Lenox, and Tilden Foundations.

Reports and Published Documents

American Federation of Labor. *Report of Proceedings of the Ninth Annual Convention of the American Federation of Labor.* Boston, December 10–14, 1889.

———. *Report of Proceedings of the Tenth Annual Convention of the American Federation of Labor.* Detroit: December 8–12, 1890.

International Typographical Union. *Report of Proceedings of the Twenty-sixth Annual Session of the International Typographical Union.* Detroit, 1878.

———. *Report of Proceedings of the Thirtieth Annual Session of the International Typographical Union.* St. Louis, [1882].

———. *Report of Proceedings of the Thirty-first Annual Session of the International Typographical Union.* Cincinnati, [1883].

———. *Report of Proceedings of the Thirty-second Annual Session of the International Typographical Union.* New Orleans, [1884].

———. *Report of Proceedings of the Thirty-fourth Annual Session of the International Typographical Union.* Pittsburgh, 1886.

Knights of Labor, Michigan. *Minutes of the Washington Literary Society* (Detroit L.A. 901), 1878–79.

———. *Record of Proceedings of the First Regular Session of the Michigan State Assembly.* Detroit, January 11–12, 1884.

———. *Record of Proceedings of the Second Regular Session of the Michigan State Assembly.* June 3–4, 1885.

————. "Report of John M. Decker, Delegate to the General Assembly, Minneapolis." Detroit: John R. Burton, 1887.

————. "Report of Joseph A. Labadie, Delegate to the General Assembly, Minneapolis." Detroit: John R. Burton, 1887.

Knights of Labor, National. *Adelphon Kruptos,* n.d., Reel No. 67, Microfilm Edition, TVP.

————. *Record of Proceedings of the Second Regular Session of the General Assembly.* St. Louis, June 14–17, 1879.

————. *Record of Proceedings of the Fourth Regular Session of the General Assembly.* Pittsburgh, September 7–11, 1880.

————. *Record of Proceedings of the Fifth Regular Session of the General Assembly.* Detroit, September 6–10, 1881.

————. *Record of Proceedings of the Sixth Regular Session of the General Assembly.* New York City, September 5–12, 1882.

————. *Record of Proceedings of the Seventh Regular Session of the General Assembly.* Cincinnati, September 4–11, 1883.

————. *Record of Proceedings of the Eighth Regular Session of the General Assembly.* Philadelphia, September 1–10, 1884.

————. *Record of Proceedings of the Ninth Regular Session of the General Assembly.* Hamilton, Ont., October 5–13, 1885.

————. *Record of Proceedings of the Tenth Regular Session of the General Assembly.* Richmond, October 4–20, 1886.

————. *Record of Proceedings of the Eleventh Regular Session of the General Assembly.* Minneapolis, October 3–19, 1887.

Michigan Federation of Labor. *First Annual Convention of the Michigan Federation of Labor, 1889. Report of Proceedings.* Lansing, February 19–21, 1889.

————. *Second Annual Convention of the Michigan Federation of Labor, 1890. Report of Proceedings.* East Saginaw, February 4–7, 1890.

Michigan State Bureau of Labor. Annual Reports. Lansing, 1884–99.

Socialist Labor Party of America. *Proceedings of the First National Convention.* Newark, December 26–31, 1877.

————. *Proceedings of the Second National Convention.* Allegheny. December 26, 1879–January 1, 1880.

————. *Records of the National Board of Appeals.* 1880–83.

Periodicals

Advance and Labor Leaf. Detroit, 1887–89. Edited by J. M. McGregor, Joseph A. Labadie, and Judson Grenell.

The Alarm. Chicago, New York, 1884–89. Edited by Albert R. Parsons and Dyer D. Lum.

American Federationist. American Federation of Labor. Indianapolis, 1894–1976.

The Citizen. Detroit, 1896–97.

The Craftsman. Washington, D.C., 1883–90. Edited by August Donath and H. V. Bisbee.

The Crisis. Indianapolis, 1885–? Published by Sam Leffingwell.

Der arme Teufel. Detroit, 1884–1900. Edited by Robert Reitzel.

The Egoist. Clinton, Iowa, 1921–25. Edited by E. H. Fulton.

The Firebrand. Mt. Juliet, Tennessee, 1903–1905; 1909–1910. Edited by Ross Winn.

The Firebrand. Portland, Ore., 1895–97. Edited by Abe Isaak.

Free Society. San Francisco, Chicago, New York, 1897–1904. Edited by Abe Isaak.

Bay City Globe. Bay City, Michigan, 1881.

Industrial Gazette. Detroit, 1894–95.

The Independent Voter. Toledo, Ohio, 1905–1906. Edited by Ben W. Johnson.

Journal of United Labor. Knights of Labor. Marblehead, Mass., Pittsburgh, Philadelphia, 1880–89.

John Swinton's Paper. New York, 1883–87. Edited by John Swinton.

Labor Enquirer. Denver, 1883–87; Chicago, 1887–88. Edited by Burnette Haskell (Denver) and Joseph Buchanan (Chicago).

Labor Leader. Boston, 1887–97. Edited by Frank K. Foster.

Labor Leaf. Detroit, 1884–87. Edited by Charles Bell and John R. Burton.

Labor Review/***. Detroit, 1880–82. Edited by Joseph A. Labadie, Henry Poole, and Judson Grenell.

Labor Star. Cleveland, 1882–83.

Liberty. Boston (1881–91), New York (1892–1908). Edited by Benjamin R. Tucker.

Liberty Library. Columbus Junction, Iowa, 1896–[97]. Edited by E. H. Fulton.

Michigan Federation of Labor Yearbook, 1896. Detroit: Thos. Smith Press.

Mother Earth. New York, 1906–18. Edited by Emma Goldman and Alexander Berkman.

Ohio Valley Budget Weekly. Wheeling, West Virginia, 1887–89.

Onward. Detroit, 1888–90. Published by John R. Burton.

Our Organette. Indianapolis, 1882–83. Published by Sam Leffingwell.

The People. Detroit, 1897–99.

The People. New York, 1896–97.

Detroit Printer. 1896–?.

Detroit Sentinel. 1897–99. Edited by W. D. Mahon and Sam Marcus.

Lansing Sentinel. 1884–85. Edited by Joseph A. Labadie

The Socialist. Detroit and Chicago, 1878–79. Edited by Judson Grenell (Detroit) and Frank Hirth (Chicago).

Solidarity. New York, 1887–88. Edited by J. E. Smith.

Detroit Spectator. 1883–84. Edited by Judson Grenell.

Detroit Times. 1881. Edited by Joseph A. Labadie and Judson Grenell.

The Trades. Philadelphia, 1879–80.

Today (later *Detroit Times*). Detroit, 1900–1903.

Truth. San Francisco, 1882–84. Edited by Burnette Haskell.

Twentieth Century. New York, 1888–98. Edited by Hugh O. Pentecost.

Typographical Journal. Indianapolis, 1889–. International Typographical Union.

Union Printer. New York, 1887–90.

The Unionist. Detroit, 1882–83. Edited by William Murtagh and Judson Grenell.

Vorbote. Chicago, 1883.

The Workman. Grand Rapids, [1883]–1893.

Booklets Published by the Labadie Shop, 1908–33

Greusel, John Hubert. *The Poor Devil: Tribute to Robert Reitzel* (1909).

Hubbard, Elbert. *Jesus Was an Anarchist* (1910).

Labadie, Joseph A. *Anarchism* (1932).

————. *Anarchism: Genuine and Asinine* (1925).

————. *Doggerel for the Underdog* (1910).

————. *Essays* (1911).

————. *Holiday Sentiments* (1932–33).

————. *I Welcome Disorder* (1911).

————. *The Might of Music* (1908).

————. *The Red Flag and Other Verses* (1910).

————. *Russian Verses* (written 1905 and 1913, published 1932 by Laurance Labadie).

————. *Sing Songs and Some That Don't* (1925).

————. *Soft Soap* (1925).

————. *Songs of the Spoiled* (1922).

————. *What Is Love?* (1910).

————. *What Is Love?* 2d ed. (1921).

————. *What Is Love? and Other Fancies* (1910).

————. *Windows* (1924).

————. *Workshop Rimes* (1911).

Labadie, Joseph A., and Edwin M. Clark. *My Friend Indeed and A Friend's Acceptance* (1922).

Perry, James V. C. *Poems* (1922).

Scott, Winfield, and Joseph A. Labadie. *A Jaunt Along the River Rouge* (1908).

————. *Off the Beaten Track* (n.d.).

Weller, Myra Pepper. *Prairie Songs* (1925)

Books

Adamic, Louis. *Dynamite: The Story of Class Violence in America.* New York: Chelsea House Publishers, n.d.

Alpern, Ron, et al. *Union Town: A Labor History Guide to Detroit.* Detroit: Workers Education Local 189, n.d.

Ashbaugh, Carolyn. *Lucy Parsons: American Revolutionary.* Chicago: Charles H. Kerr Publishing Co., 1976.

Avrich, Paul. *An American Anarchist: The Life of Voltairine de Cleyre.* Princeton: Princeton University Press, 1978.

————. *Anarchist Portraits.* Princeton: Princeton University Press, 1988.

————. *Anarchist Voices: An Oral History of Anarchism in America.* Princeton: Princeton University Press, 1995.

————. *The Haymarket Tragedy.* Princeton: Princeton University Press, 1984.

————. *Sacco and Vanzetti: The Anarchist Background.* Princeton: Princeton University Press, 1991.

Babson, Steve. *Working Detroit: The Making of a Union Town.* New York: Adama Books, 1984.

Bald, F. Clever. *Michigan in Four Centuries.* Rev. Ed. New York: Harper and Bros., 1961.

Bennett, David H. *The Party of Fear: From Nativist Movements to the New Right in American History.* New York: Vintage Books, 1990.

Blatt, Martin Henry. *Free Love and Anarchism: The Biography of Ezra Heywood.* Urbana: University of Illinois Press, 1989.

Boyer, Richard O., and Herbert M. Morais. *Labor's Untold Story.* Pittsburgh: United Electrical, Radio, and Machine Workers of America, 1988.

Brody, David, ed. *The American Labor Movement.* New York: Harper and Row, 1971.

Buchanan, Joseph R. *The Story of a Labor Agitator.* New York: The Outlook Co., 1903.

Burton, Clarence M. *The City of Detroit, 1701–1922.* Detroit: Clarke, 1922.

Chasan, Will. *Samuel Gompers: Leader of American Labor.* New York: Praeger Publishers, 1971.

Chauvin, Francis X. *Hiram Walker: His Life, His Work.* Walkerville: Hiram Walker Distillery, [1925].

Cooper, Patricia A. *Once a Cigar Maker: Men, Women, and Work Culture in Americn Factories, 1900–1918.* Urbana: University of Illinois Press, 1987.

Cornwell, William C. *Greenbacks, The Cause of All Our Trouble.* Buffalo: Greenback Publishing Co., n.d. [1896].

Coughlin, Michael E., et al., eds. *Benjamin R. Tucker and the Champions of Liberty.* St. Paul: Michael E. Coughlin, 1987.

DeLeon, David. *The American as Anarchist: Reflections on Indigenous Radicalism.* Baltimore: Johns Hopkins University Press, 1978.

Denissen, Rev. Fr. Christian. *The Genealogy of the French Families of the Detroit River Region, 1701–1936.* Rev. Ed. Detroit: Detroit Society for Genealogical Research, 1987.

Destler, Charles M. *American Radicalism.* Chicago: Quadrangle Books, 1966.

Dewey, A. M. *Industrial Leaders of Today.* Detroit: A. M. Dewey, 1888.

Donaldson, Randall Paul. "Robert Reitzel (1849–1898) and His German-American Periodical *Der arme Teufel*" Ph.D. diss., Johns Hopkins University, 1976.

Drinnon, Richard. *Rebel in Paradise: A Biography of Emma Goldman.* New York: Harper and Row, 1976.

Dubofsky, Melvyn. *Industrialism and the American Worker, 1865–1920.* Arlington Heights, Ill.: Harlan Davidson, 1985.

Dubofsky, Melvyn, and Warren Van Tine, eds. *Labor Leaders in America.* Urbana: University of Illinois Press, 1987.

Dulles, Foster Rhea, and Melvyn Dubofsky. *Labor in America.* Arlington Heights: Harlan Davidson, Inc., 1984.

Dunham, Betty J. *Oliver Township History.* Kalkaska: Rowell Printing, 1985.

Ely, Richard T. *The Labor Movement in America.* New York: Thomas Y. Crowell and Co., 1886.

Falk, Candace. *Love, Anarchy and Emma Goldman.* New York: Holt, Rinehart and Winston, 1984.

Farmer, Silas. *History of Detroit and Wayne County and Early Michigan.* Detroit: S. Farmer and Company, 1890.

Fink, Leon. *Workingmen's Democracy: The Knights of Labor and American Politics.* Urbana: University of Illinois Press, 1983.

Fink, Gary M., ed. *Biographical Dictionary of American Labor Leaders.* Westport, Conn.: Greenwood Press, 1984.

Foner, Philip S. *History of the Labor Movement in the United States,* 2 vols. New York, International Publishers, 1947, 1975.

Garlock, Jonathan. *Guide to the Local Assemblies of the Knights of Labor.* Westport, Conn.: Greenwood Press, 1982.

Ginger, Ray. *The Bending Cross: A Biography of Eugene Victor Debs.* New Brunswick, N.J.: Rutgers University Press, 1949.

Glazer, Sidney. *Detroit: A Study in Urban Development.* New York: Bookman Associates, 1965.

———. "Labor and Agrarian Movements in Michigan, 1876–1896." Ph.D. diss., University of Michigan, 1932.

Goldman, Emma. *Living My Life.* New York: Dover Publications, 1970; reprint of 1931.

Gompers, Samuel. *Seventy Years of Life and Labor,* revised and edited by Philip Taft and John A. Sessions. New York: E. P. Dutton, 1957.

———. *Seventy Years of Life and Labor.* New York: Augustus M. Kelley, 1967 reprint of 1925.

Graham, Marcus, ed. *Anthology of Revolutionary Poetry.* New York: Active Press, 1927.

Gutman, Herbert. *Work, Culture and Society in Industrializing America.* New York: Alfred A. Knopf, 1976.

Hillquit, Morris. *History of Socialism in the United States.* Rev. ed. New York: Dover Publications, 1971.

Holli, Melvin G., ed. *Detroit.* New York: New Viewpoints, 1976.

———. *Reform in Detroit: Hazen S. Pingree and Urban Politics.* New York: Oxford University Press, 1969.

Jacker, Corinne. *The Black Flag of Anarchy.* New York: Charles Scribner's Sons, 1968.

Katzman, David M. *Before the Ghetto: Black Detroit in the Nineteenth Century.* Urbana: University of Illinois Press, 1973.

Kealey, Gregory S., and Bryan D. Palmer. *Dreaming of What Might Be: The Knights of Labor in Ontario, 1880–1900.* Cambridge: Cambridge University Press, 1982.

Kellogg, Charles Flint. *NAACP: A History of the National Association for the Advancement of Colored People.* Baltimore: Johns Hopkins University Press, 1967.

Kornbluh, Joyce L., ed. *Rebel Voices: An I.W.W. Anthology.* Ann Arbor: University of Michigan Press, 1964.

Laslett, John H. M., and Seymour Martin Lipset, eds. *Failure of a Dream? Essays in the History of American Socialism.* Rev. ed. Berkeley: University of California Press, 1984.

Laurie, Bruce. *Artisans into Workers: Labor in Nineteenth-Century America.* New York: The Noonday Press, 1989.

Leake, Paul. *History of Detroit.* Chicago: The Lewis Publishing Co., 1912.

Levine, Susan. *Labor's True Woman: Carpet Weavers, Industrialization and Labor Reform in the Gilded Age.* Philadelphia: Temple University Press, 1984.

McLaughlin, Doris B. *Michigan Labor: A Brief History from 1818 to the Present.* Ann Arbor: Institute of Labor and Industrial Relations, University of Michigan/Wayne State University, 1970.

McNeill, George E., ed. *The Labor Movement: The Problem of Today.* Boston: A. M. Bridgeman and Co., 1887.

Madison, Charles A. *American Labor Leaders.* New York: Frederick Ungar Publishing, 1950.

———. *Critics and Crusaders.* New York: Henry Holt, 1947–48.

Mandel, Bernard. *Samuel Gompers.* Yellow Springs, Ohio: The Antioch Press, 1963.

Martin, James J. *Men Against the State: The Expositors of Individualist Anarchism in America, 1827–1908.* Colorado Springs: Ralph Myles Publisher, 1970.

———. *Laurance Labadie: Selected Essays.* Colorado Springs: Ralph Myles Publisher, 1978.

Meyer, Stephen III. *The Five Dollar Day: Labor Management and Social Control in the Ford Motor Company, 1908–1921.* Albany: State University of New York Press, 1981.

Record of Service of Michigan Volunteers in the Civil War, 1861–1865. Vol. 41. Kalamazoo: State of Michigan, 1905.

Montgomery, David. *The Fall of the House of Labor: The Workplace, the State, and American Labor Activism, 1865–1925.* Cambridge: Cambridge University Press, 1987.

Nelson, Bruce C. *Beyond the Martyrs: A Social History of Chicago's Anarchists, 1870–1900.* New Brunswick, N.J.: Rutgers University Press, 1988.

Oestreicher, Richard Jules. *Solidarity and Fragmentation: Working People and Class Consciousness in Detroit, 1875–1900.* Urbana: University of Illinois Press, 1986.

Peterson, Joyce Shaw. *American Automobile Workers, 1900–1933.* Albany: State University of New York Press, 1987.

Powderly, Terence V. *Thirty Years of Labor.* Columbus: Excelsior Publishing House, 1890.

———. *The Path I Trod.* New York: Columbia University Press, 1940.

Ramsey, Maurice M. "The Knights of Labor in Michigan, 1878–1888." Master's thesis, College of the City of Detroit, 1932.

Reichert, William O. *Partisans of Freedom: A Study in American Anarchism.* Bowling Green: Bowling Green University Popular Press, 1976.

Rocker, Rudolf. *Pioneers of American Freedom.* Los Angeles: Rocker Publications Committee, 1949.

Roediger, Dave, and Franklin Rosemont, eds. *Haymarket Scrapbook.* Chicago: Charles H. Kerr Publishing Co., 1986.

Rolland, Siegfried. "The Detroit Labor Press, 1839–89." Master's thesis, Wayne University, 1946.

Salvatore, Nick. *Eugene V. Debs: Citizen and Socialist.* Urbana: University of Illinois Press, 1982.

Schnapper, M. B. *American Labor: A Pictorial Social History.* Washington, D.C.: Public Affairs Press, 1975.

Schuster, Eunice Minette. *Native American Anarchism: A Study of Left-Wing American Individualism.* Port Townsend, Wash.: Loompanics Unlimited, 1983, reprint of 1932.

Solin, Jacob A. "The Detroit Federation of Labor, 1900–1920." Master's thesis, Wayne University, 1939.

Stark, George W. *City of Destiny.* Detroit: Arnold-Powers, Inc., 1943.

Stearn, Gerald E., ed. *Gompers.* Englewood Cliffs, N.J.: Prentice-Hall, 1971.

Taft, Philip. *The AFL in the Time of Gompers.* New York: Harper and Bros., 1957.

Tracy, George A. *History of the Typographical Union.* Albany: International Typographical Union, 1913.

Tucker, Benjamin R. *Instead of a Book: By a Man Too Busy to Write One.* New York: Haskell House Publishers, 1969 reprint of 1897.

United States Bureau of the Census. *Historical Statistics of the United States.* Washington, D.C.: GPO, 1975.

Vexler, Robert I., ed. *Detroit: A Chronological and Documentary History.* Dobbs Ferry, N.Y.: Oceana Publications, 1977.

Voss, Kim. *The Making of American Exceptionalism: The Knights of Labor and Class Formation in the Nineteenth Century.* Ithaca: Cornell University Press, 1993.

Ware, Norman J. *The Labor Movement in the United States, 1860–1895.* Gloucester: Peter Smith, 1959.

Weir, Robert E. *Beyond Labor's Veil: The Culture of the Knights of Labor.* University Park: Pennsylvania State University Press, 1996.

Wexler, Alice. *Emma Goldman: An Intimate Life.* New York: Pantheon Books, 1984.

Zunz, Olivier. *The Changing Face of Inequality: Urbanization, Industrial Development, and Immigrants in Detroit, 1880–1920.* Chicago: University of Chicago Press, 1982.

Articles

Anderson, Carlotta R. "America's Anarchists: Who They Were and What They Stood For," *the dandelion* 22 (spring 1998).

———. "Jo Labadie: Detroit's Gentle Anarchist," *Michigan History Magazine* 70 (July/August 1986): 32–39.

———. "Joseph A. Labadie (1850–1933): 'Cranky Notions' on Haymarket." *Hay-*

market Scrapbook, edited by Dave Roediger and Franklin Rosemont, 123–24. Chicago: Charles H. Kerr Publishing Co., 1986.

Brooks, Frank. "American Individualist Anarchism: What It Was and Why It Failed," *Journal of Political Ideologies* 1, no. 1 (1996): 75–95.

———. "Ideology, Strategy, and Organization: Dyer Lum and the American Anarchist Movement," *Labor History* 34, no. 1 (winter 1993): 57–83.

Conrad, Lawrence. "Jo Labadie—Poet," *Michigan History Magazine* 16, no. 2 (spring 1932): 218–24.

Conroy, Jack. "Jo Labadie, Craftsman and Poet," *The Northern Light* 1, no. 7 (November–December 1927): 159–160.

Cotkin, George B. "The Spencerian and Comtian Nexus in Gompers' Labor Philosophy: The Impact of Non-Marxian Evolutionary Thought," *Labor History* 20 (fall 1979): 510–23.

Drescher, Nuala McGann. "To Play the Hypocrite: Terence V. Powderly on the Anarchists," *Labor History* 13, no. 1 (winter 1972): 60–62.

Fine, Sidney. "The Ely-Labadie Letters," *Michigan History Magazine* 36, no. 1 (March 1952): 1–32.

———. "Anarchism and the Assassination of McKinley," reprinted in *The Underside of American History II,* edited by Thomas R. Frazier, 61–86. New York: Harcourt Brace Jovanovich, 1971.

Glazer, Sidney. "The Michigan Labor Movement," *Michigan History Magazine* 29 (1945): 73–82.

———. "Origins and Early Development of the Michigan Federation of Labor," *American Federationist* 41 (May 1934): 527–30.

Hamilton, Charles H. "Introduction: The Evolution of a Subversive Tradition." In *Benjamin R. Tucker and the Champions of Liberty,* edited by Michael E. Coughlin et al. St. Paul: Michael E. Coughlin, 1987.

Miles, Dione. "Agnes Inglis: Librarian, Activist, Humanitarian," *the dandelion* 3, no. 12 (winter 1979): 7–15.

Nold, Carl. "Anarchists: Joseph A. Labadie," *Man!* 6, no. 69 (November 1933).

Oestreicher, Richard Jules. "Robert Reitzel, *Der arme Teufel.*" In *The German-American Radical Press: The Shaping of a Left Political Culture, 1850–1940,* edited by Elliott Shore, et al., 147–67. Urbana: University of Illinois Press, 1992.

———. "Socialism and the Knights of Labor in Detroit, 1877–1886," *Labor History* 22 (1981): 5–20.

Ogg, Robert Y. "Joseph A. Labadie, First President of the Michigan Federation of Labor," *Michigan Federation of Labor Yearbook,* 1896.

Okey, R. Anne. "They All Knew Each Other: Agnes Inglis and the Labadie Collection," exhibit catalog, Special Collections Library, University of Michigan Library, 1992.

Panet, A. Philippe E. "The Labadie Family in the County of Essex, Ontario," *Essex Historical Society* 1 (1905).

Rockaway, Robert. "The Laboring Man's Champion: Samuel Goldwater of Detroit," *Bulletin of the Detroit Historical Society,* November 1970, 4–9.

Rogin, Michael. "Voluntarism: The Political Functions of an Antipolitical Doctrine." In *Labor and American Politics,* edited by Charles M. Rehmus and Doris B. McLaughlin, 108–28. Ann Arbor: University of Michigan Press, 1967.

Scanlan, Eleanor H. "The Labadie Collection," *Labor History* 6 (1965): 244–48.

Scofield, Robert G. "Anti-Anarchist Laws," *the dandelion* 5, no. 18 (spring–winter 1982): 3–11.

Stewart, R. C. "The Labadie Labor Collection," *Michigan Alumnus Quarterly Review* 53 (1947): 247–53.

Weber, Edward C. "The Labadie Collection in the University of Michigan Library," *Labor History* 31, nos. 1–2 (winter–spring 1990): 155–62.

Ziegler, Robert H. "A Letter from Jo Labadie to John R. Commons," *Labor History* 2 (1970): 345–46.

Unpublished Manuscripts

Anderson, Carlotta. "The Ancestors of Jo Labadie (Charles Joseph Antoine Labadie), Detroit Labor Leader and Anarchist 1850–1933," 1995, LC.

Burton, Clarence M. "The Labadie Family in Detroit" (genealogy), LC.

Coyne, Thomas E. "Jo Labadie: A Study in Radical Thinking," unpublished term paper, University of Michigan, 1956.

Emery, Larry. "The Story of Marie Sauvagesse and Antoine 'Badichon' Labadie," July 1997, 30p. ts., LC.

Grenell, Judson. "Autobiography." Clearwater, Fla.: n.p., 1930, 98p. ts., MSUAHC.

———. "A Foreword," March 1928, 3p. ts., LC.

Inglis, Agnes. "Reflections—Notes for a Book," 244p. ts., LC.

John, Arthur. "A History of the Labadie Collection of Labor and Radical Literature in the University of Michigan Library," term paper, University of Michigan, 1941–42.

"The Labadies of Windsor, Ontario," LC.

Oestreicher, Richard J. "The Limits of Labor Radicalism: Tom Barry and the Knights of Labor," 1981, 26p. ts.

INDEX

TITLES IN THE GREAT LAKES BOOKS SERIES

Detroit Images: Photographs of the Renaissance City, edited by John J. Bukowczyk
and Douglas Aikenhead, with Peter Slavcheff, 1989

Hangdog Reef: Poems Sailing the Great Lakes, by Stephen Tudor, 1989

Detroit: City of Race and Class Violence, revised edition, by B. J. Widick, 1989

Deep Woods Frontier: A History of Logging in Northern Michigan, by Theodore J.
Karamanski, 1989

Orvie, The Dictator of Dearborn, by David L. Good, 1989

Seasons of Grace: A History of the Catholic Archdiocese of Detroit, by Leslie
Woodcock Tentler, 1990

The Pottery of John Foster: Form and Meaning, by Gordon and Elizabeth Orear,
1990

The Diary of Bishop Frederic Baraga: First Bishop of Marquette, Michigan, edited
by Regis M. Walling and Rev. N. Daniel Rupp, 1990

Walnut Pickles and Watermelon Cake: A Century of Michigan Cooking, by Larry B.
Massie and Priscilla Massie, 1990

The Making of Michigan, 1820–1860: A Pioneer Anthology, edited by Justin L.
Kestenbaum, 1990

America's Favorite Homes: A Guide to Popular Early Twentieth-Century Homes, by
Robert Schweitzer and Michael W. R. Davis, 1990

Beyond the Model T: The Other Ventures of Henry Ford, by Ford R. Bryan, 1990

Life after the Line, by Josie Kearns, 1990

*Michigan Lumbertowns: Lumbermen and Laborers in Saginaw, Bay City, and Muske-
gon, 1870–1905,* by Jeremy W. Kilar, 1990

Detroit Kids Catalog: The Hometown Tourist by Ellyce Field, 1990

Waiting for the News, by Leo Litwak, 1990 (reprint)

Detroit Perspectives, edited by Wilma Wood Henrickson, 1991

Life on the Great Lakes: A Wheelsman's Story, by Fred W. Dutton, edited by William
Donohue Ellis, 1991

Copper Country Journal: The Diary of Schoolmaster Henry Hobart, 1863–1864, by
Henry Hobart, edited by Philip P. Mason, 1991

John Jacob Astor: Business and Finance in the Early Republic, by John Denis Haeger,
1991

Survival and Regeneration: Detroit's American Indian Community, by Edmund J.
Danziger, Jr., 1991

Steamboats and Sailors of the Great Lakes, by Mark L. Thompson, 1991

Cobb Would Have Caught It: The Golden Years of Baseball in Detroit, by Richard
Bak, 1991

Michigan in Literature, by Clarence Andrews, 1992

Under the Influence of Water: Poems, Essays, and Stories, by Michael Delp, 1992

The Country Kitchen, by Della T. Lutes, 1992 (reprint)

The Making of a Mining District: Keweenaw Native Copper 1500–1870, by David
J. Krause, 1992

Kids Catalog of Michigan Adventures, by Ellyce Field, 1993

Henry's Lieutenants, by Ford R. Bryan, 1993

Historic Highway Bridges of Michigan, by Charles K. Hyde, 1993

Lake Erie and Lake St. Clair Handbook, by Stanley J. Bolsenga and Charles E. Herndendorf, 1993

Queen of the Lakes, by Mark Thompson, 1994

Iron Fleet: The Great Lakes in World War II, by George J. Joachim, 1994

Turkey Stearnes and the Detroit Stars: The Negro Leagues in Detroit, 1919–1933, by Richard Bak, 1994

Pontiac and the Indian Uprising, by Howard H. Peckham, 1994 (reprint)

Charting the Inland Seas: A History of the U.S. Lake Survey, by Arthur M. Woodford, 1994 (reprint)

Ojibwa Narratives of Charles and Charlotte Kawbawgam and Jacques LePique, 1893–1895. Recorded with Notes by Homer H. Kidder, edited by Arthur P. Bourgeois, 1994, co-published with the Marquette County Historical Society

Strangers and Sojourners: A History of Michigan's Keweenaw Peninsula, by Arthur W. Thurner, 1994

Win Some, Lose Some: G. Mennen Williams and the New Democrats, by Helen Washburn Berthelot, 1995

Sarkis, by Gordon and Elizabeth Orear, 1995

The Northern Lights: Lighthouses of the Upper Great Lakes, by Charles K. Hyde, 1995 (reprint)

Kids Catalog of Michigan Adventures, second edition, by Ellyce Field, 1995

Rumrunning and the Roaring Twenties: Prohibition on the Michigan-Ontario Waterway, by Philip P. Mason, 1995

In the Wilderness with the Red Indians, by E. R. Baierlein, translated by Anita Z. Boldt, edited by Harold W. Moll, 1996

Elmwood Endures: History of a Detroit Cemetery, by Michael Franck, 1996

Master of Precision: Henry M. Leland, by Mrs. Wilfred C. Leland with Minnie Dubbs Millbrook, 1996 (reprint)

Haul-Out: New and Selected Poems, by Stephen Tudor, 1996

Kids Catalog of Michigan Adventures, third edition, by Ellyce Field, 1997

Beyond the Model T: The Other Ventures of Henry Ford, revised edition, by Ford R. Bryan, 1997

Young Henry Ford: A Picture History of the First Forty Years, by Sidney Olson, 1997 (reprint)

From Saginaw Valley to Tin Pan Alley: Saginaw's Contribution to American Popular Music, 1890–1955, by R. Grant Smith, 1998

Bridging the River of Hatred: The Pioneering Efforts of Detroit Police Commissioner George Edwards, 1962–1963, by Mary M. Stolberg, 1998

Toast of the Town: The Life and Times of Sunnie Wilson, by Sunnie Wilson with John Cohassey, 1998

All-American Anarchist: Joseph A. Labadie and the Labor Movement, by Carlotta R. Anderson, 1998